The American Record: Since 1941
Images of the Nation's Past

The American Record: Since 1941 Images of the Nation's Past

William Graebner

*State University of New York,
College at Fredonia*

Jacqueline Swansinger

*State University of New York,
College at Fredonia*

The McGraw-Hill Companies, Inc.

*New York   St. Louis   San Francisco   Auckland   Bogotá   Caracas
Lisbon   London   Madrid   Mexico City   Milan   Montreal   New Delhi
San Juan   Singapore   Sydney   Tokyo   Toronto*

McGraw-Hill

*A Division of The **McGraw·Hill** Companies*

THE AMERICAN RECORD: SINCE 1941
IMAGES OF THE NATION'S PAST

This book was printed on acid-free paper.

1 2 3 4 5 6 7 8 9 0   DOC DOC   9 0 9 8 7 6

ISBN 0-07-024016-7

This book was set in Times Roman by Ruttle, Shaw & Wetherill, Inc.
The editor was Lyn Uhl;
the production supervisor was Kathryn Porzio.
The cover was designed by Wanda Lubelska.
Cover photo: Elementary school children in Charlestown, Massachusetts,
during the busing crisis, c. 1975. Courtesy Boston Herald Photos.
Project supervision was done by Ruttle, Shaw & Wetherill, Inc.
R. R. Donnelley & Sons Company was printer and binder.

Library of Congress Cataloging in Publication Data

The American record: since 1941—images of the nation's past /
William Graebner, Jacqueline Swansinger, [editors].
   p.   cm.
Includes bibliographical references and index.
ISBN 0-07-024016-7
   1. United States—History—1945- —Sources.   I. Graebner,
William.   II. Swansinger, Jacqueline.
E838.3.A44   1997   96-23320
973.92—dc20

About the Editors

WILLIAM GRAEBNER is Professor of History at the State University of New York at Fredonia. He received the Frederick Jackson Turner Award from the Organization of American Historians for *Coal-Mining Safety in the Progressive Period: The Political Economy of Reform.* Another book, *A History of Retirement: The Meaning and Function of an American Institution, 1885–1978,* was published in 1980. He is also the author of *The Engineering of Consent: Democracy and Authority in Twentieth-Century America* (1987); *Coming of Age in Buffalo: Youth and Authority in the Postwar Era* (1990); and *The Age of Doubt: American Thought and Culture in the 1940s* (1991). His latest book is an edited collection, *True Stories from the American Past* (1993). In 1993, he was Fulbright Professor of American Studies at the University of Rome. He currently serves on the editorial boards of *American Studies* and *The Historian.*

JACQUELINE SWANSINGER is Associate Professor of History at the State University of New York at Fredonia, where she teaches American foreign policy. A graduate of Georgian Court College in New Jersey, she received her Ph.D. from Rutgers University. She specializes in twentieth-century U.S. history and American foreign relations, with special emphasis on economic development. Recent articles include "From Farmers to Businessmen" (*New York History*) and "A Three-Legged Race: Ethiopian Reconstruction, 1940–1944" (*Journal of World History*). She is currently working on Franco-American diplomacy during the Algerian War.

Contents

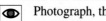

Preface

The American Record: Since 1941 is indebted to the very successful approach to studying and teaching history worked out in several editions of *The American Record: Images of the Nation's Past,* edited by William Graebner and Leonard Richards. That approach combines scholarly essays, primary sources, and a rich variety of visual materials. Throughout, we have attempted to incorporate materials with *texture:* documents that are not only striking but will also yield more than one interpretation; photographs and media stills that invite real examination and discussion; tables and graphs that have something new and interesting to contribute; and essays, such as Stephanie Coontz's account of self-reliance and the American family, Kenneth J. Heineman's analysis of the 1960s anti-war movement, William L. Van Deburg's cultural perspective on the black power movement, or Ronald P. Formisano's history of Boston busing, that are at once superb examples of recent historical scholarship and accessible to undergraduates.

We have tried to bridge the gap between the old history and the new, to graft the excitement and variety of modern approaches to history onto an existing chronological and topical framework with which most of us feel comfortable. Most of the familiar topics are here: the mid-century Red Scare, the Kennedy presidency; the Vietnam war, the counterculture, the siege mentality of the 1970s, the Reagan revolution, the cold war, and today's "new world order." But we have also chosen to take a topical approach to areas that we thought deserved special attention, including welfare and the family; the emergence of a new African-American consciousness; the Nixon-led white backlash; the "culture wars" of the 1980s; the Los Angeles rebellion of 1992; and the aesthetic of postmodernism. The role of the media in postwar life is a regular motif, presented here through materials that deal with television's early years, the 1960 presidential debates, TV families, late-night talk-show hosts, and the Reagan mystique.

Culture—high and low, popular and elite—is prominently featured, so that students may begin to appreciate the connections between rock 'n' roll and the civil rights movement or between the 1964 World's Fair and the hubris of JFK, feel the irony and cynicism of the mid-1980s in a postmodern building designed by Michael Graves, or think about why the National Air and Space Museum had so much difficulty presenting an exhibit on the dropping of the atomic bomb, a half-century after the event took place. In addition, every chapter concludes with a suggestively annotated list of films and popular songs that bear on the broader themes under discussion. Like its predecessors, this book teaches the skill of making sense out of one's whole world.

From the beginning, we realized that our approach to American history would require some adjustment for many students and teachers. It was one thing to expect a student to place an address by Harry Truman in the context of the widespread anxiety produced by World War II, the use of the atomic bomb against the Japanese, and the knowledge of the Holocaust, yet quite another to expect that same student to do the same with Mickey Spillane's crime novel, *I, the Jury* (1947). For this reason, we have offered a good deal of guidance. Introductions to primary and secondary materials are designed not just to provide basic background information, but to suggest productive avenues of interpretation. Interpretive essays and questions are intended to create a kind of mental chemistry in which students will have enough information to experience the excitement of putting things together, and yet not so much guidance that conclusions become obvious. We hope the book contains what we have tried to bring to our students over the years: a sense of the incomparable richness of the past, and of the very real pleasures of studying history and of acquiring historical knowledge.

William Graebner
Jacqueline Swansinger

CHAPTER 1

The Age of Anxiety

When older Americans reflect on the 1940s, they recall the decade in halves: the first half, dominated by World War II, a difficult time when men and women fought for democracy against the forces of tyranny; and the second half, remembered as the beginning of a long period of prosperity and opportunity that would reach into the 1960s. There is much to be said for this view of the decade. Although Americans had been reluctant to go to war (the United States remained formally neutral when France was invaded by Germany in 1940), the Japanese attack on Pearl Harbor in December 1941 brought a flush of patriotism that temporarily buried most remaining doubts. A Virginia politician announced that "we needed a Pearl Harbor—a Golgotha—to arouse us from our self-sufficient complacency, to make us rise above greed and hate." Vice President Henry Wallace was one of many who revived Wilsonian idealism. "This is a fight," he wrote in 1943, "between a slave world and a free world. Just as the United States in 1862 could not remain half slave and half free, so in 1942 the world must make its decision for a complete victory one way or another." When the United States ended the war in the Pacific by exploding atomic bombs over Hiroshima and Nagasaki, many Americans considered the act appropriate retribution for the attack at Pearl Harbor by a devious and immoral enemy.

In many ways, the war justified idealism, for it accomplished what the New Deal had not. Organized labor prospered. The name "Rosie the Riveter" described the new American woman who found war-related opportunities in the factories and shipyards. Black people—segregated by New Deal housing programs, injured as tenant farmers by New Deal farm policies, and never singled out as a group worthy of special aid—found skilled jobs in the wartime economy. They also received presidential assistance—in the form of the Fair Employment Practices Committee—in their struggle to end racially discriminatory hiring practices. A growing military budget in 1941 produced the nation's first genuinely progressive income tax legislation. Despite a serious and disruptive wave of postwar strikes that was triggered by high unemployment, for the most part the prosperity and economic growth generated by the war carried over into the late 1940s and 1950s.

Yet this *good war/good peace* view of the 1940s leaves too much unexplained and unaccounted for. It does not explain that the very patriotism that made Americans revel in wartime unity also had negative consequences. For example, on the Pacific Coast, more than 100,000 Japanese-Americans, including many American citizens, were taken from their homes and removed to distant relocation centers, where they remained for the "duration." *Good war/good peace* does not explain that the effects of combat lasted long beyond the formal end of conflict, as the Mickey Spillane excerpt in this chapter demonstrates. Nor does it reveal how thoroughly the war disrupted existing gender and race relations, setting the stage for the silly and absurd things postwar Americans did to restore the prewar status quo. And *good war/good peace* does not explain the popularity between 1942 and 1958 of *film noir,* a gloomy black-and-white film genre that pictured a world in which ordinary, decent people were regularly victimized by bad luck.

Beneath the surface of 1940s America was a pervasive anxiety. Some of this anxiety was economic; those who had experienced the great depression could never quite believe that another one wasn't around the corner. But far more important were anxieties linked to the use of the atomic bomb on the Japanese, the killing of 6 million Jews by the Nazis, the war-related deaths of 60 million people worldwide and the increasing seriousness of the cold war. These extraordinary facts and events created the most elemental form of insecurity: the knowledge that any human life could end senselessly and without warning. And many thoughtful Americans began to question—in a way they had not even during the great depression—whether history was still the story of civilization and progress, or a sad tale of moral decline. The concepts *good war* and *good peace* remained vital to Americans' understanding of their world, but they could not encompass the haunting feeling, so much a part of the late 1940s, that something very important had gone wrong.

INTERPRETIVE ESSAY

Coming Out Under Fire

Allan Bérubé

There is a school of thought that holds that almost every significant social change in the late twentieth century can be traced to World War II. In this view, the civil rights activism of the late 1950s and early 1960s was set in motion by changes in the wartime economy; the feminist movement of the late 1960s was spearheaded by the daughters of women who had experienced the war as a field of opportunity; and the campus protests of the Vietnam war era were led by young people raised in the shadow of the atomic bomb or (in a claim that appeals to conservatives) by spoiled brats brought up under the permissive, democratic child-rearing regimen popularized by Dr. Benjamin Spock in his 1946 The Common Sense Book of Baby and Child Care, *itself a product of the war.*

Allan Bérubé's account of how the nation's gay community was affected by, and responded to, government policies during and after the war fits that model in some respects. Like the stories of blacks and feminists, it is the story of an emerging community (or communities), and it is a story anchored, like the others, in wartime events and experiences. In this case, what was it about the war—and about the status and claims of the veteran—that contributed to social change? It is also a story about repression, and the intensity and character of that repression needs to be described and understood. Was the military, and later the Senate and President Dwight Eisenhower, really concerned about homosexuals? Or was the attack on the gay community a way to achieve some other purpose? Why were Americans—or their public officials—so anxious about questions of sexuality?

The massive mobilization for World War II propelled gay men and lesbians into the mainstream of American life. Ironically the screening and discharge policies, together with the drafting of millions of men, weakened the barriers that had kept gay people trapped and hidden at the margins of society. Discovering that they shared a common cause, they were more willing and able to defend themselves, as their ability to work, congregate, and lead sexual lives came under escalating attack in the postwar decade.

Long before the war a chain of social constraints immobilized many gay men and women by keeping them invisible, isolated, silent, ignorant, and trivialized. As young people they learned to hide their homosexual feelings in fear and in shame, helping to perpetuate the myth that people like them didn't exist. Locked in a closet of lies and deceptions, many people with homosexual desires mistakenly believed that they were the only ones in the world, often not even knowing what to call themselves. Isolated from each other and kept ignorant by a "conspiracy of silence" in the media, they lacked the language and ideas that could help them define themselves and understand their often vague feelings and desires. When publicly acknowledged at all, they were caricatured as "fairies" and "mannish" women, freaks whose lives were trivialized as silly and unimportant, so that many lesbians and gay men learned not to take themselves or each other seriously. Such insidious forms of social control worked quietly below the surface of everyday life through unspoken fears and paralyzing shame, coming into view only in sporadic acts of violence, arrests, school expulsions, firings, or religious condemnations.

Ironically the mobilization for World War II helped to loosen the constraints that locked so many gay people in silence, isolation, and self-contempt. Selective Service acknowledged the importance of gay men when it drafted hundreds of thousands to serve their country and broke the silence when examiners asked millions of selectees about their homosexual tendencies. The draft, together with lax recruitment policies that allowed lesbians to enter the military, placed a whole generation of gay men and women in gender-segregated bases where they could find each other, form cliques, and discover the gay life in the cities. Classification officers assigned even the most "mannish" women and effeminate men to stereotyped duties, recognizing that these previously marginal people were useful and even indispensable to the war effort. Officers confirmed the competence, value, and courage of gay soldiers when they sent many into combat, some to die, even after they had declared their homosexuality.

Changes in policy brought about similarly dramatic effects. Military officials intensified the significance of homosexuality by building a special bureaucratic apparatus to manage homosexual personnel. In the process, they inadvertently gave gay inductees and soldiers the option to avoid compulsory military service by coming out. Psychiatrists, as the military's pioneer experts on homosexuality, gave soldiers as well as military officials a biased but useful new language and set of concepts—such as the word *homosexual* and the idea of a "personality type"—that some did use to categorize homosexuals, understand homosexuality, and even define themselves. During purges interrogators terrorized suspects into breaking their protective silence, forcing them to describe their homosexual lives, to make confessions, and to name their friends and sexual partners. Officers who aggressively rooted out homosexuals and exposed them to their draft boards, company mates, and families further destroyed their ability to hide in the closet, forcing them to lead new lives as known homosexuals. As these soldiers were thrown together into psych wards and queer stockades, they endured the same hardships together in small groups, better able to perceive themselves as compatriots who were victims of the same persecution. When they were discharged as undesirables without benefits and without having been charged with any crime, gay men and women gained a cause, a target to attack, and new avenues of appeal to defend their rights as gay GIs and veterans.

Disrupted and exposed by the war, gay life in the postwar years seemed to be growing at an unprecedented rate. Gay men and lesbians often saw this growth as a sign of hope, while government officials and the press saw it as a dangerous threat. The proliferation of gay bars, the broadening of public discussion of homosexuality, the formulation of the idea that homosexuals constituted a minority, the widespread acceptance of the psychiatric model of homosexuals as sexual psychopaths, the emergence and growth of federal anti-homosexual policies and bureaucracies, and the opening of new avenues through which gay citizens could appeal government injustices against them were some of the many legacies of World War II. These changes had a powerful impact on how a nation and its people would respond to homosexuality long after the war.

The veterans of World War II were the first generation of gay men and women to experience such rapid, dramatic, and widespread changes in their lives as homosexuals. Their common experience and shared memories as a generation helped determine how they would fit into this new world. Having grown up during the depression under New Deal reforms, many had learned to view the government as a provider of social welfare programs, a tradition that continued with the 1944 Servicemen's Readjustment Act. These men and women had matured at a time when the government was waging a war against fascism and when President Roosevelt's "Four Freedoms" had come to embody the principles for which the United States and its allies were fighting. In many ways their attitudes resembled those of second-generation immigrants who were passionately pro-American and who gained legitimacy as Americans by serving in the armed forces. Despite their griping in the military, gay veterans were patriotic and proud of their service to their country. They took advantage of the GI Bill and the postwar prosperity to try to settle down as civilians into stable, secure lives and to fit into American society whenever and wherever they could.

But beneath their desire to assimilate loomed an uneasiness, a sense of possibility mixed with fear. They saw the gay life begin to grow while the military, the federal government, and the press increasingly focused public attention on them. Like the Nisei generation of Japanese-Americans, who had been interned by the government that questioned their loyalty but from which they sought approval, this generation of gay Americans felt deep conflicts during and after the war. Often blaming themselves for being arrested or losing their jobs, they retained a strong faith in their government and a desire to fit in. Yet they felt a growing sense that as veterans they were being treated unfairly when singled out for persecution and should instead be able to live their lives in peace so long as they did their jobs and didn't hurt anybody else.

By the late 1940s, however, the ability of gay men and lesbians to blend into normal life became increasingly difficult as the attention of the nation's media, government officials, and church leaders turned toward issues of conformity and deviance. As families were reunited and struggled to put their lives back together after the war, articles, books, advertisements, and the media promoted idealized versions of the nuclear family, heterosexuality, and traditional gender roles in the home and in the workplace. Accompanying this preoccupation with conformity was a fearful scapegoating of those who deviated from a narrowing ideal of the nuclear family and the American way of life. Lesbians and gay men, many of them unable or unwilling to conform to such a narrow family idea, stood out more than they had during the war as "queers" and "sex deviates."

The media and government propaganda associated homosexuals and other "sex psychopaths" with Communists as the most dangerous nonconformists—invisible enemies who could live next door and who threatened the security and safety of children, women, the family, and the nation. From 1947 to 1955 twenty-one states and the District of Columbia, following local panics over child murderers and rapists, enacted sex psychopath laws. Supported by psychiatrists interested in extending the authority of their profession further into the criminal justice system, these laws targeted personality types, including homosexuals, more than their crimes, allowed their indefinite incarceration in institutions for the mentally ill until they were cured, and often required their registration as sex offenders with police departments wherever they lived.

During the nationwide campaigns against sexual psychopaths, the terms *child molester, homosexual, sex offender, sex psychopath, sex degenerate, sex deviate,* and sometimes even *Communist* became interchangeable in the minds of the public, legislators, and local police. In such a hostile climate, gay blue-discharge veterans could feel especially threatened because the military had diagnosed them on their military records as sexual psychopaths. The local panics that followed violent sex crimes, especially those against children, sometimes ended in rounding up gay men as potential suspects. "I suppose you read about the kidnapping and killing of the little girl in Chicago," wrote Marty Klausner in a letter to a gay friend in January 1946. "I noticed tonight that they 'thought' (in their damn self-righteous way) that perhaps a pervert had done it and they rounded up all the females [gay men]— they blame us for everything."

The press added to the national hysteria by portraying gay men as molesters of children, corrupters of youths, and even perpetrators of violent sexual crimes; lesbians were sometimes portrayed as malevolent seducers of women and girls. Some pulp magazines ran antigay articles in nearly every issue with titles such as "Homosexuals Are Dangerous" and "Lesbians Prey on Weak Women." Such an image of the homosexual as a dangerous sex pervert suited the paranoid political climate in the 1950s in which the national enemy was seen as lurking within. When America had needed its men and women to fight powerful enemies overseas during World War II, the military organization had found it more useful to project the image of the homosexual man as an effeminate weakling who was incapable of fighting or killing and of the aggressive, masculine woman as a patriot.

The enforcement of sex psychopath laws had the greatest impact on gay men and lesbians who led sexual or social lives outside their homes. While arrests for violent sexual crimes did not increase significantly in the postwar years, arrests did increase for gay men who were charged with nonviolent offenses such as consensual sodomy, sexual perversion, and public indecency, as well as for both men and women charged with patronizing a gay bar, touching in public, or wearing the clothing of the other gender. Some of these people, under the new laws, were sent to prison or committed to mental hospitals, then, upon their release, forced to register as sex offenders with their local police departments. . . .

While the sex psychopath panic was under way, military officials set out to consolidate the experimental antihomosexual policies they had developed during the war, but now working unconstrained by the wartime pressure to utilize all available personnel. The Navy Department led the other branches in centralizing and refining its homosexual procedures. In September 1947, Secretary of the Navy John L. Sullivan initiated the Navy's first postwar study of the way it managed homosexual personnel, hoping that the Navy would "take the leadership in a medical attack on a problem which appears to be growing." The secretary established a special "Committee for the Review of the Procedures for the Disposition of Naval Personnel Involved in Homosexual Offenses," which proposed several reforms, most of which in July 1949 were incorporated into a directive that superseded all the homosexual policy directives that the Navy had issued during the war.

This more comprehensive directive affirmed most aspects of existing policy while extending the Navy's power over its homosexual personnel. It directed officers to consider both the active and passive partners, whether two men or two women, as equally homosexual and equally responsible for their acts. It attempted to protect heterosexuals from "malicious charges" of homosexuality by requiring a more complete system of investigation and record keeping on each case. And it tried to protect the Navy from gay dischargees' charges of unjust discrimination by requiring homosexuals to sign the following statement of consent before being discharged: "I understand that I may be deprived of virtually all rights as a veteran under both Federal and State legislation; and that I may expect to encounter substantial prejudice in civilian life." A refusal to sign this statement of consent meant that the suspect would instead be tried by court-martial on criminal charges. . . .

The Defense Department adopted the committee's recommendations, extending the reach of the military's antihomosexual net even farther. These included adopting a clear policy statement that "homosexual personnel, irrespective of sex, should not be permitted to serve in any branch of the Armed Forces in any capacity, and prompt separation of known homosexuals from the Armed Forces is mandatory." This was broader than wartime policies that had required the rehabilitation of some gay male and lesbian personnel. The committee also recommended that each branch of the armed forces give indoctrination lectures on homosexuality modeled on existing venereal disease lectures. They proposed dividing all homosexual cases into three classes—those who used force, those who were consenting adults, and those with tendencies who had committed no provable acts in the service. . . .

At the same time Congress was taking steps to increase civilian control over military disciplinary procedures. In 1950 it enacted the Uniform Code of Military Justice (UCMJ), which was designed to protect the due process rights of individual military personnel and went into effect on May 21, 1951. Congress also established an all-civilian Court of Military Appeals to review court-martial decisions. By 1951 the Uniform Code, together with the Defense Department's uniform guidelines, established the basic policies, discharge procedures, and appeal channels for the disposition of homosexual personnel that remained in effect, with periodic modifications, in all branches of the armed forces for the next four decades.

While these changes were taking place at the policy level, the military's grip on homosexual personnel was tightening in practice as well. . . . During the peacetime years from 1947 to early 1950, the rate of discharge for homosexuals more than tripled the wartime rate. Except for a sharp drop in the Navy during the Korean War—suggesting that once again the military found it expedient to utilize homosexual personnel during a time of war—the discharge rate remained at postwar levels throughout the 1950s.

Nowhere was this tightening grip after the war more dramatic than in the military's about-face treatment of lesbians. During World War II the personnel shortages had allowed large numbers of American women to enlist in the armed forces. After the war when women were encouraged to return to civilian life and reassume traditional gender roles, those unmarried women who chose to remain in the military or who enlisted during peacetime increasingly stood out as members of a deviant group that was easily stereotyped as lesbian. As the wartime constraints against antilesbian witch hunts were lifted, purges of lesbians increased. Pat Bond, a WAC stationed in Tokyo, and Sarah Davis, a WAVE stationed in Florida, were both interrogated during extensive antilesbian witch hunts in the late 1940s, and each narrowly escaped being discharged as an undesirable, Bond because she had wed a gay man in a marriage of convenience and so passed as heterosexual, Davis because she successfully denied knowing her friends. During the Tokyo purge one woman committed suicide. By the mid-1950s, Navy officials secretly acknowledged that the homosexual discharge rate had become "much higher for the female than the male."

Another dramatic shift in postwar policy and practice was the introduction of programs to give all recruits lectures on homosexuality. This was a reversal of wartime policies to protect recruits from any discussion of homosexuality, especially in the women's branches, that might arouse their curiosity. The postwar introduction of lectures expanded the military's antihomosexual apparatus by adding a system of indoctrination to the prewar criminal justice system and the wartime systems for screening, discharge, and appeal.

These lectures reflected the growing preoccupation during the 1950s with stigmatizing not only homosexuals but also any women or men who deviated from a narrow gender norm. Retreating from the psychiatric advances of the war, Navy lecturers in 1952 were instructed that homosexuality "is not to be condoned on the grounds of 'mental illness' any more than other crime such as theft, homicide or criminal assault." Postwar lectures to WAVES recruits specifically rejected the guidance, counseling, and reassignment that had been recommended to WAC officers during the war. They told WAVES recruits that first-timers were as guilty as "confirmed" lesbians, encouraged them to inform on one another and warned that homosexuality threatened their ability to assume their proper roles in life as feminine women, wives, and mothers. While the wartime lectures had minimized the differences between lesbians and other women, the postwar lectures portrayed lesbians as exotic and dangerous perverts ready to seduce any woman who was young and naive. . . .

With these and other lectures, the military began to teach millions of young men and women to accept a uniform image of homosexuals, to fear them and report them, and to police their own feelings, friendships, and environment for signs of homosexual attractions. In a word, military officials began systematically to indoctrinate in its young recruits a response that psychiatrists and the gay rights movement later identified as homophobia: the irrational fear of homosexuality and of homosexual people. This fear reinforced a set of cold war political beliefs regarding homosexuals: To ensure public safety it was necessary to discuss the "homosexual menace" openly and to increase public awareness that unidentified homosexuals could be lurking anywhere; the government had a duty to root out and eliminate them; and all citizens needed to be ever vigilant in order to identify hidden sex perverts and report them to authorities. In this context Kinsey's findings on the high incidence of homosexual behavior among American males were used to indicate the magnitude of the homosexual threat. . . .

One of the thorniest administrative problems that military officials confronted as their antihomosexual project expanded after the war was what to do with the growing lists of names that were being generated as by-products of the discharge system. Some officials proposed releasing these names to the FBI and other government agencies to protect the general public by keeping known or suspected homosexuals under government surveillance. In January 1946, during the brief period of tolerance and gratitude following the war, such a proposal from the twelfth Naval District in San Francisco was stopped by the strong objections of Navy Surgeon General Ross McIntire. He argued that turning these files over to the FBI and local police would betray "the confidence of the individuals concerned" and "would be a prostitution of the art of medicine and contrary to the ethics of the medical profession." He also argued that it would jeopardize the chances of discharged homosexual men to re-establish themselves as "useful and self-supporting citizens in civil life" and questioned whether these men "constitute any particular danger to the security of the social order as a whole." . . .

But as the names continued to accumulate, and the social and political climate became increasingly hostile to homosexuals, pressure to release the lists mounted, especially from the offices of Army and Navy intelligence. These had been largely responsible for compiling the lists of names from the confessions, seized letters, and address books of the gay men and lesbians their personnel had interrogated. As a result intelligence officers earned a reputation as being among the most antihomosexual in the armed forces. They eventually found sympathetic ears not among top military administrators but rather among senators who began their own crusade against the employment of homosexuals in the federal government.

The military organization has often served as a testing ground for social policies and programs that later have been adopted by civilian bureaucracies. The military's expansion of its antihomosexual policies during and after the war served as such a model for senators who in 1950 launched the most aggressive attack on homosexual employees that had ever taken place in the federal government. Their crusade was in sharp contrast to the sympathetic concern congressmen had expressed in 1946 for the plight of the blue-discharge veterans.

The 1950 antihomosexual hearings in the Senate began as a by-product of the cold war anticommunist scare. On February 28 Under Secretary of State John Peurifoy, testifying before a Senate Committee investigating the loyalty of government employees, admitted that most of the ninety-one State Department employees who had been dismissed as security risks were homosexual. Republicans seized the opportunity to attack the Truman administration and turned Peurifoy's revelation into a partisan issue that each month increased in intensity and even gained the support of several Democrats. For the rest of the year, new antihomosexual revelations or actions took place in Washington almost weekly. Republican Senator Kenneth Wherry of Nebraska and Democratic Senator Lister Hill of Alabama immediately formed a subcommittee to make preliminary investigations into the "Infiltration of Subversives and Moral Perverts into the Executive Branch of the United States Government." In June the full Senate authorized the formation of a subcommittee, headed by Senator Clyde Hoey of North Carolina, to investigate the "Employment of Homosexuals and Other Sex Perverts in Government." The subcommittee submitted its report to the Senate on December 16, describing its "government-wide" investigation into homosexuality as "unprecedented."

It was through the vehicle of these hearings by Senators Wherry, Hill, and Hoey that the military's policies and procedures for discharging homosexual personnel were extended to every employee of the federal government. Until these hearings, the Hoey committee reported, government administrators had never considered homosexuality to be a "personnel problem" and were grossly negligent in employing homosexuals. Some administrators actually "condoned the employment of homosexuals" based on the "false premise that what a Government employee did outside of the office on his own time . . . was his own business." Others took a "head-in-the-sand attitude toward the problem of sexual perversion," hoping to avoid dealing with an unpleasant issue by ignoring it. Civil Service Commission regulations had not explicitly mentioned homosexuals or "perverts" as candidates for removal from the federal service, making it easier for personnel officers to retain them as employees.

The result of this negligence, the Hoey committee noted, was that few homosexuals had been fired from government jobs. Instructing federal agencies to submit statistics regarding homosexual dismissals, the committee discovered that from January 1, 1947, to the end of 1950, the government had handled 4954 homosexual cases, the vast majority (4380) of which were in the military. Two-thirds of the few civilian cases during this four-year period occurred in 1950, mostly after the antihomosexual campaign had received wide publicity in March. The armed services clearly had a head start on other government agencies because they had discharged the most homosexuals and because, a decade earlier, they had been the first branch of the government to define homosexuality as a personnel problem. The committee concluded that the military's policy and procedures should be used as the model for other government agencies.

To strengthen their arguments, members of the Hoey committee invited intelligence officers—whose job it was to interrogate suspected homosexuals—to present the military's rationale for eliminating such people. They testified that male homosexual personnel were dangerous because they preyed on young boys in the service, they were high-strung and neurotic from leading double lives, and they were security risks. "This reasoning by authorities in the Armed Forces," concluded Senator Wherry, "based on years of observation and experience applies with equal force to other departments and agencies of the Government." In the areas of explicit policies, standardized procedures, uniform enforcement, constant vigilance, and coordination with law enforcement agencies regarding homosexuals, the committee regarded the armed services as the standard against which all other government agencies were compared and found lacking.

The major purpose and achievement of both the Hoey and Wherry-Hill committees, however, was to construct and promote the belief that homosexuals in the military and the government constituted security risks who, as individuals or working in conspiracy with members of the Communist party, threatened the safety of the nation. They wanted to apply this reasoning to military as well as federal personnel policies. But the military had its own rationale for excluding homosexual personnel based on the belief that they were unfit for military service and that they disrupted morale and discipline. The Navy Surgeon General's Office in 1941 and the Defense Department's 1949 Project M-46 report had both raised the security risk issue but considered it unimportant; the 1948 Navy lectures, although vehemently antihomosexual, had not mentioned the security risk issue at all. The military establishment had won the greatest war in its history without anyone in its ranks having threatened national security because of [his or her] homosexuality. Even under pressure from senators and their own intelligence officers, the initial response of military authorities was to give the security risk argument little credence except as a political issue outside the military domain.

To build their case that homosexuals were security risks, the Senate committees solicited testimony from intelligence officers working in police departments, the FBI, the CIA, and the armed forces. The senators interpreted the opinions of military intelligence officers as representing those of the armed forces and concluded, without releasing the testimony, that "all of these agencies are in complete agreement that sex perverts in Government constitute security risks." The evidence that these witnesses provided, however, was flimsy at best, consisting of one anecdote about an Austrian intelligence officer, Colonel Alfred Redl, who was blackmailed in 1912. Witnesses also referred to unspecified cases in which "Nazi and Communist agents have attempted to obtain information from employees of our Government by threatening to expose their abnormal sex activities," and reported unsubstantiated rumors that during the war Adolf Hitler had "amassed the names of homosexuals around the world" and that this list had been "acquired by Russia" after Germany's defeat.

Ironically the strongest argument for portraying homosexuals as susceptible to blackmail by Communists was the military's own success in emotionally breaking down gay men and lesbians during and after the war. Intelligence officers testified that, in their own experience, "perverts are vulnerable to interrogation by a skilled questioner and they seldom refuse to talk about themselves." Despite the fact that in all these cases the interrogators and blackmailers were officers of the United States military, not agents of enemy governments, the Hoey report concluded that homosexuals did constitute security risks. They recommended that government officials should "get sex perverts out of Government and keep them out," and that all government agencies should pool their information on homosexuals through the FBI to make this process more efficient.

The immediate impact of the 1950 antihomosexual scare in Congress on the careers of civilian government workers was dramatic. Before the investigations, from 1947 through April 1950, the government had dismissed an average of five homosexuals each month. During the second half of 1950, this rate had grown to more than sixty per month. In July Max Lerner, in a *New York Post* column entitled "Panic on the Potomac," compared these cold war "witch hunts" to the military's wartime actions against homosexuals. "In the Army it used to be called 'blue discharge,'" Lerner wrote. "The Senators call it the 'purge of the pervert.'"

While the panic generated by the Senate hearings led to an immediate increase in firings, members of Congress, as well as government and military officials, began to translate the Hoey committee's recommendations into new laws and policies. . . . But the strongest action was taken by President Dwight Eisenhower shortly after he took office. In April 1953 he signed Executive Order 10450, which tightened loyalty and security regulations and, for the first time in civil service law, explicitly stated that "sexual perversion" was necessary grounds for not hiring and for firing federal workers.

With Eisenhower's executive order the government's antihomosexual policies and procedures, which had originated in the wartime military, expanded to include every agency and department of the federal government and every private company or corporation with a government contract, such as railroad companies and aircraft plants. This affected the job security of more than six million government workers and armed forces personnel. By the mid-1950s, similar policies also had gone into effect in state and local governments, extending the prohibitions on the employment of homosexuals to over twelve million workers, more than 20 percent of the United States labor force, who now had to sign oaths attesting to their moral purity in order to get or keep their jobs. Similar policies were adopted independently by private companies and even by private organizations such as the American Red Cross, which "summarily dismissed" employees involved in homosexual conduct, whether they were "habituals, one-time offenders, or mere tendency cases." Within only a few years antihomosexual policies had spread from the military to nearly all levels of employment in the United States.

The prominent coverage given to this federal antihomosexual campaign, combined with state crusades against sexual psychopaths, contributed to a climate that fostered local panics and crackdowns. The gay and lesbian bars that had proliferated after the war became particular targets. As they emerged in more cities and multiplied in others, the legislatures of California, Michigan, and other states, which were charged with the duty of licensing and regulating liquor establishments, took steps in conjunction with local police to regulate or ban those they identified as "homo hangouts" or "resorts for sexual perverts." Highly publicized antigay crusades swept through Miami, Wichita, Boise, Portland (Oregon), Tacoma, San Francisco, and many other cities, especially where gay bars were expanding or where politicians exploited the antihomosexual climate to further their careers, leading to street sweeps and mass arrests of hundreds of people at a time.

As refugees from these local crackdowns and from federal and military purges looked for safer harbors, city after city imagined that an "invasion of homosexuals" was turning it into the homosexual capital of America. In the words of one newspaper's headline, the 1950s had turned into a "war on homosexuals," one that was more widespread and publicized than any antihomosexual campaigns that had occurred during World War II.

Under heavy attack during the postwar decade, most gay male and lesbian citizens refrained from publicly standing up for themselves, fighting for their rights, or even talking about their lives. In 1951, Donald Webster Cory, protected by his pseudonym, tried to explain why he and other gay people didn't fight back. The "worst effect of discrimination," he wrote, "has been to make the homosexuals doubt themselves and share in the general contempt for sexual inverts." When an injustice was done against them, the fear of exposure led many to accept what had happened and then "make an effort to hide their homosexuality even more carefully." When arrested in gay bar raids, most people pleaded guilty, fearful of publicly exposing their homosexuality during a trial that might prove they were innocent of any crime. Legally barred from many forms of private and government employment, from serving their country, from expressing their opinions in newspapers and magazines, from gathering in bars and other public places as homosexuals, and from leading sexual lives, gay men and women were denied the civil liberties and even the channels of protest that were open to many other minorities. To make matters worse, no civil liberties organizations were willing to speak up in their behalf. Caught in what Cory called a "vicious circle," those who were honest about their lives became outcasts and martyrs, while those who lived a lie faced the shame of their own debasement, wondering if the contempt so many people felt toward them was justified. Such conditions led to stifled anger, fear, isolation, and helplessness, not collective protest or political action.

But the postwar years were also a period of new possibilities that helped to strengthen and develop gay culture. Despite and sometimes because of the mounting political war against them, the generation of World War II gay veterans did find ways to break through their isolation. They responded to a hostile environment by expanding their "closet," making it a roomier place to live. Previous generations had invented the closet—a system of lies, denials, disguises, and double entendres—that had enabled them to express some of their homosexuality by pretending it didn't exist and hiding it from view. A later generation would "come out of the closet," learning to live as proud and openly gay men and women and demanding public recognition. But the World War II generation slowly stretched their closet to its limits, not proclaiming or parading their homosexuality in public but not willing to live lonely, isolated lives.

In increasing numbers these men and women went to gay and lesbian bars that proliferated despite new state laws designed to put them out of business. In the late 1940s gay bars opened for the first time in such medium-size cities as Kansas City, Missouri; Richmond, Virginia; Worcester, Massachusetts; and San Jose, California. These meeting places evolved into the primary gay social institution in cities after the war. By providing patrons with public spaces in which to gather, bars helped shape a sense of gay identity that went beyond the individual to the group. When patrons were caught in raids, they knew they were being arrested and harassed for gathering in public as homosexuals. Throughout the 1950s and 1960s, gay and lesbian bars became a major battleground in the fight to create public gathering places for homosexuals that were legal and free from harassment. In June 1969 gay riots in response to a routine police raid of the Stonewall Inn, a gay bar in New York's Greenwich Village, sparked the beginning of the gay liberation movement. Another gay institution, the bathhouse, also proliferated after the war, creating a relatively safe, semipublic space that affirmed gay male eroticism and provided any man an anonymous outlet for his homosexual desires.

Their widespread use of pseudonyms enabled this generation to expand the closet while minimizing the risk of being exposed. Under pen names they wrote honestly about their lives and their sexuality in books, paperbacks, magazines, and pornography. Gay men published male physique magazines, creating a market that evolved into a flourishing gay erotica industry. Lesbians wrote and devoured hundreds of lesbian romance paperbacks, which became so popular that they were sold in five-and-dimes and drugstores across the country, reaching even the loneliest, most isolated lesbian or gay man in Kansas or North Dakota.

It was in this social climate—when antihomosexual campaigns terrorized gay Americans while the expansion of gay culture and the public discussion of homosexuality opened up new possibilities—that the first signs of a continuous gay political movement and press emerged in the United States. In 1950 the Mattachine Society was organized in Los Angeles in response to the antihomosexual campaigns in Washington, police arrests in Los Angeles, the state sexual psychopath panics, the treatment of homosexuals by the military, and the crackdowns on gay and lesbian bars. In 1955 women in San Francisco started the Daughters of Bilitis, the first lesbian rights organization in the United States. The esoteric names of both of these groups hid that they were homosexual, helping to protect them from harassment. Most of their officers used personal pseudonyms as well.

Charles Rowland recalled that he and most of the other founders of the Mattachine Society had been veterans. Rowland's own interest in starting a gay organization grew indirectly out of his military experience. World War II was a war against fascism, he explained. After his discharge he continued his wartime "save the world" idealism first by organizing other veterans in the Midwest as a field representative of the liberal American Veterans Committee, then by joining the Communist party. When he fled the Midwest to Los Angeles during the anticommunist scare, it was this same idealism that led him to join original founder Harry Hay and others in starting a homosexual rights organization.

From the start the gay male and lesbian organizations published and distributed their own little magazines, which actively took on the cause of homosexual soldiers and veterans. Beginning in 1953 issues of the predominantly gay male magazines *ONE* and *Mattachine Review* and the lesbian magazine the *Ladder,* published by the Daughters of Bilitis, included pieces on the status of lesbians and gay men in the military. They reprinted congressional testimony and newspaper clippings concerning veterans with undesirable discharges and printed anonymous interviews with lesbian and gay male veterans as well as their poems, letters, stories, and personal statements. They published editorials and advice columns, as well as news of witch hunts, changes in military policy, and accounts of individuals who appealed their bad discharges. They ran special features, including cover stories, with such titles as "Homosexuals in Uniform," "Homosexual Servicemen" and "Undesirable Discharges."

In 1954 *Mattachine Review* published an open letter to Senator Everett Dirksen, who had made an offhand complaint that it had been "no picnic" to purge homosexuals from the government. The letter's anonymous author, writing in memory of the gay soldiers who had died in World War II, captured many veterans' sense of quiet outrage at being persecuted by the government they had fought for. "Thousands of graves in France," the letter read, "many many thousand more graves on South Pacific Islands and beneath the seas, contain the sad remains of men who were brave soldiers, airmen, sailors, and marines *first* and homosexuals second. They were no less brave, they did no less to win the war for democracy, than did their heterosexual compatriots. But the democracy for which they did fight and die, and still fight and still die, and will yet fight and yet die, denies them and us our rights."

The issue of military discrimination remained of vital concern to the growing gay rights movement. In 1966 the first nationwide protest by gay male and lesbian organizations in the United States was one that opposed the military's discrimination against gay personnel and veterans. But by this time such a position appeared old-fashioned to a baby-boom generation of gay activists who, as the Vietnam War heated up, began to question why homosexuals wanted to join the military at all. . . .

The military's policy remains staunchly antihomosexual while many other bureaucracies, from federal agencies to private corporations, have abandoned similar stands and have even adopted policies of nondiscrimination. It defines homosexuality as a threat to the very essence of the military organization, and the bureaucracy that puts this ideology into practice both legalizes and reinforces the social hostility toward homosexuals that helps to keep it in place. By taking such an extreme position, policymakers make it difficult for themselves to stop excluding gay personnel without losing face and credibility, and without appearing to condone homosexuality and embrace homosexuals.

Despite the strictness of their policies, military officials can never eliminate homosexuals or homosexuality from the armed forces. During World War II military psychiatrists and other administrators began to identify some of the most common personnel problems regarding homosexuality: Gender-segregated living conditions intensify homosexual fears and tensions; the hostility that some soldiers express toward homosexuals can threaten morale and affect job performance; and sexual relations between officers and enlisted personnel, whether homosexual or heterosexual, can threaten discipline. But the solution that was developed during the war—the punitive elimination of homosexuals—only magnified the military's "homosexual problem." The discharge policy increased fear, reinforced hostility and prejudice, encouraged scapegoating and witch hunting, and helped to solidify gay men and women into a political movement against the military's exclusion of homosexuals. The discharge policy continues to intensify the importance of homosexuality as a military problem rather than make it go away.

Since the antigay policies were introduced during World War II, military officials have spent much time and resources denying that the armed forces have any significant problem with homosexuality. They have done this by erasing the history of the policies, refusing to discuss them in public, and suppressing even the friendliest internal criticism. In the process, military officials have successfully perpetuated three myths: that the armed forces always had an antigay discharge policy, that known homosexuals cannot fit into the military organization and are routinely discharged, and that organized opposition to the policy comes only from outside and not from within. A policy that appears to have existed for all time, to be unanimously supported within the military, and to allow for no exceptions is not easily abandoned.

But the military's hidden history shows that the discharge policy itself was the product of liberal reform, having been put in place in 1943 by officers who in part wanted to improve the lot of the homosexual soldier out of a sense of fairness and justice. It has always been used flexibly, being modified or completely ignored—although usually in secret—to meet the demands of fluctuating personnel needs particularly during times of war. And since its inception the discharge policy has been surrounded by internal debate.

The long tradition of dissent within the military, as old as the discharge policy itself, has continually offered alternatives to the blanket elimination of homosexuals from the military, identifying antihomosexual prejudice rather than homosexuals as the problem. In 1945 Lewis Loeser, Clements Fry, and Edna Rostow all recommended that homosexuals not be treated as a class but be accepted and integrated into the military, assigned to duty based on individual skills and talents, and discharged only if their homosexuality prevented them from doing their jobs. In 1952 a Defense Department committee appointed to review homosexual policy could not reach agreement and issued two reports, with only the dissenting minority maintaining that homosexuals constituted security risks and that no homosexuals should be retained in the service. In 1957 the Navy's Crittenden Board concluded that there was no evidence to support the idea that homosexuals as a class "cannot acceptably serve in the military" or that they were security risks. The board even suggested that homosexuals might be more reliable in espionage and other top-secret jobs than some heterosexuals.

This long tradition of dissent, however, has been accompanied by a long record of suppression. The reports of Fry and Rostow, the Crittenden Board, and virtually every other team of military researchers have been kept secret or destroyed. In September 1977, after thirty-five years of studying homosexuals and their own antihomosexual policies, Army officials stated that their files revealed "no evidence of special studies pertaining to homosexuals" and Navy officials maintained that they could not locate any of their own studies on homosexuality. It was only under orders from a federal judge in 1977 that the Crittenden Report and other Navy studies were released.

Today the same pattern of dissent and suppression continues, although it has become more public. In October 1989 members of Congress released to the press a report by researchers at the Defense Department's Personnel Security Research and Education Center (PERSEREC) in Monterey, California. The report concluded that homosexuals were no more of a security risk and no more susceptible to blackmail than heterosexuals, and that the military should consider accepting homosexuals. It recommended that the military begin research to test the hypothesis that gay men and women "can function appropriately in military units," as the military had done before it integrated blacks into the military immediately after World War II. Members of Congress released another report from the same research center that concluded that personnel discharged as homosexuals were better qualified and had fewer personal problems than the average heterosexual in the service. Defense Department officials rejected and condemned both these reports. They charged that the research was biased and technically flawed and that the researchers had exceeded their authority by criticizing policy. Refusing to participate in a public debate, the Pentagon stated that "we cannot comment on matters that remain unresolved before the court."

In 1957, the secret Crittenden Report had made nearly the same conclusions as the 1989 PERSEREC Reports. The Crittenden Report, however, recommended no change in policy because the military "should not move ahead of civilian society" in accepting homosexuals, although it advised the Navy to "keep abreast of any widely accepted changes in the attitude of society." In the three decades that followed the Crittenden Report, dramatic changes significantly altered social attitudes, leading to the rise of movements for women's rights and gay rights, the repeal of sodomy laws, and the adoption of corporate and government nondiscrimination policies. The PERSEREC Report, addressing the issue of leadership raised by the Crittenden Report, suggested that the military had fallen behind civilian society and the time had come for it to stop excluding homosexuals. Summarizing the broad changes that had taken place during the twentieth century, the report concluded that the earlier categorizations of homosexuality as "sin, crime, and sickness" were obsolete and that the military should begin to accept homosexuals as members of a "minority group." With this recommendation, the process by which the military's expanding antigay policy had pressured gay men and women to identify themselves as members of a persecuted minority had come full circle: Military researchers were now using the idea that homosexuals constituted a minority group to call for an end to the antigay policy.

The generation of gay men and women who served in World War II grew into adulthood fighting one war for their country and another to protect themselves from their government's escalating mobilization against them. When they returned to civilian life, some fought for their right to be treated fairly as patients, veterans, and citizens. For others a quiet sense of belonging was victory enough, to have the chance to fit into the country they fought for, leading ordinary but unapologetic lives. As they grow into old age and once again face their own and each other's deaths, most still blend into the world around them, while some have come out either under fire or on their own. Today they witness an expanding public debate over the military's exclusion of homosexuals. If that debate is to be at all serious, it must include a sense of history—not only of how the military established its anti-gay policy during World War II and then suppressed all internal dissent, but also of how the men and women who were the policy's first targets fought and died for their country with the rest of their generation.

SOURCES

Sex Crime Panic

The items on this and the following page are typical of the kinds of images that circulated during the nationwide panic over sexual psychopaths in the late 1940s. The first appeared as an illustration to FBI Director J. Edgar Hoover's article, "How Safe Is Your Daughter?" (1947). The second is from a brochure for schoolchildren distributed by the City of Detroit. What messages do they contain? If the photo of the three girls were made into a film, what genre would it be?

"*The nation's women and children will never be secure . . . so long as degenerates run wild*"

NEVER go with strangers when they ask for directions.

NEVER go with strangers who offer you a job with pay.

Truman on Hiroshima (August 6, 1945)

On the day the Enola Gay *released an atomic bomb over the Japanese city of Hiroshima, the White House released this statement by President Harry Truman. It is an extraordinary document, full of the twists and turns that were perhaps inevitable at this moment when the public was first introduced to the atomic bomb, told about its use at Hiroshima, and informed of its atomic future. How did Truman justify the use of this weapon? What aspects of the atomic bomb did Truman emphasize? What should or might he have said that he did not?*

Sixteen hours ago an American airplane dropped one bomb on Hiroshima, an important Japanese Army base. That bomb had more power than 20,000 tons of T.N.T. It had more than two thousand times the blast power of the British "Grand Slam" which is the largest bomb ever yet used in the history of warfare.

The Japanese began the war from the air at Pearl Harbor. They have been repaid many fold. And the end is not yet. With this bomb we have now added a new

Foreign Relations of the United States, *Potsdam,* vol. 2, Washington, D.C., 1960, pp. 1380–1381 and revolutionary increase in destruction to supplement the growing power of our armed forces. In their present form these bombs are now in production and even more powerful forms are in development.

It is an atomic bomb. It is a harnessing of the basic power of the universe. The force from which the sun draws its power has been loosed against those who brought war to the Far East.

Before 1939, it was the accepted belief of scientists that it was theoretically possible to release atomic energy. But no one knew any practical method of doing it. By 1942, however, we knew that the Germans were working feverishly to find a way to add atomic energy to the other engines of war with which they hoped to enslave the world. But they failed. We may be grateful to Providence that the Germans got the V-1s and the V-2s late and in limited quantities and even more grateful that they did not get the atomic bomb at all.

The battle of the laboratories held fateful risks for us as well as the battles of the air, land and sea, and we have now won the battle of the laboratories as we have won the other battles.

Beginning in 1940, before Pearl Harbor, scientific knowledge useful in war was pooled between the United States and Great Britain, and many priceless helps to our victories have come from that arrangement. Under that general policy the research on the atomic bomb was begun. With American and British scientists working together we entered the race of discovery against the Germans.

The United States had available the large number of scientists of distinction in the many needed areas of knowledge. It had the tremendous industrial and financial resources necessary for the project and they could be devoted to it without undue impairment of other vital war work. In the United States the laboratory work and the production plants, on which a substantial start had already been made, would be out of reach of enemy bombing, while at that time Britain was exposed to constant air attack and was still threatened with the possibility of invasion. For these reasons Prime Minister Churchill and President Roosevelt agreed that it was wise to carry on the project here. We now have two great plants and many lesser works devoted to the production of atomic power. Employment during peak construction numbered 125,000 and over 65,000 individuals are even now engaged in operating the plants. Many have worked there for two and a half years. Few know what they have been producing. They see great quantities of material going in and they see nothing coming out of these plants, for the physical size of the explosive charge is exceedingly small. We have spent two billion dollars on the greatest scientific gamble in history—we won.

But the greatest marvel is not the size of the enterprise, its secrecy, nor its cost, but the achievement of scientific brains in putting together infinitely complex pieces of knowledge held by many men in different fields of science into a workable plan. And hardly less marvelous has been the capacity of industry to design, and of labor to operate, the machines and methods to do things never done before so that the brain child of many minds came forth in physical shape and performed as it was supposed to do. Both science and industry worked under the direction of the United States Army, which achieved a unique success in managing so diverse a problem in the advancement of knowledge in an amazingly short time. It is doubtful if such another combination could be got together in the world. What has been done is the greatest achievement of organized science in history. It was done under high pressure and without failure.

We are now prepared to obliterate more rapidly and completely every productive enterprise the Japanese have above ground in any city. We shall destroy their docks, their factories, and their communications. Let there be no mistake; we shall completely destroy Japan's power to make war.

It was to spare the Japanese people from utter destruction that the ultimatum of July 26 was issued at Potsdam. Their leaders promptly rejected that ultimatum. If they do not now accept our terms they may expect a rain of ruin from the air, the like of which has never been seen on this earth. Behind this air attack will follow sea and land forces in such numbers and power as they have not yet seen and with the fighting skill of which they are already well aware.

The secretary of war, who has kept in personal touch with all phases of this project, will immediately make public a statement giving further details.

His statement will give facts concerning the sites of Oak Ridge near Knoxville, Tennessee, and at Richland near Pasco, Washington, and an installation near Santa Fe, New Mexico. Although the workers at the sites have been making materials to be used in producing the greatest of destructive force in history they have not themselves been in danger beyond that of many other occupations, for the utmost care has been taken of their safety.

The fact that we can release atomic energy ushers in a new era in man's understanding of nature's forces. Atomic energy may in the future supplement the power that now comes from coal, oil, and falling water, but at present it cannot be produced on a basis to compete with them commercially. Before that comes there must be a long period of intensive research.

It has never been the habit of the scientists of this country or the policy of this government to withhold from the world scientific knowledge. Normally, therefore, everything about the work with atomic energy would be made public.

But under present circumstances it is not intended to divulge the technical processes of production or all the military applications, pending further examination of possible methods of protecting us and the rest of the world from the danger of sudden destruction.

I shall recommend that the Congress of the United States consider promptly the establishment of an appropriate commission to control the production and use of atomic power within the United States. I shall give further consideration and make further recommendations to the Congress as to how atomic power can become a powerful and forceful influence towards the maintenance of world peace.

I, The Jury

Mickey Spillane

To a reading public enthralled with detectives and detective stories, Mickey Spillane's 1947 best-seller, I, The Jury, *introduced one of the most famous fictional detectives of all: Mike Hammer. Hammer was different. Though he was no dummy, his methods were not those of science (like Sherlock Holmes) or of advanced technology (like the comic strip figure Dick Tracy, who debuted in the 1940s). In reading the opening chapter to the novel, use the Hammer character to help shape your understanding of the 1940s. What were Hammer's methods? Why might readers have responded enthusiastically to Hammer's ways of doing things? In addition, pay close attention to the circumstances that bring Hammer into the case and make him want to solve it. How is Hammer affected by the war? Do you see any similarity between Hammer's style and values and those of Harry Truman, expressed in the previous document? Or between Hammer and Joe McCarthy (see Chapter 2)?*

I shook the rain from my hat and walked into the room. Nobody said a word. They stepped back politely and I could feel their eyes on me. Pat Chambers was standing by the door to the bedroom trying to steady Myrna. The girl's body was racking with dry sobs. I walked over and put my arms around her.

"Take it easy, kid," I told her. "Come on over here and lie down." I led her to a studio couch that was against the far wall and sat her down. She was in pretty bad shape. One of the uniformed cops put a pillow down for her and she stretched out.

Pat motioned me over to him and pointed to the bedroom. "In there, Mike," he said.

In there. The words hit me hard. In there was my best friend lying on the floor dead. The body. Now I could call it that. Yesterday it was Jack Williams, the guy that shared the same mud bed with me through two years of warfare in the stinking slime of the jungle. Jack, the guy who said he'd give his right arm for a friend and did when he stopped a bastard of a Jap from slitting me in two. He caught the bayonet in the biceps, and they amputated his arm.

Pat didn't say a word. He let me uncover the body and feel the cold face. For the first time in my life I felt like crying. "Where did he get it, Pat?"

"In the stomach. Better not look at it. The killer carved the nose off a forty-five and gave it to him low."

I threw back the sheet anyway, and a curse caught in my throat. Jack was in shorts, his one hand still clutching his belly in agony. The bullet went in clean, but where it came out left a hole big enough to cram a fist into.

Very gently I pulled the sheet back and stood up. It wasn't a complicated setup. A trail of blood led from the table beside the bed to where Jack's artificial arm lay. Under him the throw rug was ruffled and twisted. He had tried to drag himself along with his one arm, but never reached what he was after.

His police positive, still in the holster, was looped over the back of the chair. That was what he wanted. With a slug in his gut he never gave up.

I pointed to the rocker, overbalanced under the weight of the .38. "Did you move the chair, Pat?"

"No, why?"

"It doesn't belong there. Don't you see?"

Pat looked puzzled. "What are you getting at?"

"That chair was over there by the bed. I've been here often enough to remember that much. After the killer shot Jack, he pulled himself toward the chair. But the killer didn't leave after the shooting. He stood here and watched him grovel on the floor in agony. Jack was after that gun, but he never reached it. He could have if the killer didn't move it. The trigger-happy bastard must have stood by the door laughing while Jack tried to make his last play. He kept pulling the chair back, inch by inch, until Jack gave up. Tormenting a guy who's been through all sorts of hell. Laughing. This was no ordinary murder, Pat. It's as cold-blooded and as deliberate as I ever saw one. I'm going to get the one that did this."

"You dealing yourself in, Mike?"

"I'm in. What did you expect?"

"You're going to have to go easy."

"Uh-uh. Fast, Pat. From now on it's a race. I want the killer for myself. We'll work together as usual, but in the homestretch, I'm going to pull the trigger."

"No, Mike, it can't be that way. You know it."

"Okay, Pat," I told him. "You have a job to do, but so have I. Jack was about the best friend I ever had. We lived together and fought together. And by Christ, I'm not letting the killer go through the tedious process of the law. You know what happens, damn it. They get the best lawyer there is and screw up the whole thing and wind up a hero! The dead can't speak for themselves. They can't tell what happened. How could Jack tell a jury what it was like to have his insides ripped out by a dumdum? Nobody in the box would know how it felt to be dying or have your own killer laugh in your face. One arm. Hell, what does that mean? So he has the Purple Heart. But did they ever try dragging themselves across a floor to a gun with that one arm, their insides filling up with blood, so goddamn mad to be shot they'd do anything to reach the killer. No, damn it. A jury is cold and impartial like they're supposed to be, while some snotty lawyer makes them pour tears as he tells how his client was insane at the moment or had to shoot in self-defense. Swell. The law is fine. But this time I'm the law and I'm not going to be cold and impartial. I'm going to remember all those things."

I reached out and grabbed the lapels of his coat. "And something more, Pat. I want you to hear every word I say. I want you to tell it to everyone you know. And when you tell it, tell it strong, because I mean every word of it. There are ten thousand mugs that hate me and you know it. They hate me because if they mess with me I shoot their damn heads off. I've done it and I'll do it again."

There was so much hate welled up inside me I was ready to blow up, but I turned and looked down at what was once Jack. Right then I felt like saying a prayer, but I was too mad.

"Jack, you're dead now. You can't hear me any more. Maybe you can. I hope so. I want you to hear what I'm about to say. You've known me a long time, Jack.

My word is good just as long as I live. I'm going to get the louse that killed you. He won't sit in the chair. He won't hang. He will die exactly as you died, with a .45 slug in the gut, just a little below the belly button. No matter who it is, Jack, I'll get the one. Remember, no matter who it is, I promise."

When I looked up, Pat was staring at me strangely. He shook his head. I knew what he was thinking. "Mike, lay off. For God's sake don't go off half-cocked about this. I know you too well. You'll start shooting up anyone connected with this and get in a jam you'll never get out of."

"I'm over it now, Pat. Don't get excited. From now on I'm after one thing, the killer. You're a cop, Pat. You're tied down by rules and regulations. There's someone over you. I'm alone. I can slap someone in the puss and they can't do a damn thing. No one can kick me out of my job. Maybe there's nobody to put up a huge fuss if I get gunned down, but then I still have a private cop's license with the privilege to pack a rod, and they're afraid of me. I hate hard, Pat. When I latch on to the one behind this they're going to wish they hadn't started it. Some day, before long, I'm going to have my rod in my mitt and the killer in front of me. I'm going to watch the killer's face. I'm going to plunk one right in his gut, and when he's dying on the floor I may kick his teeth out.

"You couldn't do that. You have to follow the book because you're a Captain of Homicide. Maybe the killer will wind up in the chair. You'd be satisfied, but I wouldn't. It's too easy. That killer is going down like Jack did."

There was nothing more to say. I could see by the set of Pat's jaw that he wasn't going to try to talk me out of it. All he could do was to try to beat me to him and take it from there. We walked out of the room together. The coroner's men had arrived and were ready to carry the body away.

I didn't want Myrna to see that. I sat down on the couch beside her and let her sob on my shoulder. That way I managed to shield her from the sight of her fiancé being carted off in a wicker basket. She was a good kid. Four years ago, when Jack was on the force, he had grabbed her as she was about to do a Dutch over the Brooklyn Bridge. She was a wreck then. Dope had eaten her nerve ends raw. But he had taken her to his house and paid for a full treatment until she was normal. For the both of them it had been a love that blossomed into a beautiful thing. If it weren't for the war they would have been married long ago.

When Jack came back with one arm it had made no difference. He no longer was a cop, but his heart was with the force. She had loved him before, and she still loved him. Jack wanted her to give up her job, but Myrna persuaded him to let her hold it until he really got settled. It was tough for a man with one arm to find employment, but he had many friends.

Before long he was part of the investigating staff of an insurance company. It had to be police work. For Jack there was nothing else. Then they were happy. Then they were going to be married. Now this.

Pat tapped me on the shoulder. "There's a car waiting downstairs to take her home."

I rose and took her by the hand. "Come on, kid. There's no more you can do. Let's go."

She didn't say a word, but stood up silently and let a cop steer her out the door. I turned to Pat. "Where do we start?" I asked him.

"Well, I'll give you as much as I know. See what you can add to it. You and Jack were great buddies. It might be that you can add something that will make some sense."

Inwardly I wondered. Jack was such a straight guy that he never made an enemy. Even while on the force. Since he'd gotten back, his work with the insurance company was pretty routine. But maybe an angle there, though.

"Jack threw a party last night," Pat went on. "Not much of an affair."

"I know," I cut in, "he called me and asked me over, but I was pretty well knocked out. I hit the sack early. Just a group of old friends he knew before the army."

"Yeah. We got their names from Myrna. The boys are checking on them now."

"Who found the body?" I asked.

"Myrna did. She and Jack were driving out to the country today to pick a building site for their cottage. She got here at eight A.M. or a little after. When Jack didn't answer, she got worried. His arm had been giving him trouble lately and she thought it might have been that. She called the super. He knew her and let her in. When she screamed the super came running back and called us. Right after I got the story about the party from her, she broke down completely. Then I called you."

"What time did the shooting occur?"

"The coroner places it about five hours before I got here. That would make it about three fifteen. When I get an autopsy report we may be able to narrow it down ever further."

"Anyone hear a shot?"

"Nope. It probably was a silenced gun."

"Even with a muffler, a .45 makes a good-sized noise."

"I know, but there was a party going on down the hall. Not loud enough to cause complaints, but enough to cover up any racket that might have been made here."

"What about those that were here?" Pat reached in his pocket and pulled out a pad. He ripped a leaf loose and handed it to me.

"Here's a list Myrna gave me. She was the first to arrive. Got here at eight thirty last night. She acted as hostess, meeting the others at the door. The last one came about eleven. They spent the evening doing some light drinking and dancing, then left as a group about one."

I looked at the names Pat gave me. A few of them I knew well enough, while a couple of the others were people of whom Jack had spoken, but I had never met.

"Where did they go after the party, Pat?"

"They took two cars. The one Myrna went in belonged to Hal Kines. They drove straight up to Westchester, dropping Myrna off on the way. I haven't heard from any of the others yet."

Both of us were silent for a moment, then Pat asked, "What about a motive, Mike?"

I shook my head. "I don't see any yet. But I will. He wasn't killed for nothing. I'll bet this much, whatever it was, was big. There's a lot here that's screwy. You got anything?"

"Nothing more than I gave you, Mike. I was hoping you could supply some answers."

I grinned at him, but I wasn't trying to be funny. "Not yet. Not yet. They'll come though. And I'll relay them on to you, but by that time I'll be working on the next step."

"The cops aren't exactly dumb, you know. We can get our own answers."

"Not like I can. That's why you buzzed me so fast. You can figure things out as quickly as I can, but you haven't got the ways and means of doing the dirty work. That's where I come in. You'll be right behind me every inch of the way, but when the pinch comes I'll get shoved aside and you slap the cuffs on. That is, if you can shove me aside. I don't think you can."

"Okay, Mike, call it your own way. I want you in all right. But I want the killer, too. Don't forget that. I'll be trying to beat you to him. We have every scientific facility at our disposal and a lot of men to do the leg work. We're not short in brains, either," he reminded me.

"Don't worry, I don't underrate the cops. But cops can't break a guy's arm to make him talk, and they can't shove his teeth in with the muzzle of a .45 to remind him that you aren't fooling. I do my own leg work, and there are a lot of guys who will tell me what I want to know because they know what I'll do to them if they don't. My staff is strictly ex officio, but very practical."

That ended the conversation. We walked out into the hall where Pat put a patrolman on the door to make sure things stayed as they were. We took the self-operated elevator down four flights to the lobby and I waited while Pat gave a brief report to some reporters.

My car stood at the curb behind the squad car. I shook hands with Pat and climbed into my jalopy and headed for the Hackard Building, where I held down a two-room suite to use for operation.

Dark Victory: A Visual Essay

Four of the illustrations in this grouping feature Americans dealing in ordinary ways with the fact of World War II. The fifth is an illustration from a high school yearbook for 1946 (a year of transition: the war was over, the cold war not yet recognizable). What does each illustration reveal about the era? About the war? About relations between men and women?

Soldier home on furlough, Brown Summit, North Carolina, May 1944.
Standard Oil (New Jersey) Collection, University of Louisville Photographic Archives.

Mrs. Ella Watson, government charwoman, Washington, D.C., August 1942.
Photo by Gordon R. Parks. Library of Congress.

The Tanner Family—Velma, Jimmie, and their son—at home in the Humble Oil Company "Poor Boy" Camp, Tomball, Texas, 1945.
Standard Oil (New Jersey) Collection, University of Louisville Photographic Archives.

A barmaid in Great Falls, Montana, 1944.
Standard Oil (New Jersey) Collection, University of Louisville Photographic Archives.

Riverside High School *Skipper*, Buffalo, New York, 1946.

SUGGESTIONS FOR VIEWING AND LISTENING

Best Years of Our Lives (1946)
Returning vets classic. Stories of the male psyche, concerns and anxieties about veterans.

Gentleman's Agreement (1947)
The subject is postwar anti-semitism. Gregory Peck pretends to be a Jew. One lesson is that being a Jew is no more than playing a role.

Detour (1945)
Low-budget *film noir.* The specter of contingency.

Frank Sinatra, "The House I Live In" (1945)
Sinatra sang this at high schools. Mythic, but a catalog of 1940s issues.

Roy Brown, "Good Rockin' Tonight" (1947)
A popular musical style called "jump blues." Listen for the origins of rock 'n' roll.

Glenn Miller, "American Patrol" (1942)
From the big band era, which lasted only a decade. Listen for democracy, individualism, and the cohesion of wartime.

CHAPTER 2

Cold War, Cold War at Home

The end of World War II marked a clear American military and economic success. But it also created a power vacuum in Europe and a sense of insecurity about the immediate future in Washington. Some prominent Americans, like Henry Luce, the publisher of *Life* magazine, welcomed the opportunity to inaugurate an "American Century," an era where the United States was challenged to embrace world leadership and create an environment conducive to American commercial growth and development. Should the nation fail to grasp this opportunity, Luce argued, it might find itself, as it had after World War I, hostage to the fortunes of fascist, totalitarian, or Communist nations that were less keen on peace, commercial development, and democracy.

Throughout World War II, Washington's major policies were consistent with Luce's vision of an American Century. At the Bretton Woods Conference in April 1944, the World Bank, the International Monetary Fund, and a system of currency exchange were created, all aimed at facilitating and stabilizing the free flow of trade. A further American diplomatic priority was world stability, addressed through the renewed commitment to collective security as defined by the United Nations, another agency given new life by the allies' military success.

America held one other high card in its hand, in addition to its immense military and economic and financial establishments. In August 1945, American technology and science were proved superior when the first atomic bomb was exploded over Hiroshima. In sole possession of a startling new weapon that redefined warfare, Americans felt they had a sure winner. It was, however, frustratingly difficult to find combat situations where the bomb could be profitably employed, especially since it took months to build each one. The preponderance of the American contribution in funding the war, in ending the conflict in the Pacific, and in creating the monetary environment of the future seemed to indicate that the American Century had commenced.

Yet August 1945 did not immediately usher in a secure, stable world for American workers. The problems inherent in converting the American economy to peacetime production, the demobilization of millions of servicemen, and the shift in the labor force as returning servicemen displaced recently hired women and minorities, meant a period of inflation and insecurity for a nation only too familiar with the economic hardships of the recent depression. Americans became aware, once again, that they could win the war and lose the peace. The clear military victory of 1945 was followed by inconclusive diplomacy, as the allies were unable to agree on the structure of postwar Germany; American factories were in danger of cutting production for lack of clients; and the shared goals and ideals of wartime were giving way to socialism and state economies among the allies.

As these concerns grew and multiplied, President Truman took action. In March 1947, he boldly asked Congress for $400 million in aid to Greece and Turkey. The general anxiety and sense of crisis among the American public regarding recent world events coalesced into active fear of the Soviet Union and Communist regimes. The cold war had officially begun.

Within two months, the Truman administration would call for the largest foreign aid program in the history of the United States: the Marshall Plan. The intent was to save the economies of Europe and indirectly to provide markets to sustain America's production. In 1948, the first arguments for American defense of Europe were heard; in 1949, the North Atlantic Treaty Organization was formed, and military containment was born. The American decision to reconstruct western Europe led the Soviet Union to retaliate by forming its own east European bloc. Truman's response to the crisis of 1947 institutionalized a military, economic, and diplomatic contest between the United States and the Soviet Union.

The 1952 election of Dwight D. Eisenhower redefined the problem. Republicans accused Truman of misunderstanding the nature of the fight; what Democrats called a relatively short-term crisis was, the Republicans argued, a long-term, ideological struggle between the forces of communism and capitalism—a struggle that threatened, if not dealt with correctly, to destroy the very foundations of American society. In this contest to the death, America's future lay in maintaining budgetary balance, military superiority, and a clear moral definition of its goals. If a "clear and present danger" existed in America's future, then all of America's promises of freedom, democracy, and individualism had to be placed on hold until security was won.

The acute insecurity expressed in the elections of 1950 and 1952 blurred the lines between foreign policy and domestic policy. Once the concept of America under siege became political consensus, dissension in actions or thoughts could easily be seen as treason, offering aid and comfort to the enemy, deeds worthy of prosecution and punishment. This was the climate that led to the growth of McCarthyism and its excesses.

INTERPRETIVE ESSAY

Two Halves of the Same Walnut (1947–1948)

Walter LaFeber

The origins of the cold war have been widely debated by historians and politicians. A central controversial question remains: who was to blame? The Soviet Union, for its aggressive, imperial, military activities in eastern Europe after World War II? Or the United States, anxious about its economic future and insecure about Soviet ideology, seeking to preemptively contain Soviet power? Were both countries driven by domestic imperatives, each blind to the security and economic needs of the other?

The enunciation of the Truman Doctrine stands as the opening salvo and the defining ethos of the cold war. Alone, it defines an altruistic American response to Soviet aggression "to support free peoples who are resisting attempted subjugation by armed minorities or by outside pressures." But, when Walter LaFeber, an eminent historian of the revisionist school, analyzes the Truman Doctrine in combination with the Marshall Plan, the overall intent of the policy is less humanitarian, more economically self-interested, and infinitely more complicated. Although criticized by many as a great giveaway program, the Marshall Plan provided huge markets for American products, especially munitions.

America's economic picture in 1945 was muddled. The sudden, early end of the war brought about by the atomic explosions at Hiroshima and Nagasaki ended all chances of a gradual conversion to a peacetime economy. Instead, policies originally expected to develop over months were approved over a weekend. The Office of War Mobilization and Reconversion reported that unemployment might reach 8 million by 1946. Demobilization ran at a precipitous rate, as Truman himself announced that 2 million men would be home by Christmas 1945. The biggest economic problem of all was inflation, which reached 18.2 percent in 1946. America's gross national product was growing, but American workers could not afford to purchase American products. American exports in 1947 accounted for one-third of the world's exports, and many worried that unless trade continued to expand, another depression would descend. But Europe, America's best customer and historic trading partner, was not recovering, and some governments were actually espousing socialist and communist programs. Was it time for America to stake out a new policy and take on responsibility for

America, Russia, and the Cold War: 1945–1972, 7th edition, McGraw-Hill, Inc., New York, 1993, pp. 49–73. © 1993. Used with the permission of McGraw-Hill.

Europe's economic health? And if so, how could Congress and the people be
convinced to indulge such a expensive, entangling endeavor?

On March 12, 1947, President Truman finally issued his own declaration of cold
war. Dramatically presenting the Truman Doctrine to Congress, he asked Americans to join in a global commitment against communism. The nation responded. A
quarter of a century later, Senator J. William Fulbright declared, "More by far than
any other factor the anti-communism of the Truman Doctrine has been the guiding
spirit of American foreign policy since World War II."

An odd circumstance, however, must be explained if the Truman Doctrine is to
be understood. The Soviet Union had been less aggressive in the months before the
president's pronouncement than at any time in the postwar period. Stalin consoli-
dated his hold over Rumania and Poland through manipulated elections, and at
home Soviet propagandists encouraged Western socialists and other "proletarians"
to undertake revolutionary action. But throughout the winter of 1946–1947, the
Soviet [leaders] acted cautiously. State Department officials privately believed that
"the USSR is undergoing serious economic difficulties," which have led to "the
less aggressive international attitude taken by Soviet authorities in recent weeks."
This policy was only "a temporary retreat." Nonetheless, the problems seemed so
great that the Russians gave military discharges to "hundreds of thousands of
young men [who] will now become available for labor force in industry, agriculture and construction." Stalin reduced his 12 million military men of 1945 to between 3 and 4 million in 1947. (American forces dropped from 10 million to 1.4
million, but Americans enjoyed a monopoly of atomic weapons.) Russian military
levels would go no lower, for the Red Army was Stalin's counter to Truman's
atomic bomb. Poised in Eastern Europe, the troops threatened to take the continent
hostage in case of atomic attack on Russia. Stalin had no navy capable of long-
range offensive strikes. The fleet depended on 300 submarines geared for defensive purposes.

Truman's immediate problem was not the threat of a Russian invasion. As
Dean Acheson privately remarked, the Russians would not make war with the
United States "unless they are absolutely out of their minds."* The greater danger
was that Stalin might be proven correct when he indicated the Communists could
bide their time since a "general crisis" was becoming so "acute" in the West that it
would sweep away "atom-dollar" diplomacy. Communist party power rose steeply
in Europe, particularly in France, where the first cabinet of the new Fourth Republic contained four Communists, including the minister of defense. Chaotic conditions in former colonial areas also opened exceptional opportunities to revolutionaries. The two gems of the British crown, India and Egypt, shattered the empire
with drives for independence. They were soon joined by Pakistan, Burma, Ceylon
[Sri Lanka], and Nepal. France began a long, futile, eight-year war to regain Indochina. The Dutch faced full-scale revolution in Indonesia. The Middle East was
in turmoil over the determination of a half-dozen countries to be totally indepen-

---

*Undersecretary Dean Acheson would be secretary of state from 1949 to 1953.

dent, as well as over the influx of 100,000 Jews who hoped to establish a homeland in Palestine.

In late 1946 and early 1947, American officials gave increasing attention to these newly emerging areas. Europe could not be fully stabilized until England, France, and the Netherlands settled their colonial problems. The State Department also assumed that the American economy, as well as the economy of the western community, which depended upon American prosperity, demanded a proper settlement of these conflicts. In a speech in November 1946, [Assistant Secretary of State] Will Clayton explained that the expansion in the domestic economy and the "depletion of our natural resources" would make the United States much more dependent on the importation of raw materials and minerals. Many of these came from the newly emerging areas. "No nation in modern times," the assistant secretary of state warned, "can long expect to enjoy a rising standard of living without increased foreign trade." Adolf Berle, economist, adviser to Roosevelt and Truman, and State Department official, declared in late 1946 that the Soviet [Union] and the United States had begun a battle for the allegiance of the less industrialized nations. "Within four years the world [will] be faced with an apparent surplus in production beyond any previously known," Berle explained. If American surpluses were used to "take the lead in material reconstruction" of the newly emerging countries, the United States could level off those "cycles of 'boom and bust' which disfigured our prewar economy."

"Boom and bust" already threatened. The American economy sagged, and unemployment rose in early 1946 before some expansion began. State Department experts worried that the improvement was temporary, for it rested on a $15 billion American export trade, nearly four times the level of the 1930s. Most of these exports were rebuilding western Europe, but the Europeans were rapidly running out of dollars to pay for the goods. When its remaining dollars and gold were spent, Europe would stagnate, then perhaps grasp at socialism to save itself. Americans would face the loss of their most vital market and probably the return of the 1930s with all the attendant political consequences. Truman understood this by early 1947, but a tax-cutting Republican Congress and his own low popularity seemed to block any action.

The turn came on Saturday morning, February 21, 1947, when a British embassy official drove to the near-deserted State Department building. He informed Acheson that because of its own economic crisis (more than half its industry was quiet), England could not provide the $250 million of military and economic support needed by Greece and Turkey. As Secretary of State George Marshall later observed, "It was tantamount to British abdication from the Middle East with obvious implications as to their successor."

American officials were not taken by surprise. From 1944 until early 1947 they had closely watched the British attempt to regain control of Greece become bogged down in a Greek civil war. On one side was a conservative-monarchical group supported by London. On the other was the National Liberation Front (NLF), with Communist leadership, which had gained popularity and power by leading resistance efforts against the Nazis. By 1947 the NLF received support from Yugoslav Communist leader Josep Broz (Marshal Tito). The Yugoslav was not motivated by affection for his fellow Communists in Greece. Rather, he hoped to annex parts of Greece to a large Yugoslav federation. Stalin was not directly involved and indeed developed a strong dislike for Tito's ambitions.

But as NLF strength grew, the United States did become involved. Throughout 1946 it sent special missions, poured in $260 million of aid, and sided with the British. Drawing on this experience, the State Department was able to work out a detailed proposal for assistance within a week after Acheson received the British message. After only nineteen days, Truman could appear before Congress with a complete program. Clearly, the president's request on March 12 for $400 million in Greek and Turkish aid (the Truman Doctrine speech) was not a sudden, drastic departure in American foreign policy.

But the reasoning in Truman's speech was radically new. That reasoning was worked out by American officials who had long been waiting for this opportunity. As they developed the speech, "they found release from the professional frustrations of years," as one later declared. "It seemed to those present that a new chapter in world history had opened and they were the most privileged of men." Those words help explain why the officials made certain choices. For example, they could have determined simply that Greece was in a civil war and therefore the United States had no business intervening. Or they could quietly have asked Congress to continue aid to Greece and Turkey while transferring to those nations weapons left from the war. The administration, however, rejected those alternatives, choosing instead to appear dramatically before Congress to request support for a global battle against communism. A White House adviser remarked that the message would be "the opening gun in a campaign to bring people up to [the] realization that the war isn't over by any means."

As State Department officials prepared drafts of the speech, Truman, Secretary of State Marshall, and Acheson met with congressional leaders. It was not a warm audience. The Republicans were busily cutting taxes 20 percent and chopping $6 billion from Truman's already tight budget. The legislators remained unmoved until Acheson swung into the argument that the threat was not a Greek civil war but Russian communism; its aim was the control of the Middle East, South Asia, and Africa; and this control was part of a communist plan to encircle and capture the ultimate objective, Germany and Europe. It was a struggle between liberty and dictatorship. By defending Greece and Turkey, therefore, Americans were defending their own freedoms. "The Soviet Union was playing one of the greatest gambles in history at minimal cost," Acheson concluded. "We and we alone are in a position to break up the play."

The congressmen were stunned. Silence followed until Arthur Vandenberg (now chairman of the Senate Foreign Relations Committee) told Truman that the message must include Acheson's explanation. As the senator advised, the president "scared hell" out of the American people. Insofar as public opinion was concerned, this tactic worked well for Truman (at least until three years later when Senator Joseph McCarthy and others turned the argument around and accused the administration of too gently handling such a horrible danger). The president also won over

Congress with assurances that the United States would not only control every penny of America's aid to Greece but run the Greek economy by controlling foreign exchange, budget, taxes, currency, and credit.

Inside the State Department, however, Acheson ran into opposition. George Kennan, the top expert on Soviet affairs, objected bitterly to sending military assistance to nations such as Turkey that had no internal Communist problems and bordered the Soviet Union. Unlike economic help, military aid could be provocative. Acheson rejected the argument. The opportunity to build Turkey's military strength was too good to miss. Thus in the words of one official, "Turkey was slipped into the oven with Greece because that seemed the surest way to cook a tough bird." Kennan also protested against the harsh ideological tone and open-ended American commitment in the speech drafts. He was joined by Secretary of State Marshall and Charles Bohlen, another expert on Russia, who told Acheson that "there was a little too much flamboyant anticommunism in the speech." Acheson stood his ground. Marshall was informed that Truman believed the Senate would not approve the doctrine "without the emphasis on the Communist danger."

Acheson, however, carefully kept the central economic factors out of the speech. He and Truman wanted a simple ideological call to action that all could understand, not a message that might trigger arguments over American oil holdings in the Middle East. The economic interests were nevertheless crucial. As State Department official Joseph Jones noted, if Greece and similar key areas "spiral downwards into economic anarchy, then at best they will drop out of the United States orbit and try an independent nationalistic policy; at worst they will swing into the Russian orbit," and the result would be a depression worse than that of the 1930s.

Jones's insight was incorporated into a major speech made by Truman at Baylor University on March 6. The address provided the economic dimension to the Truman Doctrine pronounced six days later. The president frankly declared that if the expansion of state-controlled economies (such as the Communists') was not stopped, and an open world marketplace restored for private businessmen, depression would occur and the government would have to intervene massively in the society. Americans could then bid farewell to both their traditional economic and personal freedoms. "Freedom of worship—freedom of speech—freedom of enterprise," Truman observed. "It must be true that the first two of these freedoms are related to the third." For "Peace, freedom and world trade are indivisible." He concluded, "We must not go through the thirties again." The president had given the economic reasons for pronouncing the Truman Doctrine. The Baylor speech (written by Acheson and Will Clayton) explained why Americans, if they hoped to preserve their personal freedom, had to rebuild the areas west of the iron curtain before these lands collapsed into anarchy, radical governments, or even communism.

The Truman Doctrine speech itself laid out the ideological and political reasons for the commitment. The president requested $400 million for military and economic aid, but he also asked for something else. Truman warned Congress that the world must now "choose between alternative ways of life." He urged Americans to commit themselves to helping "free peoples" and to opposing "totalitarian regimes." This request, plus Truman's failure to place any geographical limits on where Americans must commit themselves (Africa as well as Germany? Southeast Asia as well as western Europe?), raised criticism.

Robert Taft of Ohio, the Senate's Republican leader, accused Truman of dividing the world into communist and anticommunist zones, then said flatly, "I do not want war with Russia." On the left, Henry Wallace, traveling in Europe, accused Truman of "reckless adventury" that would cost the world "a century of fear." Senator Vandenberg rushed to the president's defense by calling Wallace an "itinerant saboteur." But such fear was not only on Taft's and Wallace's minds. Shortly before the speech, Acheson told J. Robert Oppenheimer, a leading scientist in the atomic weapons field, "We are entering an adversary relationship with the Soviet [Union]," and "we should bear that in mind" while making atomic plans.

Congress wriggled uncomfortably. As Senator Vandenberg began closed-door hearings on what he called "the most fundamental thing that has been presented to Congress in my time," Acheson hedged on whether the Truman Doctrine had any limitations. "If there are situations where we can do something effective, then I think we must certainly do it." But he was clear on one issue: "I think it is a mistake to believe that you can, at any time, sit down with the Russians and solve questions." Only when the West built insuperable bastions of strength would Stalin listen to American terms. Acheson assumed Russia was primarily responsible for the Greek revolution. After all, said Lincoln MacVeagh, United States ambassador to Greece, "Any empire that bases itself on revolution always has expansionist tendencies." (The ambassador was alluding to the revolution of 1917, not 1776.) This view of Soviet involvement was wrong. The Greek problem was caused by internal forces and fueled by Tito for his own purposes. But this point made little difference. The administration asked for a commitment against communism anywhere, not just against the Soviet [Union].

That caused a special problem in Greece, for as MacVeagh admitted, "the best men" in Greece "are the heads of the Communist movement. . . . That is the sad part of it." But Americans had to keep on "trying to make bricks without straw . . . or you are going to lose the country." The Greek government became so brutal that the State Department privately warned it must stop torturing its political prisoners or "the president's program" would be damaged. When criticized for helping the Greek and Turkish right-wing parties, however, Truman could simply ask Americans whether they preferred "totalitarianism" or "imperfect democracies." This settled that question.

The president and Acheson mousetrapped those in Congress who wanted to be both anticommunist and penny pinchers. As a leading Democrat chuckled privately, of course the Republicans "didn't want to be smoked out. . . . They don't like Communism but still they don't want to do anything to stop it. But they are all put on the spot now and they all have to come clean." The president, moreover, had moved so quickly that Congress had no choice but to give him increased powers. "Here we sit," mourned Vandenberg, "not as free agents," but dealing with something "almost like a Presidential request for a declaration of war." "There is precious little we can do," the senator concluded, "except say 'yes.'" Vandenberg was correct. Congress's acceptance of Truman's definition of crisis marked the point in the cold war when power in foreign policy formulation began shifting rapidly from Capitol Hill to the White House.

Nine days after his speech, Truman helped ensure his victory by announcing a loyalty program to ferret out security risks in government. The first such peacetime program in American history, it was so vaguely defined that political ideas and long-past associations were suddenly made suspect. Most ominously, the accused would not have the right to confront the accuser. Truman thus strikingly dramatized the communist issue, exerting new pressure on Congress to support his doctrine. By mid-May Congress had passed his request by large margins.

The Truman Doctrine was a milestone in American history for at least four reasons. First, it marked the point at which Truman used the American fear of communism both at home and abroad to convince Americans they must embark upon a cold war foreign policy. This consensus would not break apart for a quarter of a century. Second, as Vandenberg knew, Congress was giving the president great powers to wage this cold war as he saw fit. Truman's personal popularity began spiraling upward after his speech. Third, for the first time in the postwar era, Americans massively intervened in another nation's civil war. Intervention was justified on the basis of anticommunism. In the future, Americans would intervene in similar wars for supposedly the same reason and with less happy results. Even Greek affairs went badly at first, so badly that in late 1947 Washington officials discussed sending as many as two divisions of Americans to save the situation. That proved unnecessary, for when Yugoslavia left the Communist bloc in early 1948, Tito turned inward and stopped aiding the rebels. Deprived of aid, the Greek left wing quickly lost ground. But it had been close, and Americans were nearly involved massively in a civil war two decades before their Vietnam involvement. As it was, the success in Greece seemed to prove that Americans could, if they wished, control such conflicts by defining the problem as "Communist" and helping conservatives remain in power.

Finally, and perhaps most important, Truman used the doctrine to justify a gigantic aid program to prevent a collapse of the European and American economies. Later such programs were expanded globally. The president's arguments about anticommunism were confusing, for the western economies would have been in grave difficulties whether or not communism existed. The complicated problems of reconstruction and the United States dependence on world trade were not well understood by Americans, but they easily comprehended anticommunism. So Americans embarked upon the cold war for the good reasons given in the Truman Doctrine, which they understood, and for real reasons, which they did not understand. Thus, as Truman and Acheson intended, the doctrine became an ideological shield behind which the United States marched to rebuild the western political-economic system and counter the radical left. From 1947 on, therefore, any threats to that western system could be easily explained as communist inspired, not as problems that arose from difficulties within the system itself. That was the most lasting and tragic result of the Truman Doctrine.

The president's program evolved naturally into the Marshall Plan. Although the speech did not limit American effort, Secretary of State Marshall did by concentrating the administration's attention on Europe. Returning badly shaken from a foreign ministers conference in Moscow, the secretary of state insisted in a nation-wide broadcast that western Europe required immediate help. "The patient is sinking," he declared, "while the doctors deliberate." Personal conversations with Stalin had convinced Marshall that the Russians believed Europe would collapse. Assuming that the United States must lead in restoring Europe, Marshall appointed a policy planning staff under the direction of George Kennan to draw up policies.

Kennan later explained the basic assumption that underlay the Marshall Plan and, indeed, the entire range of America's postwar policies between 1947 and the mid-1950s. Excluding the United States, Kennan observed,

> there are only four aggregations which are major ones from the standpoint of strategic realities [that is, military and industrial potential] in the world. Two of those lie off the shores of the Eurasian land mass. Those are Japan and England, and two of them lie on the Eurasian land mass. One is the Soviet Union and the other is that of central Europe. . . .
>
> Viewed in absolute terms, I think the greatest danger that could confront the United States security would be a combination and working together for purposes hostile to us of the central European and the Russian military-industrial potentials. They would really create an entity . . . which could overshadow in a strategic sense even our own power. It is not anything, I think, which would be as easy of achievement as people often portray it as being here. I am not sure the Russians have the genius for holding all that together. . . . Still, they have the tendency of political thought, of Communist political expansion.

Building on this premise, round-the-clock conferences in May 1947 began to fashion the main features of the Marshall Plan. Kennan insisted that any aid, particularly military supplies, be limited and not given to just any area where Communists seemed to be enjoying some success. The all-important question then became how to handle the Russians. Ostensibly, Marshall accepted Kennan's advice to "play it straight" by inviting the Soviet bloc. In reality, the State Department made Russian acceptance improbable by demanding that economic records of each nation be open to scrutiny. For good measure Kennan also suggested that the [Soviet Union's] devastated economy, weakened by war and at that moment suffering from drought and famine, participate in the plan by shipping Soviet goods to Europe. Apparently no one in the State Department wanted the Soviet [Union] included. Russian participation would vastly multiply the costs of the program and eliminate any hope of its acceptance by a purse-watching Republican Congress, now increasingly convinced by Truman that Communists had to be fought, not fed.

Acheson's speech at Cleveland, Mississippi, in early May and Marshall's address at Harvard on June 5 revealed the motives and substance of the plan. In preparing for the earlier speech, Acheson's advisers concluded that American exports were rapidly approaching the $16 billion mark. Imports, however, amounted to only half that amount, and Europe did not have sufficient dollars to pay the difference. Either the United States would have to give credits to Europeans or they would be unable to buy American goods. The president's Council of Economic Advisers predicted a slight business recession, and if, in addition, exports dropped in any substantial amount, "the effect in the United States," as one official wrote, "might be most serious." Acheson underlined these facts in his Mississippi speech.

At Harvard, Marshall urged Europeans to create a long-term program that would "provide a cure rather than a mere palliative." On June 13 British Foreign Minister Ernest Bevin accepted Marshall's suggestion that Europeans take the initiative. Bevin traveled to Paris to talk with French Foreign Minister Georges Bidault. The question of Russian participation became uppermost in their discussions. *Pravda* had labeled Marshall's speech as a Truman Doctrine with dollars, a useless attempt to save the American economy by dominating European markets. Bidault ignored this; pressured by the powerful French Communist party and fearful that Russia's absence might compel France to join the Anglo-Saxons in a divided Europe dominated by a resurrected Germany, he decided to invite [Soviet Foreign Minister Vyacheslao] Molotov. The Russian line immediately moderated.

On June 26 Molotov arrived in Paris with eighty-nine economic experts and clerks, then spent much of the next three days conferring over the telephone with Moscow officials. The Russians were giving the plan serious consideration. Molotov finally proposed that each nation individually establish its own recovery program. The French and British proposed instead that Europe as a whole create the proposal for American consideration. Molotov angrily quit the conference, warning that the plan would undermine national sovereignty, revive Germany, allow Americans to control Europe, and, most ominously, divide "Europe into two groups of states . . . creating new difficulties in the relations between them." Within a week after his return to Moscow, the Soviet [Union] set [its] own "Molotov Plan" in motion. The Poles and the Czechs, who had expressed interest in Marshall's proposal, now informed the Paris conference that they could not attend because it "might be construed as an action against the Soviet Union."

As the remaining sixteen European nations hammered out a program for Marshall to consider, the United States moved on another front: it determined to revive Germany quickly. In late 1946 the Americans and British had overridden French opposition to merge economically the United States and British zones in Germany. Administrative duties were given to Germans. By mid-July 1947 Washington officials so rapidly rebuilt German industry that Bidault finally pleaded with Marshall to slow down or else the French government would never survive to carry through the economic recovery program. The United States nevertheless continued to rebuild German nonmilitary industry to the point where the country would be both self-sufficient and able to aid the remainder of western Europe. On September 22, the Paris meeting completed its work, pledging increased production, tariff reductions, and currency convertibility in return for American aid. The State Department could view its successes in Germany during the summer as icing on the cake.

The European request for a four-year program of $17 billion of American aid now had to run the gauntlet of a Republican Congress, which was dividing its attention between slashing the budget and attacking Truman, both in anticipation of the presidential election only a year away. In committee hearings in late 1947 and early 1948, the executive presented its case. Only large amounts of government money that could restore basic facilities, provide convertibility of local currency into dollars, and end the dollar shortage would stimulate private investors to rebuild Europe, administration witnesses argued. Then a rejuvenated Europe could offer many advantages to the United States: eradicate the threat of continued nationalization and socialism by releasing and stimulating the investment of private capital; maintain demand for American exports; encourage Europeans to produce strategic goods, which the United States could buy and stockpile; preserve European and American control over Middle Eastern oil supplies from militant nationalism, which might endanger the weakened European holdings; and free Europeans from economic problems so they could help the United States militarily. It would all be like magic.

George Kennan summarized the central problem in a note to Acheson. "Communist activities" were not "the root of the difficulties of Western Europe" but rather "the disruptive effects of the war on the economic, political, and social structure of Europe." So in the final plan Italy, with Europe's largest Communist party, received less aid than other, more economically important nations. In this sense the plan revolved around a rebuilt and autonomous Germany. As Secretary of State Marshall told Congress, "The restoration of Europe involved the restoration of Germany. Without a revival of German production there can be no revival of Europe's economy. But we must be very careful to see that a revived Germany can not again threaten the European community." The Marshall Plan offered a way to circumvent allied restrictions on German development, for it tied the Germans to a general European program and then offered vast sums to such nations as France that might otherwise be reluctant to support reconstructing Germany.

The Marshall Plan served as an all-purpose weapon for Truman's foreign policy. It charmed those who feared a slump in American exports and who believed, communist threat or no communist threat, that American and world prosperity rested on a vigorous export trade. A spokesman for the National Association of Manufacturers, for example, appeared considerably more moderate toward communism than some government officials when he argued that Europe suffered not from "this so-called communistic surge," but from a "production problem" that only the Marshall Plan could solve. Appropriately, Truman named as administrator of the plan Paul Hoffman, a proven entrepreneur who, as Acheson once observed, preached a "doctrine of salvation by exports with all the passion of an economic Savonarola." The plan also attracted a group, including Reinhold Niebuhr, which placed more emphasis upon the containment of communism. The plan offered all things to all people. Or almost all, for Henry Wallace decided to oppose it in late 1947 on the grounds that only by channeling aid through the United Nations could calamitous relations between the United States and the Soviet Union be avoided.

The Marshall Plan now appears not the beginning but the end of an era. It marked the last phase in the administration's use of economic tactics as the primary means of tying together the Western world. The plan's approach, that peaceful and positive approach which Niebuhr applauded, soon evolved into military alliances. Truman proved to be correct in saying that the Truman Doctrine and the Marshall Plan "are two halves of the same walnut." Americans willingly acquiesced as the military aspects of the doctrine developed into quite the larger part.

Why such programs could so easily be transformed into military commitments was explained by George Kennan in a well-timed article appearing in July 1947 under the mysterious pseudonym Mr. "X." Washington's most respected expert on Soviet affairs, Kennan (who once called Niebuhr "the father of us all") had warned throughout the early 1940s against any hope of close postwar cooperation with Stalin. In early 1946 he sent a long dispatch to Washington from Moscow suggesting that at the "bottom of the Kremlin's neurotic view of world affairs is the traditional and instinctive Russian sense of insecurity." In post-1917 Russia, this became highly explosive when mixed with Communist ideology and "Oriental secretiveness and conspiracy." This dispatch brought Kennan to the attention of Secretary of the Navy James Forrestal, who helped bring the diplomat back to Washington and then strongly influenced Kennan's decision to publish the "X" article.

The article gave the administration's view of what made the Russians act like Communists. The analysis began not by emphasizing "the traditional Russian sense of insecurity" but by assuming that Stalin's policy was shaped by a combination of Marxist-Leninist ideology, which advocated revolution to defeat the capitalist forces in the outside world, and the dictator's determination to use "capitalist encirclement" as a rationale to regiment the Soviet masses so that he could consolidate his own political power. Kennan belittled such supposed "encirclement," although he recognized Nazi-Japanese hatred of the Soviet [Union] during the 1930s. (He omitted mentioning specifically the American and Japanese intervention in Russia between 1918 and 1920 and the United States attempt to isolate the Soviet [Union] politically through the 1920s.) Mr. "X" believed Stalin would not moderate communist determination to overthrow the western governments. Any softening of the Russian line would be a diversionary tactic designed to lull the west. For in the final analysis Soviet diplomacy "moves along the prescribed path, like a persistent toy automobile wound up and headed in a given direction, stopping only when it meets some unanswerable force." Endemic Soviet aggression could thus be "contained by the adroit and vigilant application of counterforce at a series of constantly shifting geographical and political points." The United States would have to undertake this containment alone and unilaterally, but if it could do so without weakening its prosperity and political stability, the Soviet party structure would undergo a period of immense strain climaxing in "either the break-up or the gradual mellowing of Soviet power."

The publication of this article triggered one of the more interesting debates of the cold war. Walter Lippmann was the dean of American journalists and one of those who did not accept the "two halves of the same walnut" argument. He condemned the military aspects of the Truman Doctrine while applauding the Marshall Plan because he disagreed with Kennan's assessment of Soviet motivation. And that, of course, was a crucial point in any argument over American policy. In a series of newspaper articles later collected in a book entitled *The Cold War,* Lippmann argued that Soviet policy was molded more by traditional Russian expansion than by Communist ideology. "Stalin is not only the heir of Marx and of Lenin but of Peter the Great, and the Czars of all the Russians." Because of the victorious sweep of the Red Army into Central Europe in 1945, Stalin could accomplish what the czars for centuries had only hoped to obtain. This approach enabled Lippmann to view the Soviet advance as a traditional quest for national security and, in turn, allowed him to argue that Russia would be amenable to an offer of withdrawal of both Russian and American power from central Europe. The fuses would thus be pulled from that explosive area.

Lippmann outlined the grave consequences of the alternative, the Mr. "X"–Truman Doctrine policy: "unending intervention in all the countries that are supposed to 'contain' the Soviet Union"; futile and costly efforts to make "Jeffersonian democrats" out of eastern European peasants and Middle Eastern and Asian warlords; either the destruction of the United Nations or its transformation into a useless anti-Soviet coalition; and such a tremendous strain on the American people that their economy would have to be increasingly regimented and their men sent to fight on the perimeter of the Soviet bloc. The columnist warned that if Mr. "X" succeeded in applying counterforce to the "constantly shifting geographical and political points," the Soviet [Union] would perforce be allowed to take the initiative in the cold war by choosing the grounds and weapons for combat. Finally, Lippmann, like the administration, emphasized Germany's importance, but he differed by observing that Russia, which controlled eastern Germany, could, at its leisure, outmaneuver the west and repeat the 1939 Nazi-Soviet pact of offering the ultimate reward of reunification for German cooperation. "The idea that we can foster the sentiment of German unity, and make a truncated Germany economically strong," Lippmann wrote, "can keep her disarmed, and can use her in the anti-Soviet coalition is like trying to square the circle."

Lippmann was profound, but he had no chance of being persuasive. By the end of August 1947, the State Department rejected Lippmann's proposals for disengagement in Germany. American officials instead assumed that the "one world" of the United Nations was "no longer valid and that we are in political fact facing a division into two worlds." The "X" article also indicated the administration was operating on another assumption: economic development could not occur until "security" was established. This increasing concern with things military became evident in late 1947 when Kennan suggested that the United States change its long-standing hostility to Franco's government in Spain in order to cast proper military security over the Mediterranean area. A year earlier the United States had joined with Britain and France in asking the Spanish people to overthrow Franco by political means because his government was pro-Nazi and totalitarian. Kennan's suggestion marked the turn in Spanish-American relations, which ended in close military cooperation after 1950.

The quest for military security also transformed American policy in Asia. With Chiang Kai-shek's decline, the State Department searched for a new partner who could help stabilize the far east. The obvious candidate was Japan, which from the 1890s until 1931 had worked closely with Washington. It was also the potential industrial powerhouse of the area, the Germany of the Orient. Since 1945 the United States had single-handedly controlled Japan. The Soviet [Union] had been carefully excluded. Even Australia was allowed to send occupation forces only after promising not to interfere with the authority of General Douglas MacArthur, head of the American government in Japan. MacArthur instituted a new constitution (in which Japan renounced war for all time), then conducted elections that allowed him to claim that the Japanese had overwhelmingly repudiated communism. To the general, as to Washington officials, this was fundamental. In 1946 MacArthur privately compared America in its fight against communism to the agony of Christ at Gethsemane, for "Christ, even though crucified, nevertheless prevailed."

He added that Japan was becoming "the western outpost of our defenses." In 1947–1948 Japan received the "two halves of the same walnut" treatment. The State Department decided to rebuild Japanese industry and develop a sound export economy. At the same time, American bases on the islands were to be expanded and maintained until, in one official's words, "the at present disarmed soldiers of Japan are provided with arms and training to qualify them to preserve the peace." As in Europe, economic development and security moved hand in hand as Americans buttressed the Pacific portion of their system. . . .

Of special importance to Truman's "security" effort, the president transformed what he termed "the antiquated defense setup of the United States" by passing the National Security Act through Congress in July 1947. This bill provided for a single Department of Defense to replace the three independently run services, statutory establishment of the Joint Chiefs of Staff, a National Security Council to advise the president, and a Central Intelligence Agency to correlate and evaluate intelligence activities. James Forrestal, the stepfather of Mr. "X" and the leading advocate among presidential advisers of a tough military approach to cold war problems, became the first secretary of defense. Forrestal remained until he resigned in early spring 1949. Two months later on the night of May 22, Forrestal, suffering from mental and physical illness, jumped or accidentally fell to his death from the twelfth floor of the Bethesda Naval Hospital.

The military and personal costs of the Truman Doctrine–Mr. "X" policy would be higher than expected. And the cost became more apparent as Truman and J. Edgar Hoover (director of the Federal Bureau of Investigation) carried out the president's Security Loyalty program. Their search for subversives accelerated after Canadians uncovered a Soviet spy ring. During hearings in the Senate on the appointment of David E. Lilienthal as chairman of the Atomic Energy Commission, the first major charges of "soft on communism" were hurled by Robert Taft [in part] because of Lilienthal's New Deal background. . . .

Since the Iranian and Turkish crises of 1946, the Soviet [Union] had not been active in world affairs. But Molotov's departure from the Marshall Plan conference in Paris during July 1947 marked the turn. Russian attention was riveted on Germany. The Politburo interpreted the Marshall Plan to mean the American "intention to restore the economy of Germany and Japan on the old basis [of pre-1941] provided it is subordinated to interests of American capital." Rebuilding Europe through the plan and tying it closer to American economic power threatened Stalin's hope of influencing west European policies. Incomparably worse, however, was linking that Europe to a restored western Germany. This not only undercut Soviet determination to keep this ancient enemy weak, as well as divided, but vastly increased the potential of that enemy, tied it to the forces of "capitalist encirclement," and revived the memories of two world wars.

Molotov quickly initiated a series of moves to tighten Soviet control of the bloc. A program of bilateral trade agreements, the so-called Molotov Plan, began to link the bloc countries and Russia in July 1947. The final step came in January 1949, when the Council for Mutual Economic Assistance (COMECON) provided the Soviet answer to the Marshall Plan by creating a centralized agency for stimulating and controlling bloc development. As a result of these moves, Soviet trade with the east European bloc, which had declined in 1947 to $380 million, doubled in 1948, quadrupled by 1950, and exceeded $2.5 billion in 1952. Seventy percent of east European trade was carried on with either the Soviet Union or elsewhere within the bloc.

Four days after his return from Paris, Molotov announced the establishment of the Communist Information Bureau (Cominform). Including Communists from Russia, Yugoslavia, France, Italy, Poland, Bulgaria, Czechoslovakia, Hungary, and Rumania, the Cominform provided another instrument for increasing Stalin's control. This was his answer to the Czech and Polish interest in joining the Marshall Plan. In late August, a month before the first Cominform meeting, Soviet actions in Hungary indicated the line that would be followed. After a purge of left-wing anticommunist political leaders, the Soviet [Union] directly intervened by rigging elections. All anticommunist opposition disappeared. Three weeks later at the Cominform meeting in Warsaw, [Cominform leader Andrei] Zhdanov formally announced new Soviet policies in a speech that ranks next to Stalin's February 9, 1946, address as a Russian call to cold war.

Zhdanov's analysis of recent international developments climaxed with the announcement that American economic power, fattened by the war, was organizing western Europe and "countries politically and economically dependent on the United States, such as the Near-Eastern and South-American countries and China" into an anticommunist bloc. The Russians and the "new democracies" in eastern Europe, Finland, Indonesia, and Vietnam meanwhile formed another bloc, which "has the sympathy of India, Egypt and Syria." In this way, Zhdanov again announced the rebirth of the "two-camp" view of the world, an attitude that had dominated Russian policy between 1927 and 1934 when Stalin bitterly attacked the west, and a central theme in the dictator's speech of February 1946. In some respects Zhdanov's announcement resembled the "two-world" attitude in the United States. The mirror image was especially striking when Zhdanov admonished the socialist camp not to lower its guard. "Just as in the past the Munich policy united the hands of the Nazi aggressors, so today concessions to the new course of the United States and the imperialist camp may encourage its inspirers to be even more insolent and aggressive."

Following Zhdanov's call to action, the Cominform delegates sharply criticized French and Italian Communists, who seemed to want a more pacific approach, and, once again following the disastrous practices of the 1927–1934 era, ordered all members to foment the necessary strikes and internal disorder for the elimination of independent socialist, labor, and peasant parties in their countries. The meeting was the high-water mark of the tough Zhdanov line in Soviet foreign policy. Its effect was soon felt not only in bloc and west European countries but inside Russia as well. Stalin cleansed Soviet economic thinking by discrediting and removing from public view Eugene Varga, a leading Russian economist who had angered the Politburo by warning that Marxists were wrong in thinking that the western economies would soon collapse.

American officials fully understood why the Soviet [Union was] trying these new policies. As Secretary of State Marshall told Truman's cabinet in November 1947, "The advance of Communism has been stemmed and the Russians have been compelled to make a reevaluation of their position." America was winning its eight-month cold war. But the [Soviet Union's] difficulties provided an excuse for Congress, which was not anxious to send billions of dollars of Marshall Plan aid to Europe if the Russians posed no threat. Congress dawdled as the plan came under increased criticism. Taft urged that good money not be poured into a "European TVA." On the other side of the political spectrum, Henry Wallace labeled it a "Martial Plan." In speeches around the country, Marshall tried to sell the program for its long-term economic and political benefits. His arguments fell on deaf ears. The American economy seemed to be doing well. Just weeks before the 1948 presidential campaign was to begin, Truman faced a major political and diplomatic defeat.

And then came the fall of Czechoslovakia. The Czechs had uneasily coexisted with Russia by trying not to offend the Soviet [Union] while keeping doors open to the west. This policy had started in late 1943, when Czech leaders signed a treaty with Stalin that, in the view of most observers, obligated Czechoslovakia to become a part of the Russian bloc. President Eduard Beneš and Foreign Minister Jan Masaryk, one of the foremost diplomatic figures in Europe, had nevertheless successfully resisted complete communist control. Nor had Stalin moved to consolidate his power in 1946 after the Czech Communist party emerged from the parliamentary elections with 38 percent of the vote, the largest total of any party. By late 1947 the lure of western aid and internal political changes began to pull the Czech government away from the Soviet [Union]. At this point Stalin, who like Truman recalled the pivotal role of Czechoslovakia in 1938, decided to put the 1943 treaty into effect. Klement Gottwald, the Czech Communist party leader, demanded the elimination of independent parties. In mid-February 1948 Soviet armies camped on the border as Gottwald ordered the formation of a wholly new government. A Soviet mission of top officials flew to Prague to demand Beneš's surrender. The Communists assumed full control on February 25. Two weeks later Masaryk either committed suicide or, as Truman believed, was the victim of "foul play."

Truman correctly observed that the coup "sent a shock throughout the civilized world." He privately believed, "We are faced with exactly the same situation with which Britain and France was faced in 1938–9 with Hitler." In late 1947 Hungary had been the victim of a similar if less dramatic squeeze. Within two months, new opportunities would beckon to the Cominform when the Italian election was held. On March 5 a telegram arrived from General Clay in Germany. Although "I have felt and held that war was unlikely for at least ten years," Clay began, "within the last few weeks, I have felt a subtle change in Soviet attitude which . . . gives me a feeling that it may come with dramatic suddenness." For ten days, government intelligence worked furiously investigating Clay's warnings and on March 16 gave Truman the grim assurance that war was not probable within sixty days. Two days before, on March 14, the Senate had endorsed the Marshall Plan by a vote of 69 to

17. As it went to the House for consideration, Truman, fearing the "grave events in Europe [which] were moving so swiftly," decided to appear before Congress.

In a speech remarkable for its repeated emphasis on the "increasing threat" to the very "survival of freedom," the president proclaimed the Marshall Plan "not enough." Europe must have "some measure of protection against internal and external aggression." He asked for Universal Military Training, the resumption of Selective Service (which he had allowed to lapse a year earlier), and speedy passage of the Marshall Plan. Within twelve days the House approved authorization of the plan's money.

With perfect timing and somber rhetoric, Truman's March 17 speech not only galvanized passage of the plan but accelerated a change in American foreign policy that had been heralded the previous summer. Congress stamped its approval on this new military emphasis by passing a Selective Service bill. Although Universal Military Training, one of Forrestal's pet projects, found little favor, a supposedly penny-proud Congress replaced it with funds to begin a seventy-group Air Force, 25 percent larger than even Forrestal had requested.

Perhaps the most crucial effect of the new policy, however, appeared in the administration's determination to create great systems that would not only encourage military development but would also compel the western world to accept political realignments as well. The first of these efforts had been the Rio Pact and the new policies toward Japan. The next, somewhat different, and vastly more important effort would be the North Atlantic Treaty Organization (NATO).

SOURCES

Cold War at Home

During the Army-McCarthy hearings of 1954, McCarthy (far right) *blocked an attempt by Army Counsel Joseph Welch* (far left) *to obtain names of Mc-Carthy's office staff. McCarthy charged "a smear campaign" was under way against "anyone working with exposing communists." District of Columbia Public Library.*

Tail Gunner Joe: The Wheeling Address

Joseph McCarthy

McCarthyism is the name applied to the second Red Scare, a period of politi-cal repression in America, epitomized by the career of Senator Joseph Mc-Carthy. "Tail gunner Joe" was elected as the junior senator from Wisconsin in

From U.S., Congress, Senate, *Congressional Record*, 81st Cong., 2d sess., 1950, 96, 1954, 1946, 1957.

1946 and received little recognition until his speech in Wheeling, West Virginia, in February 1950. For the next four years, he chaired Senate committee meetings where he accused first the Truman administration, and later the Eisenhower administration, of harboring known Communists and probable spies in the government. He was censured by his colleagues in the Senate in 1954 and faded into obscurity.

McCarthy did not create the atmosphere of suspicion and anticommunism given his name. Indeed, years before McCarthy came on the scene, the Truman administration had instituted its own loyalty-security program (1947) and stepped up the use of the Smith Act throughout 1948 to prosecute Americans suspected of subversive thinking. Congress also contributed with the hearings of the House Un-American Activities Committee (HUAC) and the Alger Hiss investigation and trials (1948). Yet McCarthy was surely the most notorious opportunist of the era. His tactics of demagoguery, insinuation, and guilt by association defined the means by which thousands of Americans were denied their civil rights. Worse still, a public insecure about the postwar world accepted his vision of conspiracy and sanctioned his attacks.

The following is a sample of McCarthy's tactics against the State Department. How does Senator McCarthy define the threat to American security? What proof does he offer that the State Department is filled with known Communists? What were the elements of his success? Was his failure inevitable? Or could he have become more powerful than he was?

Ladies and gentlemen, tonight as we celebrate the one hundred and forty-first birthday of one of the greatest men in American history, I would like to be able to talk about what a glorious day today is in the history of the world. As we celebrate the birth of this man who with his whole heart and soul hated war, I would like to be able to speak of peace in our time, of war being outlawed, and of worldwide disarmament. These would be truly appropriate things to be able to mention as we celebrate the birthday of Abraham Lincoln.

Five years after a world war has been won, men's hearts should anticipate a long peace, and men's minds should be free from the heavy weight that comes with war. But this is not such a period—for this is not a period of peace. This is a time of the "cold war." This is a time when all the world is split into two vast, increasingly hostile armed camps—a time of a great armaments race.

Today we can almost physically hear the mutterings and rumblings of an invigorated god of war. You can see it, feel it, and hear it all the way from the hills of Indochina, from the shores of Formosa, right over into the very heart of Europe itself.

The one encouraging thing is that the "mad moment" has not yet arrived for the firing of the gun or the exploding of the bomb which will set civilization about the final task of destroying itself. There is still a hope for peace if we finally decide that no longer can we safely blind our eyes and close our ears to those facts which are shaping up more and more clearly. And that is that we are now engaged in a showdown fight—not the usual war between nations for land areas or other material gains, but a war between two diametrically opposed ideologies.

The great difference between our western Christian world and the atheistic Communist world is not political, ladies and gentlemen, it is moral. There are other differences, of course, but those could be reconciled. For instance, the Marxian idea of confiscating the land and factories and running the entire economy as a single enterprise is momentous. Likewise, Lenin's invention of the one-party police state as a way to make Marx's idea work is hardly less momentous.

Stalin's resolute putting across of these two ideas, of course, did much to divide the world. With only those differences, however, the east and the west could most certainly still live in peace.

The real, basic difference, however, lies in the religion of immoralism—invented by Marx, preached feverishly by Lenin, and carried to unimaginable extremes by Stalin. This religion of immoralism, if the Red half of the world wins—and well it may—this religion of immoralism will more deeply wound and damage mankind than any conceivable economic or political system. . . .

Today we are engaged in a final, all-out battle between communistic atheism and Christianity. The modern champions of communism have selected this as the time. And, ladies and gentlemen, the chips are down—they are truly down. . . .

Ladies and gentlemen, can there be anyone here tonight who is so blind as to say that the war is not on? Can there be anyone who fails to realize that the Communist world has said, "The time is now"—that this is the time for the showdown between the democratic Christian world and the Communist atheistic world?

Unless we face this fact, we shall pay the price that must be paid by those who wait too long.

Six years ago, at the time of the first conference to map out the peace—Dumbarton Oaks—there was within the Soviet orbit 180 million people. Lined up on the antitotalitarian side there were in the world at that time roughly 1,625,000,000 people. Today, only six years later, there are 800 million people under the absolute domination of Soviet Russia—an increase of over 400 percent. On our side, the figure has shrunk to around 500 million. In other words, in less than six years the odds have changed from 9 to 1 in our favor to 8 to 5 against us. This indicates the swiftness of the tempo of Communist victories and American defeats in the cold war. As one of our outstanding historical figures once said, "When a great democracy is destroyed, it will not be because of enemies from without, but rather because of enemies from within."

The truth of this statement is becoming terrifyingly clear as we see this country each day losing on every front.

At war's end we were physically the strongest nation on earth and, at least potentially, the most powerful intellectually and morally. Ours could have been the honor of being a beacon in the desert of destruction, a shining living proof that civilization was not yet ready to destroy itself. Unfortunately, we have failed miserably and tragically to arise to the opportunity.

The reason why we find ourselves in a position of impotency is not because our only powerful potential enemy has sent men to invade our shores, but rather because of the traitorous actions of those who have been treated so well by this nation. It has not been the less fortunate or members of minority groups who have been selling this nation out, but rather those who have had all the benefits that the wealthiest nation on earth has had to offer—the finest homes, the finest college education, and the finest jobs in government we can give.

This is glaringly true in the State Department. There the bright young men who are born with silver spoons in their mouths are the ones who have been worst.

Now I know it is very easy for anyone to condemn a particular bureau or department in general terms. Therefore, I would like to cite one rather unusual case—the case of a man who has done much to shape our foreign policy.

When Chiang Kai-shek was fighting our war, the State Department had in China a young man named John S. Service. His task, obviously, was not to work for the communization of China. Strangely, however, he sent official reports back to the State Department urging that we torpedo our ally Chiang Kai-shek and stating, in effect, that communism was the best hope of China.

Later, this man—John Service—was picked up by the Federal Bureau of Investigation for turning over to the Communists secret State Department information. Strangely, however, he was never prosecuted. However, Joseph Grew, the under secretary of state, who insisted on his prosecution, was forced to resign. Two days after Grew's successor, Dean Acheson, took over as under secretary of state, this man—John Service—who had been picked up by the FBI and who had previously urged that communism was the best hope of China, was not only reinstated in the State Department but promoted. And finally, under Acheson, placed in charge of all placements and promotions.

Today, ladies and gentlemen, this man Service is on his way to represent the State Department and Acheson in Calcutta—by far and away the most important listening post in the far east. . . .

This, ladies and gentlemen, gives you somewhat of a picture of the type of individuals who have been helping to shape our foreign policy. In my opinion the State Department, which is one of the most important government departments, is thoroughly infested with Communists.

I have in my hand fifty-seven cases of individuals who would appear to be either card-carrying members or certainly loyal to the Communist party, but who nevertheless are still helping to shape our foreign policy. . . .

This brings us down to the case of one Alger Hiss who is important not as an individual any more, but rather because he is so representative of a group in the State Department. It is unnecessary to go over the sordid events showing how he sold out the nation which had given him so much. Those are rather fresh in all of our minds.

However, it should be remembered that the facts in regard to his connection with this international Communist spy ring were made known to the then Under Secretary of State Berle three days after Hitler and Stalin signed the Russo-German alliance pact. At that time one Whittaker Chambers—who was also part of the spy ring—apparently decided that with Russia on Hitler's side, he could no longer betray our nation to Russia. He gave Under Secretary of State Berle—and this is all a matter of record—practically all, if not more, of the facts upon which Hiss's conviction was based.

Under Secretary Berle promptly contacted Dean Acheson and received word in return that Acheson (and I quote) "could vouch for Hiss absolutely"—at which time the matter was dropped. And this, you understand, was at a time when Russia was an ally of Germany. This condition existed while Russia and Germany were invading and dismembering Poland, and while the Communist groups here were screaming "warmonger" at the United States for their support of the allied nations.

Again in 1943, the FBI had occasion to investigate the facts surrounding Hiss's contacts with the Russia spy ring. But even after that FBI report was submitted, nothing was done.

Then late in 1948—on August 5—when the Un-American Activities Committee called Alger Hiss to give an accounting, President Truman at once issued a presidential directive ordering all government agencies to refuse to turn over any information whatsoever in regard to the Communist activities of any government employee to a congressional committee.

Incidentally, even after Hiss was convicted—it is interesting to note that the president still labeled the exposé of Hiss as a "red herring."

If time permitted, it might be well to go into detail about the fact that Hiss was Roosevelt's chief advisor at Yalta when Roosevelt was admittedly in ill health and tired physically and mentally. . . .

Of the results of this conference, Arthur Bliss Lane of the State Department had this to say: "As I glanced over the document, I could not believe my eyes. To me, almost every line spoke of a surrender to Stalin."

As you hear this story of high treason, I know that you are saying to yourself, "Well, why doesn't the Congress do something about it?" Actually, ladies and gentlemen, one of the important reasons for the graft, the corruption, the dishonesty, the disloyalty, the treason in high government positions—one of the most important reasons why this continues is a lack of moral uprising on the part of the 140 million American people. In the light of history, however, this is not hard to explain.

It is the result of an emotional hangover and a temporary moral lapse which follows every war. It is the apathy to evil which people who have been subjected to the tremendous evils of war feel. As the people of the world see mass murder, the destruction of defenseless and innocent people, and all of the crime and lack of morals which go with war, they become numb and apathetic. It has always been thus after war.

However, the morals of our people have not been destroyed. They still exist. This cloak of numbness and apathy has only needed a spark to rekindle them. Happily, this spark has finally been supplied.

As you know, very recently the secretary of state proclaimed his loyalty to a man guilty of what has always been considered as the most abominable of all crimes—of being a traitor to the people who gave him a position of great trust. The secretary of state in attempting to justify his continued devotion to the man who sold out the Christian world to the atheistic world, referred to Christ's Sermon on the Mount as a justification and reason therefor, and the reaction of the American people to this would have made the heart of Abraham Lincoln happy.

When this pompous diplomat in striped pants, with a phony British accent, proclaimed to the American people that Christ on the Mount endorsed communism, high treason, and betrayal of a sacred trust, the blasphemy was so great that it awakened the dormant indignation of the American people.

He has lighted the spark which is resulting in a moral uprising and will end only when the whole sorry mess of twisted, warped thinkers are swept from the national scene so that we may have a new birth of national honesty and decency in government.

The Kitchen Debate, 1959

In July 1959, Vice President Richard Nixon was officially invited to Moscow to open the first American National Exhibition, held as part of a cultural exchange program initiated at Geneva in 1955. The central exhibit was a full-scale model of a six-room ranch-style house, with labor-saving appliances and devices meant to represent the typical American home.

Nixon intended to use the exhibition's picture of domestic affluence to demonstrate the stability and endurance of the American way of life. The exhibit offered an argument: that it was capitalism, not the ideology of socialism, that would improve the condition of working people everywhere.

Unofficially, the vice president was to let Soviet Premier Nikita Khrushchev know that Washington expected some movement on the Berlin discussions before the premier would receive an invitation to the United States. Behind the vice president's visit was the Soviet threat to reach a separate peace with East Germany in order to evict the allies from Berlin. West Berlin's prosperity and economic development were proving both an embarrassment to the Soviet system and a personal embarrassment to its leader.

Once again, the separation between foreign policy and domestic politics was blurred. The kitchen debate exemplified how affluence and mass consumption were all grist for the mill of American cold war politics: the ideology of capitalism, the American way of life, could win the cold war. After twelve years of pursuing containment, Nixon showed the American public that the diplomatic issues separating the United States and the Soviet Union could be easily understood in terms of dishwashers, toasters, and televisions.

Did the kitchen debate come to grips with differences between the two systems? What do you make of Khrushchev's comment that the Soviet Union does not have the "capitalist attitude toward women"?

Following is an account of the informal exchanges in Moscow yesterday between Vice President Richard M. Nixon and Premier Nikita S. Khrushchev. It was compiled from dispatches of the *New York Times,* the Associated Press, United Press International and Reuters. . . .

A TRADE OF GIBES ABOUT TRADE

On arriving at the gate of the American National Exhibition later in the morning, Mr. Khrushchev voiced a gibe about the United States ban on the shipment of strategic goods to the Soviet Union.

KHRUSHCHEV: "Americans have lost their ability to trade. Now you have grown older and you don't trade the way you used to. You need to be invigorated."

NIXON: "You need to have goods to trade."

The statesmen went on to look at equipment for playing back recordings. Mr. Nixon took a cue from it.

NIXON: "There must be a free exchange of ideas."

Mr. Khrushchev responded with a remark touching on the reporting of his speeches on his recent Polish tour.

Mr. Nixon said he was certain that Mr. Khrushchev's speeches and those of Frol R. Kozlov, a first deputy premier, had been fully reported in the West.

Khrushchev (indicating cameras, recording the scene on videotape): "Then what about this tape?" (smiling). "If it is shown in the United States it will be shown in English and I would like a guarantee that there will be a full translation of my remarks."

Mr. Nixon said there would be an English translation of Mr. Khrushchev's remarks and added his hope that all his own remarks in the Soviet Union would be given with full translations in that country.

KHRUSHCHEV: "We want to live in peace and friendship with Americans because we are the two most powerful countries, and if we live in friendship then other countries will also live in friendship. But if there is a country that is too war-minded we could pull its ears a little and say: Don't you dare; fighting is not allowed now; this is a period of atomic armament; some foolish one could start a war and then even a wise one couldn't finish the war. Therefore, we are governed by this idea in our policy—internal and foreign. How long has America existed? Three hundreds years?"

NIXON: "One hundred and fifty years."

THEY WILL WAVE AS THEY PASS U.S.

KHRUSHCHEV: "One hundred and fifty years? Well, then, we will say America has been in existence for 150 years and this is the level she has reached. We have existed not quite forty-two years and in another seven years we will be on the same level as America.

"When we catch you up, in passing you by, we will wave to you. Then if you wish we can stop and say: Please follow us. Plainly speaking, if you want capitalism you can live that way. That is your own affair and doesn't concern us. We can still feel sorry for you but since you don't understand us—live as you do understand.

"We are all glad to be here at the exhibition with Vice President Nixon. . . . I think you will be satisfied with your visit and if—I cannot go without saying it—if you would not take such a decision [proclamation by the United States Government of Captive Nations Week, a week of prayer for peoples enslaved by the Soviet Union] which has not been thought out thoroughly, as was approved by Congress, your trip would be excellent. But you have churned the water yourselves—why this was necessary God only knows.

"What happened? What black cat crossed your path and confused you? But that is your affair, we do not interfere with your problems. [Wrapping his arms about a Soviet workman] Does this man look like a slave laborer? [Waving at others] With men with such spirit how can we lose?"

EXCHANGE OF IDEAS URGED BY NIXON

NIXON (POINTING TO AMERICAN WORKMEN): "With men like that we are strong. But these men, Soviet and American, work together well for peace, even as they have worked together in building this exhibition. This is the way it should be.

"Your remarks are in the tradition of what we have come to expect—sweeping and extemporaneous. Later on we will both have an opportunity to speak and consequently I will not comment on the various points that you raised, except to say this—this color television is one of the most advanced developments in communications that we have.

"I can only say that if this competition in which you plan to outstrip us is to do the best for both of our peoples and for peoples everywhere there must be exchange of ideas. After all, you don't know everything—"

KHRUSHCHEV: "If I don't know everything, you don't know anything about communism except fear of it."

NIXON: "There are some instances where you may be ahead of us, for example in the development of the thrust of your rockets for the investigation of outer space; there may be some instances in which we are ahead of you—in color television, for instance."

KHRUSHCHEV: "No, we are up with you on this, too. We have bested you in one technique and also in the other."

NIXON: "You see, you never concede anything."

KHRUSHCHEV: "I do not give up."

APPEARANCES ON TV ARE SUGGESTED

NIXON: "Wait till you see the picture. Let's have far more communication and exchange in this very area that we speak of. We should hear you more on our television. You should hear us more on yours."

KHRUSHCHEV: "That's a good idea. Let's do it like this. You appear before our people. We will appear before your people. People will see and appreciate this."

NIXON: "There is not a day in the United States when we cannot read what you say. When Kozlov was speaking in California about peace, you were talking here in somewhat different terms. This was reported extensively in the American press. Never make a statement here if you don't want it to be read in the United States. I can promise you every word you say will be translated into English."

KHRUSHCHEV: "I doubt it. I want you to give your word that this speech of mine will be heard by the American people."

NIXON (SHAKING HANDS ON IT): "By the same token, everything I say will be translated and heard all over the Soviet Union?"

KHRUSHCHEV: "That's agreed."

NIXON: "You must not be afraid of ideas."

KHRUSHCHEV: "We are telling you not to be afraid of ideas. We have no reason to be afraid. We have already broken free from such a situation."

NIXON: "Well, then, let's have more exchange of them. We are all agreed on that. All right? All right?"

KHRUSHCHEV: "Fine. [Aside] Agree to what? All right, I am in agreement. But I want to stress what I am in agreement with. I know that I am dealing with a very good lawyer, I also want to uphold my own miner's flag so that the coal miners can say, 'Our man does not concede.'"

NIXON: "No question about that."

KHRUSHCHEV: "You are a lawyer for capitalism and I am a lawyer for communism. Let's compete."

VICE PRESIDENT PROTESTS FILIBUSTER

NIXON: "The way you dominate the conversation you would make a good lawyer yourself. If you were in the United States Senate you would be accused of filibustering."

NIXON (HALTING KHRUSHCHEV AT MODEL KITCHEN IN MODEL HOUSE): "You had a very nice house in your exhibition in New York. My wife and I saw and enjoyed it very much. I want to show you this kitchen. It is like those of our houses in California."

KHRUSHCHEV (AFTER NIXON CALLED ATTENTION TO A BUILT-IN PANEL-CONTROLLED WASHING MACHINE): "We have such things."

NIXON: "This is the newest model. This is the kind which is built in thousands of units for direct installation in the houses."

He added that Americans were interested in making life easier for their women. Mr. Khrushchev remarked that in the Soviet Union they did not have "the capitalist attitude toward women."

NIXON: "I think that this attitude toward women is universal. What we want to do is make easier the life of our housewives."

Moscow, 1959. Soviet Premier Nikita Khrushchev and Vice President Richard Nixon, on television at the American National Exhibition.
Library of Congress.

He explained that the house could be built for $14,000 and that most veterans had bought houses for between $10,000 and $15,000.

NIXON: "Let me give you an example you can appreciate. Our steel workers, as you know, are on strike. But any steel worker could buy this house. They earn $3 an hour. This house costs about $100 a month to buy on a contract running twenty-five to thirty years."

KHRUSHCHEV: "We have steel workers and we have peasants who also can afford to spend $14,000 for a house." He said American houses were built to last only twenty years, so builders could sell new houses at the end of that period. "We build firmly. We build for our children and grandchildren."

Mr. Nixon said he thought American houses would last more than twenty years, but even so, after twenty years many Americans want a new home or a new kitchen, which would be obsolete then. The American system is designed to take advantage of new inventions and new techniques, he said.

KHRUSHCHEV: "This theory does not hold water."

He said some things never got out of date—furniture and furnishings, perhaps, but not houses. He said he did not think that what Americans had written about their houses was all strictly accurate.

GADGETRY DERIDED BY KHRUSHCHEV

NIXON (POINTING TO TELEVISION SCREEN): "We can see here what is happening in other parts of the home."

KHRUSHCHEV: "This is probably always out of order."

NIXON: "Da [yes]."

KHRUSHCHEV: "Don't you have a machine that puts food into the mouth and pushes it down? Many things you've shown us are interesting but they are not needed in life. They have no useful purpose. They are merely gadgets. We have a saying, if you have bedbugs you have to catch one and pour boiling water into the ear." . . .

NIXON (HEARING JAZZ MUSIC): "I don't like jazz music."

KHRUSHCHEV: "I don't like it either."

NIXON: "But my girls like it." . . .

RUSSIANS HAVE IT TOO, PREMIER ASSERTS

KHRUSHCHEV: "The Americans have created their own image of the Soviet man and think he is as you want him to be. But he is not as you think. You think the Russian people will be dumbfounded to see these things, but the fact is that newly built Russian houses have all this equipment right now. Moreover, all you have to do to get a house is to be born in the Soviet Union. You are entitled to housing. I was born in the Soviet Union. So I have a right to a house. In America if you don't have a dollar—you have the right to choose between sleeping in a house or on the pavement. Yet you say that we are slaves of communism." . . .

NIXON: "To us, diversity, the right to choose, the fact that we have 1,000 builders building 1,000 different houses, is the most important thing. We don't have one decision made at the top by one government official. This is the difference."

Selling America

The two photographs that follow are idealizations of American life, created by the United States Information Agency, the international propaganda arm of the American government. In a sense, they were weapons in the cold war. As you look at them, try to think of connections between them and the "kitchen debate" between Richard Nixon and Nikita Khrushchev. According to the second photograph, what apparent relationship exists between technology and domestic bliss and harmony? What idealized notions of youth culture are present in the first photograph? Is there some connection between this photograph and Nixon's and Khrushchev's disavowal of jazz in the "kitchen debate"? between the photograph and the emergence of rock 'n' roll (Chapter 3)?

Original caption: "Washington, D.C.—Brennan Jacques, a typical American
teenager, has his own orchestra, the 'Fabulous Esquires,' composed of youngsters
aware of what their schoolmates like and do not like in current music. Here, young
Jacques plays the piano for a group of young people, who have gathered around him.
1957."

Original caption: "Takoma Park, Maryland—In the living room of their home, the A.
Jackson Cory family and some friends watch a television program. Some sociologists
claim the growing popularity of television will tend to make family life stronger and
make the home the center of the family's recreation. 1950."
United States Information Agency photo, National Archives.

SUGGESTIONS FOR VIEWING AND LISTENING

On the Waterfront (1954)
Should Terry Malloy rat on his friends? Should Elia Kazan, who directed the film,
have testified before the House Un-American Activities Committee (HUAC)?

Salt of the Earth (1954)
Directed by Herbert Biberman, who had been blacklisted by Hollywood for his refusal
to cooperate with HUAC. The story of Mexican-American zinc miners.

The Day The Earth Stood Still (1951)
A cold war feast. Nuclear testing, science, invasion anxieties, a Christian parable.

Patti Page, "Mockin' Bird Hill" (1951)
Waltzes—and simplicity—were in vogue at the height of the cold war.

Sammy Kaye, "In the Mission of St. Augustine" (1953)
Americans were more religious than ever.

Bill Hayes, "Ballad of Davy Crockett" (1955)
Cold war nationalism and imperialsim. "His land was biggest, and his land was best."

CHAPTER 3

The Eisenhower Consensus

Reason, objectivity, dispassion—these were the qualities and values that twice elected Dwight Eisenhower to the presidency. His appeal was bipartisan. In 1948 and 1952, politicians of both major parties sought to nominate this man with the "leaping and effortless smile" who promised the electorate a "constitutional presidency"—immune from the ideological harangues of European dictators, American demagogues, and New Deal presidents—and a secure economy—immune from major dislocations.

To replace the disjointed and unpredictable insecurity of depression, war, and ideological struggle, he offered Americans a society based on consensus. In the consensual society, major disagreements over important issues such as race, class, and gender were presumed not to exist. Conflict—serious conflict, about who had power and who did not—was considered almost un-American.

By 1960, it was clear that Eisenhower, and the nation at large, had not sought to create or maintain the consensual society through any radical departures from the past. The cold war, anticommunism, the welfare state—all inherited from his Democratic predecessor, Harry Truman—were not so much thrown aside as modulated or refined.

Anticommunism was central to the consensus, for the existence of a powerful enemy helped define the consensus and to deflect attention from the economic and social issues on which there could be no easy agreement. Joseph McCarthy would cease to be a factor after 1954, but otherwise, anticommunism was almost as much a part of the Eisenhower years as it had been of Truman's. The purges that cleansed most labor unions of Communist influence were completed when Ike took office, but cold war attitudes permeated the labor movement throughout the decade. The Committee on Un-American Activities of the House of Representatives (HUAC) would never know the acclaim it had mustered in the late 1940s, but each year it received more money from Congress and continued to function. In 1959, the Supreme Court refused to declare HUAC in violation of the First Amendment. New organizations—Robert Welch's John Birch Society and the Christian Anti-Communist Crusade, for example—emerged to carry on the struggle against internal subversion. Welch labeled Eisenhower a "dedicated, conscious agent of the Communist conspiracy."

Those who feared that the first Republican president since Herbert Hoover would grasp the opportunity to dismantle the welfare state had misunderstood both Eisenhower and the function of government at midcentury. If only intuitively, Eisenhower knew that what was left of the New Deal could not be eliminated without risking serious social and economic disruption. Countercyclical programs like old-age insurance and unemployment insurance were maintained or expanded; the Council of Economic Advisers, created in the Employment Act of 1946 to provide the president with his own planning staff, remained; spending for military hardware and interstate highways was expected to create jobs. Republicans did manage a rollback of New Deal policies in the areas of taxation and agriculture.

There was in much of this a pervasive element of acceptance—acceptance of American institutions as they were or as Americans wished they were. The power of the large corporation was accepted, its influence invited. Many agreed with General Motors president Charles E. Wilson, who during Senate hearings to confirm his nomination as secretary of defense said, "I thought what was good for our country was good for General Motors, and vice versa." Effective government was often conceptualized as the product of big business, big labor, and big government, each checking and balancing the others. The antitrust emphasis of the later New Deal was all but forgotten. Instead, Americans took comfort in John Kenneth Galbraith's theory of countervailing power, which postulated a self-regulating economy in which some big businesses (such as Sears, Roebuck) countervailed others (such as General Electric), leaving government the limited task of fine-tuning an economic system whose basic structure was virtually guaranteed to be competitive.

It followed that a wide variety of social problems—racism, unemployment, poverty, urban life, and the cult of domesticity, which suffocated women—were ignored, denied, accepted, or left in abeyance to be handled by some future generation. Throughout the 1950s, social commentators affirmed that America's central problems were ones of boredom, affluence, and classlessness. *The Midas Plague*, a science-fiction novel, described a world in which goods were so easily produced and so widely available that consuming had become a personal duty, a social responsibility, and an enormous and endless burden. David Riesman's *Lonely Crowd*, an influential study published in 1950, argued that the age of scarcity had ended; Americans would henceforth be concerned with leisure, play, and the "art of living." For many analysts of American society, the new conditions of life had eliminated the old conflicts between capital and labor and ushered in the "end of ideology." Economic growth—so the theory went—would increase the size of the total product to be distributed and soon result in a society consisting mainly of white-collar workers.

Beneath the surface of the consensual society, there were some currents that disturbed many Americans. Despite a landmark Supreme Court decision in 1954 ordering the racial integration of public schools with "all deliberate speed," black Americans remained outside the American system, gathering energies for a spectacular assault on the traditions of prejudice and exploitation. Women did not resist so overtly, but a growing body of scholarly literature suggests that many women were at best ambivalent about the June Cleaver (*Leave It to Beaver*) and Margaret Anderson (*Father Knows Best*) images that were television's contribution to the consensual society. Everyone was concerned about an apparent alienation among many young people, an alienation that expressed itself sometimes frighteningly as juvenile delinquency, sometimes just as a mystifying lack of energetic affirmation, most often in an affinity for a new music called rock 'n' roll. Following the launch of the Soviet satellite *Sputnik* in 1957, Americans began to ask whether this technological defeat reflected a general withering of national purpose (a theme taken up by Eisenhower's successor, John Kennedy). As the decade wore on, it became obvious, too, that millions of Americans were not participating in the prosperity the administration proclaimed. Eisenhower's farewell address would be silent on most of these issues; but its discussion of the military-industrial complex was perhaps Eisenhower's way of acknowledging that the consensus he had tried so hard to preserve—indeed, to create—was fundamentally unstable. If so, the next decade would prove him right.

INTERPRETIVE ESSAY

Rebels Without a Cause?
Teenagers in the 1950s

Beth Bailey

Against images of Elvis Presley's contorted torso, of Little Richard's scream-ing black sexuality, of Cleveland disc jockey Alan Freed introducing a gener-ation of eager young people to the erotic pleasures of rhythm and blues, Beth Bailey offers a very different perspective on American youth in the 1950s. Using dating behavior to understand the emerging postwar youth culture, Bailey suggests that young people were responding to a climate of insecurity that had deep historical roots. Furthermore, she identifies the quest for secu-rity with a revised, "50s" version of the American dream that also encom-passed family and suburbia. In short, Bailey seems to suggest that the youth of the 1950s were as attuned to consensual values as any other group.

While reading the essay, consider some of these questions: Does Bailey's argument apply to most American youths, or only to those who were white and middle class? What did parents find objectionable in this youth behavior, and why? Might "going steady" be understood as both a form of acquies-cence in dominant values and a kind of resistance? And how can one square Bailey's perspective with the Presley, Little Richard, and Freed images men-tioned above?

The United States emerged from the Second World War the most powerful and af-fluent nation in the world. This statement, bald but essentially accurate, is the given foundation for understanding matters foreign and domestic, the cold war and the age of abundance in America. Yet the sense of confidence and triumph sug-gested by that firm phrasing and by our images of soldiers embracing women as confetti swirled through downtown streets obscures another postwar reality. Un-derlying and sometimes overwhelming both bravado and complacency were voices of uncertainty. America at war's end was not naively optimistic.

The Great War had planted the seeds of the great depression. Americans won-dered if hard times would return as the war boom ended. (They wouldn't.) The First World War had not ended all wars. Would war come again? (It would, both cold and hot.) And the fundamental question that plagued postwar America was, would American citizens have the strength and the character to meet the demands of this new world?

Postwar America appears in stereotype as the age of conformity—smug, mate-rialistic, complacent, a soulless era peopled by organization men and their

Beth Bailey, "Rebels Without a Cause? Teenagers in the 1950s," *History Today* vol. 40, February 1990, pp. 25–31.

(house)wives. But this portrait of conformity exists only because Americans created it. Throughout the postwar era Americans indulged in feverish self-examination. Experts proclaimed crises, limned the American character, poked and prodded into the recesses of the American psyche. Writing in scholarly journals and for an attentive general public, theorists and social critics suggested that America's very success was destroying the values that had made success possible. Success, they claimed, was eroding the ethic that had propelled America to military and industrial supremacy and had lifted American society (with significant exceptions seen clearly in hindsight) to undreamed-of heights of prosperity.

At issue was the meaning of the American dream. Did the American dream mean success through individual competition in a wide-open free marketplace? Or was the dream only of the abundance the American marketplace had made possible—the suburban American dream of two cars in every garage and a refrigerator-freezer in every kitchen? One dream was of competition and the resulting rewards. The *making* of the self-made man—the process of entrepreneurial struggle—was the stuff of that dream. Fulfillment, in this vision, was not only through material comforts, but through the prominence, social standing, and influence in the public sphere one achieved in the struggle for success.

The new-style postwar American dream seemed to look to the private as the sphere of fulfillment, of self-definition and self-realization. Struggle was not desired, but stasis. The dream was of a private life—a family, secure, stable, and comfortable—that compensated for one's public (work) life. One vision highlighted risk; the other security. Many contemporary observers feared that the desire for security was overwhelming the "traditional" American ethic. In the dangerous postwar world, they asserted, the rejection of the public, of work and of risk would soon destroy America's prosperity and security.

The focus for much of the fear over what America was becoming was, not surprisingly, youth. Adult obsession with the new postwar generation took diverse forms—from the overheated rhetoric about the new epidemic of juvenile delinquency (too many rebels without causes) to astringent attacks on the conformity of contemporary youth. These critiques, though seemingly diametrically opposed, were based on the shared assumption that young people lacked the discipline and get-up-and-go that had made America great.

Perhaps nowhere in American culture do we find a richer statement of concern about American youth and the new American dream than in the debates that raged over "going steady," an old name for a new practice that was reportedly more popular among postwar teenagers than "bop, progressive jazz, hot rods and curiosity (slight) about atomic energy." The crisis over the "national problem" of going steady is not merely emblematic—an amusing way into a serious question. "Going steady" seemed to many adults the very essence of the problem, a kind of leading indicator of the privatization of the American dream. Social scientists and social critics saw in the new security-first courtship patterns a paradigm for an emerging American character that, while prizing affluence, did not relish the risks and hard work that made it possible.

Certainly the change in courtship patterns was dramatic. And it was not hard to make a connection between the primary characteristics of teenagers' love lives and what they hoped to get out of American life in general. Before the Second World

War, American youth had prized a promiscuous popularity, demonstrating competitive success through the number and variety of dates they commanded. Sociologist Willard Waller, in his 1937 study of American dating, gave this competitive system a name: "the campus rating complex." His study of Pennsylvania State University detailed a "dating and rating" system based on a model of public competition in which popularity was the currency. To be popular, men needed outward, material signs: an automobile, proper clothing, the right fraternity membership, money. Women's popularity depended on building and maintaining a reputation for popularity. They had to *be seen* with popular men in the "right" places, indignantly turn down requests for dates made at the "last minute," and cultivate the impression they were greatly in demand.

In *Mademoiselle*'s 1938 college issue, for example, a Smith college senior advised incoming freshmen to "cultivate an image of popularity" if they wanted dates. "During your first term," she wrote, "get 'home talent' to ply you with letters, invitations, telegrams. College men will think, 'She must be attractive if she can rate all that attention.' " And at Northwestern University in the 1920s, competitive pressure was so intense that co-eds made a pact not to date on certain nights of the week. That way they could preserve some time to study, secure in the knowledge they were not losing ground in the competitive race for success by staying home.

In 1935, the Massachusetts *Collegian* (the Massachusetts State College student newspaper) ran an editorial against using the library for "datemaking." The editors proclaimed: "The library is the place for the improvement of the mind and not the social standing of the student." Social standing, not social life: on one word turns the meaning of the dating system. That "standing" probably wasn't even a conscious choice shows how completely these college students took for granted that dating was primarily concerned with competition and popularity. As one North Carolina teenager summed it up:

> Going steady with one date
> Is okay, if that's all you rate.

Rating, dating, popularity, competition: catchwords hammered home, reinforced from all sides until they seemed a natural vocabulary. You had to rate in order to date, to date in order to rate. By successfully maintaining this cycle, you became popular. To stay popular, you competed. There was no end; the competitive process defined dating. Competition was the key term in the formula—remove it and there was no rating, dating, or popularity.

In the 1930s and 1940s, this competition was enacted most visibly on the dance floor. There, success was a dizzying popularity that kept girls whirling from escort to escort, "cut in" on by a host of popular men. Advice columns, etiquette books, even student handbooks told girls to strive to be "once-arounders," to never be left with the same partner for more than one turn around the dance floor. On the dance floor, success and failure were easily measured. Wallflowers were dismissed out of hand. But getting stuck—not being "cut in" on—was taken quite seriously as a sign of social failure. Everyone noticed, and everyone judged.

This form of competitive courtship would change dramatically. By the early 1950s, "cutting in" had almost completely disappeared outside the deep south. In

1955, a student at Texas Christian University reported, "To cut in is almost an insult." A girl in Green Bay, Wisconsin, said that her parents were "astonished" when they discovered that she hadn't danced with anyone but her escort at a "formal." "The truth was," she admitted, "that I wasn't aware that we were supposed to."

This 180-degree reversal took place quickly—during the years of the Second World War—and was so complete by the early 1950s that people under eighteen could be totally unaware of the formerly powerful convention. It signaled not simply a change in dancing etiquette but a complete transformation of the dating system as well. Definitions of social success as promiscuous popularity based on strenuous competition had given way to new definitions, which located success in the security of a dependable escort.

By the 1950s, early marriage had become the goal for young adults. In 1959, 47 percent of all brides married before they turned nineteen, and up to 25 percent of students at many large state universities were married. The average age at marriage had risen to 26.7 for men and 23.3 for women during the lingering depression, but by 1951 the average age at marriage had fallen to 22.6 for men, 20.4 for women. And younger teens had developed their own version of early marriage.

As early as 1950, going steady had completely supplanted the dating-rating complex as the criterion for popularity among youth. A best-selling study of American teenagers, *Profile of Youth* (1949) reported that in most high schools the "mere fact" of going steady was a sign of popularity "as long as you don't get tied up with an impossible gook." The *Ladies' Home Journal* reported in 1949 that "every high school student . . . must be prepared to fit into a high-school pattern in which popularity, social acceptance and emotional security are often determined by the single question: does he or she go steady?" A 1959 poll found that 57 percent of American teens had gone or were going steady. And, according to *Cosmopolitan* in 1960, if you didn't go steady, you were "square."

The new protocol of going steady was every bit as strict as the old protocol of rating and dating. To go steady, the boy gave the girl some visible token, such as a class ring or letter sweater. In Portland, Oregon, steadies favored rings (costing from $17 to $20). In Birmingham, Michigan, the girl wore the boy's identity bracelet, but never his letter sweater. In rural Iowa, the couple wore matching corduroy "steady jackets," although any couple wearing matching clothing in California would be laughed at.

As long as they went steady, the boy had to call the girl a certain number of times a week and take her on a certain number of dates a week (both numbers were subject to local convention). Neither boy nor girl could date anyone else or pay too much attention to anyone of the opposite sex. While either could go out with friends of the same sex, each must always know where the other was and what he or she was doing. Going steady meant a guaranteed date for special events, and it implied greater sexual intimacy—either more "necking" or "going further."

In spite of the intense monogamy of these steady relationships, teenagers viewed them as temporary. A 1950 study of 565 seniors in an eastern suburban high school found that 80 percent had gone or were going steady. Out of that number, only eleven said they planned to marry their steady. In New Haven, Connecticut, high school girls wore "obit bracelets." Each time they broke up with a boy, they added a disc engraved with his name or initials to the chain. In Louisiana, a girl would embroider her sneakers with the name of her current steady. When they broke up, she would clip off his name and sew an X over the spot. An advice book from the mid-1950s advised girls to get a "Puppy Love Anklet." Wearing it on the right ankle meant that you were available, on the left that you were going steady. The author advised having "Going Steady" engraved on one side, "Ready, Willing 'n Waiting" on the other—just in case the boys could not remember the code. All these conventions, cheerfully reported in teenager columns in national magazines, show how much teenagers took it for granted that going steady was a temporary, if intense, arrangement.

Harmless as this system sounds today, especially compared to the rigors of rating and dating, the rush to go steady precipitated an intense generational battle. Clearly some adult opposition was over sex: going steady was widely accepted as a justification for greater physical intimacy. But more fundamentally, the battle over going steady came down to a confrontation between two generations over the meaning of the American dream. Security versus competition. Teenagers in the 1950s were trying to do the unthinkable—to eliminate competition from the popularity equation. Adults were appalled. To them, going steady, with its extreme rejection of competition in favor of temporary security, represented all the faults of the new generation.

Adults, uncomfortable with the "cult of happiness" that rejected competition for security, attacked the teenage desire for security with no holds barred. As one writer advised boys, "To be sure of anything is to cripple one's powers of growth." She continued, "To have your girl always assured at the end of a telephone line without having to work for her, to beat the other fellows to her is bound to lessen your powers of personal achievement." A male adviser, campaigning against going steady, argued: "Competition will be good for you. It sharpens your wits, teaches you how to get along well in spite of difficulties." And another, writing in *Esquire*, explained the going steady phenomenon this way: "She wants a mate; he being a modern youth doesn't relish competition."

As for girls, the argument went: "She's afraid of competition. She isn't sure she can compete for male attention in the open market: 'going steady' frees her from fear of further failures." The author of *Jackson's Guide to Dating* tells the story of "Judith Thompson," a not-especially-attractive girl with family problems, who has been going steady with "Jim" since she was fourteen. Lest we think that poor Judith deserves someone to care for her or see Jim as a small success in her life, the author stresses that going steady is one more failure for Judith. "Now that Judith is sixteen and old enough to earn money and help herself in other ways to recover from her unfortunate childhood, she has taken on the additionally crippling circumstance of a steady boyfriend. How pathetic. The love and attention of her steady boyfriend are a substitute for other more normal kinds of success." What should Judith be doing? "A good deal of the time she spends going steady with Jim could be used to make herself more attractive so that other boys would ask her for dates."

There is nothing subtle in these critiques of going steady. The value of competition is presumed as a clear standard against which to judge modern youth. But there is more here. There is a tinge of anger in these judgments, an anger that may well stem from the differing experiences of two generations of Americans. The competitive system that had emerged in the flush years of the 1920s was strained by events of the 1930s and 1940s. The elders had come of age during decades of depression and world war, times when the competitive struggle was, for many, inescapable. Much was at stake, the cost of failure all too clear. While youth in the period between the wars embraced a competitive dating system, even gloried in it, as adults they sought the security they had lacked in their youth.

Young people and their advocates made much of the lack of security of the postwar world, self-consciously pointing to the "general anxiety of the times" as a justification for both early marriage and going steady. But the lives of these young people were clearly more secure than those of their parents. That was the gift their parents tried to give them. Though the cold war raged it had little immediate impact on the emerging teenage culture (for those too young to fight in Korea, of course). Cushioned by unprecedented affluence, allowed more years of freedom within the protected youth culture of high school and ever-more-frequently college, young people did not have to struggle so hard, compete so ferociously as their parents had.

And by and large, both young people and their parents knew it and were genuinely not sure what that meant for America's future. What did it mean—that a general affluence, at least for a broad spectrum of America's burgeoning middle class, was possible without a dog-eat-dog ferocity? What did *that* mean for the American Dream of success? One answer was given in the runaway best seller of the decade, *The Man in the Gray Flannel Suit*, which despite the title was not so much about the deadening impact of conformity but about what Americans should and could dream in the postwar world.

The protagonist of the novel, Tom Rath (the not-so-subtle naming made more explicit by the appearance of the word "vengeful" in the sentence following Tom's introduction), has been through the Second World War, and the shadow of war hangs over his life. Tom wants to provide well for his family, and feels a nagging need to succeed. But when he is offered the chance at an old-style American dream—to be taken on as the protégé of his business-wise, driven boss, he says no. In a passage that cuts to the heart of postwar American culture, Tom tells his boss:

> I don't think I'm the kind of guy who should try to be a big executive. I'll say it frankly: I don't think I have the willingness to make the sacrifices. . . . I'm trying to be honest about this. I want the money. Nobody likes money better than I do. But I'm not the kind of guy who can work evenings and weekends and all the rest of it forever. . . . I've been through one war. Maybe another one's coming. If one is, I want to be able to look back and figure I spent the time between wars with my family, the way it should have been spent. Regardless of war, I want to get the most out of the years I've got left. Maybe that sounds silly. It's just that if I have to bury myself in a job every minute of my life, I don't see any point to it.

Tom's privatized dream—of comfort without sacrifice, of family and personal fulfillment—might seem the author's attempt to resolve the tensions of the novel (and of postwar American society). But the vision is more complex than simply affirmative. Tom's boss responds with sympathy and understanding, then suddenly loses control. "Somebody has to do the big jobs!" he says passionately. "This world was built by men like me! To really do a job, you have to live it, body and soul! You people who just give half your mind to your work are riding on our backs!" And Tom responds: "I know it."

The new American Dream had not yet triumphed. The ambivalence and even guilt implicit in Tom Rath's answer to his boss pervaded American culture in the 1950s—in the flood of social criticism and also in parents' critiques of teenage courtship rituals. The attacks on youth's desire for security are revealing, for it was in many ways the parents who embraced security—moving to the suburbs, focusing on the family. The strong ambivalence many felt about their lives appears in the critiques of youth. This same generation would find even more to criticize in the 1960s, as the "steadies" of the 1950s became the sexual revolutionaries of the 1960s. Many of the children of these parents came to recognize the tensions within the dream. The baby-boom generation accepted wholeheartedly the doctrine of self-fulfillment, but rejected the guilt and fear that had linked fulfillment and security. In the turbulence of the 1960s, young people were not rejecting the new American Dream of easy affluence and personal fulfillment, but only jettisoning the fears that had hung over a generation raised with depression and war. It turns out the 1950s family was not the new American Dream, but only its nurturing home.

SOURCES

The Suburbs

Photographs like this one, of a housing development called Levittown, on Long Island, appear in most history textbooks, usually to offer evidence of the inherent sterility of life in the new American suburbs. Yet there are those who argue that this is only a superficial impression and that up-close investigation of particular houses would reveal the effort most homeowners made to customize their homes and distinguish their properties from those of their neighbors. What do you think?

UPI.

Television

In 1949, when the following photographs were taken, television was a new medium, experiencing its first full "season." Because it was new, representations of television were in part designed to explain the medium to Americans who were curious and concerned about how it would shape their lives. What do these photographs tell us about how television was understood at midcentury? What reassurance do they offer? What might they reveal about television's place in the consensual society of the 1950s?

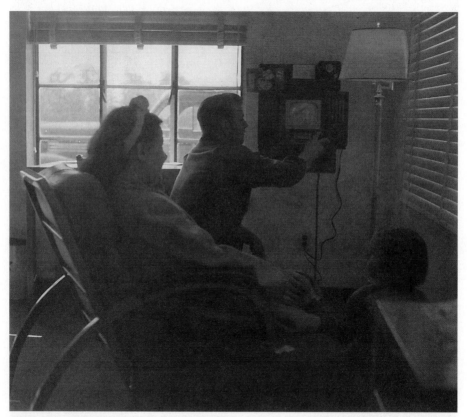

Original caption: "Inside an overnight cottage, a tourist family relaxes after unpacking luggage from car. Man adjusts television receiver as wife and child look on. This motel operator has installed TV sets in each of the cottages for guests' use." Camden, New Jersey, 1949.
United States Information Agency photo, National Archives.

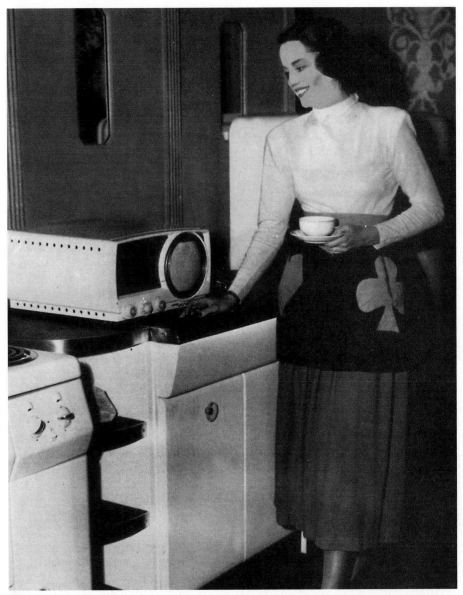

Original caption: "Terry Thomas is so interested in the first kitchen television set ever made (a product of Motorola), that she forgets her coffee." New York City, September, 1949.
National Archives.

Teen Culture
Rock 'n' Roll

The musical style called "rock 'n' roll" dates from the early 1950s. It is usually considered a sign of revolt, musical evidence that the generational rebellion that would sweep the 1960s was already under way even as Dwight Eisenhower was serving his first term. It was this. But rock 'n' roll was also essentially a white music, and a white music that was developed almost entirely from black musical styles.

The verses below—from the rock 'n' roll classic "Shake, Rattle and Roll" (1954)—allow us to inquire into the historical meaning of this new music. The verses on the left are from the original version, written by Charles Calhoun and recorded by Joe Turner for the black market. The verses on the right are from the more popular "cover" version by Bill Haley and the Comets. Both versions were hits in 1954.

Why did Haley change the words? Was rock 'n' roll part of the Eisenhower consensus, or its antithesis?

"SHAKE, RATTLE AND ROLL" (1954)

The Charles Calhoun / Joe Turner version

Get out of that bed,
And wash your face and hands. [twice]

Get into the kitchen
Make some noise with the pots and pans.

Well you wear those dresses,
The sun comes shinin' through. [twice]

I can't believe my eyes,
That all of this belongs to you.

I said over the hill,
And way down underneath. [twice]

You make me roll my eyes,
And then you make me grit my teeth.

The Bill Haley version

Get out in that kitchen,
And rattle those pots and pans. [twice]

Roll my breakfast
'Cause I'm a hungry man.

You wear those dresses,
Your hair done up so nice. [twice]

You look so warm,
But your heart is cold as ice.

[the third verse of the Calhoun/Turner version is not part of the Haley version]

Dress Right

Parents, school officials, and other adult authorities carefully monitored the behavior of 1950s youth. The Catholic church published a list of films considered morally objectionable, and many radio stations refused to play rhythm and blues or rock 'n' roll. The schools had regulations too numerous to mention, among them dress codes like the one below. Called "Dress Right," this code was designed in part by student representatives from various schools. It was in force in Buffalo in the late 1950s and emulated nationally as the Buffalo Plan. What were the purposes of the code? On what assumptions was it based? What accounts for the distinction between academic and vocational schools? From the accompanying photograph of the lunchroom at one of the city's vocational schools (with a summary of the code on the wall), what can one conclude about student attitudes toward the code?

Board of Education
Buffalo, New York
School-Community Coordination
Recommendations of the Inter High School Student Council
for Appropriate Dress of Students in High School

BOYS
ACADEMIC HIGH SCHOOLS AND
HUTCHINSON-TECHNICAL HIGH SCHOOL

Recommended:

1. Dress shirt and tie or conservative sport shirt and tie with suit jacket, jacket, sport coat, or sweater
2. Standard trousers or khakis; clean and neatly pressed
3. Shoes, clean and polished; white bucks acceptable

Not Recommended:

1. Dungarees or soiled, unpressed khakis
2. T-shirts, sweat shirts
3. Extreme style of shoes, including hobnail or "motorcycle boots"

VOCATIONAL HIGH SCHOOLS

Recommended:

1. Shirt and tie or sport shirt and tie
2. Sport shirt with sweater or jacket

The cafeteria at Buffalo's Burgard Vocational High School, with the Dress Right code on the wall.
Burgard Craftsman, 1958.

3. Standard trousers or khakis; clean and neatly pressed
4. Shoes, clean and polished; white bucks acceptable

Not Recommended:

1. Dungarees or soiled, unpressed khakis
2. T-shirts, sweat shirts
3. Extreme styles of shoes, including hobnail or "motorcycle boots"

Note: The apparel recommended for boys should be worn in standard fashion with shirts tucked in and buttoned, and ties tied at the neck. Standard of dress for boys, while in school shops or laboratories, should be determined by the school.

GIRLS
ACADEMIC AND VOCATIONAL HIGH SCHOOLS

Recommended:

1. Blouses, sweaters, blouse and sweater, jacket with blouse or sweater
2. Skirts, jumpers, suits or conservative dresses
3. Shoes appropriate to the rest of the costume

Not Recommended:

1. V-neck sweaters without blouse
2. Bermuda shorts, kilts, party-type dresses, slacks of any kind
3. Ornate jewelry
4. T-shirts, sweat shirts

Note: All recommended wear for girls should fit appropriately and modestly. Standard of dress for girls, while in school shops or laboratories, should be determined by the school.

January 24, 1956

School Sampler: An Essay in Words and Images

The items on these pages come from Buffalo, New York, school yearbooks. What does each tell us about coming of age in the 1950s—and, in the case of one of the photographs, in the early 1960s?

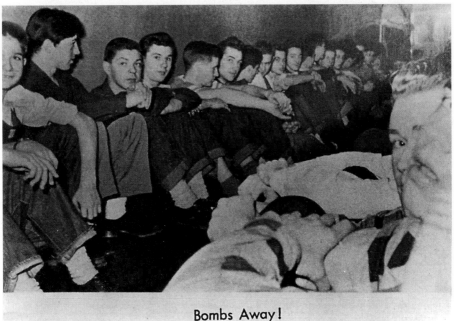

Bombs Away!

Seneca Vocational
Chieftain, 1952.

"We can't all be captains, we've got to be crew,
There's something for all of us here.
There's big work to do and there's lesser to do,
And the task we must do is the near.

If you can't be a highway then just be a trail,
If you can't be the sun be a star;
It isn't by size that you win or you fail--
Be the best of whatever you are!"

                                              --Douglas Malloch

Riverside
Skipper, 1950.

The board of the Buffalo Seminary yearbook, *The Seminaria*, beneath the image of the school's former headmistress.
The Seminaria, 1950.

A home economics class at newly integrated East High, 1954.
Eastonian.

Bishop Timon Seniors, enjoying their smoking privilege in the school cafeteria.
Talisman, 1962.

SUGGESTIONS FOR VIEWING AND LISTENING

Rebel Without a Cause (1955)
A dysfunctional family: Mom's too strong, Dad's too weak.

Magic Town (1947)
Jimmy Stewart as a public opinion pollster who discovers a small town that perfectly represents the entire United States. Postwar obsession with the predictable and typical.

The Man in the Gray Flannel Suit (1956)
Middle-aged male angst in the affluent society.

Hank Ballard & the Midnighters, "Work With Me Annie" (1954)
Suggestive r & b of the kind that seldom reached the white suburbs. The follow-up was "Annie Had a Baby."

Rover Boys, "From a School Ring to a Wedding Ring" (1956)
This sort of thinking produced the baby boom.

Buddy Knox, "Party Doll" (1957)
Reportedly banned by the Catholic Church for being too sexy. Hints of the sexual revolution of the 1960s.

CHAPTER 4

John F. Kennedy and the New Frontier

In the fall of 1960, Americans tuned their televisions to a new form of political entertainment: nationally televised presidential debates, debates that confirmed that advertising's technology of image manipulation was now a mature part of American politics. A majority of Americans participated and judged a contest between image and experience. Viewers watched the charismatic junior senator from Massachusetts, John F. Kennedy, pit his wits and good looks against the experience and record of Republican Vice President Richard Milhous Nixon.

Kennedy came to the debate with very little public baggage. Voters knew of only two certainties regarding the young candidate, both of them controversial: his religion—Roman Catholic—and his father, Joseph P. Kennedy, a self-made tycoon, former ambassador to Great Britain, and a focus of Hollywood gossip due to his association with the movie industry and actresses. Nixon's public image was less malleable, since he had been vice president during the eight years of the Eisenhower administration. Indeed, Nixon and his supporters counted on his reputation as a fierce anticommunist and a keen student of foreign policy to add to his credibility and to underline Kennedy's amateur status. In addition, knowledgeable observers knew Nixon to be an adroit user of the new television medium based on his televised "Checkers" speech in 1952, when Nixon had salvaged his place on the ticket by parading his family, and the family dog, Checkers, before television cameras.

Yet for all his experience, Nixon failed to understand how deeply the medium of television had already transformed the national landscape. In the 1940s, most Americans got their news and entertainment from the radio; by 1956, 73 percent of all American homes had a television, and many had more than one. It was becoming the medium of choice for a younger generation, and to many viewers the packaging was as important as the content. Those who listened to the debate on the radio—that is, those not affected by the televised image—believed that Nixon's thoughtfulness and intelligence had brought him victory. In contrast, the TV viewers told pollsters that Kennedy was young, witty, poised, and clearly the winner. The immediate appeal of Kennedy's good looks and wit on television seemed to make him as qualified for the presidency as did Nixon's twelve years of public experience.

The theme of Kennedy's campaign, reflected in the party platform, was the New Frontier. It was a pledge "to get the country moving again" through a new president and a new role for government, at home and abroad. In his inaugural address, Kennedy redefined the image of freedom in the world. Freedom, he explained, was to evolve from the Truman-Eisenhower struggle against Communism to include war against hunger, poverty, colonialism, and disease. Through its technology, expertise, and wealth, America would transform the world. This vision did not look to people for inspiration, but rather to an active centralized government supported by the people. Kennedy's rhetoric was glossy and inspirational, but he had no existing blueprint to transform words into deeds, nor did he create an administrative structure conducive to planning. Like the candidate who had debated only a few months before, the Kennedy program was more image than substance.

The Kennedy administration resurrected Truman's Fair Deal as its outline for domestic reform. The agenda received new impetus from Michael Harrington's *The Other America* (1962), which had "rediscovered" poverty amidst the affluence of postwar America. In response, the administration argued for a greater federal role to help poor Americans, and Congress acceded to Kennedy's wishes by passing a redevelopment act for regions in West Virginia and the Appalachians. The administration also introduced legislation for a federally funded health program, and it requested expanded aid to both elementary and secondary education, although neither of these efforts passed Congress while Kennedy was president. Another item was a request for a $5 billion appropriation for public housing, which became the basis for the Department of Housing and Urban Development (HUD) under Lyndon Johnson. The New Frontier program offered idealistic young Americans a chance to take an active part as anti-poverty workers in the National Service Corps, later to become VISTA (Volunteers in Service to America). And by 1962, the vitality of the civil rights movement had pushed the administration to commit itself to a legislative program for black Americans.

In the realm of foreign policy, the Kennedy administration sought to move away from Eisenhower's strong reliance on nuclear weapons, and to develop alternative tools, called "flexible response," which he and his advisers believed were better suited than nuclear retaliation to a postcolonial world characterized by wars of national liberation. Flexible response consisted of a broad range of military, economic, and social tactics. Kennedy expanded Fort Bragg's elite military special force, the Green Berets; created a new agency to coordinate foreign aid—the Agency for International Development (AID); and founded another volunteer youth organization, the Peace Corps, which sent young Americans to work in developing countries.

Kennedy's ability to deliver this comprehensive package of change was hampered by the geopolitical realities he inherited: a bipolar world, constructed on alliances defined by World War II, and defended by a series of regional military agreements, including NATO, SEATO, and the Baghdad Pact. Furthermore, Kennedy was young and somewhat insecure in his powers, yet he felt himself personally responsible for American foreign policy. At this stage of the cold war, and especially for a nation newly committed to sweeping programs of global change, every issue was a crisis, every decision a demonstration of manhood, and every compromise a failure. West Berlin, an enclave of American power in Soviet Eastern Europe, became for Kennedy "the great testing place of Western courage and will." A conflict over an island nation in the Caribbean brought the world to the brink of nuclear holocaust. And a war in Southeast Asia seemed critical to the national interest.

None of this was exactly predictable in 1960, but the presidential debates had offered a hint of the future: a serious and extensive exchange between the candidates on what ought to be done about Quemoy and Matsu, two tiny islands (that no one had ever heard of) off the coast of mainland China, apparently threatened by the Communists. In a world in which even the smallest parcel of land appeared central to the international balance of power, and every event promised to polish or tarnish the image of America and its young president, the nation was never far from the next crisis, the next moment of truth, the next day of judgment. In a curious way, though, Americans had already seen the future, and heard it "debated"—on their television sets.

INTERPRETIVE ESSAY

Fixation with Cuba: The Bay of Pigs

Thomas G. Paterson

The hard-earned equilibrium of cold war was temporarily threatened whenever the question of succession arose in either the U.S. or the USSR. Both sides had to pay close attention to any sign that indicated a possible escalation or relaxation of tensions between the two countries. In 1953, the death of Soviet leader Joseph Stalin and the uncertainty regarding his successor kept American policy makers anxious for several years. The Soviets were no less concerned about the transfer of the American presidency from Republican to Democratic hands in 1960, and they kept a wary eye on the situation to determine if Kennedy was to pursue Eisenhower's policy of brinkmanship, or soften his position to one resembling Truman's containment.

The new president's first public foreign policy crisis occurred just four months after his inauguration, when an invasion of Cuba, spearheaded by CIA-trained Cuban exiles, failed to ignite a rebellion against Castro and led to the capture of nearly half the force. The botched Bay of Pigs invasion and the president's acceptance of responsibility gave American voters their first impression of Kennedy's leadership and character. While Americans were willing to grant him the benefit of inexperience, policy makers throughout the world came to a variety of more negative conclusions, depending on how they answered these questions: Why had Kennedy decided to continue a policy (and a plan) initiated by Eisenhower? Did his decision to do so suggest a continuation of Eisenhower's policy on the cold war? Or was the Kennedy hard line applicable only to Cuba? Was Kennedy's decision to pursue the invasion the act of a weak, possibly uninformed, president? Or the mark of a man unable to confront his own CIA? Or, as historian Thomas Paterson suggests, was it the result of a personal fixation on Castro that kept Kennedy from caring about other issues?

The Bay of Pigs fiasco also affected Kennedy and his office. Although he took full responsibility for the failure of the invasion, and through that action gained considerable domestic support, it remained a blemish on his presidency, perhaps even a personal humiliation. What effect could this have had on later foreign policy decisions? What might be the link between the defeat at the Bay of Pigs and the Cuban missile crisis, the subject of the next selection?

"My God," muttered Richard Helms of the Central Intelligence Agency, "these Kennedys keep the pressure on about Castro." Another CIA officer heard it straight from the Kennedy brothers: "Get off your ass about Cuba." About a year after John F. Kennedy's inauguration, a member of Congress applauded "the way you are gradually strangling Castro and Communism in Cuba." In 1963 the President still sought to "dig Castro out of there." Defense Secretary Robert McNamara remembered that "we were hysterical about Castro at the time of the Bay of Pigs and thereafter." As someone said, Cuba was one of the four-letter words of the 1960s.

President Kennedy spent as much or more time on Cuba as on any other foreign policy problem. Cuba stood at the center of his Administration's admitted greatest failure, the Bay of Pigs, and its alleged greatest success, the missile crisis. A multitude of government agencies enlisted in the crusade against revolutionary Cuba: the Commerce Department administered trade restrictions; the State Department labored to rally the Organization of American States and North Atlantic Treaty Organization allies against Cuba; the Federal Bureau of Investigation spied on pro- and anti-Castro groups; the Immigration and Naturalization Service, Coast Guard, and Department of Health, Education, and Welfare handled the steady flow of exiles from the turbulent island; and the CIA launched covert operations designed to topple the Cuban government and to assassinate its leader Fidel Castro. Contrary to some Kennedy memoirists and scholars who have claimed that Kennedy was often trapped by a bureaucracy he could not control and distracted by other time-consuming issues, the President was knowledgeable, engaged, and influential on matters Cuban.

Why did President Kennedy and his chief advisers indulge such a fixation with Cuba and direct so many United States resources to an unrelenting campaign to monitor, harass, isolate, and ultimately destroy Havana's radical regime? One answer springs from a candid remark by Robert F. Kennedy. Looking back at the early 1960s, he wondered "if we did not pay a very great price for being more energetic than wise about a lot of things, especially Cuba." The Kennedys' famed eagerness for action became exaggerated in the case of Cuba. They always wanted to get moving on Cuba, and Castro dared them to try. Some Euopeans thought that "we kept slapping at Castro because he'd had the effrontery to thumb his nose at us," recalled one American diplomat. The popular, intelligent, but erratic Cuban leader, whose *barbudos* (bearded ones) came down from the Sierra Maestra Mountains in January 1959 to overthrow the United States ally Fulgencio Batista, hurled harsh words at Washington and defiantly challenged the Kennedy model of evolutionary, capitalist development so evident in the Alliance for Progress. As charismatic figures charting new frontiers, the President and *Jefe Máximo* often personalized the Cuban-American contest. Kennedy harbored a "deep feeling against Castro," and the Cuban thought the American "an intelligent and able leader of American imperialism," and, after the Bay of Pigs invasion, he branded him a new Hitler. To Kennedy's great annoyance, Castro could not be wheedled or beaten.

Kennedy's ardent war against *Fidelismo* may also have stemmed from his feeling that Castro had double-crossed him. As a senator, Kennedy had initially joined many Americans in welcoming the Cuban Revolution as a decided advancement over the "oppressive" Batista dictatorship. Linking Castro to the legacy of Bolívar, Kennedy urged a "patient attitude" toward the new government, which he did not see as Communist. Denying repeatedly that he was a Communist, Castro had in fact proclaimed his allegiance to democracy and private property. But in the process of legitimizing his revolution and resisting United States pressure, Castro turned more and more radical. Americans grew impatient with the regime's highly charged anti-Yankeeism, postponement of elections, jailing of critics, and nationalization of property. The Cuban police state system reminded many of Hitler's and Stalin's dreaded totalitarianism. The President rejected the idea that intense United States hostility to the Cuban Revolution may have contributed to Castro's tightening political grip and flirtation with the Soviet Union. Nor did Kennedy and other Americans wish to acknowledge the measurable benefits of the revolution—improvements in education, medical care, and housing, and the elimination of the island's infamous corruption that once had been the American Mafia's domain. Instead, Kennedy officials concluded that Cuba's was a "betrayed revolution."

Richard N. Goodwin, the young White House and State Department official with responsibilities for Latin America, provided another explanation for the Kennedy fixation with Cuba. He remarked that "the entire history of the Cold War, its positions and assumptions, converged upon the 'problem of Cuba.'" Indeed, the Cold War dominated international politics, and in the zero-sum accounting of the time, a loss for "us" meant a gain for "them." As Cuban-American relations steadily deteriorated, Cuban-Soviet relations gradually improved. Not only did Americans come to believe that a once-loyal ally had jilted them for the tawdry embrace of the Soviets; they also grew alarmed that Castro sneered at the Monroe Doctrine by inviting the Soviet military to the island. When Castro, in late 1961, declared himself a Marxist-Leninist, Americans who had long denounced him as a Communist then felt vindicated. American leaders began to speak of Cuban membership in the "Sino-Soviet bloc," thus providing Communists with a "spearhead" to penetrate the Western Hemisphere. From the moment of victory, Castro had called for Cuban-style revolutions throughout Latin America, and Havana had sent agents and arms to other nations to kindle radical fires. Castro's revolutionary mission happened to coincide with Nikita Khrushchev's alarming statement that the Soviet Union supported wars of national liberation worldwide. It mattered little to Americans that the two appeals appeared independently or that Havana and Moscow differed markedly over the best method for promoting revolutionary change—the Soviets insisted on utilizing Communist parties within political systems, whereas the Cubans espoused peoples' rebellions. Cuba came to represent the Cold War in the United States's backyard, and, as such, one senator explained, it became a "target for our national frustration and annoyance with Moscow and the whole Communist conspiracy."

In addition to the Kennedy style and the Cold War, American politics influenced the Administration's Cuba policy. In the 1960 presidential campaign, Kennedy had seized the Cuban issue to counter Richard Nixon's charge that the inexperienced Democratic candidate would abandon Quemoy and Matsu to Communism and prove no match for the hard-nosed Khrushchev. "In 1952 the Republicans ran on a program of rolling back the Iron Curtain in Eastern Europe," Kennedy jabbed. "Today the Iron Curtain is 90 miles off the coast of the United States." Privately he asked, "How could *we* have saved Cuba if we had [had] the power"? but he nonetheless valued the political payback from his attack. "What the hell," he informed his aides, "they never told us how they would have saved China [in 1949]." He did recommend a controversial method to reclaim Cuba for the American system. Apparently unaware that President Dwight D. Eisenhower had initiated a clandestine CIA program to train Cuban exiles for an invasion of the island, candidate Kennedy bluntly called for just such a project.

After exploiting the Cuban issue, Kennedy, upon becoming President, could not easily have retreated. Partisan politics kept his gaze fixed on the defiant leader in the Caribbean. Hardly a press conference went by without an insistent question about Cuba. Republicans and Democrats alike peppered the White House with demands for action against Castroism. The vocal, burgeoning Cuban exile community in Florida never let the issue rest. Businessmen protested that the Cuban government nationalized American-owned property worth a billion dollars, and they grew apprehensive that the practice would become attractive in the hemisphere. The outgoing Treasury Secretary told Kennedy that "large amounts of capital now planned for investment in Latin America" were being held back, because investors were "waiting to see whether the United States can cope" with Castro's Cuba. George Meany, the cantankerous head of the AFL-CIO, decried the communization of the Cuban labor federation. The Joint Chiefs of Staff advised the President to invade Cuba. Everyone seemed eager to know when Kennedy would knock Castro off his perch, and many expected the President to act before the next election.

Overarching all explanations for Kennedy's obsession with Cuba is a major phenomenon of twentieth-century world history: the steady erosion of the authority of imperial powers, which had built systems of dependent, client, and colonial governments. The strong currents of decolonization, anti-imperialism, revolutionary nationalism, and social revolution, sometimes in combination, undermined the instruments the imperial nations had used to maintain control and order. In the 1950s France was driven from Indochina, and Great Britain's position in the Middle East receded dramatically after the Suez crisis, to cite two prominent examples.

The Cuban Revolution exemplified this process of breaking up and breaking away. American leaders reacted so hostilely to this revolution not simply because Castro and his 26th of July Movement taunted them or because domestic politics and the Cold War swayed them, but because Cuba, as symbol and reality, challenged United States hegemony in Latin America. The specter of "another Cuba" haunted President Kennedy, not just because it would hurt him politically, but because "the game would be up through a good deal of Latin America." Americans refused to accept a revolution that not only targeted Batista and their island assets but also the Monroe Doctrine and the United States's claim to political, economic, and military leadership in the hemisphere. "The revolution became anti-imperialism and freedom, the overthrow of the monoculture-militarist-dictatorship-dependence structure," remembered Carlos Franqui, a *Fidelista* who later went into exile. Given this fundamental conflict, a breakdown in Cuban-American relations was inevitable: Cuba sought independence and radical social change which would necessarily come at the expense of the United States, and the latter, not unexpectedly, defended its interests against revolutionary nationalism. As Castro put it, "the United States *had* to fight his revolution." Khrushchev, in pondering the American campaign against Cuba, once asked: "Why should an elephant be afraid of a mouse?" The Soviet leader, who certainly knew his own nation's imperial record in suppressing its neighbors when they became too independent-minded, surely knew that the answer to his question could be found in the American fear that the Cuban Revolution would become contagious and further diminish United States hegemony in the Western Hemisphere.

After the United States helped expel Spain from Cuba in 1898 and imposed the Platt Amendment on the island in 1903, Americans gained influence through military interventions, occupations, threats, economic penetration, and political manipulation. By 1959 Americans dominated Cuba's oil, telephone, mining, and electric industries and produced more than a third of its sugar. That year, too, the United States bought 74 percent of Cuba's exports and supplied 65 percent of the island's imports. Because the United States had such tremendous economic favors to dispense (especially a quota system that guaranteed Cuba sugar sales in the American market), Washington wielded political influence in Havana. The United States also stationed a military mission in Cuba and sent arms to Batista's forces. The CIA infiltrated political groups and helped Batista organize an anti-Communist police unit.

After having underestimated Castro's 26th of July Movement and the depth of the nation's unrest, the Eisenhower Administration tried to manipulate Cuba once again on the very eve of Castro's victory. With the President's blessing and CIA instructions, William D. Pawley, owner of Cuban lands and former Ambassador to Brazil, traveled to Havana to press Batista to resign in favor of a military junta in order to prevent the 26th of July Movement's imminent triumph. The Cuban President balked at this exercise of "Plattism," and Pawley's mission aborted. Even after this setback, the United States's continued sense of its strength in Cuba appeared in a CIA report that concluded that "no sane man undertaking to govern and reform Cuba would have chosen to pick a fight with the US." Because Castro did not honor traditional United States power in his nation, he must have possessed a "psychotic personality." Americans, unable or unwilling to acknowledge that the Cuban Revolution tapped deep nationalistic feelings and that their own interventionism and island interests made the United States a primary target, preferred to depict Fidel Castro as a crazed *guerrillero* whose temporarily frenzied people would toss him out when their rationality returned.

The Eisenhower Administration bequeathed to its successor an unproductive tit-for-tat process of confrontation with Cuba and a legacy of failure. In 1959–1960, with Ambassador Philip Bonsal thinking that Castro suffered "mental unbalance at times" and Eisenhower concluding that the Cuban leader "begins to look like a madman," Havana and Washington traded punch for punch. In November 1959 the President decided to encourage anti-Castro groups within Cuba to "check" or "replace" the revolutionary regime, and thus end an anti-Americanism that was "having serious adverse effects on the United States position in Latin America and corresponding advantages for international Communism." In March of the next year Eisenhower ordered the CIA to train Cuban exiles for an invasion of their homeland—this shortly after Cuba signed a trade treaty with the Soviet Union. The CIA, as well, hatched assassination plots against Castro and staged hit-

and-run attacks along the Cuban coast. As Cuba undertook land reform that struck at American interests and nationalized American-owned industries, the United States suspended Cuba's sugar quota and forbade American exports to the island, drastically cutting a once-flourishing commerce. On January 3, 1961, fearing an invasion and certain that the American embassy was a "nest of spies" aligned with counter-revolutionaries who were burning cane fields and sabotaging buildings, Castro heatedly demanded that the embassy staff be reduced to the small size of the Cuban delegation in Washington. The United States promptly broke diplomatic relations with Cuba.

Eisenhower failed to topple Castro, but American pressure accelerated the radicalization of the revolution and helped open the door to the Soviets. Moscow bought sugar, supplied technicians, armed the militia, and offered generous trade terms. Although the revolution's radicalization was probably inevitable, it was not inexorable that Cuba would end up in the Soviet camp. Hostile United States policies ensured that outcome. Revolutionary Cuba needed outside assistance to survive. "Russia came to Castro's rescue," Bonsal has concluded, "only after the United States had taken steps designed to overthrow him."

Kennedy's foreign policy troubles have sometimes been explained as inheritances from Eisenhower that shackled the new President with problems not of his own making. To be sure, Kennedy inherited the Cuban problem from Eisenhower. But he did not simply continue his predecessor's anti-Castro policies. Kennedy greatly exaggerated the Cuban threat, attributing to Castro a capability to export revolution that the Cuban leader never had and lavishing on him an attention he did not deserve. Castro was "an affront to our pride" and a "mischief maker," Walter Lippmann wisely wrote, but he was not a "mortal threat" to the United States. And because of his obsession with Cuba, Kennedy significantly increased the pressures against the upstart island. He thus helped generate major crises, including the October 1962 missile crisis. Kennedy inherited the Cuban problem—and he made it worse.

The new President actually made his first important policy choice on Cuba before he entered the White House. On the day Cuban-American relations were severed, Secretary of State Christian Herter telephoned Secretary-designate Dean Rusk and asked for Kennedy's reaction. Rusk talked with Kennedy and reported that the President-elect "would not associate himself with the Administration stand, i.e., he would not take a position for or against it at the present time. . . ." By saying nothing, Kennedy accepted a decision that reduced his own options for dealing with Cuba. The United States lost an embassy which had served as a first-hand listening post; now Washington would have to rely upon a fast diminishing number of CIA informants and deep-cover agents or upon often exaggerated information from exiles. Most important, with economic coercion having failed to bring down Castro and diplomacy now impeded, the rupture in relations elevated covert action—especially an invasion by Cuban exiles—as one of the few means left to resolve the contest with Cuba.

The questions of whether and under what conditions to approve an exile expedition dominated the President's discussion of Cuba in his first few months in office. Although Kennedy always reserved the authority to cancel the operation right up to the moment of departure, his choices, made after much deliberation, pointed in one direction: Go. National security adviser McGeorge Bundy later said that the President "really was looking for ways to make it work . . . and allowed himself to be persuaded it would work and the risks were acceptable." Not simply a prisoner of events or of the Eisenhower legacy, Kennedy associated so closely with the covert operation that it became identified as *his*. He listened to but rejected the counsel of doubting advisers, and he never revealed moral or legal qualms about violently overthrowing a sovereign government. He never requested a contingency plan to disband the exile brigade. In questioning aides, the President worried most about which methods would deliver success and whether the guiding hand of the United States could be concealed. Kennedy sought deniability of an American role, but never the demise of the project.

On March 11, Kennedy's chief advisers gathered in a critical National Security Council (NSC) meeting. CIA Director Allen Dulles and Deputy Director for Plans Richard Bissell explained plans for an invasion at the town of Trinidad, on Cuba's southern coast near the Escambray Mountains, where CIA-backed rebels were already operating. The President criticized the plan as too much like a spectacular World War II amphibious landing. He asked for something quieter, and he instructed planners that no American forces were to be used. Dulles advised that the mission had to go forward, because "we have a disposal problem." Great embarrassment would beset Washington if the exile brigade, training in Guatemala, were to disband and its members return to the United States to bellow their anger. Kennedy requested "new proposals"; he ordered the CIA to force bickering exile groups to unite behind one leader; he directed Arthur M. Schlesinger, Jr., the Harvard historian-turned-White House assistant, to draft a White Paper to justify an invasion; and he asked the State Department to gain OAS backing for strong anti-Castro measures.

Officials moved fast. The CIA devised a plan for dawn landings in the area of Bahía de Cochinos (Bay of Pigs). The existence of an air strip at the town of Playa Girón, the surrounding Zapata swamps with few access roads, and the region's sparse population made this an appealing entry site. In a Miami motel, a CIA operative bluntly forced exiles to form the Cuban Revolutionary Council under José Miró Cardona, a former foe of Batista and a onetime member of Castro's government. Schlesinger quickly produced a White Paper. Issued on April 3, this propagandistic justification for anti-Castroism condemned the Cuban radical for betraying his revolutionary promises, delivering his island to the "Sino-Soviet bloc," and attempting to subvert Latin American governments. After several high-level meetings and Dulles's assurance that the prospects for Operation Zapata were even greater than they had been for the successful CIA plot in 1954 against Guatemala, Kennedy set April 17 as D-Day.

The Bay of Pigs plan began to unravel from the start. As the brigade's old, slow freighters, obtained from the United Fruit Company, plowed their way to Cuba, B-26 airplanes took to the skies from Nicaragua. On April 15, D-Day minus 2, the brigade pilots destroyed several parked planes of Castro's meager air force. That same day, as part of a pre-invasion ploy, a lone, artificially damaged B-26 flew directly to Miami, where its pilot claimed that he had defected from the Cuban military and had just bombed his country's airfields. But the cover story soon cracked. Snooping journalists noticed that the nose cone of the B-26 was metal; Cuban planes had plastic noses. They observed too that the aircraft's guns had not been fired. The American hand was being exposed. The President, still insistent upon hiding American complicity, decided to cancel a second D-Day air strike against the remnants of the Cuban air force. CIA officials protested, because they believed the invasion force could not succeed unless Castro's few planes were knocked out. After conferring with Secretary Rusk, Kennedy stuck with his decision.

Shortly after midnight on April 17, more than 1400 commandos motored in small boats to the beaches at Bahía de Cochinos. The invaders immediately tangled with Castro's militia. Some commandos never made it, because their boats broke apart on razor-sharp coral reefs. In the air, Castro's marauding airplanes shot down two brigade B-26s and, in the water, sank ships carrying essential communications equipment and ammunition. Fighting ferociously, the brigade nonetheless failed to establish a beachhead. Would Washington try to salvage the mission? Kennedy turned down CIA appeals to dispatch planes from the nearby USS *Essex,* but he did permit some jets to provide air cover for a new B-26 attack from Nicaragua. Manned this time by American CIA pilots, the B-26s arrived an hour after the jets had come and gone. Cuban aircraft downed the B-26s, killing four Americans. With Castro's boasting that the *mercenarios* had been foiled, the final toll was grim: 114 of the exile brigade dead and 1,189 captured. A pall settled over the White House.

"How could I have been so stupid, to let them go ahead?" Kennedy asked an assistant. Stupid or not, Kennedy knew the answers to his own question. First, he dearly sought to oust Castro and score a victory in the Cold War. Second, his personality and style encouraged action. Always driven to win, Kennedy believed "that his disapproval of the plan would be a show of weakness inconsistent with his general stance." One foreign policy observer explained "how the President got such bad advice from such good advisers":

> The decision on which they were asked to advise was presented as a choice between action and inaction. . . . None of the President's advisers wants it said of him by his colleagues . . . that he . . . loses his nerve when the going gets hot. The Harvard intellectuals are especially vulnerable, the more so from being new on the scene. They are conscious of the fact that the tough-minded military suspect them of being soft-headed. They have to show that they are he-men too, that they can act as well as lecture.

Third, fear of nasty political repercussions influenced the President. Told to disband, brigade members might have refused to give up their arms or even have mutineed. In any case, Republicans would have scorned a weak-kneed Administration. Kennedy approved the operation, finally, because he felt a sense of urgency. CIA analysts advised that time was on Castro's side. Delay would permit the Soviets to strengthen the Cuban military, perhaps with MIG fighters, and the rainy season was about to begin, making military maneuver difficult. The Guatemalan president, facing awkward questions about Cuban trainees in his country, was also beseeching Washington to move the exiles out by late April.

Failures in intelligence, operations, decision-making, and judgment doomed the Bay of Pigs undertaking. Arrogant CIA architects knew too little and assumed too much about Cuba, particularly about the landing site. Although Bissell and Dulles have staunchly denied that they ever told the President that the invasion would ignite an island-wide rebellion against the Castro regime and thus ensure the ascendency of Miró's provisional government, Kennedy decision-makers nonetheless believed that the invasion would stimulate a popular revolt against an unpopular government. But the CIA did not coordinate the invasion with the anti-Castro underground in Cuba, because the agency feared leaks and the likely infiltration of opposition groups by Castro's security forces. No rebellion erupted. Kennedy and his advisers also assumed that, should the brigade prove incapable of taking territory, it could melt into the mountains and become a guerrilla army. But, because the invasion site had been shifted, the mountains now lay some 80 miles away, with impassable swamps between. Neither Kennedy nor CIA advisers had explored this problem. The guerrilla option, which, like the belief in a rebellion, probably led Kennedy to suppress doubts about the operation, was actually impossible.

CIA planners failed in other ways. If they overestimated Cuban discontent with Castro, they underestimated the effectiveness of his military. They anticipated that he would crack; in fact, he expertly led his forces at the Bay of Pigs, where he had vacationed. CIA analysts had failed to detect the coral reefs. CIA-issued equipment malfunctioned; crucial communications gear was concentrated in one ship that sunk; paratroopers did not drop far enough inland to cut off causeways. Another operational failure remained a tightly held secret. The CIA had been attempting since 1960 to kill Fidel Castro, even employing Mafia thugs for the task. The CIA activated assassination plots in March and April. It seems likely that assassination was part of the general Bay of Pigs plan. Bissell has admitted that he was hopeful "that Castro would be dead before the landing."

The most controversial operational question remains the cancelled second D-Day air strike. Post-crisis critics have complained that the President lost his nerve and made a decision that condemned the expedition to disaster. Castro and Bissell have agreed that Cuban air supremacy was important to Cuba's triumph. But was it decisive? A pre-emptive strike on D-Day against the Cuban air force would not have delivered victory to the invaders. After the first air attack, Castro had dispersed his planes; the brigade's B-26s would have encountered considerable difficulty in locating and destroying them. And, even if a D-Day assault had disabled all of Castro's planes, then what? *La brigada*'s 1400 men would have had to face Castro's army of 25,000 and the nation's 200,000 militia. The commandos most likely would not have survived the overwhelming power of the Cuban military.

A flawed decision-making system also contributed to failure. Bissell and Dulles were too emotionally committed to the project to see the shortcomings in their handiwork. CIA planners were less than candid with the President, for fear that he would terminate the project. Operation Zapata was even kept a secret from many other CIA professionals responsible for intelligence analysis. Had they been asked to assess the chances for national rebellion, for example, they probably would have reported negatively, pointing out Castro's continued popular appeal.

CIA officials also contributed to the President's thinking that American participation could be hidden and plausibly denied. But how could Kennedy ever have thought that secrecy was possible? Wishful thinking provides the best answer. "Trying to mount an operation of this magnitude from the United States," a CIA official wrote later, "is about as covert as walking nude across Times Square without attracting attention." Nonetheless, until his decision to cancel the second strike, Kennedy clung to the fiction of deniability.

The Joint Chiefs of Staff and Secretary of State also failed as advisers. Although the generals and admirals had serious reservations, they always evaluated the operation favorably. Sworn to secrecy, they did not seek close staff analysis of the CIA plan. Not "cut in" until the later stages of planning, they hesitated to "pound the desk," because the operation was "not our show." Nor did Dean Rusk provide rigorous scrutiny or press his case against the invasion. A "good soldier" who went along with the apparent consensus, he seemed to believe that he should preside over debate rather than influence it. Rusk later regretted his restraint:

> As a colonel of infantry [in the Second World War], I knew that this brigade didn't have the chance of a "snowball in hell." But I wasn't a colonel of infantry; I was sitting there in a very special cubicle. I failed President Kennedy by not insisting that he ask a question that he did not ask. He should have turned to our Joint Chiefs of Staff and said to them: "Now gentlemen, I may want to do this with U.S. forces, so you tell me what you would need. . . ." By the time the Joint Chiefs had come in with their sustained and prolonged bombing, their several divisions, a massive fleet, and their big air force, it would have become obvious to the President that that little brigade didn't have a chance at all.

One wonders, of course, why Kennedy himself did not think to ask the question. Rusk also kept departmental intelligence and Cuban specialists in the dark.

Kennedy encountered a good deal of dissenting opinion and he rejected it. Schlesinger, for example, wrote several memoranda to the President, arguing that time was actually not on Castro's side and that the Cuban leader, at least for the moment, remained popular. The skeptics included Richard Goodwin, John Kenneth Galbraith, Charles E. Bohlen, Chester Bowles, and Adlai Stevenson. In making his decision, Kennedy also bypassed Congress, further ensuring that he received limited advice. Only Senator J. William Fulbright, Foreign Relations Committee chairman, was let into the inner circle, and at that, only once. Picking up rumors of a forthcoming invasion of Cuba, Fulbright sent the President a memorandum that strongly disapproved invasion—it was "of a piece with the hypocrisy and cynicism for which the United States is constantly denouncing the Soviet Union . . . ," he wrote. Kennedy thereupon invited the Arkansas senator to attend an April 4 meeting. Fulbright spoke forthrightly to the assembled top-level advisers, chiding them for exaggerating the Cuban threat. As he had told the President earlier, the Castro regime "is a thorn in the flesh; but it is not a dagger in the heart." No one in the room agreed with Fulbright.

"Mr. President, it could have been worse," remarked a Stevenson assistant. How? "It might have succeeded." Had all gone well with the chain reaction of beachhead, rebellion, and Castro's death or departure, the victory would only have "exchanged a Castro pesthouse for a post-Castro asylum." Tainted as an American stooge, the head of the new government would have struggled to win public favor. Well-armed Castroites, including Fidel's brother Raúl and Che Guevara, would probably have initiated a protracted guerrilla war against the American-created regime. The Soviets might have helped these rebel forces, and volunteers from around the world might have swelled the resistance—like the Spanish Civil War of the 1930s, Schlesinger had warned. The United States would have had to save its puppet government through military aid, advisers, and maybe even troops. To have sustained a successful Bay of Pigs invasion, then, the Kennedy Administration probably would have had to undertake a prolonged and expensive occupation of the island.

As it was, defeat did not chasten the Administration. While a secret presidential panel investigated the disaster, Kennedy and his advisers huddled. At the April 20 Cabinet meeting, Bowles found his colleagues "almost savage." Robert Kennedy became especially agitated, and "there was an almost frantic reaction for an action program which people would grab onto." With Republicans belittling the President—Eisenhower said the story ought to be titled "Profile in Timidity and Indecision" and Nixon allowed that Kennedy should have known that "when you commit maximum U.S. prestige you have to commit maximum U.S. power to back it up," Kennedy was not sympathetic to Bowles's call for patience and caution. The Under Secretary was "yellow-bellied," press secretary Pierre Salinger snorted, "and "we're going to get him." White House aide Harris Wofford shot back: "Why don't you get those who got us into this mess?" Kennedy pushed Bowles out of the State Department later in the year.

On April 20 the beleaguered President spoke out. "Let the record show," he boomed, "that our restraint is not inexhaustible." Indeed, the United States intended to defend the Monroe Doctrine and carry on a "relentless" struggle with Communism in "every corner of the globe." In familiar words, Kennedy declared that "the complacent, the self-indulgent, the soft societies are about to be swept away with the debris of history. Only the strong . . . can possibly survive." That day, too, Kennedy ordered American military advisers in Laos to put on their uniforms to show United States resolution in the face of defeat. "A new urgency" was injected into "Kennedy's concern for counterinsurgency . . . ," recalled General Maxwell Taylor, who headed the post-crisis inquiry. Although Kennedy privately claimed that the Cuban failure deterred him from military intervention in Laos, the record of the April 22 NSC meeting demonstrates that the President chose an activist policy of confrontation with the "Communist world." Such a posture was more in line with the advice a Bundy aide offered Robert Kennedy during the Bay of Pigs crisis. When the Attorney General growled that Moscow would now judge America weak, Walt W. Rostow commented that "we would have ample opportunity to prove we were not paper tigers in Berlin, Southeast Asia, and elsewhere." This thinking also resembled the recommendations of the Taylor Study Group, which on June 13 reported secretly to the President that "we are in a life and death struggle which we may be losing," so henceforth all of the nation's Cold War resources had to be mobilized.

SOURCES

Romancing the Missiles

Robert F. Kennedy

In October 1962, U.S. spy flights over Cuba discovered the presence of Russian missile sites. President Kennedy faced an immediate crisis: how to handle the existence of a Russian threat to American hegemony within the confines of the western hemisphere—a direct breach of the Monroe Doctrine. The decision-making process during the Cuban missile crisis remains a classic example of crisis management; historians and political scientists have focused on Kennedy's control over his bureaucracy and advisers and the procedure that helped determine his course of action. Kennedy's defenders have argued that the president was cool, rational, and adamant about staying away from escalation. Critics have contended that he was an irresponsible and dogmatic cold warrior who brought the world to the brink of war.

Attorney General Robert F. Kennedy, the president's brother, was privy to much of the discussion and debate within the administration and later published a memoir of the episode, Thirteen Days. *In the following excerpt from his memoir, Kennedy discusses two documents that reveal different aspects of the complex diplomacy of the event. The first document is a transcript of a televised session of the United Nations that took place at the beginning of the crisis. It features American Ambassador Adlai Stevenson, confronting Soviet Ambassador V. A. Zorin, who has denied the presence of missiles in Cuba. Why do you think the confrontation was important in diplomatic circles? Why did it occur in a public forum? What is the tone of Stevenson's accusations? How might charges made in this episode have influenced how Soviet policy was perceived in the arena of world opinion?*

The second document Robert Kennedy presents is a letter from Soviet Premier Nikita Khrushchev to President Kennedy, received on October 26, 1962, at the height of the "quarantine" (a U.S. naval blockade of further offensive military shipments into Cuba). The letter is a personal document, sent directly to the president of the United States by the leader of the Soviet Union. How does the tone differ from that of the Zorin-Stevenson exchange? How is Khrushchev appealing to Kennedy? What impression do you have of Khrushchev and of his policy after reading this letter?

STEVENSON/ZORIN CONFRONTATION

Adlai Stevenson, at a meeting of the United Nations Security Council, publicly confronted Ambassador V. A. Zorin of the Soviet Union. President Kennedy had made arrangements for photographs of the missile sites to be furnished to Stevenson. Many newspapers around the world, and particularly in Great Britain, were openly skeptical of the U.S. position. At the urgings of Pierre Salinger, the President's Press Secretary, and of Don Wilson, representing the USIA, the President, on October 23, had released the pictures for use at the UN and for publication. Stevenson used them most skillfully in his dramatic televised confrontation with the Russians:

STEVENSON: "Well, let me say something to you, Mr. Ambassador, we do have the evidence. We have it, and it is clear and incontrovertible. And let me say something else. Those weapons must be taken out of Cuba. . . . You, the Soviet Union, have sent these weapons to Cuba. You, the Soviet Union, have created this new danger—not the United States. . . .

"Finally, Mr. Zorin, I remind you that the other day you did not deny the existence of these weapons. But today, again, if I heard you correctly, you now say that they do not exist, or that we haven't proved they exist.

"All right, sir, let me ask you one simple question. Do you, Ambassador Zorin, deny that the U.S.S.R. has placed and is placing medium- and intermediate-range missiles and sites in Cuba? Yes or no? Don't wait for the translation, yes or no?"

ZORIN: "I am not in an American courtroom, sir, and therefore I do not wish to answer a question that is put to me in the fashion in which a prosecutor puts questions. In due course, sir, you will have your answer."

STEVENSON: "You are in the courtroom of world opinion right now, and you can answer yes or no. You have denied that they exist, and I want to know whether I have understood you correctly."

ZORIN: "Continue with your statement. You will have your answer in due course."

STEVENSON: "I am prepared to wait for my answer until hell freezes over, if that's your decision. And I am also prepared to present the evidence in this room."

And with that Stevenson revealed the photographs of the Russian missiles and sites, with devastating effect.

KHRUSHCHEV LETTER TO KENNEDY

We must not succumb to "petty passions" or to "transient things," he wrote, but should realize that "if indeed war should break out, then it would not be in our power to stop it, for such is the logic of war. I have participated in two wars and know that war ends when it has rolled through cities and villages, everywhere sowing death and destruction." The United States, he went on to say, should not be concerned about the missiles in Cuba; they would never be used to attack the

United States and were there for defensive purposes only. "You can be calm in this regard, that we are of sound mind and understand perfectly well that if we attack you, you will respond the same way. But you too will receive the same that you hurl against us. And I think that you also understand this. . . . This indicates that we are normal people, that we correctly understand and correctly evaluate the situation. Consequently, how can we permit the incorrect actions which you ascribe to us? Only lunatics or suicides, who themselves want to perish and to destroy the whole world before they die, could do this."

But he went on: "We want something quite different . . . not to destroy your country . . . but despite our ideological differences, to compete peacefully, not by military means."

There was no purpose, he said, for us to interfere with any of his ships now bound for Cuba, for they contained no weapons. He then explained why they carried no missiles: all the shipments of weapons were already within Cuba. This was the first time he had acknowledged the presence of missiles in Cuba. He made reference to the landing at the Bay of Pigs and the fact that President Kennedy had told him in Vienna that this was a mistake. He valued such frankness, wrote Khrushchev, and he, too, had similar courage, for he had acknowledged "those mistakes which had been committed during the history of our state and I not only acknowledge but sharply condemned them." (President Kennedy had told him in Vienna that he was quick to acknowledge and condemn the mistakes of Stalin and others, but he never acknowledged any mistakes of his own.)

The reason he had sent these weapons to Cuba was because the U.S. was interested in overthrowing the Cuban government, as the U.S. had actively attempted to overthrow the Communist government in the Soviet Union after their revolution. Khrushchev and the Soviet people wished to help Cuba protect herself.

But then he went on: "If assurances were given that the President of the United States would not participate in any attack on Cuba and the blockade lifted, then the question of the removal or the destruction of the missile sites in Cuba would then be an entirely different question. Armaments bring only disasters. When one accumulates them, this damages the economy, and if one puts them to use, then they destroy people on both sides. Consequently, only a madman can believe that armaments are the principal means in the life of society. No, they are an enforced loss of human energy, and what is more are for the destruction of man himself. If people do not show wisdom, then in the final analysis they will come to a clash, like blind moles, and then reciprocal extermination will begin."

This is my proposal, he said. No more weapons to Cuba and those within Cuba withdrawn or destroyed, and you reciprocate by withdrawing your blockade and also agree not to invade Cuba. Don't interfere, he said, in a piratical way with Russian ships. "If you have not lost your self-control and sensibly conceive what this might lead to, then, Mr. President, we and you ought not to pull on the ends of the rope in which you have tied the knot of war, because the more the two of us pull, the tighter the knot will be tied. And a moment may come when that knot will be tied so tight that even he who tied it will not have the strength to untie it, and then it will be necessary to cut that knot, and what that would mean is not for me to explain to you, because you yourself understand perfectly of what terrible forces our countries dispose. Consequently, if there is no intention to tighten that knot, and thereby to doom the world to the catastrophe of thermonuclear war, then let us not only relax the forces pulling on the ends of the rope, let us take measures to untie that knot. We are ready for this."

A Rumor of War

Philip Caputo

Both critics and admirers credit John F. Kennedy with inspirational rhetoric. His inauguration address, speeches, and press conferences were all known for style, wit, and charm. Young people, however, were perhaps less able—or less willing—than others to discern the difference between style and substance, between rhetoric and reality; many took his words at face value. When Kennedy called on Americans in his inaugural address to act upon their ideals, to live their dreams, and to serve the nation, many young people did just that.

In the following selection, Philip Caputo explains why, as a young man in the Kennedy era, he decided to join the Marines. How would you describe his motives? What role did affluence play? What was the role of youth in his decision? Is it idealistic or cynical for older men to inspire younger men to go to war?

I joined the Marines in 1960, partly because I got swept up in the patriotic tide of the Kennedy era but mostly because I was sick of the safe, suburban existence I had known most of my life.

I was raised in Westchester, Illinois, one of the towns that rose from the prairies around Chicago as a result of post-war affluence, VA mortgage loans, and the migratory urge and housing shortage that sent millions of people out of the cities in the years following World War II. It had everything a suburb is supposed to have: sleek, new schools smelling of fresh plaster and floor wax; supermarkets full of Wonder Bread and Bird's Eye frozen peas; rows of centrally heated split-levels that lined dirtless streets on which nothing ever happened.

It was pleasant enough at first, but by the time I entered my late teens I could not stand the place, the dullness of it, the summer barbecues eaten to the lulling drone of power mowers. During the years I grew up there, Westchester stood on or near the edge of the built-up area. Beyond stretched the Illinois farm and pasture lands, where I used to hunt on weekends. I remember the fields as they were in the late fall: the corn stubble brown against the snow, dead husks rasping dryly in the wind; abandoned farm houses waiting for the bulldozers that would tear them down to clear space for a new subdivision; and off on the horizon, a few stripped sycamores silhouetted against a bleak November sky. I can still see myself roaming around out there, scaring rabbits from the brambles, the tract houses a few miles behind me, the vast, vacant prairies in front, a restless boy caught between suburban boredom and rural desolation.

The only thing I really liked about my boyhood surroundings were the Cook and DuPage County forest preserves, a belt of virgin woodland through which flowed a muddy stream called Salt Creek. It was not too polluted then, and its sluggish waters yielded bullhead, catfish, carp, and a rare bass. There was small game in the woods, sometimes a deer or two, but most of all a hint of the wild past, when moccasined feet trod the forest paths and fur trappers cruised the rivers in bark canoes. Once in a while, I found flint arrowheads in the muddy creek bank. Looking at them, I would dream of that savage, heroic time and wish I had lived then, before America became a land of salesmen and shopping centers.

That is what I wanted, to find in a commonplace world a chance to live heroically. Having known nothing but security, comfort, and peace, I hungered for danger, challenges, and violence.

I had no clear idea of how to fulfill this peculiar ambition until the day a Marine recruiting team set up a stand in the student union at Loyola University. They were on a talent hunt for officer material and displayed a poster of a trim lieutenant who had one of those athletic, slightly cruel-looking faces considered handsome in the military. He looked like a cross between an All-American halfback and a Nazi tank commander. Clear and resolute, his blue eyes seemed to stare at me in challenge. JOIN THE MARINES, read the slogan above his white cap. BE A LEADER OF MEN.

I rummaged through the propaganda material, picking out one pamphlet whose cover listed every battle the Marines had fought, from Trenton to Inchon. Reading down that list, I had one of those rare flashes of insight: the heroic experience I sought was war; war, the ultimate adventure; war, the ordinary man's most convenient means of escaping from the ordinary. The country was at peace then, but the early sixties were years of almost constant tension and crisis; if a conflict did break out, the Marines would be certain to fight in it and I could be there with them. Actually *there.* Not watching it on a movie or TV screen, not reading about it in a book, but *there,* living out a fantasy. Already I saw myself charging up some distant beachhead, like John Wayne in *Sands of Iwo Jima,* and then coming home a suntanned warrior with medals on my chest. The recruiters started giving me the usual sales pitch, but I hardly needed to be persuaded. I decided to enlist.

I had another motive for volunteering, one that has pushed young men into armies ever since armies were invented: I needed to prove something—my courage, my toughness, my manhood, call it whatever you like. I had spent my freshman year at Purdue, freed from the confinements of suburban home and family. But a slump in the economy prevented me from finding a job that summer. Unable to afford the expense of living on campus (and almost flunking out anyway, having spent half my first year drinking and the other half in fraternity antics), I had to transfer to Loyola, a commuter college in Chicago. As a result, at the age of nineteen I found myself again living with my parents.

It was a depressing situation. In my adolescent mind, I felt that my parents regarded me as an irresponsible boy who still needed their guidance. I wanted to prove them wrong. I had to get away. It was not just a question of physical separation, although that was important; it was more a matter of doing something that would demonstrate to them, and to myself as well, that I was a man after all, like the steely-eyed figure in the recruiting poster. THE MARINE CORPS BUILDS MEN was another slogan current at the time, and on November 28 I became one of its construction projects.

I joined the Platoon Leaders' Class, the Marines' version of ROTC. I was to attend six weeks of basic training the following summer and then an advanced course during the summer before I graduated from college. Completion of Officer Candidate School and a bachelor's degree would entitle me to a commission, after which I would be required to serve three years on active duty.

I was not really ambitious to become an officer. I would have dropped out of school and gone in immediately as an enlisted man had it not been for my parents' unflinching determination to have a college graduate for a son. As it was, they were unhappy. Their vision of my future did not include uniforms and drums, but consisted of my finding a respectable job after school, marrying a respectable girl, and then settling down in a respectable suburb.

For my part, I was elated the moment I signed up and swore to defend the United States "against all enemies foreign and domestic." I had done something important on my own; that it was something which opposed my parents' wishes made it all the more savory. And I was excited by the idea and I would be sailing off to dangerous and exotic places after college instead of riding the 7:45 to some office. It is odd when I look back on it. Most of my friends at school thought of joining the army as the most conformist thing anyone could do, and of the service itself as a form of slavery. But for me, enlisting was an act of rebellion, and the Marine Corps symbolized an opportunity for personal freedom and independence.

Officer Candidate School was at Quantico, a vast reservation in the piny Virginia woods near Fredericksburg, where the Army of the Potomac had been futilely slaughtered a century before. There, in the summer of 1961, along with several hundred other aspiring lieutenants, I was introduced to military life and began training for war. We ranged in age from nineteen to twenty-one, and those of us who survived OCS would lead the first American troops sent to Vietnam four years later. Of course, we did not know that at the time: we hardly knew where Vietnam was.

The first six weeks, roughly the equivalent of enlisted boot camp, were spent at Camp Upshur, a cluster of quonset huts and tin-walled buildings set deep in the woods. The monastic isolation was appropriate because the Marine Corps, as we quickly learned, was more than a branch of the armed services. It was a society unto itself, demanding total commitment to its doctrines and values, rather like one of those quasi-religious military orders of ancient times, the Teutonic Knights or the Theban Band. We were novitiates, and the rigorous training, administered by high priests called drill instructors, was to be our ordeal of initiation.

Visions of the Future: The New York World's Fair, 1964

Philip Caputo writes of the patriotic tide of the Kennedy era as a factor that motivated him to join the Marines. But there is a sense in which Kennedy's words and Caputo's decision were both part of self-confident, even ebullient American culture. One reflection of that culture was the 1964 New York World's Fair. General Motors' Futurama exhibit presented a world in which humankind was always made welcome. The most desolate places of the world were rendered accessible and productive by nuclear power, chemistry, and transportation technology, without losing their picturesque qualities. From the Arctic to the Sahara, no place could evade the science, the technology, and the domesticity of humanity—and especially, the United States. No one spoke of costs, or trade-offs, or Faustian bargains. All was possible, all was still to come.

General Motors Futurama II exhibit at 1964–1965 New York World's Fair. The future features vacation cottages in the Rockies with electronic highways running by the front door.
National Archives.

Aerial view of 1964 New York World's Fair. The unisphere in the foreground was the global symbol of the fair.
National Archives.

SUGGESTIONS FOR VIEWING AND LISTENING

The Music Man (1961)
The transformative powers of the American dream—and a good woman.

Psycho (1960)
Horror comes to the heartland. Think of the Bates Motel as halfway between Transylvania and the American suburb.

Lawrence of Arabia (1962, re-released in 1989)
A white man among natives. A fascination with empire, with Vietnam on the horizon.

Johnny Horton, "The Battle of New Orleans" (1959)
Echoes of John Kennedy's "New Frontier."

Ray Peterson, "Tell Laura I Love Her" (1960)
One of many "coffin" songs popular in this period.

Bobby Bare, "Detroit City" (1963)
The pain of the south-to-north migration that was transforming popular music and the nation.

New Christy Minstrels, "This Land Is Your Land" (1962)
Americans feeling good—perhaps too good—about themselves.

CHAPTER 5

The 1960s
Protest and War

In the 1989 film *Field of Dreams,* Ray Kinsella (Kevin Costner) turns his Iowa cornfield into a baseball park, a place where dreams come true. Ray's dream is a dream of reconciliation; he wants to "have a catch" with his father, now deceased. At the heart of Ray's dream is a nightmare—the nightmare of the 1960s—a historical moment of discord and disruption that shattered the emotional bond between father and son. To rediscover and reaffirm that bond, Ray must find his way back in time to a moment before the "sixties"—before Vietnam, before the protests, before drugs, before the riots in the cities, before college campuses became hotbeds of radicalism, before the assassinations. Before the American consensus came apart.

On one level, Ray's dream is simply a fantasy. But on another level, it expresses the feelings of millions of Americans who continue to believe that the 1960s was a time of inexcusable excess and irresponsibility, a moment of social catastrophe that permanently damaged the nation and its institutions. Some critics of the era emphasize an emerging crisis of authority, a growing lack of trust and confidence in parents, politicians, military leaders, teachers, ministers, and others whose authority was once (presumably) sacrosanct. Others argue that the upheavals of the 1960s came at a most inopportune moment, when a wealthy nation was on the verge of integrating the races, winning the war in Vietnam, and providing everyone with a decent standard of living. Still others insist that the protesters and dissidents of the 1960s were so many spoiled brats, the affluent young that had been the major beneficiaries of the Eisenhower consensus and now, ironically, sought its destruction.

Scholars, too, have offered critical perspectives. Historian George Lipsitz contends that the middle-class counterculture represented by Frank Zappa's 1967 album, *Freak Out,* spent too much time avoiding authority and "dropping out," and not enough thinking about how the lives of those less fortunate might be improved. Kenneth Cmiel describes the emergence of a problematic culture of "incivility" in which decorum and etiquette were replaced by a cult of obscenity that favored shouts of "fuck the draft." In a study of one New York State high school, sociologist Gerald Grant argues that typical 1960s' efforts at school integration and

107

student-centered learning were the ruination of a place he called "Hamilton High."
Numerous scholars on the right blame the social programs of Lyndon Johnson's
Great Society for corrupting American values and suffocating the nation under
needless layers of bureaucracy. And historian Allen J. Matusow laments what he
describes as "the unraveling of America."

One's interpretation of events in the 1960s depends a great deal on how one
evaluates the liberal consensus nurtured by Eisenhower and John Kennedy. On the
one hand, if one evaluates that consensus negatively—if, for example, one judges
it to be less a genuine consensus than a racist and sexist arrangement for the benefit of white males—then one would welcome some degree of unraveling. On the
other hand, if one believes that the rapidly growing American economy of the
early 1960s was on the verge of producing a pie large enough for everyone—an
idea called "growth liberalism"—then the efforts of the Great Society to distribute
income might appear misguided. If one holds that the racial reformism of Kennedy
and Johnson was making significant progress toward a just and integrated society,
then Stokely Carmichael's use of the slogan "black power" in 1966 would seem a
tragic error of bad timing. And if one accepts the dictum of the liberal consensus
that the only real enemy of American social and economic progress was international Communism, then one might be inclined to look more positively on the
Vietnam war, and to denounce the protesters and demonstrators that made the conflict so difficult to wage.

In contrast, Ray Kinsella's goal—to have a "catch" with Dad—seems remarkably straightforward. That is, until one remembers that their falling out had a
cause—Ray's moral objection to his father's admiration for "Shoeless" Joe Jackson, a member of the notorious Black Sox baseball team that in 1919 conspired to
throw the World Series. By insisting on that stance, Ray had chosen politics over
family, personal morality over paternal authority. He had struck a blow for truth,
and in doing so shattered some version of the liberal consensus, contained at that
moment in the understanding between father and son. As the film ends, Ray and
his father are having their catch, and all seems well. But the issue of Shoeless
Joe—a symbol, here, for the moral conflicts that infused the decade of the 1960s
and tore the nation apart—remains unresolved.

INTERPRETIVE ESSAY

Campus Wars

Kenneth J. Heineman

More than twenty years after they ended, the campus protests of the 1960s remain at the center of how Americans understand their recent history. For some, these protests were the last best hope of turning the country off the path of imperialism and militarism and reclaiming the American nation for democratic and moral purposes. For others, the same protests were just so much chaos and disorder, but with tragic consequences: the beginning of the decline of the United States as a world economic and political power, and a pervasive and irreparable fracturing of the sense of community.

Kenneth J. Heineman's analysis of these "campus wars" offers us a way to enter this larger debate. Who, he asks, were the campus protesters? Who was likely to belong to SDS (Students for a Democratic Society), and who was not? Were the campus activists, as the Nixon administration liked to claim, just pampered rich kids used to having their own way in the affluent society of the 1950s or, just as bad, trying to end the war so that they would not have to serve in it? Having determined who *they were, what conclusions can one draw about* why *they chose to become campus activists?*

As late as 1940, just 16 percent of American college-aged youth could afford to attend an institution of higher education and prestigious private and public universities restricted the admission of Catholics and Jews. Liberals, from Franklin Roosevelt to Congressman Lyndon Johnson, believed that higher education, if made financially accessible and less culturally exclusive, would enable less-privileged citizens, particularly the New Deal's core constituency of industrial workers and ethnic Catholics and Jews, to achieve upward social mobility. Therefore, the federal government began in the 1930s to provide students with education grants and exerted some moral, and later legal, pressure on universities to abolish religious quotas.

Once the United States found itself engaged in the cold war, liberals came up with additional reasons to educate larger numbers of youth. As Clark Kerr and Harlan Hatcher argued in the 1950s and early 1960s, the demands placed upon the nation by the emerging American-centered global economy, as well as by an escalating nuclear arms race, required the creation of a technologically proficient, college-educated, society. Additionally, cold war liberal intellectuals such as Arthur Schlesinger, Jr., and Daniel Bell came to view higher education as a means

Kenneth J. Heineman, *Campus Wars: The Peace Movement at American State Universities in the Vietnam Era,* New York University Press, New York, 1993, pp. 76–95, 124–125. Reprinted with the permission of New York University Press.

to create a politically centrist, classless society. Ideally, educated citizens would cease to identify themselves by their class and cultural backgrounds. This loss of identity was necessary for, to a nation locked in struggle with international communism, class and cultural consciousness served only to promote disunity and lay bare America's historic class, ethnic, religious, and racial divisiveness. In any event, cold war liberals reasoned, the end of ethnic, religious, and racial discrimination in higher education, and the fact that more youths could obtain government education aid, signaled that class and cultural distinctions among Americans were disappearing.

Guided by a cold war liberal vision of the world, in which divisive class and cultural consciousness, and radical left and right political doctrines were ideologically repugnant, the federal government successfully promoted mass education. University enrollment expanded dramatically: from two million in 1950 to nearly four million in 1960 and further to seven million in 1968. By 1970, 50 percent of all college-aged youths attended an institution of higher education. With greater numbers of youths entering the universities in the 1960s, the title "student" began to take on the connotation of an occupation, albeit a temporary one. Intellectuals ranging from psychologist Kenneth Keniston to Michigan student activist Tom Hayden, ironically mirroring their cold war counterparts, described students as part of a new social class, a class that was neither blue nor white collar and which stood apart from the larger society. Moreover, this new class had personal and political concerns that were quite different from those of workers and professionals.

In many regards, students by the 1960s did represent a new social group. Escape from parental supervision, the mounting popularity among youth of vaguely antiauthoritarian rock 'n' roll music, and the increased prevalence on the campus of marijuana and psychedelics, combined to define a student lifestyle that was distinct from mainstream society. But despite those developments, it would be misleading to categorize students only by their lifestyle. Even though cold war liberal intellectuals proclaimed the end of class and cultural differences in America, such distinctions had not disappeared. In the 1960s, students' class and cultural backgrounds helped to determine which ideas they studied and adopted and which type of lifestyle they embraced.

Ironically, students who became involved in peace protest and the New Left in the 1960s were the beneficiaries of the expansion of higher education after World War II, an expansion ideologically justified in part by the intensifying cold war. With the military escalation of the Vietnam War, many sons and daughters of blue-collar workers and ethnic Catholics and Jews revolted against the political system that had made possible their entrance into the universities. Antiwar student activists, particularly those from middle- and upper-middle-class secularized Protestant backgrounds, championed the notion of student power. Such activists considered American youth to represent a new community that had, as cold war liberals predicted, become declassed. On the other hand, there were a number of antiwar students, generally working- and lower-middle-class and often Catholic, who, while accepting in part the idea of students as a new, declassed social group, acknowledged that their class and cultural heritages informed their politics.

White student activism of the 1960s owed much to the crusading reformist spirit of the New Frontier and the civil rights movement. Activism received further stimulus with the military escalation of the Vietnam War and the subsequent loss of the universities' scholarly neutrality as it became increasingly apparent to students that American institutions of higher education, through military research projects, were tied to the defense establishment. Alienation from the impersonal "multiversity," which stressed administrative form over intellectual content, and rejection of intrusive *in loco parentis,* also contributed to the political mobilization of students. Additionally, the federal government's conflicting educational policies, bound up with the draft and the war, promoted student rebellion. Citing a desperate shortage of primary and secondary school teachers and citizens schooled in the humanities, the federal government exhorted students to go into the fields of education and the arts. At the same time, the federal government awarded student draft deferments based upon a system that ranked education and humanities majors as least essential to national security and, therefore, least worthy of military service exemptions.

University administrators unwittingly set the stage for student disaffection by placing an increased emphasis upon liberal arts and social science programs. Large numbers of college students in the 1960s pursued studies in the humanities and social sciences. Significantly, liberal arts and social science majors predominated in the ranks of protesters. This may be explained by the nature of the social sciences and the humanities, which encourage critical approaches toward analyzing authority (and attract critical students), offer no specific avenues to jobs, and require sensitivity to, and reflection on, social problems. Science and business majors primarily deal with specific problems that have absolute answers and are not accustomed to dealing with social problems whose solutions are debatable. In addition, such majors often have specific jobs open to them and, since they typically work for corporations benefiting from defense contracts, are not inclined to be critical of the government.

Contrary to contemporary stereotypes, students who became involved in anti–Vietnam War protest were not all middle class and privileged. Indeed, student peace activists came from a variety of class and cultural backgrounds. One reason that the stereotype of the affluent student antiwar activists arose was the great news media attention that privileged, secularized Protestant and Jewish, radical youths received. Such activists did exist in number at elite schools and were considered newsworthy because they represented, figuratively and literally, the children of the Establishment. Culturally secure, and the products of elite university educations, these activists operated comfortably from a position of privilege and, since economic factors did not constrict their horizons, their idealism and expectations were accordingly great. They did not have to work while in college in order to pay for tuition and, further, could afford the luxury of not being career-oriented; their parents could support them indefinitely. This privileged cultural and class background led some upper-middle-class Jewish and Protestant activists to believe that all whites were similarly advantaged and all blacks conversely disadvantaged. Convinced that they constituted the most intellectually and morally advanced segment of society, well-to-do student activists such as Bill Ayers, Diana Oughton, and Terry Robbins issued secularized jeremiads against "American imperialism," which exploited their black, brown, and yellow comrades at home and abroad. This was the class and cultural milieu that produced the most violence-prone faction of the 1960s New Left: the Weathermen.

The 1960s academic and activist melting pot also included culturally insecure and less privileged groups, particularly working- and lower-middle-class Jews and Catholics. Jewish student activists, regardless of their degree of secularization and assimilation, absorbed from their backgrounds a propensity toward political awareness and liberalism. Once uprooted from eastern Europe in the early twentieth century, Jewish immigrants confronted a culturally ambiguous environment in America. Unlike other cultural groups, which, upon gaining upward social mobility, increasingly adopted more conservative politics, Jews did not tend to forsake their commitment to civil rights, civil liberties, and trade unionism. According to a 1970 Louis Harris survey, 23 percent of Jewish students termed themselves leftist, compared to 4 percent of Protestant students.

One possible explanation for Jewish political exceptionalism lies in part in their persistent cultural anxiety, expressed by the image of the outsider who cannot accept that he has been accepted. There was some substance to Jewish cultural anxiety, given the fact that their economic success has been achieved largely in the independent professions of law, medicine, and teaching. Up to the 1970s, Protestant corporate America closed its doors to Jews and Catholics. It also must not be forgotten that for 1960s red diaper babies, 1950s McCarthyism underscored perceptions of vulnerability as well as injustice. Red diaper babies grew up with FBI harassment [and] economic hardship if their parents were blacklisted and lived in fear that their parents would be arrested and executed like Julius and Ethel Rosenberg. For these reasons, Jewish youths often interacted only with one another until entering college. Richard Flacks and Steve Max, both red diaper babies and founders of [the] SDS, were surprised to discover the existence of Midwestern Christian radicals at the 1962 Port Huron SDS convention. Indeed, Max did not meet his first Catholic until the Port Huron convention.

Catholic student activists were at once similar to, and greatly different from, Jewish student activists. Ideologically, Catholics tended to absorb from their church a reflexive distrust of communism. However, the Catholic church also taught its followers the need for community, mutual assistance, and social justice. Culturally, the parents of Catholic activists had experienced discrimination similar to that which had confronted the parents of Jewish student activists. Catholic student activists were also just as culturally insecure and insular as their Jewish counterparts. Mary Verala, a Hispanic Catholic student activist, expressed wonderment at the 1962 Port Huron convention upon meeting "my first Communist, Steve Max." In part this was because their upward mobility was largely, like that of Jews, the product of the New Deal. In addition, it is important to keep in mind that it was not until 1960 that even a Harvard-educated and wealthy Catholic could get elected president of the United States.

A final group of student activists may be broadly characterized as working and lower middle class, frequently Catholic or brought up in what Vance Packard called "low-status" Protestant denominations, Methodist, Baptist, and Lutheran. Scholars of the 1960s, as well as journalists at the time, have given short shrift to this group since they overwhelmingly attended state, rather than private, schools. For example, in 1967, 34 percent of entering Penn State students identified their parents as unskilled or skilled laborers. Nationally, just 17 percent of college students in 1966 came from working- and lower-middle-class families.

According to Richard Sennett and Jonathan Cobb, working- and lower-middle-class students whom they studied in the 1960s frequently developed feelings of cultural and intellectual inferiority vis-à-vis more economically privileged and culturally secure undergraduates. In New Left circles, these activists often found themselves condescended to and ridiculed because they were unfamiliar with the jargon employed, and authorities cited, by middle- and upper-middle-class students. Raised in a cultural milieu that placed a premium upon clear and direct discourse, less privileged activists became frustrated with the upper-middle-class students' opaque language.

Working- and lower-middle-class student activists experienced enormous psychic tensions. Not infrequently, these activists' parents did not support their decision to go to college, considering it a wasteful endeavor and an indication that they were too lazy to work. If supportive, working- and lower-middle-class parents wanted their children to concentrate on studying, not protesting, which would alienate future employers and get them in trouble with the government. Less privileged student activists, in contrast to middle- and upper-middle-class radicals, also had to concern themselves with paying for their educations since their parents had little disposable income and often opposed their enrollment in the university in the first place. This imposed limits on their degree of activism, giving rise to feelings that they were not doing enough to stop the war.

Finally, less privileged student activists, whose parents were frequently anticommunist New Deal Democrats, found themselves choosing between their new political orientation and their upbringing. Jewish student activists, at least, had generally liberal to left-of-center parents who supported their children's activism. This was not the case for working- and lower-middle-class activists who, as Texas SDS organizer Jeff Shero bitterly noted, often had to break with their past.

> If you were a New York student and became a member of SDS, it was essentially joining a political organization, which was a common experience. In Texas to join SDS meant breaking with your family, it meant being cut off—it was like in early Rome joining a Christian sect—and the break was so much more total, getting involved with something like SDS you had to be much more highly committed, and you were in a sense freed, 'cause you'd get written off. If you were from Texas, in SDS, you were a bad motherfucker, you couldn't go home for Christmas. Your mother didn't say, "Oh, isn't that nice, you're involved. We supported the republicans in the Spanish Civil War, and now you're in SDS and I'm glad to see you're socially concerned." In most of those places it meant, *"You Goddamn Communist."*

In Shero's terminology, "New York student" is to be understood as Jewish, while a "Texas student" is a stand-in for working- and lower-middle-class Catholic, Baptist, or Methodist. This quotation encompasses far more cultural tensions than just those represented by regional differences.

Student activists, their political values shaped by their varied class and cultural backgrounds, also dwelled in separate realities; there really never was one antiwar movement, or one New Left. Instead, there were in the 1960s many movements and any number of New Lefts, linked by their opposition to the Vietnam War or by their affiliation with [the] SDS, a national organization only in name. After Tom

Hayden, joined by Michigan and Oberlin College students, had completed the 1962 *Port Huron Statement,* SDS's manifesto, the privileged activists were able to get an audience with the historian and Kennedy administration adviser, Arthur Schlesinger, Jr. At this meeting they proclaimed the birth of a new social reform movement. Similarly, Todd Gitlin, an early SDS president, and the Harvard peace group TOCSIN, had a back channel into the White House at the beginning of the 1960s. Such access was not extended to most university activists. Indeed, state university student activists never dreamed that such access was possible. Moreover, such student radicals had their energies consumed at their own campuses in simply trying to gain the right to be politically active. Securing this basic right, one that state university administrators did not consider to be a right at all, involved a great deal of effort. The possibility of meeting with a White House representative, then, was so remote as to be ludicrous; they often could not even get an appointment with the dean of student affairs. Further, the ideological struggles within the SDS National Office in Chicago were of little concern to the rank-and-file activists; their attentions were focused on the local struggle for peace and social justice.

MICHIGAN STATE UNIVERSITY

Born in the Bronx to working-class German-Polish Jewish parents, Edward Gewirts (later anglicized to Garrett) entered Michigan State College in 1937. With an uncle serving as an official in the then militant American Federation of Labor, Gewirts gravitated toward campus leftist groups. Although an associate of several East Lansing radicals, Gewirts never joined the Communist party and broke off all relations with Moscow-oriented campus organizations after the 1939 Stalin-Hitler Pact—a decision he mentioned to a dean who noted his break and which subsequently saved him from "the worse ravages of the McCarthyite inquisition of the early Fifties." Eventually, Gewirts married a Methodist school teacher who supported Henry Wallace's 1948 presidential candidacy and settled in Kalamazoo, Michigan. The Garretts became active in local Democratic party politics and were frightened by the televised Army-McCarthy hearings.

The Garretts' liberalism and ties to Michigan State influenced their son's politics and led him to East Lansing in 1961. Excited by the Cuban revolution and exposed to the cold war dissent of such liberal magazines as the *Nation* and the *New Republic,* Jan Garrett, a scholarship student, joined the university's model United Nations (UN), which attracted the most socially aware students on campus. Garrett subsequently refused to participate in compulsory ROTC (Reserve Officer Training Corps), involved himself with free speech issues on the campus, and helped to revive the Young Socialist Club (YSC).

At least as early as 1961, [MSU president John Hannah] had authorized the university's Department of Public Safety (DPS) to spy upon and infiltrate activist campus organizations, sending names and photographs of student protesters to the Michigan Red Squad. One student informant infiltrated the YSC and incorrectly identified Al Meyers, a political science professor and anticommunist social democrat, as its faculty sponsor. The university also employed as informants *State News'* reporters who provided photographs and phone tips that enabled the DPS to collect several file drawers of data on student groups by the early 1960s. Garrett's efforts to revive the YSC, and invite a Communist, Robert Thompson, to speak at MSU in 1962–1963, elicited overt university hostility.

The *State News* dramatically headlined the YSC's invitation, "Young Socialists Sponsor Red." Livid, Hannah denied university facilities to Thompson, exerted pressure on the student government president to revoke the YSC's charter, and met with, and chastised, two YSC members. At that meeting, the MSU president read to the students excerpts from [the House Un-American Activities Committee's] "100 Things to Know about Communism." The MSU board of trustees, belatedly informed by Hannah that he had banned Thompson from the campus, divided, with a large minority affirming the right of a Communist to speak at the university. Trustee Don Stevens, noting that his anticommunist credentials dated from the 1930s as an activist in the Congress of Industrial Organizations (CIO), supported the YSC invitation. The Lansing ACLU (American Civil Liberties Union) and faculty activists Larrowe and Repas joined the fight to uphold free speech, as did MSU Humanist Society leader Peter Werbe, who later became an editor of the Detroit-based underground newspaper, *Fifth Estate*. Ultimately, the Delta Sigma Phi fraternity offered its backyard to Thompson and a thousand curious people gathered there, a considerable number coming to heckle his speech.

While the YSC-Hannah confrontation radicalized few students, it did serve to underscore MSU's changing political environment. Larry Lack, a Goldwater supporter who grew up in a working-class Baltimore, Maryland, neighborhood, came to MSU in 1961 and participated in the university's model UN. Partly as a result of associating in the model UN with "the sons and daughters of African revolutionaries" who had been recruited to the university by the school's aggressive international affairs programs, Lack became interested in American race relations and informally affiliated with the MSU Friends of the Student Non-Violent Coordinating Committee (SNCC). After listening to Ivanhoe Donaldson speak at MSU, Lack went south with the civil rights activist to deliver textbooks to a black college. While driving through Georgia, they were arrested and Donaldson severely beaten. Appalled, Lack moved to the left and after graduating from MSU in 1963 became a reporter for the underground newspaper, the Los Angeles *Free Press.*

Lack's radicalization was the product of an increasingly assertive civil rights movement, and part of a national as well as local process that swept up larger and larger numbers of students. In East Lansing, the MSU Friends of [the] SNCC initiated the picketing of local businesses that discriminated against the university's burgeoning African, Asian, and Latin American student population. Picketing gave way to marches on behalf of open housing in the city, culminating in the largest mass arrest in East Lansing's history in 1965. Fifty-nine students marched on city hall and wound up in the county prison. Against this backdrop of escalated protest, dozens of student volunteers took part in the Student Tutorial Education Project (STEP) and spent their summers teaching economically deprived blacks at Rust College in Holly Springs, Mississippi. In that intensely hostile and racist environment, MSU students learned how to form support networks and to sustain commitment. When such students returned to East Lansing, their experiences had prepared them to challenge the university administration and the Vietnam War.

Immediately after the march on city hall, the *State News* published the names of the students who had been arrested and "tarnished" the image of the university. Although not noted by the *State News,* at least eight of the students were members of the then straight-laced campus SDS chapter. Established in 1963 by a handful of discontented history, political science, and sociology graduate students, [the] SDS sharply criticized American cold war foreign policy and a variety of university rules and regulations. Unlike its sister chapter in Ann Arbor, [the] MSU SDS claimed a good share of working- and lower-middle-class students. Jack Sattel, a MSU SDS leader, came from a working-class, German immigrant family. In high school, Sattel "had some sense of being an outsider . . . since the majority of my friends were solidly middle class and college-bound." Upon graduation from high school, Sattel enlisted in the air force. Trained in electronics and the operation of nuclear weapons, which "scared the hell out of" him, he began "to read seriously about politics and history" and developed a new view of the nation's foreign policy. His political consciousness was heightened as a result of witnessing Japanese student peace demonstrations and developing friendships with black soldiers who were excited by the Freedom Rides. By the time Sattel left the air force in 1961 to go to MSU, he considered himself a radical.

Noticing the existence of the Young Socialist Club in the fall 1961 MSU catalogue, Sattel indicated his interest in the group on his application to the university, a fact subsequently noted in his Michigan Red Squad file. "The size and anonymity of MSU," Sattel recalled, did not disturb him "after four years in the Air Force . . . although it clearly seemed to bewilder a lot of the undergraduates and seemed to anger them." He reserved his anger "for things *outside* the university: nuclear war; racial injustice; poverty."

In 1962–1963, Sattel started to attend YSC meetings, which he came to view as:

> arcane and frustrating—arguments about sectarian left-political issues . . . however, the group did some support work for the Southern student movement, brought in some trade-unionists, began demonstrating against racial discrimination in off-campus housing, etc. It served as a way of connecting people and issues—it gave me a sense of purpose/direction while also pursuing my degree. At the same time, I always had one or two friends who were *not* political . . . with whom it was more fun to go out and raise hell. . . . Most of this group was too serious to have much fun with. I saw politics as a way to *transform* society in more open, satisfying ways; they tended to see politics as an end to itself.

It was the serious politicos of the YSC, Ed and Sheri Lessin, Paul Schiff, Brian Keleher, Harvey Goldman—a 15-year-old scholarship student—and Stu and Janet (Goldwasser) Dowty—frequent travelers to Ann Arbor and friends of Al Haber—who founded [the] MSU SDS.

In its early days, [the] MSU SDS was very much a family affair, with members frequently entering into relationships that culminated in marriage. Sue Van Eyck, whose lower-middle-class parents lived in Royal Oak, Michigan, came from a conservative Republican background, offset somewhat by the influence of her neighbor and rebellious schoolmate, Tom Hayden. The prohibitive costs of attending Michigan, and realization that she would not fit in socially with the more affluent students at Ann Arbor, led her to MSU in 1961. At the university, she was exposed to activist guest speakers and met and married Jack Sattel. Both became heavily involved in the antiwar movement: Jack as president of [the] MSU SDS and Sue as president of the East Lansing chapter of the Women's International League for Peace and Freedom.

The Sattels deeply believed in nonviolent protest and identified with community and labor union organizing. Sue had no patience for those in the MSU and the national SDS who advocated "rock throwing," describing such activists as the "sons and daughters of the ruling class" who "wanted 'to win this' and to win (bring revolution) soon . . . due to their being used to getting what they wanted if they wanted it bad enough." Jack also did not care for the upper-middle-class Columbia and Michigan SDSers who came to East Lansing in the late 1960s to sow discord within [the] MSU SDS and urge violent confrontations with the university administration. Similarly, MSU SDS member George Fish, a scholarship student from an Indianapolis, Indiana, lower-middle-class German Catholic family, railed against the elitist Michigan and National Office (Chicago) SDS travelers. Fish viewed them as "patronizing colonizers" bringing light to economically and intellectually inferior MSU SDSers. Class antagonisms between the MSU and Michigan SDS, and among MSU SDSers, mounted throughout the 1960s and contributed to the factionalism of the East Lansing chapter after upper-middle-class Columbia and Michigan SDSers seized control of the National Office in 1969.

While class conflict divided [the] MSU SDS, the East Lansing chapter was largely spared the discord resulting from overt male chauvinism. At the outset, female MSU SDSers such as Sue Sattel, Sheri Lessin, Denise Ryan, Kaye Bradley (who became a regional traveler in the south), and Carlie Tanner (later a National Office organizer) played key roles in formulating chapter policies and tactics. Initially, these women, heirs to a tradition of female subordination, had to force themselves "to speak up at meetings" and to "be taken seriously and not just get the coffee." Their efforts to influence the direction of the chapter succeeded, and they received the support of "enlightened" male SDSers who were not threatened by female assertiveness. The MSU SDS's relatively egalitarian relationship between the sexes was exceptional. In general, sexism pervaded the New Left.

An important religious-left alternative to the secular-left SDS, the University Christian Movement (UCM) emerged in East Lansing in the mid-1960s. The UCM, founded in September 1966, evolved from the religious, apolitical National Student Christian Federation. UCM's founders proclaimed that God acted on earth only through political modes; fundamental social change could be realized by activist humans working toward "community dialogue, diversity, freedom, and the abolition of bourgeois complacency through radical education." MSU UCM members, thirty in number by the fall of 1966, came from rural, moderate-to-conservative, white, evangelical Protestant families. Seemingly, their backgrounds precluded radical political activism, but their rooted home-grown religious convictions, most of all their belief that all human life was sacred, led them to disavow the war. Further, they argued that if Christian Americans truly believed in

God and democracy, they could not fight on behalf of an undemocratic, immoral South Vietnamese government.

The UCM's emphasis upon social issues, and its evangelical zeal for converting students to the cause of peace, served to bring together Catholics, Jews, Methodists, and Quakers, surmounting theological differences. This united religious front, however, had a price. UCM advisers Lynn Jondahl and Keith Pohl became the subjects of intense police surveillance, and Michigan Red Squad agents broke into the University Methodist Church to copy documents pertaining to local clergy-faculty draft counseling efforts. Moreover, older hawkish faculty and residents at the University Methodist Church resented the younger Methodists' unpatriotic, morally self-righteous opposition to the war. Methodist UCM activists found the generation gap too great to bridge and proceeded to drop out of the church. In October 1966, the University Methodist Church held three services every Sunday for eight hundred students. By 1968, only fifty students showed up for the one remaining service.

[The] MSU UCM organized students on three levels. At the first level, students formed support networks and discussed their problems in adjusting to the impersonal multiversity. Students in the first level who became interested in civil rights and peace issues graduated to the second level and joined Depth Education Groups (DEGs). Those students in the DEGs who had studied a particular social issue and had become convinced that political action was required flowed into the third level, where activist cadres were spawned. These cadres organized teach-ins, rallies, and formulated strategies with the SDS. It was through this intense, politicizing indoctrination in social interaction that a once conservative religion major from western Michigan, Dave Stockman (later President Reagan's director of the Office of Management and Budget), became a MSU antiwar leader.

Given Stockman's subsequent, controversial political career, it is necessary to point out that he in no way later set aside his commitment to social reform. The bright and energetic child of solid, conservative farmers, whether as antiwar organizer or as Reagan's budget director, possessed an ingrained distrust of the federal government, particularly of the [Defense Department]. He also consistently championed the cause of civil rights and risked his congressional seat in the 1970s by denouncing racists in his district. Sue Sattel, who worked with Stockman on the 1967 Vietnam Summer program, praised him as a committed and enthusiastic peace worker, as did Jondahl and Pohl. When a hawkish student in April 1967 denounced [the] MSU SDS as unAmerican, Stockman defended the radicals who had pledged to resist the draft as America's true patriots:

> A nation is not defined by the particular policy, of a particular administration, in power at a particular point in time. Rather, the genius of a nation is expressed in those lofty ideals and broad spiritual currents which have threaded their way through the fabric of its history. In our country these ideals are embodied in concepts like: distributive justice, limited government; individual freedom of speech, assembly and worship; and the rights to life, liberty and the pursuit of happiness. ... Many of us feel that American intervention in Vietnam runs contrary to the spirit of this historical tradition. Therefore, our commitment to the real core values and ideals that have made this nation great, demands that we oppose the war.

> There have been many expressions of this opposition. One of them being the SDS anti-draft union. . . . I think the action of many of those . . . is motivated by a broader courage than simple, blind obedience, and by a sense of responsibility to values higher than the shallow rhetoric of the present administration.

Stockman never repudiated the sentiments he expressed on behalf of [the] SDS; the Methodist populist did, however, come to loathe the organization after it became committed to violence in 1969.

A disproportionate number of students in the MSU SDS, the UCM, and the campus antiwar movement in general were National Merit Scholarship recipients. In 1963, in order to enhance the university's national prominence, MSU began a campaign to recruit greater numbers of scholarship students and to create special honors programs with close student-faculty interaction. Hundreds of highly motivated, sensitive, intelligent Merit Scholars flocked to East Lansing. Here they were soon disenchanted with the large, impersonal, bureaucratic nature of the university and with Hannah's insistence upon *in loco parentis,* which cast a shadow across every aspect of their social lives. These alienated scholars, soured by an administration promising more than it could deliver, formed mutual support groups, developed close relationships, and became reform-minded activists. In 1965, when MSU's enrollment of Merit Scholars surpassed the number attending Harvard, *Look* magazine profiled the university's academic superstars. Within a year, MSU's academic superstars had acquired a new collective label: "John Hannah's Worst Nightmares."

Hannah's nightmares filled the ranks of the Committee for Student Rights and [the] SDS and founded, in 1965, the first campus-based underground newspaper in the nation, *The Paper.* Merit Scholar-SDS reporters for *The Paper* honored Hannah with a comic strip, "Land Grant Man." Inspired by "Batman," scholarship student Steve Badrich, the product of a working-class, Yugoslavian immigrant family, conceived the idea of the comic strip. With dialogue by Jane Munn, the scrappy daughter of legendary MSU football coach and athletic director Clarence "Biggie" Munn, President "Palindrome" (Hannah), once he thumped a hoe on the floor and shouted the magic word "Poultry!" became the inept caped crusader, "Land Grant Man." Gleefully, the comic strip writers subjected Hannah's alter ego to acid trips, gang rape by sexually repressed coeds, and assault by his wife, who did not recognize him in the "Land Grant Man" costume.

The lèse-majesté explicit in "Land Grant Man" reflected the impact of events, chiefly the escalation of the Vietnam War, on activists' attitudes toward authority. It also signaled a transforming cultural-political style on the left. Activist students who entered the university in 1965 were prepared to act upon the philosophy Jack Sattel had embraced in 1962—the belief that humor and fun were integral to, and not mutually exclusive of, politics. One MSU SDSer, acting upon this idea, acquired legendary status following his summons to report for induction into the military. During his physical examination, the medical doctor ordered the SDSer to drop his pants and to bend over. The doctor noticed something protruding from the student's anus and, shocked, asked "what the hell" it was. Nonchalantly, the SDSer replied, "Oh, that's my pet rat." He was not drafted. Humor and politics were also deployed against the local news media. A group of MSU SDSers, living off-campus in the facetiously dubbed "Lenin House," learned that a news reporter was coming over to investigate rumors that [the] SDS was recruiting volunteers to fight in the North Vietnamese Army. The gullible reporter subsequently witnessed students performing military drills.

MSU student antiwar activists were overwhelmingly of northern and western European (72 percent), or Jewish (19 percent), stock, as well as male (75 percent). (See Table 5-1.) They largely majored in the liberal arts and the social sciences (76 percent) and were undergraduates (87 percent). A significant minority came from metropolitan areas (43 percent), and (46 percent) were not Michigan residents. Further, a disproportionate number were National Merit Scholarship-Honors College students (12 percent), and enrolled in the humanities and social science residential colleges (9 percent).

The significant characteristics of the MSU student antiwar movement become evident when they are compared to those of the overall student body. In 1969, 17 percent of MSU students were from out of state, while 46 percent of antiwar activists were not Michigan residents; Jews were 10 percent of the student body but 19 percent of activists; National Merit Scholarship-Honors College and residential

TABLE 5-1 MSU Antiwar Student Activists, 1965–1972 (N = 263*)

	North-West European	South-East European	Jewish			
Ethnicity	72%	9%	19%			
	Female	Male				
Gender	25%	75%				
	Liberal Arts/ Social Science	Business/ Science				
Major	76%	24%				
	Metropolitan Area	Large City		Medium City	Small City	Small Town
Residence I	43%	5%		9%	14%	30%
	In-state	Out-of-state				
Residence II	54%	46%				
	Undergraduate	Graduate				
Status	87%	13%				
	National Merit Scholar/ Honors College	Humanities and Social Science Residential College				
Specific Academic Characteristics	12%	9%				

*Of 349 names collected, I identified 263 (75%) as to majors, residence, and status. Figures reported for ethnicity and gender are derived from the entire data base.

college students constituted, respectively, 2 and 3 percent of the student body, compared to 12 and 9 percent of antiwar activists. Finally, business and science majors were underrepresented in the antiwar movement; 46 percent of the student body, and just 24 percent of peace activists.

Contrasts between the overall student body and members of [the] MSU SDS are particularly striking. (See Table 5-2.) Compared to the student body at large and non-SDS antiwar students, [the] MSU SDS had fewer south and east European Catholics, disproportionately more Jews (24 percent), and somewhat greater numbers of females, although they were underrepresented given their campus total. By contrasting *just* liberal-dovish antiwar students to radicals, we learn that fewer SDSers (16 percent) majored in business and science than [did] non-SDS antiwar students (29 percent), while a majority of the former (53 percent) came from metropolitan areas as opposed to a minority of the latter (35 percent). More SDSers claimed out-of-state residences (52 percent) than [did] non-SDS activists (42 percent), and were disproportionately National Merit Scholarship-Honors College (16 percent), and residential college (10 percent), students. [The] MSU SDS attracted to its ranks people who considered themselves culturally disfranchised from American society and the university: Jews, intellectuals, women, and urbanites transplanted into an alien environment that caused them to suffer culture shock.

To an extent, certain social characteristics of student antiwar activists and SDSers differed only slightly from those of prowar students. (See Table 5-3.) A caveat is in order. By taking a public stand in favor of military intervention in Indochina, prowar activists set themselves apart from the apathetic or anticommunist majority on campus. If we accept the fact that liberal arts and social science majors are more prone to speak out and be engaged in the political process than their career-oriented business and science counterparts, then it should be no surprise that they comprise the majority of *prowar,* as well as antiwar, activists. Nonetheless, business and science majors have a greater propensity to make a prowar, rather than antiwar, stand.

Prowar activists differed slightly from the overall MSU student body, at least in terms of majors and representation in the honors and residential colleges. On the other hand, a third of MSU prowar student activists came from out of state, nearly twice the norm, although 9 percent were Jews, nearly their proportional representation on campus. It is when prowar students are compared to non-SDS antiwar students and SDSers, in terms of gender, residential status, and enrollment in the honors and residential colleges, that contrasts become striking. Female students, if inclined to become activists, gravitated more frequently to the left than to the anticommunist center or right. Further, antiwar students, SDS and non-SDS alike, were more often from out of state than prowar students. Although there is no difference between non-SDS antiwar students and prowar students as far as metropolitan residence is concerned, there is a sharp divergence between MSU SDSers and prowar students who came from such locales: 53 percent as opposed to 35 percent. Finally, honors college and residential college students were disproportionately antiwar, rather than prowar.

While the locus of student antiwar protest and organization was largely confined to the "Old Campus," where the liberal arts and social science departments

TABLE 5-2 The MSU SDS, 1965–1970 (N = 109*)

	North-West European	South-East European	Jewish			
Ethnicity	71%	5%	24%			
	Female	Male				
Gender	29%	71%				
	Liberal Arts/ Social Science	Business/ Science				
Major	84%	16%				
	Metropolitan Area	Large City		Medium City	Small City	Small Town
Residence I	53%	4%		6%	12%	25%
	In-state	Out-of-state				
Residence II	48%	52%				
	Undergraduate	Graduate				
Status	89%	11%				
	National Merit Scholar/ Honors College	Humanities and Social Science Residential College				
Specific Academic Characteristics	16%	10%				

*Of 145 names collected, I identified 109 (75%) as to majors, residence, and status. Figures reported for ethnicity and gender are derived from the entire data base.

were situated, gaining few business and science majors on the "New Campus" across the Red Cedar River, prowar students after 1966 exercised little negative influence in shaping antiwar protest. MSU student peace activists had momentum and went on the offensive in 1966, reasonably assured that prowar student resistance would be sporadic and of little political consequence. Antiwar activists were also aided, ironically, by the outspokenness of anticommunist Vietnam Project veterans and President Hannah who, inadvertently, demonstrated the university's considerable role in creating the Indochinese conflict. Also, Hannah's zealous anticommunism, as well as his strong ties to the defense establishment, made him a perfect foil for SDSers. He was their best recruiter. Consequently, antiwar activists found that the MSU student body was relatively easy to mobilize and radicalize. . .

.

The emergence of student political activism at state schools predated the 1964 uprising at Berkeley, which, according to various scholars, spawned white student activism. Student activists at Kent State, Michigan State, and SUNY-Buffalo, their numbers varying from campus to campus, were involved in free speech protests several months prior to the Berkeley Free Speech movement. In addition, student activists at Kent State, Michigan State, and Penn State had established antiwar or-

TABLE 5-3 MSU Prowar Student Activists, 1965–1972 (N = 112*)

	North-West European	South-East European	Jewish		
Ethnicity	82%	9%	9%		
	Female	Male			
Gender	15%	85%			
	Liberal Arts/ Social Science	Business/ Science			
Major	57%	43%			
	Metropolitan Area	Large City	Medium City	Small City	Small Town
Residence I	35%	6%	11%	12%	36%
	In-state	Out-of-state			
Residence II	67%	33%			
	Undergraduate	Graduate			
Status	87%	13%			
	National Merit Scholar/ Honors College	Residential College			
Specific Academic Characteristics	2%	2%			

*Of 148 names collected, I identified 112 (76%) as to majors, residence, and status. Figures reported for ethnicity and gender are derived from the entire data base.

ganizations months, if not years, before the military escalation of the Vietnam War and the founding of the famous Berkeley Vietnam Day Committee.

Moreover, contrary to scholars who have contended that state university student activists were less articulate, intelligent, and effective than their elite-educated counterparts, the fact remains that eloquent, bright, and dynamic, as well as nationally prominent, antiwar student leaders emerged from less well-regarded universities: Carl Davidson, Clinton Deveaux, Howie Emmer, Carl Oglesby, and Andy Stapp, to list only a few. These activists contributed a moral and political approach to the peace movement, an approach shaped by their class and cultural values. Set forth by particular activists were possibilities for CIO-inspired student syndicalism and Old Testament–influenced Marxist liberation theology. However, class and cultural differences among activists, and between activists and community residents, ultimately undermined such sweeping visions, leaving in their wake political fragmentation and bitter conflict.

The influence of the local environment on the development of each campus' antiwar movement was significant. Students did react to national events and the ebb and flow of the civil rights and anti–Vietnam War movements. At the same time, though, students' tactics and perceptions of American society reflected their immediate cultural and political environment. The type of relationship antiwar students had with university administrators, prowar students, law enforcement agencies, and community residents determined the mode of dissent as well as the ways in which confrontation unfolded. Each campus was quite different from the others in such regards and bore little semblance to the so-called activist schools: Berkeley, Columbia, Harvard, and Michigan.

State university student activists greatly differed from elite university protestors as far as class and cultural origins are concerned. Activists from the less prestigious universities drew upon a diverse membership of red diaper babies, upper-middle-class secularized Protestants, and working- and lower-middle-class Catholics and Protestants. At the elite schools, student activists were overwhelmingly middle and upper middle class. Moreover, even though Jewish students represented a significant part of [the] SDS and the New Left at the state universities, their numbers, with the exception of SUNY-Buffalo, were much greater at schools such as Columbia and Michigan (anywhere from 50 to 75 percent). Finally, the state universities claimed far more Catholic student activists than the heavily WASP [White, Anglo-Saxon Protestant] elite schools.

SOURCES

Vietnam

For more than two decades, the United States tried, and failed, to create a Vietnam suitable to its own vision of the postwar world. This failure became most apparent in the 1960s, when the fighting of the war divided Americans into bitter factions. Apologists for John Kennedy believe that he would have avoided full-scale involvement. But Kennedy had remarked that a withdrawal from Vietnam would mean collapse in Southeast Asia; and by 1963 he had sent 15,000 advisers to the country, more than fifteen times Dwight Eisenhower's commitment. Lyndon Johnson also believed in the domino theory and defined the Vietnam problem as simple Communist aggression, and in 1964, he inaugurated systematic air attacks on North Vietnam. But neither the air war nor an additional half-million American troops were sufficient to bring anything resembling victory. Even before the January 1968 Tet offensive, when Viet Cong and North Vietnamese attacks on major South Vietnamese cities made clear that the American claim to be winning the war was a sham, many Americans had come to question the war in moral terms. Over 200,000 marched against the war in Washington, D.C., in 1967. When Richard Nixon in 1970 moved ground troops into Cambodia, students closed down many colleges and universities in protest. By 1973, as Nixon withdrew the last of the nation's ground troops, the Eisenhower consensus lay in ruins.

To illustrate the polarization that the Vietnam war produced, and to offer some sense of how reasonable people could find themselves at loggerheads over this conflict, we have assembled two disparate views on the war. The first, a 1965 address by President Lyndon Johnson, reveals how a socially engaged, activist president could see the war as a high priority and, indeed, allow the war to interfere with his domestic agenda. The second, a 1967 speech by the Reverend Martin Luther King, Jr., announced his opposition to the war. It was a courageous decision, for it set King apart from his own political party and identified him in certain respects with the radical, "black power" side of the civil rights movement.

How did Johnson defend the war in Vietnam? Can you find flaws or weaknesses in his argument? How did King justify his new stance of opposition? Do you find his arguments convincing?

Pattern for Peace in Southeast Asia (1965)

Lyndon Johnson

Last week seventeen nations sent their views to some two dozen countries having an interest in Southeast Asia. We are joining those seventeen countries and stating our American policy tonight, which we believe will contribute toward peace in this area of the world.

I have come here to review once again with my own people the views of the American government.

Tonight Americans and Asians are dying for a world where each people may choose its own path to change. This is the principle for which our ancestors fought in the valleys of Pennsylvania. It is a principle for which our sons fight tonight in the jungles of Vietnam.

Vietnam is far away from this quiet campus. We have no territory there, nor do we seek any. The war is dirty and brutal and difficult. And some 400 young men, born into an America that is bursting with opportunity and promise, have ended their lives on Vietnam's steaming soil.

Why must we take this painful road? Why must this nation hazard its ease, its interest, and its power for the sake of a people so far away?

We fight because we must fight if we are to live in a world where every country can shape its own destiny, and only in such a world will our own freedom be finally secure.

This kind of world will never be built by bombs or bullets. Yet the infirmities of man are such that force must often precede reason and the waste of war, the works of peace. We wish that this were not so. But we must deal with the world as it is, if it is ever to be as we wish.

The world as it is in Asia is not a serene or peaceful place.

The first reality is that North Vietnam has attacked the independent nation of South Vietnam. Its object is total conquest. Of course, some of the people of South Vietnam are participating in attack on their own government. But trained men and supplies, orders and arms, flow in a constant stream from north to south.

This support is the heartbeat of the war.

And it is a war of unparalleled brutality. Simple farmers are the targets of assassination and kidnaping. Women and children are strangled in the night because their men are loyal to their government. And helpless villages are ravaged by sneak attacks. Large-scale raids are conducted on towns, and terror strikes in the heart of cities.

The confused nature of this conflict cannot mask the fact that it is the new face of an old enemy.

Over this war—and all Asia—is another reality: the deepening shadow of Communist China. The rulers in Hanoi are urged on by Beijing. This is a regime

Speech made at Johns Hopkins University, Baltimore, Maryland, April 17, 1965, Department of State *Bulletin*, April 26, 1965, pp. 606–610.

that has destroyed freedom in Tibet, attacked India, and has been condemned by the United Nations for aggression in Korea. It is a nation that is helping the forces of violence in almost every continent. The contest in Vietnam is part of a wider pattern of aggressive purposes.

WHY ARE WE IN SOUTH VIETNAM?

Why are these realities our concern? Why are we in South Vietnam?

We are there because we have a promise to keep. Since 1954 every American president has offered support to the people of South Vietnam. We have helped to build, and we have helped to defend. Thus, over many years, we have made a national pledge to help South Vietnam defend its independence.

And I intend to keep that promise.

To dishonor that pledge, to abandon this small and brave nation to its enemies, and to the terror that must follow, would be an unforgivable wrong.

We are also there to strengthen world order. Around the globe, from Berlin to Thailand, are people whose well-being rests in part on the belief that they can count on us if they are attacked. To leave Vietnam to its fate would shake the confidence of all these people in the value of an American commitment and in the value of America's word. The result would be increased unrest and instability, and even wider war.

We are also there because there are great stakes in the balance. Let no one think for a moment that retreat from Vietnam would bring an end to conflict. The battle would be renewed in one country and then another. The central lesson of our time is that the appetite of aggression is never satisfied. To withdraw from one battlefield means only to prepare for the next. We must say in Southeast Asia—as we did in Europe—in the words of the Bible: "Hitherto shalt thou come, but no further."

There are those who say that all our effort there will be futile—that China's power is such that it is bound to dominate all Southeast Asia. But there is no end to that argument until all the nations of Asia are swallowed up.

There are those who wonder why we have a responsibility there. Well, we have it there for the same reason that we have a responsibility for the defense of Europe. World War II was fought in both Europe and Asia, and when it ended we found ourselves with continued responsibility for the defense of freedom.

Our objective is the independence of South Vietnam and its freedom from attack. We want nothing for ourselves—only that the people of South Vietnam be allowed to guide their own country in their own way. We will do everything necessary to reach that objective, and we will do only what is absolutely necessary.

In recent months attacks on South Vietnam were stepped up. Thus it became necessary for us to increase our response and to make attacks by air. This is not a change of purpose. It is a change in what we believe that purpose requires.

We do this in order to slow down aggression.

We do this to increase the confidence of the brave people of South Vietnam who have bravely borne this brutal battle for so many years with so many casualties.

And we do this to convince the leaders of North Vietnam—and all who seek to share their conquest—of a simple fact:

We will not be defeated.

We will not grow tired.

We will not withdraw, either openly or under the cloak of a meaningless agreement.

We know that air attacks alone will not accomplish all these purposes. But it is our best and prayerful judgment that they are a necessary part of the surest road to peace.

THE PATH OF PEACEFUL SETTLEMENT

We hope that peace will come swiftly. But that is in the hands of others besides ourselves. And we must be prepared for a long continued conflict. It will require patience as well as bravery—the will to endure as well as the will to resist.

I wish it were possible to convince others with words of what we now find it necessary to say with guns and planes: armed hostility is futile—our resources are equal to any challenge—because we fight for values and we fight for principle, rather than territory or colonies, our patience and our determination are unending.

Once this is clear, then it should also be clear that the only path for reasonable men is the path of peaceful settlement. Such peace demands an independent South Vietnam—securely guaranteed and able to shape its own relationships to all others—free from outside interference—tied to no alliance—a military base for no other country.

These are the essentials of any final settlement.

We will never be second in the search for such a peaceful settlement in Vietnam.

There may be many ways to this kind of peace: in discussion or negotiation with the governments concerned; in large groups or in small ones; in the reaffirmation of old agreements or their strengthening with new ones.

We have stated this position over and over again fifty times and more to friend and foe alike. And we remain ready with this purpose for unconditional discussions.

And until that bright and necessary day of peace we will try to keep conflict from spreading. We have no desire to see thousands die in battle—Asians or Americans. We have no desire to devastate that which the people of North Vietnam have built with toil and sacrifice. We will use our power with restraint and with all the wisdom that we can command.

But we will use it.

A COOPERATIVE EFFORT FOR DEVELOPMENT

This war, like most wars, is filled with terrible irony. For what do the people of North Vietnam want? They want what their neighbors also desire—food for their hunger, health for their bodies, a chance to learn, progress for their country, and an end to the bondage of material misery. And they would find all these things far more readily in peaceful association with others than in the endless course of battle.

These countries of Southeast Asia are homes for millions of impoverished people. Each day these people rise at dawn and struggle through until the night to wrest existence from the soil. They are often wracked by diseases, plagued by hunger, and death comes at the early age of forty.

Stability and peace do not come easily in such a land. Neither independence nor human dignity will ever be won, though, by arms alone. It also requires the works of peace. The American people have helped generously in times past in these works, and now there must be a much more massive effort to improve the life of man in that conflict-torn corner of our world.

The first step is for the countries of Southeast Asia to associate themselves in a greatly expanded cooperative effort for development. We would hope that North Vietnam would take its place in the common effort just as soon as peaceful cooperation is possible.

The United Nations is already actively engaged in development in this area, and as far back as 1961 I conferred with our authorities in Vietnam in connection with their work there. And I would hope tonight that the secretary-general of the United Nations could use the prestige of his great office and his deep knowledge of Asia to initiate, as soon as possible, with the countries of that area, a plan for cooperation in increased development.

For our part I will ask the Congress to join in a billion-dollar American investment in this effort as soon as it is under way. And I would hope that all other industrialized countries, including the Soviet Union, will join in this effort to replace despair with hope and terror with progress.

The task is nothing less than to enrich the hopes and existence of more than a hundred million people. And there is much to be done.

The vast Mekong River can provide food and water and power on a scale to dwarf even our own TVA [Tennessee Valley Authority]. The wonders of modern medicine can be spread through villages where thousands die every year from lack of care. Schools can be established to train people in the skills needed to manage the process of development. And these objectives, and more, are within the reach of a cooperative and determined effort.

I also intend to expand and speed up a program to make available our farm surpluses to assist in feeding and clothing the needy in Asia. We should not allow people to go hungry and wear rags while our own warehouses overflow with an abundance of wheat and corn and rice and cotton.

So I will very shortly name a special team of outstanding, patriotic, and distinguished Americans to inaugurate our participation in these programs. This team will be headed by Mr. Eugene Black, the very able former president of the World Bank.

THE DREAM OF OUR GENERATION

This will be a disorderly planet for a long time. In Asia, and elsewhere, the forces of the modern world are shaking old ways and uprooting ancient civilizations.

There will be turbulence and struggle and even violence. Great social change—as we see in our own country—does not always come without conflict.

We must also expect that nations will on occasion be in dispute with us. It may be because we are rich, or powerful, or because we have made some mistakes, or because they honestly fear our intentions. However, no nation need ever fear that we desire their land, or to impose our will, or to dictate their institutions.

But we will always oppose the effort of one nation to conquer another nation.

We will do this because our own security is at stake.

But there is more to it than that. For our generation has a dream. It is a very old dream. But we have the power, and now we have the opportunity to make that dream come true.

For centuries nations have struggled among each other. But we dream of a world where disputes are settled by law and reason. And we will try to make it so.

For most of history men have hated and killed one another in battle. But we dream of an end to war. And we will try to make it so.

For all existence most men have lived in poverty, threatened by hunger. But we dream of a world where all are fed and charged with hope. And we will help to make it so.

The ordinary men and women of North Vietnam and South Vietnam, of China and India, of Russia and America, are brave people. They are filled with the same proportions of hate and fear, of love and hope. Most of them want the same things for themselves and their families. Most of them do not want their sons to ever die in battle, or to see their homes, or the homes of others, destroyed.

Well, this can be their world yet. Man now has the knowledge—always before denied—to make this planet serve the real needs of the people who live on it.

I know this will not be easy. I know how difficult it is for reason to guide passion, and love to master hate. The complexities of this world do not bow easily to pure and consistent answers.

But the simple truths are there just the same. We must all try to follow them as best we can.

POWER, WITNESS TO HUMAN FOLLY

We often say how impressive power is. But I do not find it impressive at all. The guns and the bombs, the rockets and the warships, are all symbols of human failure. They are necessary symbols. They protect what we cherish. But they are witness to human folly.

A dam built across a great river is impressive.

In the countryside where I was born, and where I live, I have seen the night illuminated, and the kitchen warmed, and the home heated, where once the cheerless night and the ceaseless cold held sway. And all this happened because electricity came to our area along the humming wires of the REA [Rural Electrification Administration]. Electrification of the countryside—yes, that, too, is impressive.

A rich harvest in a hungry land is impressive.

The sight of healthy children in a classroom is impressive.

These—not mighty arms—are the achievements that the American nation believes to be impressive. And if we are steadfast, the time may come when all other nations will also find it so.

Every night before I turn out the lights to sleep I ask myself this question: Have I done everything that I can do to unite this country? Have I done everything I can to help unite the world, to try to bring peace and hope to all the peoples of the world? Have I done enough?

Ask yourselves that question in your homes—and in this hall tonight. Have we, each of us, all done all we can do? Have we done enough?

We may well be living in the time foretold many years ago when it was said: "I call heaven and earth to record this day against you, that I have set before you life and death, blessing and cursing: therefore choose life, that both thou and thy seed may live."

This generation of the world must choose: destroy or build, kill or aid, hate or understand. We can do all these things on a scale that has never been dreamed of before.

Well, we will choose life. And so doing, we will prevail over the enemies within man, and over the natural enemies of all mankind.

Declaration of Independence from the War in Vietnam (1967)

Martin Luther King, Jr.

Over the past two years, as I have moved to break the betrayal of my own silences and to speak from the burnings of my own heart, as I have called for radical departures from the destruction of Vietnam, many persons have questioned me about the wisdom of my path. At the heart of their concerns this query has often loomed large and loud: Why are *you* speaking about the war, Dr. King? Why are *you* joining the voices of dissent? Peace and civil rights don't mix, they say. Aren't you hurting the cause of your people, they ask. And when I hear them, though I often understand the source of their concern, I am nevertheless greatly saddened, for such questions mean that the inquirers have not really known me, my commitment or my calling. Indeed, their questions suggest that they do not know the world in which they live.

In the light of such tragic misunderstanding, I deem it of signal importance to try to state clearly why I believe that the path from Dexter Avenue Baptist Church—the church in Montgomery, Alabama, where I began my pastorage—leads clearly to this sanctuary tonight.

I come to this platform to make a passionate plea to my beloved nation. This speech is not addressed to Hanoi or to the National Liberation Front. It is not addressed to China or to Russia.

Nor is it an attempt to overlook the ambiguity of the total situation and the need for a collective solution to the tragedy of Vietnam. Neither is it an attempt to make North Vietnam or the National Liberation Front paragons of virtue, nor to overlook the role they can play in a successful resolution of the problem. While they both may have justifiable reasons to be suspicious of the good faith of the United States, life and history give eloquent testimony to the fact that conflicts are never resolved without trustful give and take on both sides.

Tonight, however, I wish not to speak with Hanoi and the NLF, but rather to my fellow Americans who, with me, bear the greatest responsibility in ending a conflict that has exacted a heavy price on both continents.

Since I am a preacher by trade, I suppose it is not surprising that I have seven major reasons for bringing Vietnam into the field of my moral vision. There is at the outset a very obvious and almost facile connection between the war in Vietnam and the struggle I, and others, have been waging in America. A few years ago there was a shining moment in that struggle. It seemed as if there was a real promise of hope for the poor—both black and white—through the Poverty Program. Then came the buildup in Vietnam, and I watched the program broken and eviscerated as if it were some idle political plaything of a society gone mad on war, and I knew that America would never invest in the necessary funds or energies in rehabilitation of its poor so long as Vietnam continued to draw men and skills and money like some demonic, destructive suction tube. So I was increasingly compelled to see the war as an enemy of the poor and to attack it as such.

Perhaps the more tragic recognition of reality took place when it became clear to me that the war was doing far more than devastating the hopes of the poor at home. It was sending their sons and their brothers and their husbands to fight and to die in extraordinarily high proportions relative to the rest of the population. We were taking the young black men who had been crippled by our society and sending them 8000 miles away to guarantee liberties in Southeast Asia that they had not found in Southwest Georgia and East Harlem. So we have been repeatedly faced with the cruel irony of watching Negro and white boys on TV screens as they kill and die together for a nation that has been unable to seat them together in the same schools. So we watch them in brutal solidarity burning the huts of a poor village, but we realize that they would never live on the same block in Detroit. I could not be silent in the face of such cruel manipulation of the poor.

My third reason grows out of my experience in the ghettos of the north over the last three years—especially the last three summers. As I have walked among the desperate, rejected, and angry young men, I have told them that Molotov cocktails and rifles would not solve their problems. I have tried to offer them my deepest compassion while maintaining my conviction that social change comes most meaningfully through nonviolent action. But, they asked, what about Vietnam? They asked if our own nation wasn't using massive doses of violence to solve its problems, to bring about the changes it wanted. Their questions hit home, and I knew that I could never again raise my voice against the violence of the oppressed in the ghettos without having first spoken clearly to the greatest purveyor of violence in the world today—my own government. . . .

And as I ponder the madness of Vietnam, my mind goes constantly to the people of that peninsula. I speak now not of the soldiers of each side, not of the junta in Saigon, but simply of the people who have been living under the curse of war for almost three continuous decades. I think of them, too, because it is clear to me that there will be no meaningful solution there until some attempt is made to know them and their broken cries.

They must see Americans as strange liberators. The Vietnamese proclaimed their own independence in 1945 after a combined French and Japanese occupation and before the Communist revolution in China. Even though they quoted the American Declaration of Independence in their own document of freedom, we refused to recognize them. Instead, we decided to support France in its reconquest of her former colony.

Our government felt then that the Vietnamese people were not "ready" for independence, and we again fell victim to the deadly western arrogance that has poisoned the international atmosphere for so long. With that tragic decision, we rejected a revolutionary government seeking self-determination, and a government that had been established not by China (for whom the Vietnamese have no great love) but by clearly indigenous forces that included some Communists. For the peasants, this new government meant real land reform, one of the most important needs in their lives.

For nine years following 1945 we denied the people of Vietnam the right of independence. For nine years we vigorously supported the French in their abortive effort to recolonize Vietnam.

Before the end of the war we were meeting 80 percent of the French war costs. Even before the French were defeated at Dien Bien Phu, they began to despair of their reckless action, but we did not. We encouraged them with our huge financial and military supplies to continue the war even after they had lost the will to do so.

After the French were defeated it looked as if independence and land reform would come again through the Geneva agreements. But instead there came the United States, determined that Ho [Chi Minh] should not unify the temporarily divided nation, and the peasants watched again as we supported one of the most vicious modern dictators—our chosen man, Premier [Ngo Dinh] Diem. The peasants watched and cringed as Diem ruthlessly routed out all opposition, supported their extortionist landlords and refused even to discuss reunification with the north. The peasants watched as all this was presided over by U.S. influence and then by increasing numbers of U.S. troops who came to help quell the insurgency that Diem's methods had aroused. When Diem was overthrown they may have been happy, but the long line of military dictatorships seemed to offer no real change—especially in terms of their need for land and peace.

The only change came from America as we increased our troop commitments in support of governments that were singularly corrupt, inept, and without popular support. All the while, the people read our leaflets and received regular promises of peace and democracy—and land reform. Now they languish under our bombs and consider us—not their fellow Vietnamese—the real enemy. They move sadly and apathetically as we herd them off the land of their fathers into concentration camps where minimal social needs are rarely met. They know they must move or be destroyed by our bombs. So they go.

They watch as we poison their water, as we kill a million acres of their crops. They must weep as the bulldozers destroy their precious trees. They wander into the hospitals, with at least twenty casualties from American firepower for each Viet Cong-inflicted injury. So far we may have killed a million of them—mostly children.

What do the peasants think as we ally ourselves with the landlords and as we refuse to put any action into our many words concerning land reform? What do they think as we test out our latest weapons on them, just as the Germans tested out new medicine and new tortures in the concentration camps of Europe? Where are the roots of the independent Vietnam we claim to be building?

Now there is little left to build on—save bitterness. Soon the only solid physical foundations remaining will be found at our military bases and in the concrete of the concentration camps we call "fortified hamlets." The peasants may well wonder if we plan to build our new Vietnam on such grounds as these. Could we blame them for such thoughts? We must speak for them and raise the questions they cannot raise. These too are our brothers.

Perhaps the more difficult but no less necessary task is to speak for those who have been designated as our enemies. What of the NLF—that strangely anonymous group we call VC or Communists? What must they think of us in America when they realize that we permitted the repression and cruelty of Diem that helped to bring them into being as a resistance group in the south? How can they believe in our integrity when now we speak of "aggression from the north" as if there were nothing more essential to the war? How can they trust us when now we charge *them* with violence after the murderous reign of Diem, and charge *them* with violence while we pour new weapons of death into their land?

How do they judge us when our officials know that their membership is less than 25 percent Communist and yet insist on giving them the blanket name? What must they be thinking when they know that we are aware of their control of major sections of Vietnam and yet we appear ready to allow national elections in which this highly organized political parallel government will have no part? They ask how we can speak of free elections when the Saigon press is censored and controlled by the military junta. And they are surely right to wonder what kind of new government we plan to help form without them—the only party in real touch with the peasants. They question our political goals, and they deny the reality of a peace settlement from which they will be excluded. Their questions are frighteningly relevant.

Here is the true meaning and value of compassion and nonviolence—when it helps us to see the enemy's point of view, to hear his questions, to know of his assessment of ourselves. For from his view we may indeed see the basic weaknesses of our own condition, and if we are mature, we may learn and grow and profit from the wisdom of the brothers who are called the opposition.

So, too, with Hanoi. In the north, where our bombs now pummel the land, and our mines endanger the waterways, we are met by a deep but understandable mistrust. In Hanoi are the men who led the nation to independence against the Japanese and the French, the men who sought membership in the French commonwealth and were betrayed by the weakness of Paris and the willfulness of the colonial armies. It was they who led a second struggle against French domination at tremendous costs, and then were persuaded at Geneva to give up, as a temporary measure, the land they controlled between the thirteenth and seventeenth parallels. After 1954 they watched us conspire with Diem to prevent elections that would have surely brought Ho Chi Minh to power over a united Vietnam, and they realized they had been betrayed again.

When we ask why they do not leap to negotiate, these things must be remembered. Also, it must be clear that the leaders of Hanoi considered the presence of American troops in support of the Diem regime to have been the initial military breach of the Geneva agreements concerning foreign troops, and they remind us that they did not begin to send in any large number of supplies or men until American forces had moved into the tens of thousands.

Hanoi remembers how our leaders refused to tell us the truth about the earlier North Vietnamese overtures for peace, how the president claimed that none existed when they had clearly been made. Ho Chi Minh has watched as America has spoken of peace and built up its forces, and now he has surely heard the increasing international rumors of American plans for an invasion of the north. Perhaps only his sense of humor and irony can save him when he hears the most powerful nation of the world speaking of aggression as it drops thousands of bombs on a poor, weak nation more than 8000 miles from its shores.

At this point, I should make it clear that while I have tried here to give a voice to the voiceless of Vietnam and to understand the arguments of those who are called enemy, I am as deeply concerned about our own troops there as anything else. For it occurs to me that what we are submitting them to in Vietnam is not simply the brutalizing process that goes on in any war where armies face each other and seek to destroy. We are adding cynicism to the process of death, for our troops must know after a short period there that none of the things we claim to be fighting for   are really involved. Before long they must know that their government has sent them into a struggle among Vietnamese, and the more sophisticated surely realize that we are on the side of the wealthy and the secure while we create a hell for the poor.

Somehow this madness must cease. I speak as a child of God and brother to the suffering poor of Vietnam and the poor of America who are paying the double price of smashed hopes at home and death and corruption in Vietnam. I speak as a citizen of the world, for the world as it stands aghast at the path we have taken. I speak as an American to the leaders of my own nation. The great initiative in this war is ours. The initiative to stop must be ours. . . .

If we continue, there will be no doubt in my mind and in the mind of the world that we have no honorable intentions in Vietnam. It will become clear that our minimal expectation is to occupy it as an American colony, and men will not refrain from thinking that our maximum hope is to goad China into a war so that we may bomb her nuclear installations.

The world now demands a maturity of America that we may not be able to achieve. It demands that we admit that we have been wrong from the beginning of our adventure in Vietnam, that we have been detrimental to the life of her people. . . .

There is something seductively tempting about stopping there and sending us all off on what in some circles has become a popular crusade against the war in Vietnam. I say we must enter that struggle, but I wish to go on now to say something even more disturbing. The war in Vietnam is but a symptom of a far deeper malady within the American spirit, and if we ignore this sobering reality we will find ourselves organizing clergy- and laymen-concerned committees for the next generation. We will be marching and attending rallies without end unless there is a significant and profound change in American life and policy.

In 1957 a sensitive American official overseas said that it seemed to him that our nation was on the wrong side of a world revolution. During the past ten years we have seen emerge a pattern of suppression which now has justified the presence of U.S. military "advisers" in Venezuela. The need to maintain social stability for our investments accounts for the counterrevolutionary action of American forces in Guatemala. It tells why American helicopters are being used against guerrillas in Colombia and why American napalm and green beret forces have already been active against rebels in Peru. With such activity in mind, the words of John F. Kennedy come back to haunt us. Five years ago he said, "Those who make peaceful revolution impossible will make violent revolution inevitable."

Increasingly, by choice or by accident, this is the role our nation has taken— by refusing to give up the privileges and the pleasures that come from the immense profits of overseas investment.

I am convinced that if we are to get on the right side of the world revolution, we as a nation must undergo a radical revolution of values. When machines and computers, profit and property rights are considered more important than people, the giant triplets of racism, materialism, and militarism are incapable of being conquered.

A true revolution of values will soon cause us to question the fairness and justice of many of our past and present policies. True compassion is more than flinging a coin to a beggar; it is not haphazard and superficial. It comes to see that an edifice that produces beggars needs restructuring. A true revolution of values will soon look easily on the glaring contrast of poverty and wealth. With righteous indignation, it will look across the seas and see individual capitalists of the west investing huge sums of money in Asia, Africa, and South America, only to take the profits out with no concern for the social betterment of the countries, and say: "This is not just." It will look at our alliance with the landed gentry of Latin America and say: "This is not just." The western arrogance of feeling that it has everything to teach others and nothing to learn from them is not just. A true revolution of values will lay hands on the world order and say of war: "This way of settling differences is not just." This business of burning human beings with napalm, of filling our nation's homes with orphans and widows, of injecting poisonous drugs of hate into the veins of peoples normally humane, of sending men home from dark and bloody battlefields physically handicapped and psychologically deranged, cannot be reconciled with wisdom, justice, and love. A nation that continues year after year to spend more money on military defense than on programs of social uplift is approaching spiritual death.

Legacies: The Monument Controversy

A decade after the last American soldiers left Vietnam in 1973, Americans quarreled again over Vietnam—this time over the shape of a monument to commemorate the war dead. The two most prominent proposals were for a sunken wall, inscribed with the names of the dead, and a statue of combat soldiers. The upshot was a memorial incorporating both designs; the statue is positioned a short distance from the wall. What was at stake in the monument controversy? What, in your opinion, is the message or theme of each design, and how might each represent a distinct understanding of the war?

The Wall Portion of the Vietnam Memorial. The design by Yale University architecture student Maya Ying Lin was the winning entry in an open competition. *National Park Service.*

The Statue Portion of the Vietnam Memorial. Sculpted by Frederick Hart.
National Park Service.

The Counterculture
The Haight-Ashbury

Charles Perry

The Haight-Ashbury is a San Francisco neighborhood, defined by the inter-
section of Haight and Ashbury streets. In the early 1960s, the area began to
attract beats and other nonconformists, but it was not until January 1967,
when some 20,000 young people came to the Haight to hear poet Allen Gins-
berg and LSD advocate Timothy Leary at the "World's First Human Be-In,"
that the Haight became a mecca for the burgeoning counterculture of hippies
and flower children.

In the selection that follows, Charles Perry looks back on the Full Moon
Public Celebration, an event that took place late in 1966. It featured the over-
sized human puppets of the Mime Troupe and a commune called the Diggers,
a group known for its efforts to distribute free food. What does the event re-
veal about the values and methods of the Haight-Ashbury counterculture? Do
you think this "celebration" made some valid point?

The Diggers' event, a Full Moon Public Celebration, had been publicized with
1,500 leaflets passed out in the Haight and another 500 in Berkeley, despite the
Diggers' distaste for the grandstanding habits of the Berkeley left. An experiment
in psychedelico-political theater and provocation, it started earlier than the other
two events and lasted, for some participants, much longer.

At 5:30 everyone in the Mime Troupe who had shown interest in the plans
gathered at the corner of Haight and Masonic, where the leaflets, headlined "PUB-
LIC NONSENSE NUISANCE PUBLIC ESSENCE NEWSENSE PUBLIC NEWS," had announced
the "intersection game" was to begin. The Mime Troupers brought the thirteen-
foot-square wooden frame, painted yellow, that they called the Frame of Reference
and through which people were required to walk before being served at the daily
free feeds. They also had the Mime Troupe's eight-foot-high satirical puppets. By
six o'clock about 600 people had gathered, including school-age trick-or-treaters
as well as hippies.

The Diggers passed out about 75 six-inch replicas of the Frame of Reference
to be worn around the neck. They performed a playlet called "Any Fool on the
Street" and then started the intersection game, which was, as it were, a lesson in
the Digger theory of ownership of the streets. Leaflets gave instructions to walk
across the intersection in different directions to form various polygons, relying on
the pedestrian's right of way over automobiles: "Don't wait don't walk (umbrella
step, stroll, cake walk, sombersault, finger-crawl, squat-jump, pilgrimage, Phylly
dog, etc.)." It was a translation of the civil rights sit-in technique directed against
automobiles, and at the same time a terrific goof.

While people were walking in close order around the sidewalks and tying up traffic, an improvised puppet drama was going on around the Frame of Reference. The giant puppets, operated with one man holding the puppet up by a pole and speaking its lines while another manipulated its hands with sticks, were bobbing absurdly around the frame and urging people to walk through it. Police had responded to the traffic jam in progress with five patrol cars and a paddy wagon. While some of the policemen began directing traffic and ordering people to clear the sidewalks, one cop, looking for the perpetrators of the nuisance, somehow decided to address the eight-foot-tall puppets.

"You are creating a public nuisance," he called up to the puppet. "We warn you that if you don't remove yourselves from the area you'll be arrested for blocking a public thoroughfare."

Street theater! Heaven-sent absurdity! The Diggers answered back through the puppets. "Who is the public?" asked one puppet, bobbing its gawky arms around.

"I couldn't care less," replied the policeman. "I'll take you in. Now move on."

"I declare myself public—I am a public," insisted the puppet. "The streets are public, the streets are free." Then the puppets walked on and the four Diggers operating them, plus the sculptor who had made them, were arrested as warned. About 200 of the crowd were still present to boo the proceedings. From inside the paddy wagon, where the puppets had with difficulty been stuffed beside their human agents, the Diggers could be heard chanting, "Public, public," on their way to Park Station.

The intersection game started up again in the meanwhile, and somebody set up a phonograph for dancing. The police drifted off about twenty minutes later, the main body of the crowd having dispersed. At Park Station the Diggers were booked for creating a public nuisance. They spent part of the night in their cells singing Mime Troupe warm-up songs such as the Italian Communist anthem "Avanti Popolo," and were released the next morning without bail.

The bust endeared the Diggers to the Berkeley left even more. The following week the *Barb* not only reported on the Halloween event but began listing the daily free food in its entertainment and events column. It reported that the Diggers were renovating a garage on Page Street where they would open a "24-hour Frame of Reference exchange" to facilitate community self-help projects, all free. The Diggers were also going to develop sewing and babysitting circles, said the *Barb,* and planned to challenge the paramilitary right-wing Minutemen to a football game. The *Barb* soon reprinted "The Ideology of Failure" and "In Search of a Frame" from the Digger broadsides.

The Counterculture: A Photo Essay

Many Americans formed opinions of the hippie counterculture by looking at photos like the ones in this visual essay. For the moment, imagine that you are a forty-year-old factory worker, trying to make some sense of the countercul-ture from these photographs. What can be learned from the pictures? What conclusions might one draw about countercultural attitudes toward gender? the body? the Vietnam war? patriotism? Should all or most of the young peo-ple in these photographs be labeled hippies? the counterculture? Why or why not?

A San Francisco hippie, peddling a local newspaper, 1967.
National Archives.

A 1970 rally against the Vietnam war, Bryant Park, New York City, April 1970.
National Archives.

Cornell University freshmen, 1972.
National Archives.

SUGGESTIONS FOR VIEWING AND LISTENING

Bonnie and Clyde (1967)
Heroic antiheroes, seeking freedom in a confining world. But, otherwise, what do Bonnie and Clyde stand for?

Midnight Cowboy (1969)
City and country.

Bob & Carol & Ted & Alice (1969)
Sexual revolution in the soulless suburbs.

Fifth Dimension, "Aquarius" (1969)
A mythic mix of rock and soul; a fantasy never realized.

Scott MacKenzie, "San Francisco (Be Sure to Wear Flowers in Your Hair)" (1967)
Middle-class schlock, but revealing of the optimism and experimentalism of the counterculture.

Jimi Hendrix, "Star Spangled Banner" (1969) (performed at Woodstock)
Sounds of Vietnam.

CHAPTER 6

From Civil Rights to Black Power

The Eisenhower consensus was not irrevocably shattered until mid-decade. The cause was race. During the 1950s, efforts by blacks to achieve integration had followed mainly legal channels, culminating in 1954 in the Supreme Court's decision in *Brown v. Board of Education* of Topeka, Kansas, declaring racial segregation in the public schools to be unconstitutional. Gradually, though, black activists adopted the tactics of direct action. In February 1960, black and white college students conducted sit-ins at the segregated lunch counters of Woolworth dime stores in Durham and Greensboro, North Carolina; in 1961 and 1962, "freedom rides" took activists into segregated bus terminals across the deep south. In August 1963, Martin Luther King, Jr., brought the civil rights movement north and sharpened its political content with an enormous march on the nation's capital. And during the "Freedom Summer" of 1964, hundreds of white college students joined black activists in Mississippi in a courageous effort to register black voters and shed light on the racist methods by which Mississippi blacks were excluded from suffrage.

This more confrontational approach made possible the legal revolution of the mid-1960s. On July 2, 1964—less than two weeks after the murder of three young Freedom Summer activists—President Lyndon Johnson signed the 1964 Civil Rights Act. Ironically, the law's voter-registration provisions were not strong enough to eliminate abuses in Mississippi and other southern states. But a provision prohibiting discrimination in employment based on race (and sex) would prove enormously important. Early the following year, a series of marches and demonstrations in Selma and Montgomery, Alabama—culminating in the arrest of King, the death of a young black activist and a white volunteer from Detroit, and the televised assault by state troopers on some 600 marchers—provided the impetus for the Voting Rights Act of 1965. Actively championed by Johnson, the law suspended literacy tests and transferred enforcement powers from the judiciary to the executive branch. Its impact was immediate and lasting. Black registration in Mississippi, for example, climbed from 7 percent in 1964 to 60 percent four years later.

In the meantime, Johnson and the Eighty-ninth Congress produced a cascade of new social programs that constituted the last great reform movement of the twentieth century. Johnson's vision went well beyond the goals of integration and elimination of discrimination that had occupied the civil rights movement since World War II. Based on an economy that seemed able to generate an unending supply of tax revenues, his Great Society promised the elimination of poverty, medical care for the aged and poor, job training for young adults, federal aid for Head Start and other programs of "compensatory education." Although the Great Society was not designed specifically to aid black Americans, its focus on those in poverty meant they benefitted disproportionately. Despite growing competition for funds from the burgeoning war in Vietnam, these programs probably had some cumulative impact on the black standard of living. Between 1966, when the Eighty-ninth Congress completed its work, and 1969, the percentage of blacks living in poverty declined from 41.8 to 32.2—roughly where it remained for the next twenty years.

Despite—or because of—this political attention, young black leaders began to question whether integration was an appropriate goal. They began to talk of Black Power and black pride. In 1965, whites who had gone south to work and protest were being forced out of the Student Non-violent Coordinating Committee (SNCC) and other organizations by blacks who wanted control over the movement. It was in this setting, too, that two of the most charismatic black leaders, Malcolm X and Martin Luther King, Jr., were shot to death. King objected to the anti-white connotations of the slogan Black Power, but he applauded efforts to build racial pride among African-Americans. When he died in Memphis in 1968, he was in the city to support the economic demands of the city's garbage workers, not to talk about integration.

This simple narrative contains no answers, but it can be useful in formulating some of the questions that emerged from this critical chapter in American history. Why did African-Americans of the mid-1960s—or, at least, a significant minority among them—move from a framework of civil rights to one of Black Power? Was the change a reasonable response to historical conditions—an appropriate next step in the long march toward equality—or a tragic blunder, destined to separate African-Americans from the American mainstream and to leave the movement isolated and vulnerable? Was Black Power the cutting edge of the multicultural society, or an early sign of what one historian has labeled the "disuniting of America"?

INTERPRETIVE ESSAY

William L. Van Deburg

Why Was There a Black Power Movement?

Until that day in June 1966, when the national news media reported Stokely Carmichael's use of the term "Black Power," white Americans were quite sure they knew what black Americans wanted. They wanted what most white Americans had: decent jobs, the right to vote, freedom from violence and intimidation, access to schools, neighborhoods, restaurants, hotels—and the American dream. Perhaps blacks still wanted these things, but for many whites and even some blacks, Black Power provoked considerable anxiety. Black writer Jules Lester was not far off the mark when he wrote, "All the whites wanted to know was if Black Power was antiwhite and if it meant killing white folks." Vice President Hubert Humphrey, whose liberal credentials on the race issue were impeccable, spoke for many Americans when he linked the slogan with racism. "We must reject calls for racism," he said, "whether they come from a throat that is white or one that is black." At the NAACP, Roy Wilkins (who was black) was equally upset. "We will have none of this," he said. "It is the father of hatred and the mother of violence. Black power can mean in the end only black death."

The urban riots of 1967 confirmed for many the violent connotation of Black Power, yet by the end of the year the phrase was also being interpreted in less threatening ways. Martin Luther King, Jr., now understood Black Power as a call for black people to gather "legitimate" political and economic power to achieve "legitimate" goals. And Time *magazine argued that Black Power was more about black culture and black pride than violence or hostility. "This kind of Negro is not anti-white,"* Time *concluded. "He is pro-black."*

In the following selection, historian William L. Van Deburg explores the emergence of the idea of Black Power. Where did the slogan come from? What meaning or meanings did it have? What connections might exist between Black Power and the rap music of the 1980s and 1990s? between Black Power and Afro-centrism? Were the efforts of African-Americans to free themselves from white cultural assumptions likely to be successful in a society dominated by a white, racist mass media?

What is needed in our country is not an exchange of pathologies, but a change of the basis of society. . . . In Negro culture there is much of value for America as a

From William L. Van Deburg, *New Day in Babylon: The Black Power Movement and American Culture, 1965–1975* (Chicago: The University of Chicago Press, 1992). © 1992 by The University of Chicago.

whole. What is needed are Negroes to take it and create of it "the uncreated consciousness of their race." In doing so they will do far more, they'll help create a
more human American.

Ralph Ellison, 1944

In the fall of 1963, John A. Williams set out in search of America. Hoping to duplicate the success of John Steinbeck's "Travels with Charley" articles, the editors of
Holiday magazine assigned the black writer to travel about the land, taking the
pulse of the country. His findings, published as *This Is My Country Too* (1965), revealed that the national character had a split personality.

On the one hand, he was taken aback by the unexpected courtesy of most hotel
desk clerks. Although only twenty-nine states had laws forbidding discrimination
in public places, he was refused lodging only once in fifteen thousand miles of
travel. He found additional hope in Atlanta's booming economy which had begun
to provide equal opportunity for skilled workers, regardless of race. In Kentucky,
he nearly drove his car off the road upon sighting his first all-black telephone line
crew. Surprised and encouraged by many of his experiences, he wrote that people
"looked you right in the eye. And I liked that."

Nevertheless, it was obvious that the spirit of America continued to be troubled by the Afro-American presence. Upon entering the South, Williams was
warned to "watch your step, keep you tongue inside your head, and *remember
where you are.*" Confederate flags on license plates, souvenir Mammy dolls, and
black road gangs reinforced a message that was driven home when a New Orleans
bartender would serve him only through "the Nigger Window." But the problem
was nationwide. Regardless of locale, white Americans evidenced their inability to
relate to dark-skinned people as individuals. Williams complained that whenever
he was introduced as a writer someone invariably would rush up and exclaim,
"You're James Baldwin!" before his own name could be announced. On one occasion, a Montana gas station attendant assumed that the five-foot-eight-inch writer
was a member of the Harlem Globetrotters, who also were in town that day. Gaffes
such as these seemed harmless, even somewhat humorous, but their cumulative effect definitely took a toll. Although he supposed it a mark of progress to be mistaken for an athlete rather than an entertainer or a musician, Williams said that
both the direct and indirect insults he received during his travels angered him
greatly. "I never know just how effective my words are, or even if they are understood," he wrote. "A physical attack would have been better."

Williams' portrait of "the paradox that is America" ended with a paean to the
beauty of the land and a warning to its people: either live up to the country's egalitarian credos or "chip them from our lives altogether." He hoped that whites would
respond to the challenge. If not, the prognosis was grim. In Chicago, he had seen
pickets in the Loop protesting de facto segregation and urging Christmas shoppers
not to patronize white-owned stores. In Atlanta, he learned that civil rights leaders
were taking "terrible psychological punishment" as they tried to keep their constituents united under the banner of nonviolence. In Detroit, a boyhood friend
drove him through the black ghetto, noting that both joblessness and gun sales
were on the increase. "Any kind of trouble comes as a diversion," observed
Williams' host. "And if they can tie that in with striking a blow for freedom, it fits

even better." In Mississippi, he was told that it was going to get worse before it got better.

After gazing into this American looking glass, Williams concluded that "grim anarchy" was but one crisis away. The great majority of whites still had no intention of sharing the American dream with their Afro-American countrymen. At the same time, the black masses were becoming estranged from their traditional middle-class leaders. Their patience was wearing thin. A potentially volatile mixture was a-brewing.

Williams had assayed his subject correctly. At mid-decade the United States was at the crossroads. Increasingly, black and white lives dovetailed. In many places, the two communities had begun to prove that they could coexist and work together for the common good. Racial "firsts" were becoming commonplace. The barriers were falling. Why, then, was there need for a Black Power movement?

Williams suggested one possible answer: there were too many barriers of too many different kinds and they were toppling too slowly. Black people no longer were awe-inspired every time they learned that a Gale Sayers had been named Rookie of the Year or that a Patricia Harris had been given an ambassadorship. They wanted to know the time and place of their own triumph over both institutional racism and the burden of everyday insults. In this respect, when they chanted "Black Power," they actually were saying "me power," "us power." They were seeking release from the psychological baggage they bore as a minority people. This was a broad and swelling sentiment, difficult to encapsulate and easily misinterpreted.

Most accounts of Black Power's rise have failed to plumb the depths of this group feeling or to understand its connection to the sphere of culture. As a result, our understanding of the movement has been colored by the plethora of negatives associated with its political components. Disappointment and disillusionment have been permitted to reign supreme as causative forces. From this perspective, black history is understood as one continual sorrow song. The energizing, soul-satisfying aspects of psychological and cultural liberation remain in the background, giving the impression that they were tributary, not foundational to the movement's overall thrust. Such an opinion is unfortunate, because it divests the Afro-American experience of its vigor, joy, and enthusiasm for life. To obtain a more accurate view of the Black Power movement, the focus must shift. Positive aspects of personal and group empowerment need to be stressed. The militant sentiment of the late sixties has to be placed in an appropriate historical and cultural framework.

As a political slogan, the term "Black Power" entered the vocabulary of most Americans only after 16 June 1966. On that date, in Greenwood, Mississippi, an assembly of civil rights workers and reporters heard Stokely Carmichael declare, "The only way we gonna stop them white men from whuppin' us is to take over. We been saying freedom for six years and we ain't got nothin'. What we gonna start saying now is Black Power!" The audience responded immediately. "Black Power!" they roared, some six hundred strong. Seizing the moment, Carmichael's associate Willie Ricks jumped to the speaker's platform. "What do you want?" he yelled. "Black Power!" the audience shouted in unison, "Black Power! Black Power! Black Power!"

It was ironic, but somehow appropriate that this chant was raised in the very heartland of black powerlessness—in a state whose governor once quipped that NAACP stood for "niggers, alligators, apes, coon and possum" and in a county whose major newspaper likened Martin Luther King to Joseph Stalin. The black and white participants in the "March Against Fear" were challenging both institutionalized and psychological bonds as they sought to complete the 200-mile walk from Memphis (Tennessee) to Jackson (Mississippi) begun by civil rights veteran James Meredith. The man who had integrated the University of Mississippi in 1962 had been wounded by three rounds from a shotgun on 6 June 1966, one day after beginning his trek down Highway 51. Immediately, black leaders such as Martin Luther King, Jr. of the Southern Christian Leadership Conference (SCLC), Floyd McKissick of the Congress of Racial Equality (CORE), and Carmichael of the Student Non-violent Coordinating Committee (SNCC) rushed to the scene. They, too, were determined to show white Mississippians that black people no longer could be driven from the voting booths by white power. Through their combined efforts, Meredith hoped that blacks would come to understand that "the old order was passing, that they should stand up as men with nothing to fear."

But, by mid-June, Carmichael and like-minded members of SNCC and CORE had concluded that they would stand alone, outside the traditional interracial alliance with its emphasis on love and nonviolence. After June 16, SNCC's staff was instructed that Black Power was to be their rallying cry for the rest of the march. At roadside rallies, supporters of the new ideological stance vied with champions of "freedom now," the SCLC slogan, in stirring up the crowds. By the time the column of marchers reached Yazoo City some were chanting, "Hey! Hey! Wattaya know! White people must go—must go!" Others distributed newly printed Black Power leaflets and placards. For a growing number, only Black Power could prevent outrages such as the attempted murder of James Meredith. "Power," as Carmichael told King, "is the only thing respected in this world, and we must get it at any cost."

As the marchers assembled at the state capitol in Jackson for their final rally on June 26, the winds of change, already gusting mightily, approached gale force. King resurrected his dream of the March on Washington, affirming the notion that someday justice would become a reality for all Mississippians. Carmichael was more impatient, more strident. He told the eleven to fifteen thousand people in attendance that blacks should build a power base so strong that "we will bring [whites] to their knees every time they mess with us." Afterward, as if throwing down a symbolic gauntlet, he approached a white SCLC staffer and shot him between the eyes with a water pistol. The opening salvo of the Black Power era had been fired. . . .

Most textbook treatments of the Black Power movement have focused on disillusionment and despair as major goads to black activism. Afro-America's shift from civil rights to Black Power has been portrayed as a bleak descent into "pessimism and even cynicism." By the mid-sixties, the high hopes of earlier years had, for most, proven illusionary. It seemed that white society had determined never to concede complete equality to blacks. Their group aspirations thwarted by unemployment, poverty, and white intransigence, urban slum dwellers expressed their isolation and alienation by lashing out in the precipitous manner characteristic of frustrated but functionally powerless masses. Frustrated by the slow pace of progress, they "express[ed] their own sense of futility" by rejecting the integrationist ethic. The Black Revolution, it was said, emerged out of a "gloomy atmosphere" in which black people increasingly regarded themselves as doomed victims of modern-day neocolonialism.

Certainly, historians are correct in noting the factor of despair in their accounts of Black Power's genesis. The nature of prevailing intergroup power relationships make it imperative that black America's deep-seated frustration be included in any listing of causal factors. By the mid-sixties, many activists were at an intellectual impasse, perplexed and disillusioned. Some had begun to question whether the federal government ever could become an effective promoter and protector of civil equality. Others had lost faith in the ability of black moderates to spur renewal in the northern ghettos. Still others were becoming skeptical of the white liberals' value to the movement in the South. In black communities, both large and small, the pressure of individual and group frustration was building behind a barrier of seemingly insoluble problems. As John A. Williams recognized, both the nation and its black citizens stood at the crossroads on issues of civil rights profession, policy, and practice.

Disillusionment with the political process stemmed from the notion that the federal officials were not doing all that they could to ensure compliance with the directives included in recent civil rights and war on poverty legislation. Skeptics claimed that the Civil Rights Act of 1964 had created little more than the illusion of progress for Afro-Americans. Instances of non-compliance were highlighted by the January 1966 murder of Sammy Younge, a twenty-one-year-old college student and civil rights worker who was shot in the back of the head after demanding to use a whites-only restroom at a Tuskegee, Alabama, gas station. While some activists continued to demand an increased federal commitment to ending open discrimination, others considered the legislation basically unenforceable. New and increasingly sophisticated legal evasions, meaningless tokenism, doomed, half-hearted searches for "qualified" minorities, and the ongoing problem of de facto segregation guaranteed further frustration. Moreover, the Johnson administration's growing commitment to the Southeast Asian war and the uneasiness evidenced within the white liberal camp after the Watts riot seemed to bode ill for increased funding of civil rights enforcement. Certainly, the failure of the Mississippi Freedom Democratic party to win official recognition and the state's delegate votes at the 1964 Democratic National Convention convinced many that nothing of substance could be expected from supposed political friends.

Black activists also found fault with the Voting Rights Act of 1965, a landmark piece of legislation whose passage through Congress was hastened by news coverage of the violent southern response to the SCLC's Selma, Alabama, voting rights campaign. Initially, however, the act was heralded as the most important political civil rights law since the Fifteenth Amendment. Black expectations were raised by the law's provisions for limiting the use of literacy tests as a suffrage qualification and for employing federal examiners and observers to register voters and monitor electoral practices. Indeed, following the law's enactment, the examiners energetically sprang into action and within a year were working in forty counties through the affected states. Southern blacks responded by packing the examiners' offices as soon as they opened each day. On the first anniversary of the law's passage, some 46 percent of adult Afro-Americans could vote in the five Deep South states to which examiners had been assigned, thereby doubling the percentage from the previous year. By 1969, approximately one million blacks had affixed their names to the registration lists. Most had been signed up by local registrars whose willingness to abide by the provisions of the law was matched only by their eagerness to avoid federal intervention in their district. In this begrudging response lay the root of a continuing problem. . . .

Adding to this clouding of the communal spirit was a growing dissatisfaction with the civil rights program favored by black moderates. The movement of the early sixties had spurred unprecedented federal interest in black America's quest to gain equality before the law, but, said critics, its leaders were too eager to claim success. The nonviolent direct action thrust had not purged or reconstructed the black ghetto, which, despite all efforts at reform, seemed to replenish itself with new victims daily. If black Americans celebrated the fact that southern brothers and sisters no longer were forced to take seats in the rear of the bus, they also were well aware that years of marches, speeches and petitions had failed to end de facto segregation in the North. To some, it seemed as if the civil rights establishment had achieved only a series of partial, localized victories, was too easily placated with tokenism, and spent an inordinate amount of energy pandering to the fears of paternalistic white allies. It was felt that the moderates' program could do little to improve the daily lives of the impacted black masses because it had failed to make significant inroads against two key components of black oppression—dependence and powerlessness.

This litany of failures and shortcomings was accompanied by a reexamination (and eventual refutation) of the moderates' goal of societal integration. According to this long-established civil rights ideal, integration would offer blacks full and equal participation in American society. In a just social order dominant and submissive roles no longer would be assigned by race. Dissimilar peoples would banish fear and hatred, learning to accept and love one another. Such was the ideal. The reality, said critics, was that the moderates had been unable to achieve interracial community. Nevertheless, they continued to promote their threadbare ideology without acknowledging its potentially harmful implications. To a frustrated mid-sixties activist, integration appeared to be a synonym for cultural assimilation.

It was believed that a committed integrationist would barter racial identity for a nice house in the suburbs. Hoping to prove themselves to whites, they appeared anxious to part company with less upwardly mobile neighbors. Whenever they did, they solidified the impression that white society's conscienceless, materialist values were superior to their own. Finding it easier to mimic than to change white America, integrationists permitted the myth of the melting pot to obscure black America's colonial status. Certainly, said critics, their own self-hatred was less easily concealed.

According to this view, the integrationists' program led not to liberation or self-determination, but to continued dependency. Barring a reciprocal (and unlikely) movement of middle-class whites to the ghetto, their exodus was certain to deprive the urban poor of talent and leadership. The whole scheme seemed a subterfuge to maintain white supremacy. As "acceptable" blacks were siphoned off into the whites' world, they were encouraged to forget their roots. In this manner, and of its own volition, the storied black vanguard consigned black cultural distinctives to history's dust bin.

Activists joined this critique of integration with a denunciation of nonviolence. Here, again, their frustration stemmed from the moderates' inability to change majoritarian behavior. Although the early-sixties crusade of love and nonviolent direct action had mobilized blacks and had placed important issues before the nation, it had not put an end to white-initiated terrrorism. By the middle of the decade, some Afro-Americans were willing to believe white people incapable of love. When it had been proffered by civil rights workers, racists returned hatred. All too often, nonviolent love was unrequited and unrewarded. If this pattern continued, the determinedly nonviolent approach to the expansion of black rights would have to be redirected. The assumption that one's adversaries possessed a modicum of compassion and an incipient sense of justice was an essential component of any doctrine which held that the national conscience could be moved to support federal civil rights initiatives. Increasingly, this seemed a false hope, a sign of black, middle-class naïveté, a dangerous presupposition.

Among those who were searching for a fresh approach to group catharsis and empowerment, the doctrine of nonviolence became stigmatized as little more than a moral exercise. Whites, most assuredly, needed to partake of the doctrine. Blacks, however, were thought to stand in danger of being rendered psychologically impotent by it. For years, Afro-America's professions of love had been mistaken for weakness. As the decade progressed, it became clear to many that the civil rights moderates had failed to recognize this clear connection between their ideological beliefs and the movement's inability to change white behavior whenever actual power was at stake. By transforming nonviolence into a way of life, they were accused of closing the door to all other approaches and, thereby, stigmatizing their people as functionally impotent.

Given the moderates' attachment to traditional views and approaches, it is scarcely surprising that they found themselves skewered by activist rhetoric. . . . Even the hallowed name of Martin Luther King, Jr., was dragged through the dirt. According to black critics, "Reverend Dr. Chickenwing" was more a chump than a champ. His attempt to involve the black masses in the "sham ethic" of passive resistance caused him to act like a fool—perhaps to disguise the fact that he was an informer and agent for "white Intelligence." Collectively, the black civil rights establishment was characterized as an inept collection of "jive-ass leaders" who subconsciously were wedded to the notion that "niggers ain't shit." For a growing number of Afro-Americans the times were proving them to be as irrelevant as their program of integration and nonviolence.

In part, dissatisfaction with black moderates stemmed from the belief that they were controlled by white liberals. To many activists, this non-black component of the civil rights coalition was more than irrelevant. White liberals were "an affliction"—an assortment of aesthetes, do-gooders, and fence-sitters who tended to confuse influence with power. Although lacking in substance and preoccupied with form and technique, they nevertheless sought always to act as power brokers—"great white fathers and mothers" who were willing to lead, but not to follow in the journey down freedom road. Motivated by guilt, they considered themselves color-blind, but this, said critics, was self-deception. Often their creed seemed to amount to little more than a mandate that one black guest be present at every important social function. Normally, they viewed Afro-Americans as victims, problems, or statistics. Seldom were people of color considered true equals—and never as creators of a distinct, viable culture. This paternalism was thought to be rooted in a guilt complex which liberals sought to alleviate by making a moral witness against overt southern bigotry. Supposedly, participation in the movement served as group therapy, making liberal whites feel guiltless and giving meaning to their sterile, middle-class suburban lives.

By mid-decade, even those whites who had rejected mainstream values found it necessary to dodge the spite-filled barbs of disenchanted former allies. College students and other members of the white counterculture were said to be more concerned with fighting for the right to wear a beard and smoke marijuana than with promoting black empowerment. Hippies in particular were criticized for practicing the technique of avoidance rather than confrontation and for attempting to appropriate the cultural argot of black America. In reality, the white counterculture was composed of "suburbanite acne pickers" who held a romanticized view of the urban black lifestyle. Under their tattered, unkempt exteriors they were mirror images of the white middle class. Unlike the poor blacks whose culture they attempted to imitate, all the hippies had to do to reap the advantages of their class was to clean up, clear out their drug-fogged brains, and rejoin the ranks of the economically secure. Surely, said a growing number of black activists, no lasting coalition could be made with such people. . . .

Nowhere was the growing black alienation from the white liberal world made more evident than in the SNCC-sponsored Mississippi Summer Projects of 1964–65. Designed to dramatize and, hopefully, to ease the plight of disfranchised, illiterate, poverty-stricken southern blacks, the Freedom Summer program of voter registration, community organization, and educational enrichment was conceptualized as an interracial effort. It was felt that the active participation of large numbers of white volunteers from northern colleges would ensure media coverage, spur financial contributions, and bring new skills, energy, and idealism to the movement. SNCC leaders assumed that Mississippi officials could not easily thwart the will of such a large assemblage. Certainly, national public opinion would not tolerate physical assaults on the offspring of Middle America. Perhaps even the interest of the federal government could be piqued. As SNCC's James Forman noted, it was high time for the nation as a whole to feel the consequences of societal racism. "We could not bring all of white America to Mississippi," he later wrote. "But by bringing in some of its children as volunteer workers, a new consciousness would feed back into the homes of thousands of white Americans as they worried about their sons and daughters confronting 'the jungle of Mississippi. . . .' "

By the fall of 1965, there were those in SNCC who suspected that their white allies were becoming more trouble than they were worth. The students seemed prone to unnecessary risk-taking and their provocative behavior sometimes endangered both themselves and their black coworkers. Moreover, it was believed that some had ulterior motives for joining the movement. Rejected and cast out of their own society, such "misfits," "beatniks," and "leftovers" journeyed South to glorify self, to become martyrs, to act like "big wheels." Harsh feelings such as these contributed to the rise of separatist, Black Power sentiment among blacks active in the Mississippi Summer Projects. By the time of the Mississippi March Against Fear, many would echo the sentiments of SNCC's John Lewis: To be effective in its attempts to liberate black America the movement had to be "black-controlled, dominated, and led."

To attribute the use of this separatist spirit within SNCC to dissatisfaction with the northern volunteers is, however, to reveal only part of the story. Certainly, the failure to create a sympathetic and lasting bond of unity between the black and white civil rights workers was significant. Nevertheless, dwelling on the negative, on this failure in interpersonal relations, obscures the cultural roots of Black Power. In truth, the empowering spirit of blackness which came to characterize the late sixties movement was evident, in embryo, in the Freedom Schools and cultural enrichment programs which operated in Mississippi during the summers of 1964 and 1965.

That Freedom Summer educational thrust was diverse and broad-based. It had to be. Black Mississippians were information-poor. For generations they had been trapped in a conspiracy of silence and avoidance that had denied them accurate information about the world around and beyond them. Their political-awareness quotient was far too low. They needed to learn how to tap available legal and medical assistance resources. Both young and old had to advance in basic literacy and computational skills. Furthermore, these improvements in the area of self-expression had to be accompanied by a quantum jump in the level of group self-awareness and esteem. It was in this latter area that the Freedom Schools were particularly important.

A Freedom School stood for everything that the state's public schools discouraged—academic freedom, intellectual curiosity, diversity of thought. Here, highly motivated black and white teachers were free to modify traditional classroom techniques. No matter what their age, students were encouraged to be creative, to express their ideas openly and without fear, to experiment. They received remedial instruction in mathematics, foreign languages, chemistry, and biology, but their learning experience was much broader than this. It was far more than informational.

For many, the schools were a sort of mental revolution—an unlocking of previously forbidden or hitherto unknown doors. They discussed the prevailing power structure of the Deep South, making direct connections between past and present. A teacher might ask, for example, "Who do you know that is like Joseph Cinqué?" and then follow up with a discussion of more contemporary black "rebels" who dared challenge southern power relationships. In exploring literacy as a means of political expression, some students wrote letters to the editors of local papers, criticizing segregation. Others engaged in role-play, pretending they were congressional supporters of civil rights legislation. Still others explored their own and their family's history, concluding: "This way of livelihood is not much different from slavery."

Like the social sciences, the language and fine arts were employed in the cause of individual and group self-discovery. In the liberating atmosphere of the Freedom School, students sang "We Shall Overcome" in French. They produced mimeographed newspapers and playscripts which revealed that new birth was being given to the self-definition ethic. Like the editors of *Freedom's Journal,* America's first black weekly, the young black Mississippians maintained that for far too long "others have done our speaking for us." Galvanized by this notion, their literary and theatrical productions resonated with pride in themselves, as re-flected in the lives of black culture heroes. Visiting performing artists from the Free Southern Theatre and the Mississippi Caravan of Music deepened these feel-ings as they presented dramatic tableaux of black history and held workshops in folk dancing and African song. For young and old, teacher and student, the Free-dom School experience solidified the notion that Afro-Americans needed to appre-ciate their own culture rather than uncritically to adopt white cultural values. When, for example, teenage civil rights workers in Canton were greeted by a heck-ler who claimed that they "wouldn't even know what to do with [freedom]" if they had it, they immediately responded: "Well, we are on the road to getting it. When we do, we'll show you all what we'll do with it. Yes, we gonna eat in your restau-rant, drive your police cars, vote and everything else." In the minds of many, the "everything else" had come to include, at a minimum, establishing and maintain-ing cultural parity. This incipient black consciousness both contributed to the rise of the tensions which eventually split black workers from white and anticipated later, more fully developed, expressions of Black Power. If the Mississippi Sum-mer Projects served as models for the organizational efforts of antiwar and women's rights activists, the Freedom Schools can be said to have served as pre-cursors of the Black Studies thrust in education. The employment of cultural forms to invigorate and nourish black pride during the Freedom Summers foreshadowed the "political" utilization of music, art, drama, and literature during the late-sixties, early-seventies heyday of Black Power.

Ultimately it is to the cultural and psychological dimensions of Afro-American life that one must look in order to obtain a satisfactory answer to the question, Why was there a Black Power movement? Yes, frustration and disappointment with the performance of federal officials, black moderates, and white liberals could be found in most black communities at mid-decade. But it was not disillusionment alone that stoked the fires of Black Power. In large measure, the movement was fueled by a psychological antidote to despair that spread a positive, empowering sense of pride throughout black America. As with earlier manifestations of the black self-definition ethic, this liberating spirit often was forwarded through cul-tural forms and served to ease feelings of discouragement and personal failure.

No torrent of tears occluded the vision of Black Power advocates. They re-sponded to the demands of their times with spirit and vigor—with an irrepressible creative force. This approach to the black condition permitted them to express neg-ative feelings, to excoriate those individuals and institutions seen as promoters of despair. But it also allowed them to build for the future. Eventually, a positive psychological foundation was laid which contributed to a long-term rise in black self-esteem. It was this essentially positive sense of individual and group empowerment that had the greatest impact on black lives in recent years.

During the late sixties and early seventies, Black Power's psychological component most often was referred to as "black consciousness" or "the new blackness." Although defined in many different ways, its core assumptions and directives were as follows:

1. To become conscious of one's blackness was a healthy psychosocial development. It was to make a positive statement about one's worth as a person. By nurturing a "significant sense of self," an individual could hope to become self-reliant, highly motivated, and goal-oriented. For many, this change in adaptive behavior could be likened to one's first sexual encounter or to a religious conversion experience. As the entire range of human emotions was called into play, they would feel "alive for the first time." No longer in doubt as to their worth as human beings, race-conscious blacks felt comfortable in "speaking up, standing tall, and thinking big."

2. This black self-actualization was accompanied by a corresponding questioning and rejection of many normative values forwarded by the majoritarian society. Such disassociative behavior was deemed necessary because assumptions of white superiority were so pervasive. Traditionally, Afro-Americans had received only negative psychological feedback from whites. Throughout American history, people of color had been treated as inferiors and dependents, forced to conform to white expectations and obliged to obey white authority. Their contributions to the nation's life and culture either had been ignored or considered little more than unthinking reactions to white stimuli. They had been denied true personhood. Rejecting this long-term contempt and sociocultural domination, those infused with the new blackness were to engage in assertive behavior. As they distanced themselves from the white world and its harmful psychosocial assumptions, they would strive to shape and master their environment rather than to submit tamely to it.

3. After declaring themselves worthy of critiquing white values, champions of black consciousness were expected to work toward a reorientation of black life. Their mandate was to create new symbols and assumptions which would guide future generations. These were to be drawn largely from the black experience. Traditional color associations would be reversed: black skin color and physical features were to be considered good, not bad characteristics. Black lifestyles and distinctive cultural forms such as religious and musical expression would be affirmed, acclaimed, and elevated in status. In this respect, the new blackness encouraged Afro-Americans to seize control of their own self-image and to validate that image via a wide array of cultural productions. Empowered by black consciousness, they would construct a new, more functional value system emanating from and fully adapted to their unique African-American culture.

4. A thoroughgoing response to this call to "collective manhood" was deemed essential to the acquisition of Black Power. Here, especially, the concept of blackness was shown to be far more than a hypothetical psychological construct. Certainly, it was no more mystical than any other form of therapy designed to serve as a goad to action. To become self-directed, to be assertive, to take pride in heritage

was to remove the negative connotations of race which long had served as a constraining psychological and social force. Whites, of course, might still factor supposed racial limitations into their plans for continued societal domination, but black people endowed with black consciousness no longer would play by the old rules. Buoyed by their new, pragmatic philosophy, they would dare to be pro-black—to look, feel, be, and *do* black. As they progressed in these consciousness-raising efforts, they would be encouraged to know that they were fulfilling an earlier, previously unanswered mandate. It was Malcolm X who had asserted that the basic need of black Americans was not to reevaluate whites (whom they knew all too well), but to seek a reevaluation of *self.* By changing their minds about themselves—by formulating a positive racial identity through self-definition and self-assertion—individual blacks could speed the process of acquiring material manifestations of group-based Black Power. . . .

On the eve of the Black Power revolution, the various social science interpretations of race in American society tended to emphasize one of two dominant themes, or a combination of them. The first stressed the black community's Americanness. In this view the impact of racism upon personality was considered superficial and transitory—subordinate to psychodynamic forces that were presumed to be universal. The Afro-American was, in effect, "a white man in a black skin." Evidencing the degree to which belief in significant group distinctives had fallen into disrepute since the intellectual community's brush with Nazism during World War II, academic supporters of this viewpoint minimized the importance of racial and cultural differences. "The Negro," they asserted, "is only an American, and nothing else. He has no values and culture to guard and protect." Despite occasional talk of psychological identification with Africa, black people were no more African than they were Irish, Danish, or Italian. They were Americans—as was their culture. Their vices and virtues, allegiances and destinies were shared with other citizens. When such sociocultural variables diverged from the mainstream it was assumed that these "peculiarities" either were exaggerations or distortions of common American traits. It was held that these aberrant traits were occasioned by white proscription and black lower-class status. With the removal of societal impediments to progress, blacks would realize their highest aspirations. As last they would be fully assimilated, becoming truly "quintessential Americans."

A second view held that the Afro-American community abounded with psychological cripples which no nation willingly would seek to claim as its own. In this view, chronic social injustice had corroded and damaged the black personality. From their earliest years as slaves of white masters blacks had been trapped in a "tangle of pathology" which had left "mutilating marks" of oppression on the Afro-American psyche. In the harsh environment of plantation slavery, Africans were "stripped bare . . . psychologically" and socialized to believe that they were inferior human beings. In this dependency-breeding atmosphere, black people had every reason to doubt their own self-worth and every incentive to wallow in shame and self-hatred. As a result, by the time slavery ended, black Americans had been socialized so thoroughly to hate both themselves and each other that group cohesion was impossible to obtain.

Minority group culture was said to be of little help in forging black unity. It was held that the Africans' "aboriginal culture" had been destroyed by the transatlantic passage. As a substitute, African-Americans subsisted on "borrowed ideals" and "foreign culture traits." When joined with the ex-slaves' ever-present sense of shame, this frustrating obsession with whiteness produced an inner desolation that was basically unchanged into modern times. Indeed, as manifested in the nation's urban ghettoes, the black American's "wretched internal life" had become an open sore. With its high incidence of juvenile delinquency, narcotic addiction, homicide, illegitimacy, and female-headed households the poverty-ridden central city served as a veritable social science laboratory for the study of a variety of chronic, self-perpetuating pathologies. To many, the black ghetto was proof positive that slavery and racism had destroyed the Afro-American family, African cultural forms, black self-esteem, and social cohesion. In this context, reconstruction of urban America necessarily involved the rehabilitation of the black psyche—an undertaking that was deemed a monumental, if not impossible task.

Not content to view themselves and their people as either black Anglo-Saxons or case studies in pathology, black social scientists and other critics questioned the assumptions upon which contemporary interpretations of the black psyche were based. . . .

Eventually, black social scientists developed what for them was a more satisfactory approach to understanding the Afro-American condition. Owing a great deal to the conceptualizations of Frantz Fanon, the black psychiatrist from Martinique who had joined a career as physician/scholar with that of political militant in the service of the Algerian revolution, they undertook the task of promoting a therapy of collective identity for black America.

Fanon, whose *Les damnés de la terre (The Wretched of the Earth)* was written during the last year of his life and published shortly before he died of leukemia in 1961, provided both revisionist social scientists and "political" Black Power militants with an ideological frame of reference. Although not specifically formulated with regard to the condition of blacks in the United States, Fanon's sociopsychological analysis contained broad implications for "colonized" peoples everywhere. With only slight interpretive readjustment, Fanon's ideas were adapted to the American scene.

Chief among these understandings were that colonialism seldom was content merely to hold a people in its grip, "emptying the native's brain of all form and content." It had to distort, disfigure, and attempt to destroy a people's history and culture. If the colonial rulers succeeded in their unholy scheme, the colonized masses were certain to become slaves of "cultural imposition"—victims of white civilization who readily admitted the inferiority of their own national heritage. Accompanied by serious psycho-affective trauma, the dire resultant would be the creation of a nation of "individuals without an anchor, without a horizon, colorless, stateless, rootless." Fortunately, wrote Fanon, it was possible for the native to thwart the colonizer's will—to be overpowered but not tamed; treated as an inferior but not convinced of one's inferiority. It was the recurring dream of such oppressed peoples to "exchange the role of the quarry for that of the hunter." When the time was ripe, when their adversaries' guard was down, they would employ violence as a cleansing and empowering force.

In a cultural context, such action involved mocking and insulting the colonizers' values—eventually "vomit[ing] them up" in an affirmation of one's own cultural integrity and psychological strength. To Fanon, culture was at the very heart of the freedom struggle. Revolution itself was a cultural undertaking with national consciousness constituting "the most elaborate form of culture." It was his belief that creators of culture had to withdraw from the temptation to mummify their art even as they shunned colonial cooptation. Instead of attaching themselves to abandoned traditions, creative artists were urged to "use the past with the intention of opening the future." They were to throw themselves body, soul, and talent into the national liberation struggle.

With this clarion call to action ringing in their ears, mid-sixties black intellectuals began to speak of Afro-America as an internal colony at war with the forces of cultural degradation and assimilation. They began to create what Fanon called "a literature of combat."

Afro-American psychologists learned both from Fanon and from their immersion in the rapidly changing world in which they lived. They believed that mainstream psychology had contributed to the worldwide domination and subjugation of peoples of color. Indeed, this "scientific colonialism" which arrogantly presumed to know *all* about black self-conception was held to be the white colonizer's "single most powerful tool of oppression." Therefore, their aim was to formulate and establish new definitions, conceptual models, and standards of normative behavior that would be free from the controlling assumptions and values of the dominant culture. Viewing Afro-American distinctives as evidence of a non-pathological "uniqueness," they sought to help blacks gain self-esteem, reach their full human potential, and begin to "master [their] environment by changing it." To spur this process of self-actualization they urged their brothers and sisters to "become black," to ground themselves in the collective identity provided by their unique group history and culture.

As formulated by these champions of "psychic revisionism," black psychology was not derived from the negative aspects of being black in white America, but rather from the positive features of traditional African philosophy. In this view, there existed a remarkably strong cultural connection between the peoples of the African diaspora. West African culture had *not* been totally destroyed by slavery. On the contrary, key components of the African worldview had survived the slave experience. The slaves' enforced isolation in the plantation South had allowed them to retain much of what was termed an "African philosophical orientation. ". . .

During the Black Power era, the notion that black culture could play a major role in the militant freedom movement was widely accepted if less than extensively footnoted. Fanon's writings, in particular, were fundamental to the development of Black Power ideology. After *The Wretched of the Earth* was translated into English and published in the United States in 1965, the black psychiatrist was canonized by Afro-American activists. Praising Fanon's analysis of the consciousness and situation of colonized peoples as well as his teaching that the oppressed had to oppose the oppressor in order to "experience themselves as men," Eldridge Cleaver termed *The Wretched of the Earth* "an historical event"—the "Bible" of the black liberation movement. Fellow Black Panther Bobby Seale claimed to have read the book six times, employing it as a guide in distinguishing "jive" cultural nationalists from those militants who correctly would utilize culture in the service of black liberation. SNCC's James Forman adjudged the dissemination and study of Fanon's ideas to be one of the five major causes for the rise of modern black nationalism while Stokely Carmichael revered Fanon as a "Patron Saint." CORE's Roy Innis agreed, lauding his promotion of black values and his willingness to speak out against the psychological aggression of the colonizers.

During the late sixties the name and image of Fanon spread far beyond the leadership elite of the movement. By the end of 1970, his book had sold some 750,000 copies. As Dan Watts, editor of *Liberator* magazine noted: "Every brother on a rooftop can quote Fanon." By adopting variants of his conceptualization, these young militants not only identified with the colonized of the world and affirmed the notion that violence could spur mental catharsis, they also acknowledged that something uniquely their own—their distinctive Afro-American culture—very well might turn out to be the most essential weapon in the struggle for Black Power. At their teacher's urging and in harmony with their own internal muse, they sought to rekindle the flame of black self-definition and thereby break the bonds of Euro-American psychological and cultural domination. Like earlier champions of change, this generation of black activists had grown tired of having outsiders speak for them. Heirs of an important Afro-American intellectual tradition, they found their own voice in and through an empowering group culture.

In the context of Black Power activism, broad-based acceptance of these principles suggests that the movement itself can be conceptualized as a revolt of culture—a contemporary activist manifestation of the long-standing divergence between black and white American cultures; between each group's distinctive "shared way of life." Life the American Revolution or the Civil War, the Black Power movement was as cultural as it was political. It involved both a contest for the control of institutions and a clash of divergent "national" identities. Both the Euro- and Afro-American cultures provided a symbolic basis for group cohesion as well as a stimulus to political mobilization. Since each forwarded a specific set of rules meant to guide human behavior, it can be said that the Black Power years witnessed a spirited conflict over the rules that would be employed to govern black America. Black activists, purporting to represent both themselves and the less vocal members of their constituency, pitted their shared worldview and standards of conduct against those of the colonizers. Seeking self-definition through various types and degrees of separation from white society, they hoped to complete the irrepressible quest for independence in thought and deed that had been thwarted so many times in the past.

SOURCES

The Faces of Stokely Carmichael

These photographs of Stokely Carmichael were taken in 1966 and 1970. What point does each photograph make? How is Carmichael presented in each case? Taken together, what do they reveal about the impact of Black Power? about the late 1960s?

Stokely Carmichael, speaking from a flatbed truck in Will Rogers Park in Watts, a section of Los Angeles, in November 1966. He called on the people of Watts to form their own city and their own police force.
National Archives.

Stokely Carmichael, speaking in 1970. By the time this photograph was taken, Carmichael had adopted a Pan African perspective and moved to West Africa with his wife, Miriam Makeba.
UPI/Bettmann.

Riots

In the midst of the reform enthusiasm of 1965—only days after Johnson signed the Voting Rights Act, just two months after Johnson had promised to pursue "equality as a fact and result" for black Americans—an event took place that changed the face of American race relations. A minor summer incident involving police in Watts, a black section of Los Angeles, set off five days of looting and rioting that left thirty-four people dead. Within two years, over a hundred major urban riots took place in the nation's urban ghettos, some of them in large cities such as Newark and Detroit, but many others in smaller communities, including Grand Rapids, Michigan; Plainfield, New Jersey; Dayton, Ohio; and Tucson, Arizona.

In March 1968, the National Advisory Commission on Civil Disorders, appointed by President Johnson the previous July, issued its encyclopedic report on the disturbances. Two sections from the report are reprinted here. The first is a brief narrative of the Watts riot. The second profiles rioters and counterrioters in Newark and Detroit.

From these materials, what conclusions can one draw about the causes of the riots? Were the riots the product of desperate poverty? of increasing affluence? Were they, as some suggested at the time, simply "commodity riots," in which the central goal was to obtain the "things" that others had? Were the rioters making a political statement? Were they racially motivated? What links can you make between the riots and Black Power?

Report of the National Advisory Commission on Civil Disorders, 1968

In the spring of 1965, the Nation's attention shifted back to the South. When civil rights workers staged a nonviolent demonstration in Selma, Alabama, police and state troopers forcibly interrupted their march. Within the next few weeks racists murdered a white clergyman and a white housewife active in civil rights.

In the small Louisiana town of Bogalusa, when Negro demonstrators attacked by whites received inadequate police protection, the Negroes formed a self-defense group called the "Deacons for Defense and Justice."

As late as the second week of August, there had been few disturbances outside the South. But, on the evening of August 11, as Los Angeles sweltered in a heat wave, a highway patrolman halted a young Negro driver for speeding. The young man appeared intoxicated, and the patrolman arrested him. As a crowd gathered, law enforcement officers were called to the scene. A highway patrolman mistakenly struck a bystander with his billy club. A young Negro woman, who was accused of spitting on the police, was dragged into the middle of the street.

When the police departed, members of the crowd began hurling rocks at passing cars, beating white motorists, and overturning cars and setting them on fire. The police reacted hesitantly. Actions they did take further inflamed the people on the streets.

The following day, the area was calm. Community leaders attempting to mediate between Negro residents and the police received little cooperation from municipal authorities. That evening the previous night's pattern of violence was repeated.

Not until almost 30 hours after the initial flareup did window smashing, looting, and arson begin. Yet the police utilized only a small part of their forces.

Few police were on hand the next morning when huge crowds gathered in the business district of Watts, 2 miles from the location of the original disturbance, and began looting. In the absence of police response, the looting became bolder and spread into other areas. Hundreds of women and children from five housing projects clustered in or near Watts took part. Around noon, extensive firebombing began. Few white persons were attacked; the principal intent of the rioters now seemed to be to destroy property owned by whites in order to drive white "exploiters" out of the ghetto.

The chief of police asked for National Guard help, but the arrival of the military units was delayed for several hours. When the Guardsmen arrived, they, together with police, made heavy use of firearms. Reports of "sniper fire" increased. Several persons were killed by mistake. Many more were injured.

Thirty-six hours after the first Guard units arrived, the main force of the riot

Report of the National Advisory Commission on Civil Disorders, March 1, 1968 (Wash., D.C.: GPO, 1968).

had been blunted. Almost 4,000 persons were arrested. Thirty-four were killed and hundreds injured. Approximately $35 million in damage had been inflicted.

The Los Angeles riot, the worst in the United States since the Detroit riot of 1943, shocked all who had been confident that race relations were improving in the North, and evoked a new mood in Negro ghettos across the country. . . .

THE RIOT PARTICIPANT

It is sometimes assumed that the rioters were criminal types, overactive social deviants, or riffraff—recent migrants, members of an uneducated underclass, alienated from responsible Negroes, and without broad social or political concerns. It is often implied that there was no effort within the Negro community to attempt to reduce the violence.

We have obtained data on participation from four different sources:

- Eyewitness accounts from more than 1,200 interviews in our staff reconnaissance survey of 20 cities;
- Interview surveys based on probability samples of riot area residents in the two major riot cities—Detroit and Newark—designed to elicit anonymous self-identification of participants as rioters, counterrioters or noninvolved;
- Arrest records from 22 cities; and
- A special study of arrestees in Detroit.

Only partial information is available on the total numbers of participants. In the Detroit survey, approximately 11 percent of the sampled residents over the age of 15 in the two disturbance areas admittedly participated in rioting; another 20 to 25 percent admitted to having been bystanders but claimed that they had not participated; approximately 16 percent claimed they had engaged in counterriot activity; and the largest proportion (48 to 53) claimed they were at home or elsewhere and did not participate. However, a large proportion of the Negro community apparently believed that more was gained than lost through rioting, according to the Newark and Detroit surveys.

Greater precision is possible in describing the characteristics of those who participated. We have combined the data from the four sources to construct a profile of the typical rioter and to compare him with the counterrioter and the noninvolved.

The Profile of a Rioter

The typical rioter in the summer of 1967 was a Negro, unmarried male between the ages of 15 and 24. He was in many ways very different from the stereotype. He was not a migrant. He was born in the state and was a lifelong resident of the city in which the riot took place. Economically his position was about the same as his Negro neighbors who did not actively participate in the riot.

Although he had not, usually, graduated from high school, he was somewhat better educated than the average inner-city Negro, having at least attended high school for a time.

Nevertheless, he was more likely to be working in a menial or low status job as an unskilled laborer. If he was employed, he was not working full time and his employment was frequently interrupted by periods of unemployment.

He feels strongly that he deserves a better job and that he is barred from achieving it, not because of lack of training, ability, or ambition, but because of discrimination by employers.

He rejects the white bigot's stereotype of the Negro as ignorant and shiftless. He takes great pride in his race and believes that in some respects Negroes are superior to whites. He is extremely hostile to whites, but his hostility is more apt to be a product of social and economic class than of race; he is almost equally hostile toward middle class Negroes.

He is substantially better informed about politics than Negroes who were not involved in the riots. He is more likely to be actively engaged in civil rights efforts, but is extremely distrustful of the political system and of political leaders.

The Profile of the Counterrioter

The typical counterrioter, who risked injury and arrest to walk the streets urging rioters to "cool it," was an active supporter of existing social institutions. He was, for example, far more likely than either the rioter or the noninvolved to feel that this country is worth defending in a major war. His actions and his attitudes reflected his substantially greater stake in the social system; he was considerably better educated and more affluent than either the rioter or the noninvolved. He was somewhat more likely than the rioter, but less likely than the noninvolved, to have been a migrant. In all other respects he was identical to the noninvolved.

Characteristics of Participants

Race   Of the arrestees 83 percent were Negroes; 15 percent were whites. Our interviews in 20 cities indicate that almost all rioters were Negroes.

Age   The survey data from Detroit, the arrest records, and our interviews in 20 cities, all indicate that the rioters were late teenagers or young adults. In the Detroit survey, 61.3 percent of the self-reported rioters were between the ages of 15 and 24, and 86.3 percent were between 15 and 35. The arrest data indicate that 52.5 percent of the arrestees were between 15 and 24, and 80.8 percent were between 15 and 35.

Of the noninvolved, by contrast, only 22.6 percent in the Detroit survey were between 15 and 24, and 38.3 percent were between 15 and 35.

Sex   In the Detroit survey, 61.4 percent of the self-reported rioters were male. Arrestees, however, were almost all male—89.3 percent. Our interviews in 20 cities indicate that the majority of rioters were male. The large difference in proportion between the Detroit survey data and the arrestee figures probably reflects either selectivity in the arrest process or less dramatic, less provocative riot behavior by women.

Family Structure   Three sources of available information—the Newark survey, the Detroit arrest study, and arrest records from four cities—indicate a tendency for rioters to be single. The Newark survey indicates that rioters were single—56.2 percent—more often than the noninvolved—49.6 percent.

The Newark survey also indicates that rioters were more likely to have been divorced or separated —14.2 percent—than the noninvolved—6.4 percent. However, the arrest records from four cities indicate that only a very small percentage of those arrested fall into this category.

In regard to the structure of the family in which he was raised, the self-reported rioter, according to the Newark survey, was not significantly different from many of his Negro neighbors who did not actively participate in the riot. Twenty-five and five-tenths percent of the self-reported rioters and 23 percent of the noninvolved were brought up in homes where no adult male lived.

Region of Upbringing   Both survey data and arrest records demonstrate unequivocally that those brought up in the region in which the riot occurred are much more likely to have participated in the riots. The percentage of self-reported rioters brought up in the North is almost identical for the Detroit survey—74.4 percent— and the Newark survey—74 percent. By contrast, of the noninvolved, 36 percent in Detroit and 52.4 percent in Newark were brought up in the region in which the disorder occurred.

Data available from five cities on the birthplace of arrestees indicate that 63 percent of the arrestees were born in the North. Although birthplace is not necessarily identical with place of upbringing, the data are sufficiently similar to provide strong support for the conclusion.

Of the self-reported counterrioters, however, 47.5 percent were born in the North, according to the Detroit survey, a figure which places them between self-reported rioters and the noninvolved. Apparently, a significant consequence of growing up in the South is the tendency toward noninvolvement in a riot situation, while involvement in a riot, either in support of or against existing social institutions, was more common among those born in the North.

Residence   Rioters are not only more likely than the noninvolved to have been born in the region in which the riot occurred, but they are also more likely to have been long-term residents of the city in which the disturbance took place. The Detroit survey data indicate that 59.4 percent of the self-reported rioters, but only 34.6 percent of the noninvolved, were born in Detroit. The comparable figures in the Newark survey are 53.5 percent and 22.5 percent.

Outsiders who temporarily entered the city during the riot might have left before the surveys were conducted and therefore may be underestimated in the survey data. However, the arrest data, which are contemporaneous with the riot, suggest that few outsiders were involved: 90 percent of those arrested resided in the riot city, 7 percent lived in the same state, and only 1 percent were from outside the state. Our interviews in 20 cities corroborate these conclusions.

Income   In the Detroit and Newark survey data, income level alone does not seem to correlate with self-reported riot participation. The figures from the two cities are not directly comparable since respondents were asked for individual income in Detroit and family income in Newark. More Detroit self-reported rioters (38.6 percent) had annual incomes under $5,000 per year than the noninvolved (30.3 percent), but even this small difference disappears when the factor of age is taken into account.

In the Newark data, in which the age distributions of self-reported rioters and the noninvolved are more similar, there is almost no difference between the rioters, 32.6 percent of whom had annual incomes under $5,000, and the noninvolved, 29.4 percent of whom had annual incomes under $5,000.

The similarity in income distribution should not, however, lead to the conclusion that more affluent Negroes are as likely to riot as poor Negroes. Both surveys were conducted in disturbance areas where incomes are considerably lower than in the city as a whole and the surrounding metropolitan area. Nevertheless, the data show that rioters are not necessarily the poorest of the poor.

While income fails to distinguish self-reported rioters from those who were not involved, it does distinguish counterrioters from rioters and the noninvolved. Less than 9 percent of both those who rioted and those not involved earned more than $10,000 annually. Yet almost 20 percent of the counterrioters earned this amount or more. In fact, there were no male self-reported counterrioters in the Detroit survey who earned less than $5,000 annually. In the Newark sample there were seven respondents who owned their own homes; none of them participated in the riot. While extreme poverty does not necessarily move a man to riot, relative affluence seems at least to inhibit him from attacking the existing social order and may motivate him to take considerable risks to protect it.

Education   Level of schooling is strongly related to participation. Those with some high school education were more likely to riot than those who had only finished grade school. In the Detroit survey, 93 percent of the self-reported rioters had gone beyond grade school, compared with 72.1 percent of the noninvolved. In the Newark survey the comparable figures are 98.1 and 85.7 percent. The majority of self-reported rioters were not, however, high school graduates.

The counterrioters were clearly the best educated of the three groups. Approximately twice as many counterrioters had attended college as had the noninvolved, and half again as many counterrioters had attended college as rioters. Considered with the information on income, the data suggest that counterrioters were probably well on their way into the middle class.

Education and income are the only factors which distinguish the counterrioter from the noninvolved. Apparently, a high level of education and income not only prevents rioting but is more likely to lead to active, responsible opposition to rioting.

Employment The Detroit and Newark surveys, the arrest records from four cities, and the Detroit arrest study all indicate that there are no substantial differences in unemployment between the rioters and the noninvolved.

Unemployment levels among both groups were extremely high. In the Detroit survey, 29.6 percent of the self-reported rioters were unemployed; in the Newark survey, 29.7 percent; in the four-city arrest data, 33.2 percent; and in the Detroit arrest study, 21.8 percent. The unemployment rates for the noninvolved in the Detroit and Newark surveys were 31.5 and 19.0 percent.

Self-reported rioters were more likely to be only intermittently employed, however, than the noninvolved. Respondents in Newark were asked whether they had been unemployed for as long as a month or more during the last year. Sixty-one percent of the self-reported rioters, but only 43.4 percent of the noninvolved, answered, "yes."

Despite generally higher levels of education, rioters were more likely than the noninvolved to be employed in unskilled jobs. In the Newark survey, 50 percent of the self-reported rioters, but only 39.6 percent of the noninvolved, had unskilled jobs.

Attitudes About Employment The Newark survey data indicate that self-reported rioters were more likely to feel dissatisfied with their present jobs than were the noninvolved.

Only 29.3 percent of the rioters, compared with 44.4 percent of the noninvolved, thought their present jobs appropriate for them in responsibility and pay. Of the self-reported rioters, 67.6 percent, compared with 56.1 percent of the noninvolved, felt that it was impossible to obtain the kind of job they wanted. Of the self-reported rioters, 69 percent, as compared with 50 percent of the noninvolved, felt that racial discrimination was the major obstacle to finding better employment. Despite this feeling, surprising numbers of rioters (76.9 percent) responded that "getting what you want out of life is a matter of ability, not being in the right place at the right time."

Racial Attitudes The Detroit and Newark surveys indicate that rioters have strong feelings of racial pride, if not racial superiority. In the Detroit survey, 48.6 percent of the self-reported rioters said that they felt Negroes were more dependable than whites. Only 22.4 percent of the noninvolved stated this. In Newark, the comparable figures were 45 and 27.8 percent. The Newark survey data indicate that rioters wanted to be called "black" rather than "Negro" or "colored" and were somewhat more likely than the noninvolved to feel that all Negroes should study African history and languages.

To what extent this racial pride antedated the riot or was produced by the riot is impossible to determine from the survey data. Certainly the riot experience seems to have been associated with increased pride in the minds of many participants. This was vividly illustrated by the statement of a Detroit rioter:

Interviewer: You said you were feeling good when you followed the crowds?
Respondent: I was feeling proud, man, at the fact that I was a Negro. I felt like

I was a first-class citizen. I didn't feel ashamed of my race because of what they did.

Similar feelings were expressed by an 18-year-old Detroit girl who reported that she had been a looter:

Interviewer: What is the Negro then if he's not American?

Respondent: A Negro, he's considered a slave to the white folks. But half of them know that they're slaves and feel that they can't do nothing about it because they're just going along with it. But most of them they seem to get it in their heads now how the white folks treat them and how they've been treating them and how they've been slaves for the white folks.

Along with increased racial pride there appears to be intense hostility toward whites. Self-reported rioters in both the Detroit and Newark surveys were more likely to feel that civil rights groups with white and Negro leaders would do better without the whites. In Detroit, 36.1 percent of the self-reported rioters thought that this statement was true, while only 21.1 percent of the noninvolved thought so. In the Newark survey, 51.4 percent of the self-reported rioters agreed; 33.1 percent of the noninvolved shared this opinion.

Self-reported rioters in Newark were also more likely to agree with the statement, "Sometimes I hate white people." Of the self-reported rioters, 72.4 percent agreed; of the noninvolved, 50 percent agreed.

The intensity of the self-reported rioters' racial feelings may suggest that the recent riots represented traditional interracial hostilities. Two sources of data suggest that this interpretation is probably incorrect.

First, the Newark survey data indicate that rioters were almost as hostile to middle-class Negroes as they were to whites. Seventy-one and four-tenths percent of the self-reported rioters, but only 59.5 percent of the noninvolved, agreed with the statement, "Negroes who make a lot of money like to think they are better than other Negroes." Perhaps even more significant, particularly in light of the rioters' strong feelings of racial pride, is that 50.5 percent of the self-reported rioters agreed that "Negroes who make a lot of money are just as bad as white people." Only 35.2 percent of the noninvolved shared this opinion.

Second, the arrest data show that the great majority of those arrested during the disorders were generally charged with a crime relating to looting or curfew violations. Only 2.4 percent of the arrests were for assault and 0.1 percent were for homicide, but 31.3 percent of the arrests were for breaking and entering—crimes directed against white property rather than against individual whites.

Political Attitudes and Involvement Respondents in the Newark survey were asked about relatively simple items of political information, such as the race of prominent local and national political figures. In general, the self-reported rioters were much better informed than the noninvolved. For example, self-reported rioters were more likely to know that one of the 1966 Newark mayoral candidates was a Negro. Of the rioters, 77.1 percent—but only 61.6 percent of the noninvolved—

identified him correctly. The overall scores on a series of similar questions also reflect the self-reported rioters' higher levels of information.

Self-reported rioters were also more likely to be involved in activities associated with Negro rights. At the most basic level of political participation, they were more likely than the noninvolved to talk frequently about Negro rights. In the Newark survey, 53.8 percent of the self-reported rioters, but only 34.9 percent of the noninvolved, said that they talked about Negro rights nearly every day.

The self-reported rioters also were more likely to have attended a meeting or participated in civil rights activity. Of the rioters, 39.3 percent—but only 25.7 percent of the noninvolved—reported that they had engaged in such activity.

In the Newark survey, respondents were asked how much they thought they could trust the local government. Only 4.8 percent of the self-reported rioters, compared with 13.7 percent of the noninvolved, said that they felt they could trust it most of the time; 44.2 percent of the self-reported rioters and 33.9 percent of the noninvolved reported that they could almost never trust the government.

In the Detroit survey, self-reported rioters were much more likely to attribute the riot to anger about politicians and police than were the noninvolved. Of the self-reported rioters, 43.2 percent—but only 19.6 percent of the noninvolved—said anger against politicians had a great deal to do with causing the riot. Of the self-reported rioters, 70.5 percent, compared with 48.8 percent of the noninvolved, believed that anger against the police had a great deal to do with causing the riot.

Perhaps the most revealing and disturbing measure of the rioters' anger at the social and political system was their response to a question asking whether they thought "the country was worth fighting for in the event of a major world war." Of the self-reported rioters, 39.4 percent in Detroit and 52.8 percent in Newark shared a negative view. In contrast, 15.5 percent of the noninvolved in Newark shared this sentiment. Almost none of the self-reported counterrioters in Detroit—3.3 percent—agreed with the self-reported rioters.

Some comments of interviewees are worthy of note:

Not worth fighting for—if Negroes had an equal chance it would be worth fighting for.

Not worth fighting for—I am not a true citizen so why should I?

Not worth fighting for—because my husband came back from Vietnam and nothing had changed.

Panther Power: A Photo Essay

The photographs on these pages depict aspects of the Black Panther Party for Self-Defense, an organization founded by Huey Newton and Bobby Seale in October 1966. A ten-point platform issued at the time included standard demands for black self-determination, full employment, decent housing, and education, but also some that were not so standard, including the exemption of black men from military service, the release of all black men held in prisons and jails, and a United Nations supervised plebiscite in which "black colonial subjects" in the United States would determine their own destiny. The Black Panther party was perhaps best known for the open bearing of weapons, for a program of free breakfasts for schoolchildren, and for a series of violent confrontations with local police departments, most initiated by the police with the intent of destroying an organization considered dangerous.

What can be learned from these images about the Black Panther Party? about the Black Panthers' relationship to whites? What insight do the photographs offer into the Panthers' curious popularity? What in these photographs might have caused authorities the greatest alarm?

Original caption: Inside the "Liberation School" it's lunchtime and the youngsters practice their various salutes. 12/20/69.
UPI/Bettmann.

Original caption: SAN FRANCISCO. Two members of the Black Panther Party are met on steps of State Capital in Sacramento, May 2, 1967, by Police Lt. Ernest Holloway who informs them they will be allowed to keep their weapons as long as they cause no trouble and not disturb the peace. Earlier several members had invaded the Assembly chambers and had their guns taken away. Whatever else the Black Panther Party may be, it is a party dedicated to changing the existing order.
UPI/Bettmann.

Black Panther convention, Lincoln Memorial, June 1970.
Library of Congress.

Black Panther convention, Lincoln Memorial, June 1970.
Library of Congress.

SUGGESTIONS FOR VIEWING AND LISTENING

Guess Who's Coming to Dinner (1967)
Middle-class white woman informs her parents of her engagement to a black man. Sidney Poitier still in favor—but not for long.

Night of the Living Dead (1968)
Unstoppable flesh-eating zombies. Echoes of Vietnam and the civil rights movement, signs of the failure of religion.

Cotton Comes to Harlem (1970)
Black director Ossie Davis presents a black detective working in Harlem, all in a new "black" style.

Supremes, "Nothing but Heartaches" (1966)
Motown: the sound of work rhythms on Detroit's assembly lines, made for car radios.

James Brown, "Say It Loud—I'm Black and I'm Proud" (1968)
Race pride, Black Power.

Percy Sledge, "When a Man Loves a Woman" (1966)
Soul music hits #1 on the pop charts for the first time—a cultural milestone.

CHAPTER 7

Twilight of Consensus

The post–World War II generation lived the American dream. Its members experienced what seemed to be permanent economic growth and prosperity and believed these conditions to be the defining fact of their, and their children's, lives. This assumption was confirmed by America's soaring gross national product (GNP), which went from $13 billion in 1945 to $500 billion in 1960, and to nearly $1 trillion in 1970. Rising productivity meant a dramatically improved standard of living for many Americans (in 1945, a practicing dentist could expect a median income of about $5,450; in 1960, $13,000; and by 1970, over $28,000). Many voters saw this prosperity not as a quirk of victory in the war, but as a reward for national virtue—as the product of superior, democratic institutions that generated success, affluence, and rising social status for the great majority of the nation's citizens. And they believed that even race, that quintessential American dilemma, would yield, eventually and inevitably, to the successful march of the American economic and political system.

The passage of the Civil Rights Act of 1964, which outlawed racial, religious, and sexual discrimination in private businesses, was a culmination of this confident mindset. But consensus on ensuring civil rights (if, indeed, there was such a consensus) did not explain how these rights were to be maintained. How would American society achieve equality before the law? President Lyndon Johnson offered a solution that emphasized concrete results. "We seek not just legal equity but human ability," he said, "not just equality as a right and a theory but equality as a fact and equality as a result." To achieve "equality as a result," the Johnson administration targeted benefits at groups living in poverty and, in the 1964 civil rights law, committed the nation to opposing discrimination based on race, religion, and gender. These categories—and others, including age, ethnicity, and disability—soon became the focus of individuals and groups seeking to change social biases or overcome injustices. African-Americans, Hispanics, Native Americans, women, religious sects, the disabled, and others brought themselves to the attention of the courts in order to locate their groups within the parameters of the legislation and to obtain public recognition of their plight.

175

As group after group successfully litigated a definition of who they were, and obtained legal redress and access, the discourse of American politics began to pivot toward voters left out of the civil rights formulation, those who could make no reasonable claim to minority status. Millions of Americans, many of them unsure of the meaning of events in the tumultuous late 1960s, identified with Richard M. Nixon's appeal to the Quiet Majority during his 1968 campaign.

At first glance, Nixon was an unlikely representative for the mass of dissatisfied Americans who by 1969 were being called the Silent Majority. He was primarily a politician, defined by twenty years of service in Washington, all of it as part of a Republican party that had long been identified more with big business than with ordinary working people. Yet, by background, by financial standards, and even more by his constant struggle to achieve, Nixon embodied the self-made man. He was middle class through and through: raised in a modest Quaker household, college on scholarship and hard work, a struggling young lawyer, marriage to a schoolteacher. Nixon would experience success, but it was a certain kind of success, based on striving and moxy rather than position and place. Nixon's version of the American dream had consequences. On the one hand, it made him insecure, resentful, and perpetually unfulfilled. On the other hand, it made him curiously able to speak for a growing number of white working-class and middle-class Americans—the Silent Majority—who were coming to feel that they had been bypassed by the political revolution of the 1960s.

As Nixon understood, the Silent Majority was a useful symbol to a host of disparate voters whose only commonality lay in their status as outsiders. It included all those not clearly delineated by ethnic or minority definitions. It did not formulate or express a belief, but rather brought together a group of voters who had, over the previous six to eight years, seen their world slip away from familiar moorings. For this group, the sights and sounds of the 1960s—massive demonstrations against a curious war in Asia, Black Panthers carrying guns into the California statehouse, Yippies throwing dollar bills off the balcony at the New York Stock exchange, the huge outdoor Woodstock concert, where young people danced in the rain and bathed publicly in the nude—simply made no sense. And many who identified themselves with the Silent Majority believed that the federal government had devoted too much effort and spent too much money advancing the interests of black people.

Nonetheless, the Silent Majority had not given up on certain parts of Franklin Delano Roosevelt's New Deal vision. They still believed in social security, unemployment insurance, and other elements of the welfare state and its safety net. Following the economic chaos of 1971–1973, when the economy went into a tailspin and the nation proved vulnerable to a boycott of its oil supply by the Organization of Petroleum Exporting Countries (OPEC), an organization dominated by third world countries, the Silent Majority favored some government action to relieve the middle class. Nixon understood. People wanted a secure future. They wanted to send their children to college. They wanted to help the old and the poor. Although they resented what they considered to be unfair assistance to undeserving minorities, they believed in ending blatant segregation.

Nixon appealed to these voters by emphasizing his own belief in discipline, the work ethic, respect for one's elders, and law and order. In line with increased citizen responsibility for social policy, he favored the growth of federal regulatory agencies such as the Environmental Protection Agency (EPA) and the Occupational Safety and Health Administration (OSHA). In an attempt to shrink government bureaucracies, he dismantled the old welfare case system and substituted fixed cash payments to welfare recipients, creating the largest welfare endowment in the twentieth century. Nixon also indexed social security to inflation, helping many elderly, yet expanding the cost of the program.

After the passion, the dissent, the protests, the riots, and the excitement of the 1960s, the next decade appears remarkably tame. The big events were political: Watergate, the near impeachment and subsequent resignation of Nixon, a scandal involving ITT, the Hartford Insurance Company, and officials in the Justice Department. These were all typical Washington events, featuring the voter as spectator, not participant. Things seemed to have quieted down, too, in the popular culture, where events such as the Monterey Pop festival and Woodstock yielded to the singer-songwriters and disco of the 1970s. Indeed, one historian refers to the decade as a period when "it seemed like nothing happened."

In reality, a huge transformation occurred. The social movements of the 1960s—including civil rights and black nationalism, feminism, environmentalism, and consumerism—continued apace, now joined by aggressive movements representing Native Americans and gay people. What was new in the 1970s was a sense of betrayal felt by many Americans, who had approved of, or tolerated, the social changes of the 1960s on the assumption that an expanding economy would support them. But the economy did not cooperate. After 1971, the United States ceased to be the sole economic superpower, and Americans were forced to acknowledge that their country was one of a group of industrial nations sharing responsibility for the economic health of the earth and competing in global markets. In this new climate of world competition and economic insecurity, the social changes and movements that had once seemed reasonable, or perhaps had not even been noticed, now seemed unjust or to have gone too far. The backlash had begun.

INTERPRETIVE ESSAY
Ronald P. Formisano

Boston Against Busing

In Brown v. the Board of Education of Topeka, Kansas *(1954), the United States Supreme Court rejected the premise that "separate but equal" was acceptable in education, and it instructed schools to integrate with "all deliberate speed," a curiously ambiguous phrase that foreshadowed all sorts of problems. In the mid-1950s most Americans believed this to be a reasonable way to deal with the "southern problem," but within a decade, it was a remedy applied to the remainder of the country. Local solutions were usually worked out by boards of education, school districts, parents, and students.*

Ronald Formisano's Boston Against Busing, *from which the following selection is taken, examines these developments in the city of Boston, where many residents felt betrayed by the content of forced busing orders issued by the courts. Their dissatisfaction stemmed from geographical restrictions (only the city was involved, not the suburbs), the neighborhoods affected (working-class or upwardly mobile ethnic), and the lack of participatory decision-making (by court order rather than through the electorate).*

On June 21, 1974, Federal District Judge Wendell Arthur Garrity, Jr. ruled on a class action suit brought by black parents against the Boston School Committee and Board of Education. The decision ended a decade-long struggle by anti-busing voters in Boston to resist the 1965 Massachusetts Racial Imbalance Act, which forced schools to balance their racial and ethnic populations. Garrity's decision included a court-ordered plan to desegregate Boston schools in time for the September opening in 1974. This initial plan, Phase I, bused thousands of students in Boston. The most controversial portion of the plan was the pairing of Roxbury High School, in the urban black ghetto, and South Boston High School, center of the Irish-dominated white bastion against busing. The linking of these two schools created a furious reaction and was seen by many moderate voters as a punitive action. Phase II, the next stage of busing, was begun in February 1975. Garrity wanted moderate community members involved in developing plans for the coming school year. A master plan was proposed in March, but it sacrificed continued advances in the number of students bused in exchange for community stability. Judge Garrity rejected this vision and was persuaded by past evidence and the expert advice of two Boston University professors to increase the number of students participating in busing. The community's original willingness to at

*least consider Phase II turned into disillusionment between March and May
1975 and refueled the radical position against desegregation.*

   *Formisano's essay describes the reactions of several Boston neighbor-
hoods that were included in the city's busing plan. It also raises questions
about the motives behind desegregating America. Does desegregation apply
to all Americans or just to the poor, those who are less educated, and those
who dwell in cities? What role does the middle class play in defining where,
and for whom, busing is necessary? Can urban centers be guided, pressured,
or forced to deal with race because they are communities of public endeavor,
while suburbs, as private sanctums of individuals, are allowed to maintain
their own mores and laws? Does living in a city mean one has fewer rights
than the owner of a ranch house near the mall?*

During the 1970s the name of South Boston became synonymous with resistance
to school desegregation. Not only did Southie militants make the drab, old high
school on Dorchester Heights a symbol of racial strife, but Southie's activists carried the war to other neighborhoods, to hated enemy territory in the suburbs, to
corridors of power in the state legislature and city hall, and beyond, more persis-
tently and passionately than any other group. To this day the South Boston Information Center continues the crusade against "forced busing" and for "neighborhood schools." . . .

   Southie, Charlestown, mostly Italian East Boston on the other side of Boston
harbor, and perhaps Hyde Park all constituted "defended neighborhoods."
Bounded to varying degrees by physical barriers, defended neighborhoods shared
a sense of separateness from the city. Each in itself contained many tribal domains
of ethnicity, class, and turf, identified often with squares, corners, or parishes, but
all shared an impulse to stop time, to resist change, and to hold fast to an ideal of
society as it had been before the upheavals of the 1960s. . . .

   No neighborhood was monolithic: each contained various factions, each used
different methods. Yet busing forced each neighborhood into confrontation with
the outside world, and, as Suttles has pointed out, "it is in their 'foreign relations'
that communities come into existence and have to settle on an identity and a set of
boundaries which oversimplify their reality." Antibusing led to such definition and
oversimplification. South Boston was surely the most antibusing of the neighborhoods, but it came to seem even more so because of the repression of many who
were not whole-hog resisters.

   Differences in neighborhood styles are important because most white Bostonians were so overwhelmingly opposed in principle to the court orders. Five surveys
taken between October 1973 and July 1975 in six "neighborhoods" registered levels of opposition to two-way busing from 86 percent to 91 percent. These figures
were slightly higher than those appearing in various polls and surveys nationally
during the mid-1970s.

   A poll of nine neighborhoods completed in August 1975 found that in no area
did a majority strongly approve of busing, while strong disapproval (over 70 percent) centered in five of the nine: South Boston, Charlestown, East Boston, Hyde
Park, and West Roxbury/Roslindale. (The poll's neighborhood groupings are arbi-

trary and obviously too large in the case of West Roxbury/Roslindale, but they do allow for a contrast with the relatively self-contained localities.) Dorchester/Mattapan and Jamaica Plain strongly disapproved by 55 and 54 percent, respectively, while only just over a third did so in Central Boston and Roxbury. Yet in the latter two, both heavily minority, levels of strong approval registered only 23 and 27 percent, respectively.

Even in the defended neighborhoods, however, conflict existed over the question of resistance versus compliance. "Some people say that there is nothing you can do about the situation, so go along with it," said Hyde Park's state representative, Angelo Scaccia. "Others say, 'like hell, it's wrong and we are going to fight it' . . . there is no middle ground." Yet despite the pressure of polarization, diversity of opinion and action existed even within the most ostensibly unified enclaves.

DEFENDED NEIGHBORHOODS: SOUTH BOSTON

. . . "Southie meant strong community pride, a fierce loyalty to one another, a distrust of any change, and—among some—a suspicion of those who might be different." South Bostonians shared "a chauvinistic pride. It is like the Marine Corps compared to the U.S. Army. . . . People like to say they are from South Boston." Neighborhood defense that cut across class and ethnic lines certainly helps to explain Southie's tenacious resistance. Yet something peculiarly Irish impressed itself on the antibusing protest that in South Boston raged for some three years or more. Like the unreconcilables of the Confederacy's Lost Cause, a romantic aura of resistance for the sake of resistance emanated from the boasts of Southie pride.

Remarkably, antibusers engaged in protest despite recognizing that fighting would not change the situation. The 1973–75 surveys found that few protesters believed their actions would end busing. The majority in fact saw that goal as unattainable. . . .

An Irish Catholic tradition, termed "collective calculated violence" by one historian, to redress social and economic grievances or to subvert unjust laws, reaches back at least to peasant movements in prefamine Ireland. Irish history is littered with the bones of rebels and fighters who took on overwhelming foes and insurmountable odds. Thus as Jimmy Breslin observed in September 1975, busing was "the perfect fight for the Irish. They were doomed before they started. Therefore they can be expected to fight on." . . .

But if Irish traditions stamped themselves on Southie's protest, South Boston was not homogeneously Irish. Poles and Lithuanians had settled there as early as the late nineteenth century, along with some Italians and scattered Jews. In the 1970s Southie contained a Greek church, an Albanian cathedral, and at least three small Protestant churches. But local politics and culture carried a distinctly Irish aura. Southie had served as one major base from which the Catholic Irish had spread out to wrest control of city politics from Yankee Protestants.

South Boston was no more homogeneously working class than it was Irish. At the Point or upper end a middle- and upper-middle class occupied substantial town houses, some ringing the high school and commanding a lovely ocean view. The lower end, however, fended off spreading industrial development and held four housing projects, one dating from the 1930s. In 1970, not surprisingly, Southie's population of 38,500 (98 percent white) had a higher percentage of families on public assistance than the city average, a higher school dropout rate, more young unemployed males, and a median family income well below the city's. A psychiatrist who worked in the high school observed a different Southie from the one of which its politicians boasted, in which alcoholism was common as were families in the projects headed by single mothers. That Southie "has very little, it really does."

Though the middle class on "the Heights" sent their offspring to parochial or private schools and projected a "keep-the-shamrock-flying respectability," Southie's style, when confronting the outside world, was distinctly working class and tough. Southie kids learned early to be skillful with their fists. A state trooper posted at the high school in 1976 told of growing up there: "I literally had to fight my way from corner to corner. My last name was Lithuanian, though I had an Irish mother. The kids would mispronounce my last name and I would fight." Some graduated to more lethal weapons and to gangs. One neighborhood gang, the Mullens, seems to have existed at several levels, from recreational to criminal, with some toughs tied in with organized crime. During 1974 rumors frequently reached City Hall that the Mullens—meaning those who were armed and dangerous— planned to add their own mayhem to the protests. . . .

Southie had been drawing the wagons in a circle for at least a decade before 1974. Children had grown up hearing as much about the black threat as of the need to defeat "Eastie" in the annual Thanksgiving football game. Southie activists had preached antibusing at rallies, street corners, coffee shops, and the many bars and taverns. In April 1974, when an estimated twenty-five thousand marched on the capitol to urge repeal of the Racial Imbalance Act, five thousand South Bostonians led the way. Most of the buttons, bumper stickers, signs, and T-shirts protesters wore originated in South Boston.

Southie activists pioneered in organizing a smoothly functioning telephone network with which to mobilize the neighborhood, and South Boston also took the lead in establishing the first antibusing "information center" in the city, which several other neighborhoods soon imitated. The idea for such a clearinghouse and rumor-control headquarters arose from Southie's distrust of city hall. During the first days of Phase 1, South Bostonians would call rumor control at city hall "and always get a reply that everything was fine." According to Nancy Yotts of the SBIC [South Boston Information Center], "we started calling it the 'hunky dory' center and decided to set up our own."

Southie's emphasis on unity and collective action meant that antibusing militants demanded absolute conformity from their neighbors. Sensitivity to issues of loyalty and betrayal ran deep in the Irish cultural heritage, and that too impressed itself on Southie's protest. As the legendary ward boss of New York's Tammany Hall, G. W. Plunkitt, once said, "The Irish, above all people in the world, hates [*sic*] a traitor." Southie's solidarity also fed off shared feelings of being put upon. "We're always fighting to keep from going under," said Hicks's lieutenant Virginia Sheehy. "But we do have solidarity. . . . if we don't look out for Southie, nobody else will."

Although the district was actually sharply divided on boycotting and many parents would have preferred to send their children to school, the school boycott worked more effectively in Southie than elsewhere. Some parents kept children at home simply out of fear. One mother in the Old Colony Housing project kept five children out of school for the entire first year, with the kids living "just like a continuation of summer." When she sent them for Phase 2 she bought an expensive police radio to monitor the schools from her kitchen. At the first hint of trouble, she could be at the schools in fifteen or twenty minutes. Other parents sent out children only to have them return and report that there was "trouble at the school." Sometimes this amounted to their being harassed for trying to attend. One white boy (of two) who rode the bus to Roxbury on the first day of school had the misfortune of being interviewed by reporters and having his name broadcast. "I don't have to tell you," wrote his mother to Judge [Wendell] Garrity, "about the threats to his life if the 'nigger lover' boards the bus again. It seems he'll 'have his head blown apart' and 'be brought home to us in a box.'" . . .

One mother, a tower of strength in 1974–75 who "stuck her neck out" to be on a biracial council, threw in the towel just before Phase 2 began, lamenting, "I tried, God knows I tried but like so many others I cannot take another year like the passed [*sic*] one," a year "of notoriety" and "harassment." James O'Sullivan persevered and became a CCC [Citywide Coordinating Council] member during 1976, despite continued hate letters and calls, public abuse, and damage to his property. As one thoughtful college youth, who himself remained silent, said, "People can't speak out in South Boston. Not if you want to live."

Of course the voices of moderation in Southie were overpowered for reasons other than militant pressure. What many saw as the obtuseness of the court, the unjustness of the law, and the heavy-handedness of the police also silenced or converted some moderates. As one woman said at a parent-teacher meeting at Southie High in December 1974, "I was all for making desegregation work until last Wednesday, when I was chased down the street by a horse." . . .

But the focus of violence in Southie was the high school, an ancient structure that sat on Dorchester Heights where George Washington had placed the cannons that drove the British from Boston. For at least three years an atmosphere of hatred and violence prevailed in the school. Ione Malloy taught English there, and kept a diary that provides a chilling chronicle of the hell endured by students, teachers, and administrators. The fear, anguish, and torment of the students, including the troublemakers, is painfully evident. The teenagers enjoyed little chance to develop good will on their own because adults—in Southie and then in Roxbury in retaliation—coached and bent them into belligerence. By the start of Phase 2 some blacks were campaigning to get the school closed and moved to a neutral site, while Southie militants complained that this was the cause of trouble at the school.

The war over Southie High raged on and on, although it is difficult to see why anyone thought that blacks would be gaining much from a school (no matter what the dedication of individual staff) that was rundown, poorly equipped, and populated mostly by lower-class white children, few of whom went on to higher education. But generations of working-class families loved it. For the daughters who married soon after graduation and the sons who went to work in blue-collar jobs,

Southie High later evoked the fondest memories. For these immobile people the high school functioned as a socializing experience, reinforcing neighborhood values and identity and providing a shared cache of memories and traditions. Some dedicated teachers did work hard at Southie High, but "quality education" was not what Southie was all about. Before the threat of desegregation, parental interest in educational matters was minimal. But everyone in South Boston knew whether its football or hockey teams were winning—as they usually did.

Sports consumed the entire neighborhood, with athletic leagues from midget hockey to adult softball in profusion. But "the main thing was football," especially the annual Thanksgiving Day game with Italian East Boston, where one of the city's major ethnic and territorial rivalries could be played out on the gridiron. Even a schoolgirl athlete who played basketball and softball found her greatest thrill in becoming a cheerleader—"all the girls tried out for cheerleading." No incipient feminism here. And Southie athletes wore their letter sweaters long past their school days, emblems of their best memories. In 1973 the Thanksgiving contest determined the district title, but in 1974 there was no game between the schools. Instead, two football clubs, the South Boston "Chippewas" and the East Boston "Fittons," played a game whose halftime festivities were turned into an antibusing rally, with the proceeds of the game going to the antibusing cause.

The presence of many poor and working-class families in Southie contributed to the emphasis on public schools, which in turn fed the obsession with sports, which accounted in part for the weakness of parochial schools. Educational opportunity and social mobility had little to do with what Southie High symbolized to its constituents. The relative lack of alternatives for Southie residents in the form of parochial schools or suburban refuges mattered little where Southie High was concerned because they did not wish to give it up. What was being torn away from them, they felt, had much to do with identity, turf, loyalty, and community relationships. The militants thus decided that if the school was no longer theirs, it would not be anyone else's, and for three years a sort of scorched earth policy turned the building into a wasteland.

Once ROAR [Restore Our Alienated Rights] determined to allow no peace in the school, the pattern of incidents became clear: whenever the numbers of students present would climb during periods of calm, new disruptions would send attendance figures plummeting. Early on many students stopped by the South Boston Information Center after school to file reports, as well as for counseling and coaching. During 1974–75 the SBIC had ROAR members directly in the school, including as an aid Warren Zaniboni, chief of the "South Boston Marshals" and sometime [Louise Day] Hicks bodyguard. (Ironically, Zaniboni was keeping his two daughters out of school.) When white students staged walkouts, one white girl told her teacher, "the white kids have to go, or they'll get beaten up." In 1972 white football players told of "getting a bad name," presumably because they were allowing blacks on the team (in order to have a team) and were leading students back into school after boycotts. In November 1975 [South Boston High's] Headmaster [William] Reid testified in court that most student demands, black and white, were prepared with the assistance of adults. . . .

Garrity's two Boston University experts, Dentler and Scott, had advised the judge that any school—and Southie High in particular—could be *"turned around overnight"* (italics mine) with a new reform administration. But the situation did not improve after Judge Garrity put the school in receivership, removed Reid, and recruited to replace him the progressive Jerome Winegar from Minnesota (the chant "Go Home, Jerome" now entered Southie's repertoire). As federal and state money poured in for new programs, the turbulence continued. Indeed, there was actually less integration in the school in year three than in year one. Soon the new headmaster was saying that he would need "six to seven years" to change things. The most commonly heard comment from students of both complexions, meanwhile, was "I hate this school." One Southie senior boy said "If anyone asks me if I've ever 'done time,' I'll tell them, 'Yeah, *I've* done time.'" On May 31, 1977, nine buses carrying a total of 115 black students pulled up, an average of 12 per bus. Malloy observed; "School opens for the personnel: 35 troopers, 55 transitional and security aides, 120 teachers and administrators, 3 secretaries, kitchen staff, as well as peripheral personnel." Winegar summed up the third year: "Anyone who thought this place could change in a year was dreaming."

Eventually, as expert Dentler put it, the high school was "taken away" from those it had served for generations. To those who "lost" the school, desegregation seemed "almost like punishment." Said state representative Michael Flaherty of the court order, *"We're being punished for what we are."* (Italics mine.) Flaherty meant that Southie was the type of place viewed as an anachronism by the technocrats, bureaucrats, and developers. South Boston's basic flaw, its popular Senator Billy Bulger averred in 1973, was to be "too successful in providing what neighborhoods should provide," and this true neighborhood based on family and personal ties stood in the way of "the concepts of homogenization of lifestyle pursued by our planners, social scientists and engineers."

South Bostonians believed they were being punished also because they were seen as racists. The unrestrained expression of bigotry in South Boston cannot be denied: the racist graffiti repeatedly painted on the high school, the obscene racist chants of mobs, the stonings and beatings of blacks who strayed into Southie, the harassment of the few blacks or Hispanics who still lived there by the early 1970s, the ugly incidents perpetrated against interracial groups taking part in the St. Patrick's Day parades of 1964 and 1965, and the insensitivity to blacks' situation in society measured in polls during these years and expressed often in the *South Boston Tribune*. Hostility to blacks had been escalating for at least a decade before 1974, and Southie's leaders tended to be more tolerant of the haters and moral pygmies in their midst than those in other neighborhoods. . . .

Many South Bostonians who did not hate blacks as such, feared poor black youths and black neighborhoods as sources of crime and violence. This fear was real, not just a cover for "purely" racial feelings. However exaggerated the perception, many whites, not only South Bostonians, saw black Roxbury as crime infested, and some who had lived on its borders or fled from districts engulfed by the ghetto had been mugged or terrorized by poor black youths. One parent told Ione Malloy that his boy was scheduled to be bused to Roxbury the following year: "I worked nine years in Roxbury as a street cleaner, and I'll never let him go there." . .

Irish Catholics' perceptions of the unrestrained sexuality of ghetto culture further intensified fears of blacks. Many whites associated ghetto blacks with promiscuity, teenage pregnancy, single-parent families, and prostitution. Irish Catholics, for a variety of reasons, have tended to be puritanical in sexual matters and have cloaked "sins of the flesh" with an aura of taboo. Desegregation raised the specter of friendships and even sexual intercourse between Southie's white daughters and black males, about whose sexual prowess Boston's white men believed old myths and made nervous jokes. This fear seldom found direct expression, but as William A. Henry III pointed out, was often subtly played upon. Henry argued that no one addressed sexual fears more explicitly than Southie's own Louise Hicks, who "almost invariably spoke of 'this terrible, terrible, forcible busing.' The customary term of opprobrium was, of course, 'forced' busing. That language carried a political message of helpless rage. Hicks's inventive choice of word called to mind instead the charge of 'forcible rape.' Busing was not just a symbolic rape of a parent's control. It might, Hicks was telling us, lead to an actual rape as some high school girl, however pure of heart, by her very unattainable beauty incited the purportedly uncontrollable sexuality of young black men."

The sexual theme arose implicitly in the epithet of "nigger lover" that fell on even the police and teachers who were just doing their jobs. One policeman in front of Southie confronted an old woman yelling obscenities who taunted him by saying that she hoped that when he got home he found his wife "in bed with a nigger." . . .

DEFENDED NEIGHBORHOODS: CHARLESTOWN

Like South Boston, Charlestown's high school occupied a central place in the Town's geography and emotions. It too sat on a hill, next to a historic monument to revolutionary patriotism, an antiquated and dilapidated anachronism that was the focus of a community pride which to many outsiders also seemed a throwback to another era. It too seemed a place where time had stood still.

Charlestown qualified perhaps even more as an urban village, with fifteen to seventeen thousand persons packed into one square mile of a hilly peninsula. Over the years Italians and others had moved in and intermarried with the predominant Irish Catholics, so that everybody was related to everybody else. Thus loyalty to "Our Town" transcended anything necessarily Irish or Catholic. Although excluded from Phase 1, Townies served notice early that the advent of busing there would be no cakewalk. Warned one Townie on the eve of Phase 2: "Charlestown's resistance to busing this fall will make South Boston look as peaceful as Vatican City."

Treated partly as a dumping-ground for institutions unwanted elsewhere, Charlestown had been closed in by ugly steel and concrete bridges and highways built mainly for the convenience of others, and a noisy, dirty elevated railway had been thrust through its heart. In the 1930s bulldozers made way for a large housing project, over the screams of many of those displaced, and by the 1960s the project had deteriorated into a cauldron of social disorganization. In the 1970s it would provide militant antibusing leaders and many young street warriors. Despite its vaunted solidarity, however, a split in Charlestown clearly emerged between poor and middle-class antibusers. . . .

Opposition to busing was much more intense, in part because race was involved. In the early 1970s, too, a national economic downturn hit Charlestown particularly hard, with the closing of the historic Charlestown navy yard. Now, too, the housing project reflected urban malaise. In 1973, 68 percent of the project's families had no father and 80 percent were on some kind of public relief. Many of the families were refugees from "urban renewal" elsewhere in the city. The project people, moreover, burned with resentment against other Townies, especially the hilltoppers, whom they knew looked down on them as "riffraff" and "project rats." And it was the housing project's residents who were affected the most by the court order because as those with the least resources they were least able to escape.

When antibusing activities began in Charlestown, however, the rowdy elements were not in evidence. In 1973 a middle-class group organized a chapter of the Massachusetts Citizens Against Forced Busing, which included the publishers and editor of the *Charlestown Patriot* and mothers from lace-curtain households. By fall 1974, however, new impulses broke through and on September 25, three hundred Townies organized the Charlestown branch of ROAR, christened it Powder Keg, and elected as head Pat Russell, a mother from the project. When asked about the chapter's name, Russell replied, "because we have a short fuse."

In September 1975, when busing finally came to Charlestown, a massive police presence forestalled a "Second Battle of Bunker Hill" but also angered many Townies and stiffened their backs. Mothers' prayer marches and confrontations with the police, protest demonstrations, and chaos in the high school continued through the year. As in Southie, ROAR was "calling the shots" in the high school, though here too the black students gradually fought back. In April 1976, the celebrated spearing with an American flag of black lawyer Theodore Landsmark on City Hall Plaza was perpetrated by a Charlestown youth who with friends had joined Southie youngsters for a protest march [see photo essay, p. 199].

Despite the similarities with Southie, explicit racism was less freely expressed in Charlestown. *The Patriot* and moderate leaders urged that Charlestown not disfigure itself with obscene graffiti. These remonstrations were often ignored, but that they were made at all suggests the Town's different style. The Town's pragmatism could be seen in the politicking of Maurice Gillen, a thirty-five-year-old meter reader with Boston Edison. Nonviolent and no racist, Moe Gillen was a quintessential Townie, born there, married to one, and residing nested among his and his wife's relatives. He fervently opposed busing as the offspring of addle-headed planners and ivory tower experts, and his wife was a founding member of Powder Keg. But Gillen believed it was foolish not to try to broker as mild a plan of desegregation as possible, and he helped organize a broad-based task force, including the state representative, members of the clergy, parents, and several militants, to negotiate with the court.

Although stunned by the original masters' plan, which made their high school into a magnet for technical training and required heavy busing in and out, Gillen hung in and steered a wary course among Charlestown's bristling factions. Eventually, his committee won concessions, most notably the high school's being continued as a district school, though the level of busing remained high. When Gillen accepted Judge Garrity's invitation to serve on the Citywide Coordinating Committee, four militant members of his group resigned in protest. But the coalition had held together long enough for moderates to play a significant role.

Although moderates were harassed less than in Southie, militants frustrated initial attempts to elect biracial councils, while some Townie parents experienced enough pressure to make them change their minds about independent action. Terry Wrenn, wife of an elevator mechanic and mother of five, with four children in parochial schools in 1975, attended a meeting of the court's citywide council. Wrenn distrusted the top ROAR leaders as well as the school committee ("For years they knew busing was coming and they sat on their ass. I voted for those idiots"). She also fiercely opposed busing, but when screaming neighbors called on the phone to berate her for attending the meeting, "I came off the thing, and that's not like me." In fact, Wrenn received calls just because she had been seen talking to a reporter: "They said they thought it wasn't too good an idea to talk to the press." . . .

As middle-class moderates withdrew from both the resistance and the schools Powder Keg meanwhile had spawned a splinter group called the Defense Fund, dominated by men, whose purpose was to raise money for the legal defense of young Townies arrested at the high school or in the streets. One Defense Fund member wrote to the *Patriot* that "we're tired of marching, praying, demonstrating."

Racism as surely contributed to neighborhood defense in Charlestown as in Southie, as did fear of black ghetto culture. Racial violence in Charlestown during these years was often virulent, from rock throwings, to beatings, to the shooting of a black football player. But a powerful class dynamic was also at work among the powerless who felt they were trapped as others were not. "How can it be the law of the land, as we are told," wrote one Charlestown mother to Judge Garrity, "when you can move less than 1 mile away and be out from under this law?" . . .

THE ITALIANS: EAST BOSTON AND THE NORTH END

Whites of Italian ancestry lived throughout Boston, including Southie and Charlestown. They were most concentrated, however, in East Boston, a heavily three-decker, working-class neighborhood of just over thirty-eight thousand in 1970 that lay across Boston harbor and that was connected to the city by two tunnels. "Eastie's" geography, social character, and intensely hostile response to the threat of busing certainly qualified it as a defended neighborhood. Its geography and perhaps its reputation also seem to have caused it ultimately to be left out of Phases 1 and 2.

But during the mid-1970s an enormous amount of antibusing energy poured out of East Boston, led predominantly by Elvira "Pixie" Palladino, who won election to the school committee in 1975. . . .

For a time the antibusing imperative managed to bridge over the longstanding rivalry between Italian East Boston and Irish South Boston. Joining Eastie in this alliance to a lesser degree was the Italian North End, a picturesque corner of the city best known for its markets, restaurants, and festivals.

As Irish Catholic culture clashed with African-American black ghetto culture (or, usually, with images of that culture), so too did the Italian-American ethos with its emphasis on family honor and *ben educato,* that is, proper raising and correct bearing. Italian concepts of "good education" did not tend to stress an Anglo-Protestant achievement ethic geared to economic mobility or moving away from one's roots. Italians tended not, thusly, to pursue formal education as did, for example, Jews earlier and African-Americans later. Indeed, East Boston produced one of the lowest proportions in the city of high school graduates, and probably no more than 10 percent of Italians went on to accredited colleges. Italian parents did stress that their children learn not to dishonor the family.

The importance of avoiding shame to Italians can be seen vividly in the fact that in 1970 only 7 percent of families in East Boston were receiving Aid to Families with Dependent Children (a mere 3 percent in the North End), even though almost a quarter of the families in these districts had family incomes of under $3,000 per year. Italians, of course, tended to avoid both divorce and welfare. Meanwhile, they perceived black families as unstable and dependent on welfare. This perception had much to do with the threat posed by desegregation, particularly the prospect of having children bused into black neighborhoods. . . .

Busing created a deep split in East Boston. Some of Pitaro's former allies worked to implement the court orders or distanced themselves from militant antibusers. Some were antibusing and the Massport-highway wars had toughened them: "Anyone who is still living here after the loss of Wood Island Park, noise of Logan Airport, and the smells from the oil tanks and large trucks," wrote one mother to Judge Garrity, "is never going [to move or to bus]. As a life-long resident you will not tell me what to do with my children." Already East Bostonians had joined demonstrations against the Racial Imbalance Act and the district had voted heavily for hard-liners on the school committee. After Garrity's decision, a ROAR chapter sprang up led by Palladino; her militants established an information center and began to plan for alternative schools.

A small group of moderates also functioned. East Bostonians for Quality Education (EBQUE) announced its intention to work for peaceful implementation. Evelyn D. Morash, a member of the liberal Board of Education and a leader of EBQUE, of course was harassed: she received threatening phone calls and windows in her home were broken. A nephew of Palladino's and the son of Charlestown antibuser Tom Johnson were actually arrested for making obscene phone calls, but nothing came of it. Yet EBQUE fought back, sending around leaflets to smooth Phase 2 arguing that "busing will not go away." EBQUE, however, hardly reflected local sentiment. In January 1975 an antibusing HSA [Home School Assn., an equivalent of the PTA] meeting and bake sale attracted some three hundred parents, while an EBQUE meeting mustered about three dozen persons, many of whom were clergy, teachers, and other professionals, with parents of school children accounting for only half a dozen.

Yet neither did Palladino's ROAR completely reflect community attitudes. As early as December 1974 a group of twenty-five activists left the ROAR Information Center. The defectors said that while they thoroughly disliked the court order, they wanted some "middle ground" way of coping with what was now an irreversible situation. These moderates advocated a "foster parent" plan to insure the safe passage of black children into East Boston. They remained opposed, however, to sending their own children out. . . .

Ironically, many observers outside of East Boston perceived it as potentially explosive—primarily because of stereotypes held regarding the predominantly Italian population. A state trooper at Southie High remarked casually regarding Eastie: "Over there they'll use bullets." That organized crime was associated in the popular mind with Italians, and that in fact it had been most entrenched and lethal in the North End and East Boston, certainly fostered this impression. Yet, ironically, the North End itself was low key about busing. A small antibusing group, North End Voices for Equal Rights (NEVER), participated in some ROAR demonstrations but opposed violence and even boycotts. The North End's relative restraint could be traced in part to having most of its children already in parochial schools, and because Phase 1 affected it primarily by busing in some 250 mostly Chinese students. The Chinese regard for ancestry and family and their well-known work ethic eased their acceptance by the Italians. . . .

SEMISUBURBIA: HYDE PARK

If you will offer something better than my neighborhood school, I would gladly accept.
    No way will my family climb down the ladder. We are going up not down, no matter what you order.

—Mr. and Mrs. R. D., Hyde Park, to Judge Garrity, Oct. 16, 1974

The basic fact of life for the residents of Canarsie was the precariousness of their hold on middle-class status, the recency of their arrival in that exalted position, and the intense fear that it might be taken from them.

—Jonathan Rieder, Canarsie

Buses can take a rider a long way from downtown Boston to neighborhoods that seem almost suburban but are still part of the city. Hyde Park is such a place, not isolated or cohesive enough to qualify, strictly speaking, as a defended neighborhood, yet ardently antibusing and conscious of turf. With a population of about thirty-eight thousand (overwhelmingly white, though a few blacks could be found in the schools) in 1970, Hyde Park resists clear-cut classification, a hybrid best characterized as semisuburban. Working-class families of Irish, Italian, and other backgrounds, moving up from housing projects or low-rent districts, found in Hyde Park affordable housing and a within-city version of the suburbs. For many, it meant having arrived.

Hyde Park parents thus often reacted to the court order with intense resentment born of the fear that it would take away from them all that they had gained. Thomas O'Connell, a father of seven and owner of a two-story house that he had built himself, had spent fourteen years in public housing. Similarly, Joseph LoPiccolo, a welfare investigator for the state, had enrolled his daughter in a private school rather than have her bused. On school's opening day in 1974 he watched the buses come in and said bitterly: "I worked three jobs just to be near this school and this church. Now it's all being taken away from me."

Proximity to suburbs that were excluded from busing fueled this strong strain of resentment. "When I bought my home I had three things in mind," one father wrote to Judge Garrity, "namely the church, the school, and the shopping center. . . . [My children] will never be bused against my wishes. . . . If you are so concerned about the so called minority, as a beginner you might consider building some low income housing out in Wellesley and the rest of suburbia. You people are the real villains who have discriminated against the minority for years and years."

Antibusing organization was strong, and in August 1974 some eight hundred parents gathered at a municipal building and voted to hold a two-week boycott of schools. Both the MCAFB [Mass Citizens Against Forced Busing] and ROAR were active, the latter structured Southie-style with a pyramid network of phone callers. Leaders of Hyde Park's ROAR worked prominently in the citywide organization and marshaled troops for demonstrations. Different factions, however, coexisted easily in Hyde Park, and local groups tried everything from lobbying and legal appeals to alternative schools and boycotts.

In overcrowded Hyde Park High School the pattern resembled that in the defended neighborhoods. Although mobs did not gather routinely and clash with police, violence erupted inside throughout the school year. After the mid-October stabbing of a white by a black, fifty to sixty police officers were stationed inside. The police presence and the installation of metal detectors caused white attendance to rise, but after the December vacation fighting, riots, arrests, and police invasions continued to the end of the year. Although trouble did not reach levels as high as at Southie or Charlestown, incidents continued. . . .

Between 1970 and 1980, as some black families moved in, residential white flight increased. The white population fell from over thirty-eight thousand to about thirty-two thousand while the black population went from .4 to 7 percent of the total. Tensions rose and in 1982 journalists described some blocks as hostile "racial frontier[s]." The high school by then was 85 percent black. Thus, like their suburban cousins, most semisuburban white Hyde Parkers simply escaped from the schools.

WEST ROXBURY

During 1986 a movement arose in the black neighborhood of Roxbury to secede from the city. In a referendum on the issue the vote went strongly against establishing a new municipality, which would have been named "Mandela" after the South African black nationalist. A joke went around Boston at the time, to the effect that if the referendum passed, then in West Roxbury a secession movement would develop, with the new city to be named "Botha."

The subject of racism in West Roxbury has its less funny side. In 1982 a black woman and her young son drove to a West Roxbury home to buy used furniture. Stopping to ask directions, the thirty-two-year-old city planner encountered white youths who told her she was in West Roxbury not Roxbury, and "they told me if I bought the house 'they'd kill me.'" That night the house was painted with obscenities and slogans such as "Keep West Roxbury White."

Such a story gives West Roxbury the flavor of a defended neighborhood. Was there as much racism in West Roxbury as in Southie? Perhaps, but West Roxbury expressed its opposition to desegregation in ways very different from Southie. Of course Southie had its moderates and West Roxbury its militants, and in comparing them one uses ideal types. But West Roxbury's antibusing movement was predominantly moderate, middle class, and individualistic.

One of the first "streetcar suburbs," West Roxbury was about as suburban as a Bostonian could get in the city. For the upwardly mobile it was, said Alan Lupo in 1974, "one of the last outposts. . . . a big sprawling ward at the southern tip of the city. . . . There are probably some Yankees left . . . and certainly some Protestants, there is an increasing number of Jews forced out of the neighborhoods to the north. But . . . West Roxbury is a largely Catholic community, whose members number politicians, well-paid appointed officials, civil servants, police, firemen, realtors, small business proprietors, doctors, and those blue-collar guys who will mortgage their grandmothers to live there."

West Roxbury's population increased in the decade before 1970 more than any other part of the city. Its median family income ranked second while its portion of residents completing high school ranked first. Employees of the state, federal, or city governments, or utilities headed 60 percent of the households. The neighborhood was far from uniformly middle class, but of a population of over thirty-one thousand, only seventy-seven were black.

In a 1975 poll the neighborhood ranked high in "outrage" over busing, and close to 80 percent agreed with the statement that forced busing violated constitutional rights (just 6 percent behind Southie). On one issue, however, West Roxbury parted company with the most militant neighborhoods: was it more important that order be maintained as Phase 2 was carried out, or was it more important that protest continue even if some violence happened to take place? Southie had the most who would continue to protest at the risk of violence, 26 percent (61 percent opted for peace), East Boston was second with 18 percent, Charlestown was third with 16 percent, and further down West Roxbury-Roslindale tied for sixth place with only 11 percent, while 81 percent there chose peace, only 7 percent less than in Roxbury. "The lace curtain Irish," said one councillor, "are very, very opposed to the court order, but they are not marchers or demonstrators." Thus, West Roxburyites could join antibusing militants in other neighborhoods in establishing a private, alternative school (West Roxbury Academy), but mob scenes outside the high school were not to be.

West Roxbury's middle-class parents had long shown intense involvement in the schools. Local HSAs vibrated with concern for education well before they became geared up for antibusing. In the spring of 1973 many residents joined the throngs that marched on the state house seeking repeal of the Racial Imbalance Act. In 1974 ten buses took demonstrators from the Robert Gould Shaw School, and the total participating from West Roxbury-Roslindale was estimated at two thousand. Meanwhile, some local activists moved on into Massachusetts Citizens Against Forced Busing.

But despite the anger that seethed also in West Roxbury, most neighborhood leaders emphasized order and safety. . . .

ROAR members lived throughout West Roxbury and Roslindale, and a local branch of ROAR came into being in October 1974 as the Tri-Neighborhood Association (TNA). The group held a dance and then a Sunday afternoon rally at Billings Field on November 3, where three thousand turned out to listen to speeches from leading antibusers. The enthusiasm resplendent at sunny Billings Field, however, faded with the winter snows. Though activists and the *Transcript* boosted the ROAR-sponsored March on Washington in March 1975, antibusing was waning. . . .

Moderation outweighed militancy in West Roxbury, and common ground existed there, if anywhere, for a middle-course solution to desegregation such as that embodied in the unrevised masters' plan. Strong support existed also for the position worked out by attorneys for the Boston HSA. They conceded that the Boston School Committee had been guilty of discrimination in the twenty-two schools for which plaintiffs and the court had provided evidence. They pleaded, however, that desegregation remedies be limited to the schools to which segregative practices had applied. In Boston, in 1975, that too was a moderate position.

Once the court rejected the masters' plan, however, the dominant reaction in West Roxbury to busing, according to state representative Michael Connolly, was "to get out from under. Either move out of the city or take their children out of the public schools." A West Roxbury lawyer wrote to Garrity that he and his wife had grown up in West Roxbury and after his attending Harvard Law School they had decided not to move to the suburbs despite "some of the difficulties and unfashionableness of living in the city." They hoped to send their children to the same schools they had attended. Now, their community activities allowed them to see that many worried parents were making plans to move out or place their children in private schools. They too were contemplating moving, especially because of the hazards threatening their nine-year-old daughter. At her Roslindale school, he had learned, a young black girl had been beaten by other black girls for associating with white children. His daughter, in an adjacent class, "is being constantly threatened physically (struck *at least* once in the face) and tormented and verbally abused by a group of black girls—all for reasons unknown. Many people have advised me that I would be further jeopardizing her physical safety if I tried . . . to have the school principal and teachers to admonish the black girls."

Far from being militant, this parent had hoped for a plan "which can be embraced by both blacks and whites." He could have added, as did another West Roxbury parent of similar views writing to the judge: "I share with you the dream that this City can have children learning and living together in friendship. However, how is this possible if there are not enough white youngsters in the public schools[?]"

In September 1975 local officials were talking of a "mass exodus," particularly by parents of elementary school children. By 1977 the publisher of the *Transcript*, James G. Colbert, described the impact of white flight on the Randall G. Morris School. Ten years ago it was one of the best in the city. Now it was "just another mediocre elementary school with severe disciplinary problems." School officials claimed that its racial composition was 58 percent black, 40 percent white, and 2 percent other, but this was misleading because it included two classes of all-white kindergarten children. Many white parents sent their children there for kindergarten only, then sent them elsewhere to avoid their being bused. Subtracting kindergarten, there were only 35 white children to be integrated with 137 black in grades one to five. Thus, one first grade classroom, for example, contained 15 black children and 1 white. Another had 13 black and 2 white. And so it went in other grades. "Under the guidelines laid down by Judge Garrity all the regular classes at the Randall Morris School from grades 1 through grade 5 are illegally segregated by needless and wasteful busing." . . .

Antibusing was much more individualistic in West Roxbury, and parents reacted more to the impact of busing on their families than on the neighborhood as a whole. Consequently, West Roxbury was pluralist and tolerant by comparison with Southie. Irish Catholic and working-class impulses fused in the latter to present a visage to the outside world of clannishness, cohesiveness, and strong distrust of outsiders. There was actually more division in Southie than the world was permitted to see. As one West Roxbury ROAR activist said, "We in West Roxbury were as opposed to busing as Southie . . . but they have Southie pride. They will hide a lot of things to save their pride." Southie put more emphasis on "sticking together." . . .

The question asked earlier: "Was there as much racism in West Roxbury as in Southie?" is the wrong question. And the fact that West Roxbury/Roslindale also scored lower than Southie and East Boston on poll questions that revealed "insensitivity to blacks" is also not particularly important here. For one thing, it is possible that middle-class types in suburban settings do much better at hiding their real feelings from pollsters. But the essential differences between West Roxbury and Southie should not be seen in any case exclusively in moral terms. West Roxburyites possessed not only the inclination but the resources to escape from busing, by moving out of the city or placing their children in private schools, or in nearby suburban refuges. Too many in South Boston lacked resources and safe retreats, and Southie also lacked the refuge a well-developed parochial school system could provide.

SOURCES

Workers Fight Back

In late April and early May 1970, the nation's newspapers printed documents revealing that the Nixon administration was engaged in a secret invasion of Cambodia. The public response was both immediate and angry. The anger arose from the belief, held by many voters, that the United States and its president were working toward getting out of Vietnam. The invasion of Cambodia denied the implicit promise of the election of 1968 and left many Americans disheartened. Students took to the streets, marching and demonstrating against the expansion of the war.

Unfortunately, these protests coincided with a growing public intolerance toward behavior characterized as unlawful and disorderly. In Ohio, at Kent State University, the tragic result was the death of four students, shot by Ohio National Guardsmen. Many Americans were shocked and distressed that American soldiers would fire on fellow citizens, and they believed that the American government had gone too far.

Others, like the construction workers who took part in the events of May 8, 1970, described below as reported in the New York Times, *offered a different perspective. Do you detect any empathy between the student protesters and the construction workers? Why was there so much heat in this contest? Was it a matter of age differences? How did construction workers explain their right to protest when they did not accept the right of students to do so?*

As the weeks went on, the story of hard hats versus students took on a life of its own, reappearing in city after city, paper after paper. How do you explain this phenomenon?

War Foes Here Attacked By Construction Workers

Helmeted construction workers broke up a student antiwar demonstration in Wall Street yesterday, chasing youths through the canyons of the financial district in a wild noontime melee that left about 70 persons injured.

The workers then stormed City Hall, cowing policemen and forcing officials to raise the American flag to full staff from half staff, where it had been placed in mourning for the four students killed at Kent State University on Monday.

At nearby Pace College a group of construction workers who said they had been pelted with missiles by students from the roof, twice invaded a building, smashing windows with clubs and crowbars and beating up students.

Earlier the workers ripped a Red Cross banner from the gates of Trinity Church and tried to tear down the flag of the Episcopal Church.

"This is senseless," said the Rev. Dr. John Vernon Butler, rector of Trinity Parish. "I suppose they thought it was a Vietcong flag."

Twice Father Butler ordered the gates closed against menacing construction workers.

Inside the church, doctors and nurses from the New York University Medical Center had set up a first-aid station, treating 40 to 60 youths who had been beaten by the workers.

The Mayor issued a statement saying that "a mob came perilously close to overwhelming the police guard at City Hall."

He added his "deep regrets" that the day of memory for the four students killed by Ohio National Guardsmen at Kent had been defiled by violence.

The police said that six persons had been arrested and that 19 persons, including four patrolmen, had been injured. However, Beekman-Downtown Hospital alone reported that 23 persons had been brought by ambulance from the Wall Street area suffering from cuts and bruises, none of them serious.

Fighting Erupts

It was about five minutes to noon when Wall Street suddenly erupted in a melee of fist-fighting that entrapped thousands of employees headed for lunch.

Starting at 7:30 A.M., hundreds of youths, mostly from New York University and others from Hunter College and city high schools, gathered at Broad and Wall Streets in a demonstration demanding the immediate withdrawal of American troops from Vietnam and Cambodia, the immediate release of all "political prisoners in America" and the cessation of military-oriented work by the universities.

All accounts agree that the demonstration was without violence until the construction workers reached the scene.

The construction workers, most of them wearing brown overalls and orange and yellow hard hats, descended on Wall Street from four directions. A thin line of policemen had blocked off the steps of the Federal Hall National Memorial at Nassau and Wall Streets, from about a thousand students who were sitting on the sidewalk and pavement listening to speakers denounce the war abroad and repression at home.

The morning was chilly, with a light rain. But toward noon the sky lightened and the day became warm and humid. The students were in good humor; they cheered a Broad Street lawyer, Charles F. Appel, 56 years old, who told the youths: "You brought down one President and you'll bring down another."

Then came the moment of confrontation. The construction workers, marching behind a cluster of American flags, swept the policemen aside and moved on the students. The youths scattered, seeking refuge in the lunch-hour crowds.

The workers sought them out, some selecting those youths with the most hair and swatting them with their helmets.

There did not seem to be more than 200 construction workers, but they were reinforced by hundreds of persons who had been drawn into the march by chants of "All the way, U.S.A." and "Love it or leave it."

On reaching the Federal Hall National Memorial, the workers at first pushed halfheartedly against the police line. "All we want to do is put our flag up on those steps," one worker said quietly to Inspector Harold Schryner. "If you try, there'll be blood to pay," the inspector replied.

But within two minutes the workers had surged over the memorial's steps, planting American flags on the statue of George Washington. Then they out-flanked the police, driving demonstrators before them and hitting the youths with their helmets.

A Staged Assault?

From his 32d-floor office at 63 Wall Street, Edward Shufro of the brokerage firm of Shufro, Rose & Ehrman watched through binoculars two men in gray suits and gray hats who, he said, seemed to be directing the workers.

"These guys were directing the construction workers with hand motions," Mr. Shufro said.

At Exchange Place, Robert A. Bernhard, a partner at Lehman Brothers, tried to protect a youth from assault by a worker. The worker grabbed Mr. Bernhard and pushed him against a telephone pole.

A man who came to the aid of Mr. Bernhard was himself attacked by a worker and struck with a pair of pliers. Bleeding from a head wound the man was taken to Beekman-Downtown Hospital.

Near City Hall, a Wall Street lawyer, Michael Berknap, 29, a Democratic can-didate for the State Senate, was beaten and kicked by a group of construction workers yelling, "Kill the Commie bastards." He was treated at Beekman-Down-town Hospital with his right eye completely closed, a large welt on his head and five bootmarks on his back.

Mr. Berknap said the police had stood by and made no attempt to stop the assault.

"These people are rampaging and the police are not arresting them," he com-plained.

Among the student demonstrators taken to Trinity Church for first aid was Drew Lynch, a teacher in the Human Resources Administration's Brooklyn street program.

Mr. Lynch had both eyes blackened and was bleeding from the mouth. He said "at least four" workers had pummeled him to the street, then kicked him.

"A policeman finally grabbed me by the collar, dragged me away, and said: 'Get out of here,'" Mr. Lynch said.

The workers led a mob to City Hall, where an unidentified mailman went to the roof and raised the flag that Mayor Lindsay had ordered lowered to half staff for the slain students. The crowd cheered wildly.

But moments later an aide to Mayor Lindsay, Sid Davidoff, stalked out on the roof and lowered the flag again.

The mob reacted in fury. Workers vaulted the police barricades, surged across the tops of parked cars and past half a dozen mounted policemen. Fists flailing they stormed through the policemen guarding the barred front doors.

Uncertain whether they could contain the mob, the police asked city officials to raise the flag. Deputy Mayor Richard R. Aurelio, in charge during the absence of Mayor Lindsay, who was at Gracie Mansion, ordered the flag back to full staff.

Two plainclothes policemen, Pat Mascia and Bob Rudion, and the City Hall custodian, John Zissel, walked out on the roof and struggled with the flapping lanyard.

As the flag went up, the workers began singing "The Star-Spangled Banner." A construction worker yelled to the police: "Get your helmets off."

Grinning sheepishly, about seven of 15 police who were on City Hall steps, removed their helmets.

Meanwhile, a group of workers had charged Pace College, across the street from City Hall Park, angered by a peace banner hanging from the roof. Some of them gained the roof of the modernistic four-story building, seized the banner and brought it down to the street, where it was burned. Others smashed windows in the lobby of the college and beat some students.

The scuffle over the flag at City Hall was accompanied by chants of "Lindsay's a Red."

"Stop being juveniles," a Lindsay aide, Donald Evans, admonished a construction worker.

"What do you mean, being juvenile?" he replied, punching Mr. Evans on the chin.

Flags and Symbols: A Photo Essay

A symbol is a presentation/representation of more complex, multifaceted ideas. As such, a symbol might be used to help bind people together, or to raise partisan consciousness. In the United States, during the first half of the twentieth century, the symbolic power of the flag was almost exclusively a call to patriotism and conformity to existing political leadership. During the 1960s, the flag took on new symbolic meanings. Some groups used the flag to assert their own claims to be more dedicated to the nation and its interests than those in positions of authority. Others used the flag as a symbol of what they believed to be a bankrupt American nationalism. Still others paraded the flag to evoke a past when—supposedly—everything was good and decent. All of these representations were part of a struggle for the political consciousness of the American people. In this struggle, not only flags but also flowers, bombs, guns, long hair, hard hats, and even children were used symbolically.

In the photographs in this section, people are protesting, demonstrating, or simply portraying their private beliefs in public. The first photo is of construction workers chasing students in the streets. What is the symbol of the construction worker? What is the symbol of the student? What is the message conveyed by the picture? Does anyone have a flag?

**Construction workers, carrying flags, rush an antiwar rally at the Subtreasury Build-
ing in the financial center in New York City, May 1970.**
The New York Times. Carl T. Gossett, Jr./NYT Pictures.

  *The second photograph is from the Boston busing controversy described
by Ronald Formisano. The young man holding the flagstaff is against busing.
What is happening? Is the positioning of the flag reminiscent of any particular
weapon? Why is the situation—a white man threatening a black man—ironic?*
  *The third item in this series is a publicity photograph from Stanley
Kubrick's* Full Metal Jacket *(1987). It features Joker, the film's protagonist,
wearing a peace symbol on the lapel of his combat fatigues and a helmet
marked "born to kill," a phrase taken from Marine training. What contradictory symbolism does Joker represent? What does this photograph tell us about
how the Vietnam war was understood in the mid-1980s?*

Pulitzer Prize photograph by Stanley Forman: an antibusing protester threatens to impale a man with a flagstaff. April 1976.
Boston Globe.

Joker in Stanley Kubrick's *Full Metal Jacket* (1987) wearing his Marine flak helmet marked "born to kill" while sporting a peace symbol on his lapel.
Museum of Modern Art.

The Emerging Republican Majority

Kevin Phillips

Richard Nixon won the election of 1968 with 43 percent of the popular vote. The Democratic contender was Hubert H. Humphrey, Lyndon Johnson's vice president, and a third candidate, Alabama's George Wallace, ran as a populist. Nixon's election surprised many people and was initially seen as a fluke, a digression in the strong Democratic pattern of the previous forty years.

In the following brief essay, Kevin Phillips, author of the The Emerging Republican Majority *(1969), analyzes the election of 1968. He concludes that Nixon's victory was not just an aberration resulting from temporary voter discontent, but rather an indication of a sea change in American politics. Phillips posits that the coalition of workers, ethnic immigrants, and blacks that swept FDR to victory in 1932 was dissolving. How does Phillips account for the breakdown? According to the electoral map, what was the core of the new coalition? What policies would the coalition be likely to promote? How did the alliance hold together over time? What is most likely to dismantle it?*

Far from being the tenuous and unmeaningful victory suggested by critical observers, the election of Richard M. Nixon as President of the United States in November, 1968, bespoke the end of the New Deal Democratic hegemony and the beginning of a new era in American politics. To begin with, Nixon was elected by a Republican Party much changed from that deposed in 1932; and such party metamorphosis has historically brought a fresh political cycle in its wake. Secondly, the vastness of the tide (57 per cent) which overwhelmed Democratic liberalism—George Wallace's support was clearly an even more vehement protest against the Democrats than was Nixon's vote—represented an epochal shifting of national gears from the 61 per cent of the country's ballots garnered in 1964 by Lyndon Johnson. This repudiation visited upon the Democratic Party for its ambitious social programming, and inability to handle the urban and Negro revolutions, was comparable in scope to that given conservative Republicanism in 1932 for its failure to cope with the economic crisis of the Depression. And ironically, the Democratic debacle of 1968 followed the Party's most smashing victory—that of 1964—just as the 1932 toppling of the Grand Old Party succeeded the great landslide of 1928. . . .

The principal force which broke up the Democratic (New Deal) coalition is the Negro socioeconomic revolution and liberal Democratic ideological inability to cope with it. Democratic "Great Society" programs aligned that party with many Negro demands, but the party was unable to defuse the racial tension sundering the nation. The South, the West and the Catholic sidewalks of New York were the focal points of conservative opposition to the welfare liberalism of the federal government; however, the general opposition which deposed the Democratic Party came in large part from prospering Democrats who objected to Washington dissipating

Kevin Phillips, *The Emerging Republican Majority* (New Rochelle: Arlington House, 1969).

their tax dollars on programs which did them no good. The Democratic Party fell victim to the ideological impetus of a liberalism which had carried it beyond programs taxing the few for the benefit of the many (the New Deal) to programs taxing the many on behalf of the few (the Great Society).

Back in 1932, the Democratic Party took office with a popular mandate to develop a new governmental approach to the problems of economic and social welfare which the Depression had brought into painful focus. Basically, Roosevelt's New Deal liberalism invoked government action to deal with situations from which the government had hitherto remained aloof; i.e., the malpractice of corporations, unemployment, malnutrition, lack of rural electricity, collapsed farm prices and managerial intolerance of organized labor. But in the years since 1932, federal interventionism has slowly changed from an innovative policy into an institutionalized reflex. Great Society liberalism propounded federally controlled categorical grant-in-aid programs and bureaucratic social engineering as the answer to crises big and little just as inevitably as Calvin ("The business of America is business") Coolidge sermonized laissez faire economics during the formative period of the Depression. And just as the political inability of laissez faire Republicanism to handle the post-1929 economic crisis signaled the end of one cycle and the beginning of another, so did the breakdown of New Deal liberalism in the face of a social and urban crisis which clearly demands its own ideological innovation. In all likelihood, 1968 marks the beginning of an era of decentralizing government, whereby Washington can regain the public confidence necessary to mobilize the inchoate American commitment to housing, education and employment opportunity.

Gone are the days when a conservative Establishment—Wall Street, the Episcopal Church, the great metropolitan newspapers, the U.S. Supreme Court and Manhattan's East Side—harassed Franklin D. Roosevelt and his fledgling New Deal. Today, these same institutions, now liberal, vent their spleen on populist conservatism. The contemporary Establishment reflects the institutionalization of the innovative political impetus of thirty years ago: the middle-aged influence and affluence of the New Deal. This is a good sign of change. By the time a once-popular political upheaval has become institutionalized in the partners' rooms of Wall Street and the salons of Fifth Avenue, a counter-movement has invariably taken hold in the ordinary (now middle-class) hinterlands of the nation.

A fourth and last theory on which a new political cycle can be predicated rests on the post-1945 migration of many white Americans (including many of the traditionally Democratic white ethnic groups) to suburbia and the Sun Belt states of Florida, Texas, Arizona and California. This trend parallels, and is partially a result of, concurrent Southern Negro migration to the principal cities of the North. The Negro problem, having become a national rather than a local one, is the principal cause of the breakup of the New Deal coalition.

Previous American population shifts have generally triggered major political changes: (1) The rise of the trans-Appalachian "New West" in the early Nineteenth Century overpowered the conservatism of the Eastern Seaboard and provided the base of Jacksonian democracy. (2) The admission of California, Oregon and the Yankee-settled Farm states to the Union tipped the balance against the South and subsequently buoyed the Republicans throughout the post–Civil War era. (3) The expansion of the United States across the plains and Rocky Mountains added new Republican states to the Union, while the vast influx of European immigrants whose sweat ran the mills and factories of the Northeast laid down a vital foundation for the 1896-1932 era of industrial Republicanism. And (4) the coming of age of urban and immigrant America, rendered more painful by the Depression, established a national Democratic hegemony rooted in the cities which lasted from 1932 to 1968. Today, the interrelated Negro, suburban and Sun Belt migrations have all but destroyed the old New Deal coalition. . . . Some Northern cities are nearly half Negro, and new suburbia is turning into a bastion of white conservatism; moreover, growing Northern-based Negro political influence has prompted not only civil rights measures obnoxious to the South but social legislation and programs anathema to the sons and daughters of Northern immigrants. As in the past, changing population patterns have set the scene for a new political alignment.

American voting patterns are a kaleidoscope of sociology, history, geography and economics. Of course, the threads are very tangled and complex, but they can be pulled apart. The "science" in political science is not entirely a misnomer; voting patterns can be structured and analyzed in such a way as to show an extraordinary amount of social and economic behaviorism at work. Once the correct framework has been erected, national voting patterns can be structured, explained, correlated and predicted to a surprising degree. The trick is to build the framework.

For a century, the prevailing cleavages in American voting behavior have been ethnic and cultural. Politically, at least, the United States has not been a very effective melting pot. In practically every state and region, ethnic and cultural animosities and divisions exceed all other factors in explaining party choice and identification. From New York City, where income level has only minimally influenced the mutual hostility of Jews and Irish Catholics; to Wisconsin, where voting analysis requires an ethnic map of the state's Welsh, Belgian, French, Swiss, Finnish, Polish, Dutch, German, Danish, Swedish, Norwegian and Yankee populations; to Missouri, where partisanship has long pivoted on Virginian, New England, hillbilly and German settlement patterns and ensuing Civil War sympathies—everywhere ethnic, regional and cultural loyalties constitute the principal dynamics of American voting. Inasmuch as most of the Catholic ethnic groups live in Northern states where the rural Protestant population—their obvious political opposition—has been Republican, they have generally voted Democratic. Today these loyalties are ebbing along with the Republicanism of the Yankee countryside.

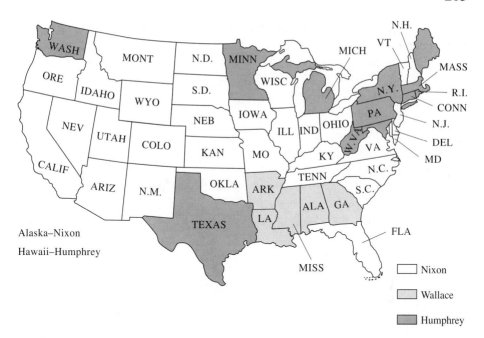

Alaska–Nixon

Hawaii–Humphrey

Nixon

Wallace

Humphrey

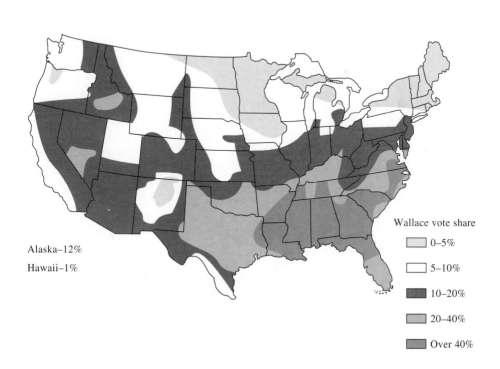

Alaska–12%

Hawaii–1%

Wallace vote share

0–5%

5–10%

10–20%

20–40%

Over 40%

SUGGESTIONS FOR VIEWING AND LISTENING

Chinatown (1974)
Corrupt 1940s Los Angeles. Americans thinking about politics during the Watergate scandal.

Nashville (1975)
The country music recording industry as a vehicle for exploring American social and political institutions and the American dream.

Straw Dogs (1971)
The flesh-eating zombies of *Night of the Living Dead* (1968) have become the working class.

Merle Haggard, "Okie from Muskogee" (1969)
The white working class attacks the counterculture.

Bruce Springsteen, "Thunder Road" (1974)
The white working class, mythologized.

Crosby, Stills, Nash and Young, "Ohio" (1970)
The Nixon administration meets the anti-war movement, this time on the Kent State University campus.

CHAPTER 8

America Under Siege

The enthusiasms of the 1960s—the Vietnam war, the Great Society's War on Poverty, the civil rights movement, the counterculture's vision of an alternative way of life, the effort to put a human being on the moon—will always provoke controversy. What can be said with assurance is that all of these ventures were underwritten by an ebullient, high-wage economy that was on its last legs.

The signs of an economy in distress appeared early. In 1965, corporate profits turned downward. In 1968, the United States for the first time imported more automobiles than it exported. In 1970, the percentage of American workers in labor unions reached a postwar peak of 26.8 and began a long decline, and the following year, the nation experienced its first international trade deficit since 1893. The most widely recognized of these signposts of decline was put into place on October 16, 1973, when the Arab-dominated Organization of Petroleum Exporting Countries (OPEC) responded to American intervention in the Arab-Israeli war by cutting off oil shipments to the United States, Japan, and western Europe. By early 1974 the stock market was in free fall and problems of inflation and economic stagnation had surfaced that would last nearly another decade.

There are many different theories about why this decline occurred. Liberal scholars generally contend that the combination of Vietnam and the social programs of the Great Society (that is, the desire to have both guns and butter) initiated the harmful inflationary spiral. Conservatives usually respond that the nation lost its competitive advantage when it became captive to powerful labor unions and then, during the Johnson presidency, overcommitted to costly and bureaucratic social programs. Others argue that the root of the problem was America's growing loss of control over developing nations, including the Arab states.

Whatever the cause, the "American Century" that publisher Henry Luce had proclaimed during World War II had ended, well short of the century mark. At this moment, when the American people desperately needed leadership, they got something they didn't need: Watergate. Watergate had its origins in 1969, when the Nixon administration embarked on a campaign to isolate and discredit the peace movement. By 1971 those charged with this responsibility had moved to the Committee for the Reelection of the President (CREEP), where they were working with former Attorney General John Mitchell in an illegal effort to gather information on political opponents. In June 1972, five CREEP operatives were apprehended at the

Democratic National Committee headquarters in Washington's Watergate apartment complex. It was an election year, and officials of the Nixon administration denied involvement. Two years later, when the president's own tape recordings revealed that he had conspired to cover up the break-in, a humiliated Nixon resigned. His legacy (although it owed something to Lyndon Johnson's lack of candor in handling the war in Vietnam) was a new and troublesome attitude toward politics: credibility. Simply put, he didn't have any. Many Americans no longer believed what the politicians told them.

Given the depressed economic conditions of the decade, the crisis of confidence in politics, and the working-class-led backlash against the social reform energies of the sixties, it is not surprising that little progress was made on "reform" fronts in the seventies. To be sure, powerful lobbies of the elderly were able to bring their constituents tangible gains: a new system that indexed social security to changes in the cost of living and a 1978 law that abolished mandatory retirement in most employment. Campaigns for gay rights and women's rights also remained vital through the 1970s. And environmental issues proved able to generate an ongoing consensus for continued government action, perhaps because those issues were consistent with the emerging idea of limits.

But on the critical issues that the sixties had courageously and optimistically raised to prominence—poverty, racism, the decaying inner cities—the consensus was washing away. What was left was a new and probably mistaken reliance on forced busing and affirmative action as solutions to these ills. These solutions relied too much on the sacrifices of the white working class and, in the case of busing, on schools that were educationally inadequate no matter who attended them. They were solutions bound to fail.

Above all it was an age of survival, of getting by until things got better, of coming to terms with limited opportunities. This was the world of Bruce Springsteen, who emerged as a pop idol in 1974 with the album *Born to Run.* Springsteen offered something like existential hope. Although he depicted the America of the 1970s as a "jungleland" of desperation, he also believed that faith, passion, and a moving automobile might be enough to produce "magic in the night," perhaps even some more permanent form of escape. As for disco, there was no more consensus over the music than anything else in the 1970s, and its origins in the gay and black communities in the early part of the decade did not endear it to the white working class. Yet disco was enormously popular because it spoke so clearly to the question of survival, with the darkened discotheque a haven of refuge from a difficult world and the pulsating, irrepressible beat a pacemaker for the walking (or dancing) wounded. In the words of the Bee Gees' 1977 hit, it all came down to "stayin' alive."

Jimmy Carter spoke this language, too, and for four years (1977–1980) he ministered to the needs of the population like Mom with a bowl of chicken soup. He worked at labeling the nation's illness—a "malaise" in one speech, a "crisis of purpose" in another. And he patiently explained to Americans how they could survive the new regime of limits by conserving energy and living simpler lives. It was not bad advice at all, and for a time Americans responded enthusiastically to a president who at least seemed honest and credible. But Carter could not solve the riddle of "stagflation"—high rates of inflation and unemployment at the same time. Nor could he do anything much about the Iranian militants who in 1979 took

John Travolta in his famous disco-dancing pose in *Saturday Night Fever* (1977). Travolta's characters were ordinary guys whose main task was to achieve a modicum of self-respect, and whose triumphs were limited ones—learning to ride a mechanical bull or winning a dance contest—won in bars and discos.
The Bettmann Archive.

52 American hostages and held them for 444 days—the last in what seemed a long series of national humiliations. By 1980, Americans wanted more than survival, and they were willing to listen to anyone who promised to give them back the nation they had lost.

INTERPRETIVE ESSAY

Environmental Politics

Samuel P. Hays

In the following essay, historian Samuel P. Hays outlines the transition from a turn-of-the-century "conservation" approach to natural resources, to a post-1960 "environmental era." This broad historical overview makes it possible to understand environmental concerns not just as another 1960s issue that happened to survive into the 1970s, but also as a product of major and ongoing changes in the lives of most Americans. Why, then, did environmental matters remain potent issues in the 1980s, whereas public housing, urban "renewal," and other ingredients of Lyndon Johnson's Great Society had virtually disappeared from the political agenda? What great historical forces underpinned the environmental era? In what other ways have those forces changed today's world?

The historical significance of the rise of environmental affairs in the United States in recent decades lies in the changes that have taken place in American society since World War II. Important antecedents of those changes, to be sure, can be identified in earlier years as "background" conditions on the order of historical forerunners. But the intensity and force, and most of the substantive direction of the new environmental social and political phenomenon, can be understood only through the massive changes that occurred after the end of the war—and not just in the United States but throughout advanced industrial societies. . . .

THE CONSERVATION AND ENVIRONMENTAL IMPULSES

Prior to World War II, before the term "environment" was hardly used, the dominant theme in conservation emphasized physical resources, their more efficient use and development. The range of emphasis evolved from water and forests in the late nineteenth and early twentieth centuries, to grass and soils and game in the 1930s. In all these fields of endeavor there was a common concern for the loss of physical productivity represented by waste. The threat to the future that that "misuse" implied could be corrected through "sound" or efficient management. Hence in each field there arose a management system that emphasized a balancing of immediate

From Samuel P. Hays, "From Conservation to Environment: Environmental Politics in the United States Since World War Two," *Environmental Review,* vol. 6, no. 2, fall 1982, pp. 14–41. Reprinted with permission by American Society for Environmental History.

in favor of more long-run production, the coordination of factors of production under central management schemes for the greatest efficiency. All this is a chapter in the history of production rather than of consumption, and of the way in which managers organized production rather than the way in which consumers evolved ideas and action amid the general public.

Enough has already been written about the evolution of multiple-purpose river development and sustained-yield forestry to establish their role in this context of efficient management for commodity production. But perhaps a few more words could be added for those resources that came to public attention after World War I. Amid the concern about soil erosion, from both rain and wind, the major stress lay in warnings about the loss of agricultural productivity. What had taken years to build up over geologic time now was threatened with destruction by short-term practices. The soil conservation program inaugurated in 1933 gave rise to a full-scale attack on erosion problems that was carried out amid almost inspired religious fervor. . . .

Perhaps the most significant vantage point from which to observe the common processes at work in these varied resource affairs was the degree to which resource managers thought of themselves as engaged in a common venture. It was not difficult to bring into the overall concept of "natural resources" the management of forests and waters, of soils and grazing lands, and of game. State departments of natural resources emerged, such as in Michigan, Wisconsin, and Minnesota, and some university departments of forestry became departments of natural resources—all this as the new emphases on soils and game were added to the older ones on forests and waters. By the time of World War II a complex of professionals had come into being, with a strong focus on management as their common task, on the organization of applied knowledge about physical resources so as to sustain output for given investments of input under centralized management direction. This entailed a common conception of "conservation" and a common focus on "renewable resources," often within the rubric of advocating "wise use" under the direction of professional experts.

During these years another and altogether different strand of activity also drew upon the term "conservation" to clash with the thrust of efficient commodity management. Today we frequently label it *preservation* as we seek to distinguish between the themes of efficient development symbolized by Gifford Pinchot and natural environment management symbolized by John Muir. Those concerned with national parks and the later wilderness activities often used the term *conservation* to describe what they were about. In the Sierra Club the "conservation committees" took up the organization's political action in contrast with its outings. And those who formed the National Parks Association and later the Wilderness Society could readily think of themselves as conservationists, struggling to define the term quite differently than did those in the realm of efficient management. . . .

Prior to World War II the natural environment movement made some significant gains. One thinks especially of the way in which Pinchot was blocked from absorbing the national parks under his direction in the first decade of the century and then, over his objections, advocates of natural environment values succeeded in establishing the National Park Service in 1916. Then there was the ensuing struggle of several decades in which an aggressive Park Service was able to engage the Forest Service in a contest for control of land and on many occasions won. . . .

After the war a massive turnabout of historical forces took place. The complex of specialized fields of efficient management of physical resources increasingly came under attack amid a new "environmental" thrust. It contained varied components. One was the further elaboration of the outdoor recreation and natural environment movements of prewar, as reflected in the Wilderness Act of 1964, the Wild and Scenic Rivers Act of 1968, and the National Trails Act of the same year, and further legislation and administrative action on through the 1970s. But there were other strands even less rooted in the past. The most extensive was the concern for environmental pollution, or *environmental protection* as it came to be called in technical and managerial circles. While smoldering in varied and diverse ways in this or that setting from many years before, this concern burst forth to national prominence in the mid-1960s and especially in air and water pollution. And there was the decentralist thrust, the search for technologies of smaller and more human scale, which complement rather than dwarf the more immediate human setting. . . . The search for a "sense of place," for a context that is more manageable intellectually and emotionally amid the escalating pace of size and scale had not made its mark in earlier years as it did in the 1970s to shape broad patterns of human thought and action.

One of the most striking differences between these postwar environmental activities, in contrast to the earlier conservation affairs, was their social roots. Earlier one can find little in the way of broad popular support for the substantive objectives of conservation, little "movement" organization, and scanty evidence of broadly shared conservation values. The drive came from the top down, from technical and managerial leaders. . . . [I]n sharp contrast, the environmental era displayed demands from the grass-roots, demands that are well charted by the innumerable citizen organizations and studies of public attitudes. One of the major themes of these later years, in fact, was the tension that evolved between the environmental public and the environmental managers, as impulses arising from the public clashed with impulses arising from management. This was not a new stage of public activity per se, but of new values as well. The widespread expression of social values in environmental action marks off the environmental era from the conservation years.

It is useful to think about this as the interaction between two sets of historical forces, one older that was associated with large-scale management and technology, and the other newer that reflected new types of public values and demands. The term *environment* in contrast with the earlier term *conservation* reflects more precisely the innovations in values. The technologies with which those values clashed in the postwar years, however, were closely aligned in spirit and historical roots with earlier conservation tendencies, with new stages in the evolution from the earlier spirit of scientific management of which conservation had been an integral part. A significant element of the historical analysis, therefore, is to identify the points of tension in the environmental era between the new stages of conservation

as efficient management as it became more highly elaborated, and the newly evolving environmental concerns, which displayed an altogether different thrust. . .
.

There was, for example, the changing public conception of the role and meaning of forests. The U.S. Forest Service, and the entire community of professional foresters, continued to elaborate the details of scientific management of wood production; it took the form of increasing input for higher yields and came to emphasize especially even-aged management. But an increasing number of Americans thought of forests as environments for home, work, and play, as an environmental rather than as a commodity resource, and hence to be protected from incompatible crop-oriented strategies. Many of them bought woodlands for their environmental rather than their wood production potential. But the forestry profession did not seem to be able to accept the new values. The Forest Service was never able to "get on top" of the wilderness movement to incorporate it in "leading edge" fashion into its own strategies. As the movement evolved from stage to stage the Service seemed to be trapped by its own internal value commitments and hence relegated to playing a rear-guard role to protect wood production. . . .

There was one notable exception to these almost irreconcilable tensions between the old and the new in which a far smoother transition occurred—the realm of wildlife. In this case the old emphasis on game was faced with a new one on nature observation or what came to be called a *nongame* or *appreciative* use of wildlife. Between these two impulses there were many potential arenas for deep controversy. But there was also common ground in their joint interest in wildlife habitat. The same forest that served as a place for hunting also served as a place for nature observation. . . . As a result of this shared interest in wildlife habitat it was relatively easy for many "game managers" to shift in their self-conceptions to become "wildlife managers." . . .

If we examine the values and ideas, then, the activities and programs, the directions of impulses in the political arena, we can observe a marked transition from the pre–World War II conservation themes of efficient management of physical resources, to the post–world war environmental themes of environmental amenities, environmental protection, and human-scale technology. Something new was happening in American society, arising out of the social changes and transformation in human values in the postwar years. These were associated more with the advanced consumer society of those years than with the industrial manufacturing society of the late nineteenth and the first half of the twentieth centuries. Let me now root these environmental values in these social and value changes.

THE ROOTS OF NEW ENVIRONMENTAL VALUES

The most immediate image of the "environmental movement" consists of its "protests," its objections to the extent and manner of development and the shape of technology. From the media evidence one has a sense of environmentalists blocking "needed" energy projects, dams, highways, and industrial plants, and of complaints of the environmental harm generated by pollution. Environmental action seems to be negative, a protest affair. This impression is also heavily shaped by the "environmental impact" mode of analysis, which identifies the "adverse effects" of development and presumably seeks to avoid or mitigate them. The question is one of how development can proceed with the "least" adverse effect to the "environment." From this context of thinking about environmental affairs one is tempted to formulate an environmental history based upon the way in which technology and development have created "problems" for society to be followed by ways in which action has been taken to cope with those problems.

This is superficial analysis. For environmental impulses are rooted in deep-seated changes in recent America, which should be understood primarily in terms of new positive directions. We are at a stage in history when new values and new ways of looking at ourselves have emerged to give rise to new preferences. These are characteristic of advanced industrial societies throughout the world, not just in the United States. They reflect two major and widespread social changes. One is associated with the search for standards of living beyond necessities and conveniences to include amenities made possible by considerable increases in personal and social "real income." The other arises from advancing levels of education, which have generated values associated with personal creativity and self-development, involvement with natural environments, physical and mental fitness and wellness and political autonomy and efficacy. Environmental values and objectives are an integral part of these changes. . . .

The "environmental impulse" . . . reflects a desire for a better "quality of life," which is another phase of the continual search by the American people throughout their history for a higher standard of living. Environmental values are widespread in American society, extending throughout income and occupational levels, areas of the nation, and racial groups, somewhat stronger in the middle sectors and a bit weaker in the very high and very low groupings. There are identifiable "leading sectors" of change with which they are associated as well as "lagging sectors." They tend to be stronger with younger people and increasing levels of education and move into the larger society from those centers of innovation. They are also more associated with particular geographical regions such as New England, the Upper Lakes states, the Upper Rocky Mountain region, and the far west, while the south, the Plains states, and the lower Rockies constitute "lagging" regions. Hence one can argue that environmental values have expanded steadily in American society, associated with demographic sectors that are growing rather than with those that are more stable or declining.

Within this general context one can identify several distinctive sets of environmental tendencies. One was the way in which an increasing portion of the American people came to value natural environments as an integral part of their rising standard of living. They sought out many types of such places to experience, explore, enjoy, and protect; high mountains and forests, wetlands, ocean shores, swamplands, wild and scenic rivers, deserts, pine barrens, remnants of the original prairies, places of relatively clean air and water, more limited "natural areas." Interest in such places was not a throwback to the primitive, but an integral part of the modern standard of living as people sought to add new "amenity" and "aesthetic" goals and desires to their earlier preoccupation with necessities and conveniences. These new consumer wants were closely associated with many others of a similar kind such as in the creative arts, recreation and leisure in general, crafts, indoor and household decoration, hi-fi sets, the care of yards and gardens as living space, and amenity components of necessities and conveniences. Americans experienced natural environments both emotionally and intellectually, sought them out for direct personal experience in recreation, studied them as objects of scientific and intellectual interest, and desired to have them within their community, their region, and their nation as symbols of a society with a high degree of civic consciousness and pride.

A new view of health constituted an equally significant innovation in environmental values, health less as freedom from illness and more as physical and mental fitness, of feeling well, of optimal capability for exercising one's physical and mental powers. The control of infectious diseases by antibiotics brought to the fore new types of health problems associated with slow, cumulative changes in physical condition, symbolized most strikingly by cancer, but by the 1980s ranging into many other conditions such as genetic and reproductive problems, degenerative changes such as heart disease and deteriorating immune systems. All this put more emphasis on the nonbacterial environmental causes of illness but, more importantly, brought into health matters an emphasis on the positive conditions of wellness and fitness. There was an increasing tendency to adopt personal habits that promoted rather than threatened health, to engage in physical exercise, to quit smoking, to eat more nutritiously, and to reduce environmental threats in the air and water that might also weaken one's wellness. [One] result of this concern [was] the rapid increase in the business of health food stores, which reached $1.5 billion in 1979. . . .

These new aesthetic and health values constituted much of the roots of environmental concern. They came into play in personal life and led to new types of consumption in the private market, but they also led to demands for public action both to enhance opportunities, such as to make natural environments more available and to ward off threats to values. The threats constituted some of the most celebrated environmental battles: power and petrochemical plant siting, hardrock mining and strip mining, chemicals in the workplace and in underground drinking water supplies, energy transmission lines and pipelines. Many a local community found itself faced with a threat imposed from the outside and sought to protect itself through "environmental action." But the incidence and intensity of reaction against these threats arose at a particular time in history because of the underlying changes in values and aspirations. People had new preferences and new personal and family values that they did not have before. . . .

Still another concern began to play a more significant role in environmental affairs in the 1970s—an assertion of the desirability of more personal family and community autonomy in the face of the larger institutional world of corporate industry and government, an affirmation of smaller in the face of larger contexts of organization and power. This constituted a "self-help" movement. It was reflected in numerous publications about the possibilities of self-reliance in production of food and clothing, design and construction of homes, recreation and leisure, recycling of wastes and materials, and use of energy through such decentralized forms as wind and solar. These tendencies were far more widespread than institutional and thought leaders of the nation recognized since their world of perception and management was far removed from community and grass-roots ideas and action. The debate between "soft" and "hard" energy paths seemed to focus much of the controversy over the possibilities of decentralization. But it should also be stressed that the American economy, while tending toward more centralized control and management, also generated products that made individual choices toward decentralized living more possible and hence stimulated this phase of environmental affairs. While radical change had produced large-scale systems of management it had also reinvigorated the more traditional Yankee tinkerer who now found a significant niche in the new environmental scheme of things.

Several significant historical tendencies are integral parts of these changes. One involves consumption and the role of environmental values as part of evolving consumer values. At one time, perhaps as late as 1900, the primary focus in consumption was on necessities. By the 1920s a new stage had emerged, which emphasized conveniences in which the emerging consumer durables, such as the automobile and household appliances, were the most visible elements. This change meant that a larger portion of personal income, and hence of social income and production facilities were now being devoted to a new type of demand and supply. By the late 1940s a new stage in the history of consumption had come into view. Many began to find that both their necessities and conveniences had been met and an increasing share of their income could be devoted to amenities. The shorter work week and increasing availability of vacations provided opportunities for more leisure and recreation. Hence personal and family time and income could be spent on amenities. Economists were inclined to describe this as *discretionary income*. The implications of this observation about the larger context of environmental values is that it is a part of the history of consumption rather than of production. That in itself involves a departure from traditional emphases in historical analysis.

Another way of looking at these historical changes is to observe the shift in focus in daily living from a preoccupation with work in earlier years to a greater role for home, family and leisure in the postwar period. Public opinion surveys indicate a persistent shift in which of these activities respondents felt were more important, a steady decline in a dominant emphasis on work and a steady rise in those activities associated with home, family, and leisure. One of the most significant aspects of this shift was a divorce in the physical location of work and home. For most people in the rapidly developing manufacturing cities of the nineteenth century the location of home was dictated by the location of work. But the widespread use of the automobile, beginning in the 1920s, enabled an increasing number of people, factory workers as well as white-collar workers, to live in one place and to work in another. The environmental context of home, therefore, came to be an increasingly separate and distinctive focus for their choices. Much of the environmental movement arose from this physical separation of the environments of home and work.

One can identify in all this a historical shift in the wider realm of politics as well. Prior to World War II the most persistent larger context of national political debate involved the balance among sectors of production. From the late nineteenth century on the evolution of organized extra-party political activity, in the form of "interest groups," was overwhelmingly devoted to occupational affairs, and the persistent policy issues involved the balance of the shares of production that were to be received by business, agriculture, and labor, and subsectors within them. Against this array of political forces consumer objectives were woefully weak. But the evolution of new types of consumption in recreation, leisure, and amenities generated quite a different setting. By providing new focal points of organized activity in common leisure and recreational interest groups, and by emphasizing community organization to protect community environmental values against threats from external developmental pressures, consumer impulses went through a degree of mobilization and activity that they had not previously enjoyed. In many an instance they were able to confront developmentalists with considerable success. Hence environmental action reflects the emergence in American politics of a new effectiveness for consumer action not known in the years before the war.

One of the distinctive aspects of the history of consumption is the degree to which what once were luxuries, enjoyed by only a few, over the years became enjoyed by many—articles of mass consumption. . . . And so it was with environmental amenities. What only a few could enjoy in the nineteenth century came to be mass activities in the mid-twentieth, as many purchased homes with a higher level of amenities around them and could participate in outdoor recreation beyond the city. Amid the tendency for the more affluent to seek out and acquire as private property the more valued natural amenity sites, the public lands came to be places where the opportunity for such activities remained far more accessible to a wide segment of the social order.

A major element of the older, pre–World War II "conservation movement," efficiency in the use of resources, also became revived in the 1970s around the concern for energy supply. It led to a restatement of rather traditional options, as to whether or not natural resources were limited, and hence one had to emphasize efficiency and frugality, or whether or not they were unlimited and could be developed with unabated vigor. Environmentalists stressed the former. It was especially clear that the "natural environments" of air, water, and land were finite, and that increasing demand for these amid a fixed supply led to considerable inflation in price for those that were bought and sold in the private market. Pressures of growing demand on limited supply of material resources appeared to most people initially in the form of inflation; this trend of affairs in energy was the major cause of inflation in the entire economy. The great energy debates of the 1970s gave special focus to a wide range of issues pertaining to the "limits to growth." Environmentalists stressed the possibilities of "conservation supplies" through greater energy productivity and while energy producing companies objected to this as a major policy alternative, industrial consumers of energy joined with household consumers in taking up efficiency as the major alternative. In the short run the "least cost" option in energy supply in the private market enabled the nation greatly to reduce its energy use and carried out the environmental option.

In accounting for the historical timing of the environmental movement one should emphasize changes in the "threats" as well as in the values. Much of the shape and timing of environmental debate arose from changes in the magnitude and form of these threats from modern technology. That technology was applied in increasing scale and scope, from enormous drag-lines in strip mining, to 1000-megawatt electric generating plants and "energy parks," to superports and large-scale petrochemical plants, to 765-kilovolt energy transmission lines. And there was the vast increase in the use and release into the environment of chemicals, relatively contained and generating a chemical "sea around us" that many people consider to be a long-run hazard that was out of control. The view of these technological changes as threats seemed to come primarily from their size and scale, the enormity of their range of impact, in contrast to the more human scale of daily affairs. New technologies appeared to constitute radical influences, disruptive of settled community and personal life, of a scope that was often beyond comprehension, and promoted and carried through by influences "out there" from the wider corporate and governmental world. All this brought to environmental issues the problem of "control," of how one could shape more limited personal and community circumstance in the face of large-scale and radical change impinging from afar upon daily life.

STAGES IN THE EVOLUTION OF
ENVIRONMENTAL ACTION

Emerging environmental values did not make themselves felt all in the same way or at the same time. Within the context of our concern here for patterns of historical change, therefore, it might be well to secure some sense of stages of development within the post–World War II years. The most prevalent notion is to identify Earth Day in 1970 as the dividing line. There are other candidate events, such as the publication of Rachel Carson's *Silent Spring* in 1962 and the Santa Barbara oil blowout in 1969. But in any event definition of change in these matters seems to be inadequate. Earth Day was as much a result as a cause. It came after a decade or more of underlying evolution in attitudes and action without which it would not have been possible. Many environmental organizations, established earlier, experienced considerable growth in membership during the 1960s, reflecting an expanding concern. The regulatory mechanisms and issues in such fields as air and water pollution were shaped then; for example the Clean Air Act of 1967 established the character of the air quality program more than did that of 1970. General public awareness and interest were expressed extensively in a variety of public forums and in the mass media. Evolving public values could be observed in the growth of the outdoor recreation movement that reached back into the 1950s and the search for amenities in quieter and more natural settings, in the increasing number of people who engaged in hiking and camping or purchased recreational lands and homes on the seashore, by lakes and in woodlands. This is not to say that the entire scope of environmental concerns emerged fully in the 1960s. It did not. But one can observe a gradual evolution rather than a sudden outburst at the turn of the decade, a cumulative social and political change that came to be expressed vigorously even long before Earth Day.

We might identify three distinct stages of evolution. Each stage brought a new set of issues to the fore without eliminating the previous ones, in a set of historical layers. Old issues persisted to be joined by new ones, creating over the years an increasingly complex and varied world of environmental controversy and debate. The initial complex of issues that arrived on the scene of national politics emphasized natural environment values in such matters as outdoor recreation, wildlands, and open space. These shaped debate between 1957 and 1965 and constituted the initial thrust of environmental action. After World War II the American people, with increased income and leisure time, sought out the nation's forests and parks, its wildlife refuges, its state and federal public lands, for recreation and enjoyment. Recognition of this growing interest and the demands upon public policy that it generated, led Congress in 1958 to establish the National Outdoor Recreational Review Commission, which completed its report in 1962. Its recommendations heavily influenced public policy during the Johnson administration. . . .

During the 1950s many in urban areas had developed a concern for urban overdevelopment and the need for open space in their communities. . . . The concern for open space extended to regional as well as community projects, involving a host of natural environment areas ranging from pine barrens to wetlands to swamps to creeks and streams to remnants of the original prairies. Throughout the 1960s there were attempts to add to the national park system, which gave rise to new parks such as Canyonlands in Utah, new national lakeshores and seashores, and new national recreation areas.

These matters set the dominant tone of the initial phase of environmental concern until the mid-1960s. They did not decline in importance, but continued to shape administrative and legislative action as specific proposals for wilderness, scenic rivers, or other natural areas emerged to be hotly debated. Such general measures as the Eastern Wilderness Act of 1974 . . . and the Alaska National Interest Lands Act of 1980 testified to the perennial public concern for natural environmental areas. . . . One might argue that these were the most enduring and fundamental environmental issues throughout the two decades. While other citizen concerns might ebb and flow, interest in natural environment areas persisted steadily. That interest was the dominant reason for membership growth in the largest environmental organizations. The Nature Conservancy, a private group that emphasized acquisition of natural environment lands, grew in activity in the latter 1970s and reached 100,000 members in 1981. . . .

Amid this initial stage of environmental politics there evolved a new and different concern for the adverse impact of industrial development with a special focus on air and water pollution. This had long evolved slowly on a local and piecemeal basis, but emerged with national force only in the mid-1960s. In the early part of the decade air and water pollution began to take on significance as national issues, and by 1965 they had become highly visible. The first national public opinion poll on such questions was taken in that year, and the president's annual message in 1965 reflected, for the first time, a full-fledged concern for pollution problems. Throughout the rest of the decade and on into the 1970s these issues evolved continually. Federal legislation to stimulate remedial action was shaped over the course of these seven years, from 1965 to 1972, a distinct period that constituted the second phase in the evolution of environmental politics, taking its place alongside the previously developing concern for natural environment areas.

The legislative results were manifold. Air pollution was the subject of new laws in 1967 and 1970; water pollution in 1965, 1970, and 1972. The evolving concern about pesticides led to revision of the existing law in the Pesticides Act of 1972. The growing public interest in natural environment values in the coastal zone, and threats to them by dredging and filling, industrial siting, and offshore oil development first made its mark on Congress in 1965 and over the next few years shaped the course of legislation, which finally emerged in the Coastal Zone Management Act of 1972. Earth Day in the spring of 1970 lay in the middle of this phase of historical development, both a result of the previous half-decade of activity and concern and a new influence to accelerate action. . . .

Yet this new phase was shaped heavily by the previous period in that it gave primary emphasis to the harmful impact of pollution on ecological systems rather than on human health—a concern that was to come later. In the years between 1965 and 1972 the interest in "ecology" came to the fore to indicate the intense public interest in potential harm to the natural environment and in protection against disruptive threats. The impacts of highway construction, electric power plants, and industrial siting on wildlife, on aquatic ecosystems, and on natural environments in general played a major role in the evolution of this concern. . . . The major concern for the adverse effect of nuclear energy generation in the late 1960s involved its potential disruption of aquatic ecosystems from thermal pollution rather than the effect of radiation on people. The rapidly growing ecological concern was an extension of the natural environment interests of the years 1957 to 1965 into the problem of the adverse impacts of industrial growth.

Beginning in the early 1970s still a third phase of environmental politics arose, which brought three other sets of issues into public debate: toxic chemicals, energy, and the possibilities of social, economic, and political decentralization. These did not obliterate earlier issues, but as some natural environment matters and concern over the adverse effects of industrialization shifted from legislative to administrative politics, and thus became less visible to the general public, these new issues emerged often to dominate the scene. They were influenced heavily by the seemingly endless series of toxic chemical episodes, from PBBs in Michigan to kepone in Virginia to PCBs on the Hudson River, to the discovery of abandoned chemical dumps at Love Canal and near Louisville, Kentucky. These events, however, were only the more sensational aspects of a more deep-seated new twist in public concern for human health. Interest in personal health and especially in preventive health action took a major leap forward in the 1970s. It seemed to focus especially on such matters as cancer and environmental pollutants responsible for a variety of health problems, on food and diet on the one hand and exercise on the other. From these interests arose a central concern for toxic threats in the workplace, in the air and water, and in food and personal habits that came to shape some of the overriding issues of the 1970s on the environmental front. It shifted the earlier emphasis on the ecological effects of toxic pollutants to one more on human health effects. Thus, while proceedings against DDT in the late 1960s had emphasized adverse ecological impacts, similar proceedings in the 1970s focused primarily on human health.

The energy crisis of the winter of 1973–1974 brought a new issue to the fore. Not that energy matters had gone unnoticed earlier, but their salience had been far more limited. After that winter they became more central. They shaped environmental politics in at least two ways. First, energy problems brought material shortages more forcefully into the realm of substantive environmental concerns and emphasized more strongly the problem of limits that these shortages imposed upon material growth. The physical shortages of energy sources such as oil in the United States, the impact of shortages on rising prices, the continued emphasis on the need for energy conservation all helped to etch into the experience and thinking of Americans the "limits" to which human appetite for consumption could go. Second, the intense demand for development of new energy sources increased significantly the political influence of developmental advocates in governmental, corporate, and technical institutions that had long chafed under both natural environment and pollution control programs. This greatly overweighted the balance of political forces so that environmental leaders had far greater difficulty in being heard. . . .

Lifestyle issues also injected a new dimension into environmental affairs during the course of the 1970s. They became especially visible in the energy debates, as the contrast emerged between highly centralized technologies on the one hand and decentralized systems on the other. Behind these debates lay the evolution of new ideas about organizing one's daily life, one's home, community, and leisure activities and even work—all of which had grown out of the changing lifestyles of younger Americans. It placed considerable emphasis on more personal, family, and community autonomy in the face of the forces of larger social, economic, and political organization. The impact and role of this change was not always clear, but it emerged forcefully in the energy debate as decentralized solar systems and conservation seemed to be appropriate to decisions made personally and locally—on a more human scale—contrasting markedly with high-technology systems that leaders of technical, corporate, and governmental institutions seemed to prefer. Issues pertaining to the centralization of political control played an increasing role in environmental politics as the 1970s came to a close. . . .

From the beginning of [the Reagan] administration, the new governmental leaders made clear their conviction that the "environmental movement" had spent itself, was no longer viable, and could readily be dismissed and ignored. During the campaign the Reagan entourage had often refused to meet with citizen environmental groups, and in late November it made clear that it would not even accept the views of its own "transition team," which was made up of former Republican administration environmentalists who were thought to be far too extreme. Hence environmentalists of all these varied hues faced a hostile government that was not prone to be evasive or deceptive about that hostility. Its antienvironmental views were expressed with enormous vigor and clarity.

We can well look upon that challenge as an historical experiment that tested the extent and permanence of the changes in social values that lay at the root of environmental interest. By its opposition the Reagan administration could be thought of as challenging citizen environmental activity to prove itself. And the response, in turn, indicated a degree of depth and persistence that makes clear that environmental affairs stem from the extensive and deep-seated changes we have been describing. Most striking perhaps have been the public opinion polls during 1981 pertaining to revision of the Clean Air Act. On two occasions, in April and in September, the Harris poll found that some 80 percent of the American people favor at least maintaining that act or making it stricter, levels of positive environmental opinion on air quality higher than for polls in the 1960s or 1970s. . . .

We might take this response to the Reagan administration challenge, therefore, as evidence of the degree to which we can assess the environmental activities of the past three decades as associated with fundamental and persistent change, not a temporary display of sentiment, which causes environmental values to be injected into public affairs continuously and even more vigorously in the face of political adversity. The most striking aspect of this for the historian lies in the way in which it identifies more sharply the social roots of environmental values, perception, and action. Something is there, in a broad segment of the American people that shapes the course of public policy in these decades after World War II that was far different from the case earlier. One observes not rise and fall, but persistent evolution, changes rooted in personal circumstance, which added up to broad social changes out of which "movements" and political action arise and are sustained. Environmental affairs take on meaning as integral parts of a "new society" that is an integral element of the advanced consumer and industrial order of the last half of the twentieth century.

SOURCES

New-Style Feminism

Modern feminism emerged in the early 1960s, with John Kennedy's Commission on the Status of Women, the Equal Pay Act of 1963, and the publication that year of Betty Friedan's The Feminine Mystique. *During the 1960s, feminists emphasized their exclusion from the mainstream—from politics, from the professions, from Princeton and Yale, from ordinary good jobs. Through the National Organization for Women (NOW) and other organizations, they demanded equality in the workplace and assailed the idea, captured in the phrase "the feminine mystique," that women could live full, rich lives in purely domestic roles. By the 1970s, vocal critics of this position had emerged. Some believed that there could be no equality that did not involve significant changes in the family and domestic relations. Others rejected the assumption, implicit in the earlier view, that women should strive to be like men. This new-style feminism emphasized that feminists should understand, value, and utilize their qualities as* women.

Our Bodies, Ourselves *(1971) was part of this new brand of feminism. What kinds of information did the book contain? Why did the women who wrote the book think it was necessary? What connection is there between its publication and the* Roe v. Wade *decision, handed down by the Supreme Court in 1973, which made invalid all laws prohibiting abortion during the first three months of pregnancy?*

Our Bodies, Ourselves

The Boston Women's Health Book Collective

PREFACE

A Good Story

The history of this book, *Our Bodies, Ourselves*, is lengthy and satisfying.

It began at a small discussion group on "women and their bodies" that was part of a women's conference held in Boston in the spring of 1969. These were the early days of the women's movement, one of the first gatherings of women meeting specifically to talk with other women. For many of us it was the very first time we got together with other women to talk and think about our lives and what we could do about them. Before the conference was over some of us decided to keep on meeting as a group to continue the discussion, and so we did.

In the beginning we called the group "the doctor's group." We had all experienced similar feelings of frustration and anger toward specific doctors and the medical maze in general, and initially we wanted to do something about those doctors who were condescending, paternalistic, judgmental, and noninformative. As we talked and shared our experiences with one another, we realized just how much we had to learn about our bodies. So we decided on a summer project—to research those topics that we felt were particularly pertinent to learning about our bodies, to discuss in the group what we had learned, then to write papers individually or in small groups of two or three, and finally to present the results in the fall as a course for women on women and their bodies.

As we developed the course we realized more and more that we were really capable of collecting, understanding, and evaluating medical information. Together we evaluated our reading of books and journals, our talks with doctors and friends who were medical students. We found we could discuss, question, and argue with each other in a new spirit of cooperation rather than competition. We were equally struck by how important it was for us to be able to open up with one another and share our feelings about our bodies. The process of talking was as crucial as the facts themselves. Over time the facts and feelings melted together in ways that touched us very deeply, and that is reflected in the changing titles of the course and then the book—from *Women and Their Bodies* to *Women and Our Bodies* to, finally, *Our Bodies, Ourselves.*

When we gave the course we met in any available free space we could get—in day schools, in nursery schools, in churches, in our homes. We expected the course to stimulate the same kind of talking and sharing that we who had prepared the course had experienced. We had something to say, but we had a lot to learn as well; we did not want a traditional teacher-student relationship. At the end of ten to twelve sessions—which roughly covered the material in the current book—we found that many women felt both eager and competent to get together in small groups and share what they had learned with other women. We saw it as a never-ending process always involving more and more women. . . .

You may want to know who we are. We are white, our ages range from twenty-four to forty, most of us are from middle-class backgrounds and have had at least some college education, and some of us have professional degrees. Some of us are married, some of us are separated, and some of us are single. Some of us have children of our own, some of us like spending time with children, and others of us are not sure we want to be with children. In short, we are both a very ordinary and a very special group, as women are everywhere. We are white middle-class women, and as such can describe only what life has been for us. But we do realize that poor women and nonwhite women have suffered far more from the kinds of misinformation and mistreatment that we are describing in this book. In some ways, learning about our womenhood from the inside out has allowed us to cross over the socially created barriers of race, color, income, and class, and to feel a sense of identity with all women in the experience of being female.

We are twelve individuals and we are a group. (The group has been ongoing for three years, and some of us have been together since the beginning. Others came in at later points. Our current collective has been together for one year.) We know each other well—our weaknesses as well as our strengths. We have learned through good times and bad how to work together (and how not to as well). We recognize our similarities and differences and are learning to respect each person for her uniqueness. We love each other.

Many, many other women have worked with us on the book. A group of gay women got together specifically to do the chapter on lesbianism. Other papers were done still differently. For instance, along with some friends the mother of one woman in the group volunteered to work on menopause with some of us who have not gone through that experience ourselves. Other women contributed thoughts, feelings, and comments as they passed through town or passed through our kitchens or workrooms. There are still other voices from letters, phone conversations, a variety of discussions, etc., that are included in the chapters as excerpts of personal experiences. Many women have spoken for themselves in this book, though we in the collective do not agree with all that has been written. Some of us are even uncomfortable with part of the material. We have included it anyway, because we give more weight to accepting that we differ than to our uneasiness. We have been asked why this is exclusively a book about women, why we have restricted our course to women. Our answer is that we are women and, as women, do not consider ourselves experts on men (as men through the centuries have presumed to be experts on us). We are not implying that we think most twentieth-century men are much less alienated from their bodies than women are. But we know it is up to men to explore that for themselves, to come together and share their sense of themselves as we have done. We would like to read a book about men and their bodies.

We are offering a book that can be used in many different ways—individually, in a group, for a course. Our book contains real material about our bodies and ourselves that isn't available elsewhere, and we have tried to present it in a new way—an honest, humane, and powerful way of thinking about ourselves and our lives. We want to share the knowledge and power that comes with this way of thinking, and we want to share the feelings we have for each other—supportive and loving feelings that show we can indeed help one another grow.

From the very beginning of working together, first on the course that led to this book and then on the book itself, we have felt exhilarated and energized by our new knowledge. Finding out about our bodies and our bodies' needs, starting to take control over that area of our life, has released for us an energy that has overflowed into our work, our friendships, our relationships with men and women, for some of us our marriages and our parenthood. In trying to figure out why this has had such a life-changing effect on us, we have come up with several important ways in which this kind of body education has been liberating for us and may be a starting point for the liberation of many other women.

First, we learned what we learned equally from professional sources—textbooks, medical journals, doctors, nurses—and from our own experiences. The facts were important, and we did careful research to get the information we had not had in the past. As we brought the facts to one another we learned a good deal, but in sharing our personal experiences relating to those facts we learned still more. Once we had learned what the "experts" had to tell us, we found that we still had a lot to teach and to learn from one another. For instance, many of us had "learned" about the menstrual cycle in science or biology classes—we had perhaps even memorized the names of the menstrual hormones and what they did. But most of us did not remember much of what we had learned. This time when we read in a text that the onset of menstruation is a normal and universal occurrence in young girls from ages ten to eighteen, we started to talk about our first menstrual periods. We found that, for many of us, beginning to menstruate had not felt normal at all, but scary, embarrassing, mysterious. We realized that what we had been told about menstruation and what we had not been told, even the tone of voice it had been told in—all had had an effect on our feelings about being female. . . .

Learning about our bodies in this way really turned us on. This is an exciting kind of learning, where information and feelings are allowed to interact. It has made the difference between rote memorization and relevant learning, between fragmented pieces of a puzzle and the integrated picture, between abstractions and real knowledge. We discovered that you don't learn very much when you are just a passive recipient of information. We found that each individual's response to information is valid and useful, and that by sharing our responses we can develop a base on which to be critical of what the experts tell us. Whatever we need to learn now, in whatever area of our life, we know more how to go about it.

A second important result of this kind of learning has been that we are better prepared to evaluate the institutions that are supposed to meet our health needs— the hospitals, clinics, doctors, medical schools, nursing schools, public health departments, Medicaid bureaucracies, and so on. For some of us it was the first time we had looked critically, and with strength, at the existing institutions serving us. The experience of learning just how little control we had over our lives and bodies, the coming together out of isolation to learn from each other in order to define what we needed, and the experience of supporting one another in demanding the changes that grew out of our developing critique—all were crucial and formative political experiences for us. We have felt our potential power as a force for political and social change.

The learning we have done while working on *Our Bodies, Ourselves* has been such a good basis for growth in other areas of life for still another reason. For women throughout the centuries, ignorance about our bodies has had one major consequence—pregnancy. Until very recently pregnancies were all but inevitable, biology *was* our destiny—that is, because our bodies are designed to get pregnant and give birth and lactate, that is what all or most of us did. The courageous and dedicated work of people like Margaret Sanger started in the early twentieth century to spread and make available birth control methods that women could use, thereby freeing us from the traditional lifetime of pregnancies. But the societal expectation that a woman above all else will have babies does not die easily. When we first started talking to each other about this we found that that old expectation had nudged most of us into a fairly rigid role of wife-and-motherhood from the moment we were born female. Even in 1969 when we first started the work that led to this book, we found that many of us were still getting pregnant when we didn't want to. It was not until we researched carefully and learned more about our reproductive systems, about birth-control methods and abortion, about laws governing birth control and abortion, not until we put all this information together with what it meant to us to be female, did we begin to feel that we could truly set out to control whether and when we would have babies.

This knowledge has freed us to a certain extent from the constant, energy-draining anxiety about becoming pregnant. It has made our pregnancies better, because they no longer happen to us; we actively choose them and enthusiastically participate in them. It has made our parenthood better, because it is our choice rather than our destiny. This knowledge has freed us from playing the role of mother if it is not a role that fits us. It has given us a sense of a larger life space to work in, an invigorating and challenging sense of time and room to discover the energies and talents that are in us, to do the work we want to do. And one of the things we most want to do is to help make this freedom of choice, this life space, available to every woman. That is why people in the women's movement have been so active in fighting against the inhumane legal restrictions, the imperfections of available contraceptives, the poor sex education, the highly priced and poorly administered health care that keeps too many women from having this crucial control over their bodies.

There is a fourth reason why knowledge about our bodies has generated so much new energy. For us, body education is core education. Our bodies are the physical bases from which we move out into the world; ignorance, uncertainty—even, at worst, shame—about our physical selves create in us an alienation from ourselves that keeps us from being the whole people that we could be. Picture a woman trying to do work and to enter into equal and satisfying relationships with other people—when she feels physically weak because she has never tried to be strong; when she drains her energy trying to change her face, her figure, her hair, her smells, to match some ideal norm set by magazines, movies, and TV; when she feels confused and ashamed of the menstrual blood that every month appears from some dark place in her body; when her internal body processes are a mystery to her and surface only to cause her trouble (an unplanned pregnancy, or cervical cancer); when she does not understand nor enjoy sex and concentrates her sexual drives into aimless romantic fantasies, perverting and misusing a potential energy because she has been brought up to deny it. Learning to understand, accept, and be responsible for our physical selves, we are freed of some of these pre-occupations and can start to use our untapped energies. Our image of ourselves is on a firmer base, we can be better friends and better lovers, better *people*, more self-confident, more autonomous, stronger, and more whole.

OUR CHANGING SENSE OF SELF

Changing Our Internalized Sexist Values

When we started talking to each other we came to realize how deeply ingrained was our sense of being less valuable than men.

> In my home I always had a sense that my father and brother were more important than my mother and myself. My mother and I shopped, talked to each other, and

had friends over—this was considered silly. My father was considered more important—he did the real work of the world.

Rediscovering Activity

Talking to each other, we realized that many of us shared a common perception of men—that they all seemed to be able to turn themselves on and to do things for themselves. We tended to feel passive and helpless and to expect and need men to do things for us. We were trained to give our power over to men. We had reduced ourselves to objects. We remained children, helpless and giving other people power to define us and objectify us.

As we talked together we realized that one of our central fantasies was our wish to find a man who could turn us on, to do for us what we could not do for ourselves, to make us feel alive and affirm our existence. It was as if we were made of clay and man would mold us, shape us, and bring us to life. This was the material of our childhood dreams: "Someday my prince will come." We were always disappointed when men did not accomplish this impossible task for us. And we began to see our passive helpless ways of handing power over to others as crippling to us. What became clear to us was that we had to change our expectations for ourselves. There was no factual reason why we could not assert and affirm our own existence and do and act for ourselves.

There were many factors that affected our capacity to act. For one, the ideal woman does less and less as her class status rises. Most of us, being middle class, were brought up not to do very much. Also, the kind of activity that is built into the traditional female role is different in quality from masculine activity. Masculine activity (repairing a window, building a house) tends to be sporadic, concrete, and have a finished product. Feminine activity (comforting a crying child, preparing a meal, washing laundry) tends to be repetitive, less tangible, and have no final durable product. Here again our sense of inferiority came into play. We had come to think of our activity as doing nothing—although essential for maintaining life—and of male activity as superior. We began to value our activity in a new way. We and what we did were as valuable as men and what they did.

On the other hand, we tried to incorporate within us the capacity to do more "male" product-oriented activity. . . .

We have also come to enjoy physical activity as well as mental and emotional activity. Again, the realm of physical strength is traditionally male. Once again we realized that we were active in our own ways, but we did not value them. As we looked at the details of our lives—the shopping and the cleaning—we realized that we used up a lot of physical energy every day but that we had taken it for granted and thought of it as nothing. We did avoid heavy, strenuous activity. . . .

We are learning to do new things—mountain climbing, canoeing, karate, auto mechanics.

Rediscovering Our Separateness

. . . During this period of building up our own sense of ourselves we tried to find out what we were like on our own, what we could do on our own. We discovered resources we never thought we had. Either because we had been dependent on men to do certain things for us or because we had been so used to thinking of ourselves as helpless and dependent, we had never tried.

It is hard. We are forever fighting a constant, inner struggle to give up and become weak, dependent, and helpless again. . . .

As we have come to feel separate we try to change old relationships and/or try to enter new relationships in new ways. We now also feel positive about our needs to be dependent and connect with others. We have come to value long-term commitments, which we find increasingly rare in such a changing society, just as we value our new separateness.

Visualizing Feminism

The photographs on this and the following page illustrate the enormous changes that occurred in feminism between 1945 and 1975. The first photograph, of a display celebrating the one hundredth anniversary of the Women's Rights Convention at Seneca Falls, New York, reflects the ambivalence of women's position at mid-century. The second, of a 1971 rally in Washington, D.C., reveals no ambivalence at all. Look at the photographs carefully. What can be learned from each of them?

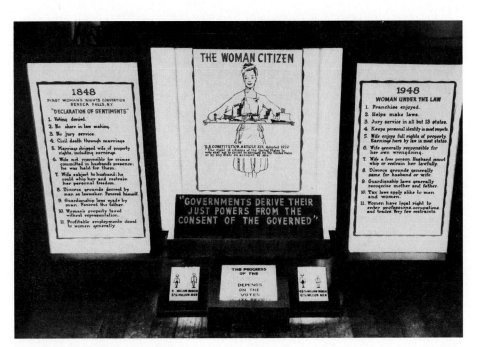

National Archives, Women's Bureau.

Dennis Brack/Black Star.

Graduating Seniors

To come of age in the 1970s was often to feel cheated, deprived not only of the economic opportunities that one's older brothers and sisters had had, but of the sense of adventure, of open-ended possibilities, that was part of life for the previous generation. Some social critics have argued that the diminished expectations that characterized the era produced a population of narcissists, committed only to their own lives and divorced from social commitment.

Transcribed below are the mid-decade commencement addresses of two bright and concerned graduating seniors of rural high schools in western New York, south of Buffalo. How does each speaker understand the climate of the era? Are the speeches optimistic or pessimistic? Do you hear evidence of narcissism in either address?

Valedictory Address, Clymer Central, 1975
"March to the Beating of Your Own Drums"

Dorothy L. Rowan

Mr. Swan, Reverend Sellers, Reverend DeGerlando, Mr. Fergus, Mr. Jaeger, Members of the Board of Education, Faculty, Parents and Relatives, Fellow Graduates:

Archives, SUNY, College at Fredonia. Reprinted with permission of Dorothy R. Babcock.

Most of us feel a great accomplishment at being here tonight. We have spent the last twelve years of our lives in school, and for most of us, in this school. This accomplishment is shadowed, though, by the thought that this is the last time any of us will be active members of Clymer Central School.

None of us could have made it here tonight without the help and encouragement of our families, teachers, and friends. They all influenced the decisions we have made and have tried to guide us with their knowledge and experience.

Each of us is a separate individual with a mind and will of our own. Through all time each person has been created differently with the specific intention of individuality. Sometimes, however, it seems that instead of emphasizing individuality, our society encourages conformity.

A person's goal in life should not be to keep up with the "Joneses," and therefore be a success, but to be totally himself and to succeed in being himself. Success should not be a goal, but the result of developing and exercising qualities of character. Success is not what we do, but what we are; not what our actions are, but what our attitudes are. Those who seem to have success did not seek it, and those who make it their life's aim never seem to hit target.

We should all aim for our own personal success; a goal we set for ourselves, not one set by someone else.

Seniors, especially, should be encouraged to think for themselves, not to decide what they think someone else wants them to decide, although sometimes that is easier. It is hard to make decisions because you always risk making the wrong choice.

But there never seems to be enough time even to sit down and think. Americans have been justly accused of always rushing around in order to "save" time, but you wonder if in the end you are not actually wasting more time than you are saving.

A comparison was made between an *Alice in Wonderland* character and time. The Red Queen, rushing through the Looking-Glass Wonderland with Alice in hand kept crying, "Faster! Faster! Don't try to talk. Faster!" Maybe the Red Queen is another name for our time. We ought to try to catch our breath long enough to ask ourselves if all this activity indicates achievement.

Also, there is an example of a certain pilot who, in answer to a passenger's question, "How're we doing?" he replied, "We're lost, but we're making good time!"

Time is a very precious thing and should never be taken for granted; you may realize, too late, how much you could have done with the time you have wasted. Time can never be brought back, so each minute should be spent carefully and wisely. Kipling's poem "If" stated how personal success could be achieved and that the main way to do this is to strive for individuality. He says a person can mature only if he lives his life according to his own mind and morals, not of those around him, he must see life in perspective and learn to live among all the conformities and immoralities he may see, but yet not let his own life be touched by it. He must keep his individuality, not just to be different, but because he should live according to his own mind.

If a man can do all this, then as Kipling says in the last line of his poem, "Yours is the Earth and everything that's in it. And, which is more—you'll be a man, my son."

Thoreau once said, "Everyone marches to the beating of his own drums." He said it a long time ago, but it really applies to all men, no matter when they lived. And it is especially important for us to listen to what he said because with our standard of living and all the rush for fame and fortune we sometimes forget we are individuals. And we tend to think of ourselves along with a group of other persons instead of just an individual. We should sit down and think for a few minutes about where we are really going and what we are really doing.

The most important thing today is for everyone to "march to the beating of his own drums."

Valedictory Address, Pine Valley Central, 1976

Carson J. Leikam

For quite some time now, especially in the last couple of years, our parents, teachers, and others who are already wise to the ways of the world, have been telling us that it's going to be tough once we get out there. They aren't going to have to tell us much longer—we're going to find out soon. Once we get out there it's not going to become "our world"; we're going to have to compete with everybody else, making it just that much tougher.

Here we are—the class of '76, all fairly confident that we're going to succeed in the world. How many of us are going to be able to keep that confidence when every place we go employers tell us that they have no openings for employment. Sociologists tell us that the strain of many jobs is almost unbearable. Is it as unbearable as having bills come in with no money to pay them off? Is it as unbearable as having a Ph.D. and being unable to get a job because of too much specialization? I can't number the times I've looked in the job section of the paper and found that I must have experience before an employer will hire me. How does one get experience without first getting hired?

I'm not pessimistic, but I won't say that the world isn't. The class of '76 knows it's tough out there, but that by itself isn't going to stop us! Probably some of you are thinking: "How can he stand up there and talk about how tough the world is? Only after he's been out there and really felt the pressure and the competition, only then will he know just how tough it is!" Well, people who think like that haven't had a son or daughter in high school for a while, because the pressure and competition in high school can be quite phenomenal. Hopefully, our years at Pine Valley have been more than just taking notes, reading books, and writing papers. If that's it, then our education to date has been totally worthless. But if our education has stressed competition, recognition for novel ideas, praise for excellent work, discussions and assignments that relate to the "world out there," then it has been very beneficial. Our education will have prepared us even more for the

Archives, SUNY, College at Fredonia. Reprinted with permission of Carson J. Leikam, Supervisor, Building & Fuel/Niagara Mohawk Power Corp.

trials to come if all these things have been combined in a manner that makes the student feel the need to succeed.

Someone might think that that's a pretty brutal way to assess one's years in school. Well, if it wasn't tough, if we didn't have to think for ourselves, if we didn't have to get in there and really dig to stay on top, then that brutal world out there is going to chew us to pieces.

Our attitude toward reality, toward the way things are, is going to have much to do with our success or failure. Sure, it's a tough world to make a living in, but we can't go out into the world with the attitude that since those who came before us made the world the way it is, then it's their responsibility to fix it up. "To err is human." Therefore we should remember that we're all capable of error. If we tackle life with the attitude that we're here now, and if we get in gear, then maybe we can shift things in the right direction. It's going to have to be a team effort, with everybody giving his utmost to put this world back on course. If we don't, the finger won't be pointed at any certain person or group as being to blame for creating the mess that we seem to be headed for right now. If we don't, it's not going to be much of a world by the time people start pointing those accusing fingers.

There are people starving to death, people living in run-down apartments with paper-thin walls and having only the bare necessities. Some don't even have that much. It's not just in Africa, underdeveloped countries of Europe, sections of Asia and South America—it's right here in the good ole USA. Let's get our country back on its feet—let's aid our own poor and deprived. Once we're strong again, we can put out our hand and help the less fortunate countries of the world. But we aren't going to be able to extend that helping hand if it turns into a mass of accusing fingers—pointing at us and the slow deterioration of our country, economically, socially, physically, and maybe most important of all—morally. The weak cannot help the weak. It is my belief that we should make ourselves strong again—the definite number one of the world. Then, we will be ready to help the other people and nations of our troubled world.

How can we do this? By exercising the qualities that I know the class of '76 has—an attitude of working together and pulling toward that common goal; to use that attitude to get out and do our part in a team effort. We need to get that nationalistic feeling—not as a show-off in the world of nations, but that feeling of unity and solidarity. Everybody forward, all at once.

I can't say "Never fear! The world is now in the hands of the class of '76!," because it's not. Even if it were in our hands I don't think I could say "Never fear." But I can say that if this country gets it together and makes a genuine effort like the class of '76 has made to attain its goals—that's going to help. With the attitude of our class of '76, the ability and desire to work together, the diligence, the high moral standard, and a real trust in our Lord, we can help steer this world right back on course.

They say that history repeats itself and goes in a pattern; that no great civilization has lasted for much more than two hundred years. There's no doubt that this country is definitely great. But, there also is no doubt that the bicentennial class of '76 with the help of the other people of this magnificent land, will not allow the death of our American civilization, but will struggle to ensure a more secure, richer heritage for us and for our descendants.

Film and Culture

In an era of VCRs, movie rentals, and cable television, students increasingly carry with them substantial knowledge of the history of film—enough, we hope, to have some fun with the lists that follow. Do the films on the 1970s list reflect some of the seventies themes discussed in this chapter, such as survival, narcissism, environmentalism, and the retreat from social reformism? What other themes might one suggest? The original Superman *was a product of the 1930s. How do you explain the reemergence of the character in the 1970s? Can you see any difference between the films of the 1960s and those of the 1970s?*

TOP TEN MONEYMAKING FILMS FROM THE SEVENTIES

1. *Star Wars* (1977)
2. *Jaws* (1975)
3. *Grease* (1978)
4. *The Exorcist* (1973)
5. *The Godfather* (1972)
6. *Superman* (1978)
7. *The Sting* (1973)
8. *Close Encounters of the Third Kind* (1977)
9. *Saturday Night Fever* (1977)
10. *National Lampoon Animal House* (1978)

Runners-up

1. *Smokey and the Bandit* (1977)
2. *One Flew Over the Cuckoo's Nest* (1975)
3. *American Graffiti* (1973)
4. *Rocky* (1976)
5. *Jaws II* (1978)
6. *Love Story* (1970)
   Towering Inferno (1975)
8. *Every Which Way But Loose* (1978)
9. *Heaven Can Wait* (1978)
10. *Airport* (1970)

TOP TEN MONEYMAKING FILMS FROM THE SIXTIES

1. *The Sound of Music* (1965)
2. *The Graduate* (1968)

Cobbett S. Steinberg, *Film Facts* (New York: Facts on File, 1980), pp. 13–14.

 3. *Doctor Zhivago* (1965)
 4. *Butch Cassidy and the Sundance Kid* (1969)
 5. *Mary Poppins* (1964)
 6. *Thunderball* (1965)
 7. *Funny Girl* (1968)
 8. *Cleopatra* (1963)
 9. *Guess Who's Coming to Dinner?* (1968)
10. *The Jungle Book* (1967)

Runners-up

 1. *2001: A Space Odyssey* (1968)
 2. *Goldfinger* (1964)
 3. *Bonnie and Clyde* (1967)
 4. *The Love Bug* (1969)
 5. *It's a Mad, Mad, Mad, Mad World* (1963)
 6. *Midnight Cowboy* (1969)
 7. *The Dirty Dozen* (1967)
 8. *The Valley of the Dolls* (1967)
    The Odd Couple (1968)
10. *West Side Story* (1961)

SUGGESTIONS FOR VIEWING AND LISTENING

Jaws (1975)
Science, once capable of any conquest, meets its match.

American Graffiti (1973)
The limits imposed by class, culture, and fate.

Friday the 13th (1980)
From the golden age of the modern horror film (1978–1983). Promiscuity, irresponsibility, and the 1960s are bad; family is good.

Billy Joel, "My Life,"(1979)
Male freedom and narcissism; group values yield to high individualism.

Gloria Gaynor, "I Will Survive" (1979)
A female, feminist rejoinder to "My Life," as well as a comment on gender relations in the black community.

Charlene, "I've Never Been to Me" (1976)
The backlash against feminism, already under way.

CHAPTER 9

Family Politics
and the Welfare State

In the wake of Watergate, the defeat in Vietnam, the Arab oil boycott, the energy crisis, rising levels of personal violence, confrontations over forced busing, and other signs of national distress, Americans combed the social landscape for help in understanding what it was that was happening to them, and what they might do about it. It was an increasingly conservative era—between Richard Nixon's election in 1968 and George Bush's defeat in 1992, only Jimmy Carter broke the Republican hold on the presidency—and, in addition to abortion, two issues focused the new conservatism and stimulated national debate. One was the "decline" of the family; the other was the growth of the welfare state, particularly the program known as "welfare."

Evidence of family decline seemed incontrovertible. Between 1966 and 1976, the divorce rate doubled. Young people were getting married later and having fewer children, and for most of the 1970s the birthrate was too low to naturally replace the population. In what became known as the *Moynihan Report* (1965), future Senator Daniel Patrick Moynihan argued that family deterioration was a particular problem in the black community, where soaring rates of divorce, teenage pregnancy, and father desertion had resulted in a very high percentage of black families headed by women. By 1980, almost a quarter of the American population was living alone, and less than 10 percent of all families conformed to the pattern that once had seemed standard: a working husband, a domestic wife, and two children.

All of this bothered liberals almost as much as it did conservatives. "We need a better life to make us better servants of the people," said Jimmy Carter to a gathering of federal employees. "So those of you living in sin I hope you'll get married. Those of you who have left your spouses, go back home. And those of you who don't remember your children's names, get reacquainted." Even so, there were important differences over what the statistics meant and what, if anything, to do about the "problem." Far from lamenting the decline of the traditional family, gays, lesbians, and some feminists celebrated the emergence of new kinds of families that were not based on patriarchy. Within the black community, the *Moynihan Report*

234

was widely criticized for suggesting that female-headed households were somehow dysfunctional, and especially for blaming the family for problems that were more clearly related to poverty and unemployment among urban blacks. "While it is convenient to argue that family instability causes poverty," said National Urban League President John Jacob in 1986, "it is more accurate to say that *poverty causes family instability.*" Without denying that divorce could harm young children, there were those who defended the practice on the grounds that an unhappy marriage could be equally damaging. Indeed, in the late 1980s, Hallmark Cards was selling a coffee mug emblazoned with the words, "Tis better to have loved and lost than to be stuck with a real loser for the rest of your entire, miserable existence!"

The earnestness with which the political right approached the family issue was comically revealed in 1992, when Vice President Dan Quayle, a Republican, announced that the title character of the CBS comedy *Murphy Brown* "[mocks] the importance of fathers by bearing a child alone and calling it just another 'life style choice.'" The right—especially the New Christian Right which emerged as a political force in the mid-1970s—had long made the family and its decline central to their worldview. Jerry Falwell, Jim Bakker, Pat Robertson, and other television evangelists advocated a return to what they insisted was the traditional family: a strong, authoritative man, a submissive woman, and obedient children. Some Christian conservatives blamed the decline of the family on men who had somehow abrogated their authority; others condemned feminism for feminizing men and disturbing the natural gender roles in which strong families were grounded; and many others believed that the national government, the public schools, and the media were implicated in the decline of the traditional family. The right-to-life movement was complex and diverse, but some of its appeal after *Roe v. Wade* (1973) derived from the conviction that the ability to choose not to bear a child after conception severed the natural relationship between sex and procreation and therefore allowed reckless men to evade family responsibilities.

No less controversial was the government program known today as "welfare" or Aid to Families with Dependent Children (AFDC). Welfare had its origins in the Progressive Era, when forty states passed mothers' pension laws that gave money to mothers for the support of children in cases where fathers were dead or absent. In 1935, the program took its current shape when New Deal legislation provided for federal matching funds. Welfare remained of minor concern to most Americans until the 1960s, when the welfare rolls grew from about 2.5 million recipients in 1957, to nearly 12.5 million in 1970. Although the number of Americans on welfare had stabilized somewhat by 1980, AFDC was often at the center of larger concerns about poverty, race, the role of government, the work ethic, and national decline.

In the quarter century after 1970, dozens of proposals for changes in the welfare system were made and debated, but with little result. Some consensus emerged among Republicans and Democrats that a way should be found to put welfare recipients to work, but that idea proved difficult to implement, and beyond it there was only disagreement. There was controversy over why the welfare system had experienced such explosive growth in the 1960s. On the right, scholars and politicians argued that welfare's growth occurred because liberals had given up on the free enterprise system. Convinced that economic growth could never eliminate poverty or unemployment, Johnson administration liberals had committed themselves to a dramatic expansion of many aspects of the welfare state. On the left, some argued that welfare was a cheap way out—one that stopped short of tackling the tough problems of racial discrimination, structural unemployment, and inner-city housing—while others contended that welfare was a reasonable and necessary response to a variety of social problems that had emerged in the early 1960s as a result of the migration of millions of black workers from southern farms to northern cities.

There was disagreement, too, about welfare's impact. Critics on the right faulted welfare for impairing the work ethic and producing a dependent population locked in a cycle of poverty. Liberals maintained that problems with the work ethic had more to do with the nature of most low-wage work; that the expansion of welfare in the mid-1960s was remarkably successful in reducing poverty; and that, far from encouraging dependency, welfare had made it possible for millions of people (most of them women) to live independently—independently of demeaning, low-wage jobs, and independently of men—for the first time.

These debates over the family and welfare were not about any one thing. They were partly about the different ways in which Americans understood the recent past, whether as a growing set of problems requiring government intervention, or as some imagined moment of near perfection, when families were "traditional" and everyone wanted to work. They were partly about race, in that it was usually assumed (and wrongly) that the "welfare" problem was a black problem and that family "decline" was most advanced within the black community. They were partly about liberalism—about whether, or how, government should intervene to promote a better society. And they were, perhaps, ultimately about what had gone wrong with America and what, if anything, could be done about it.

INTERPRETIVE ESSAY

Stephanie Coontz

We Always Stood on Our Own Two Feet
Self-Reliance and the American Family

Speaking to the National Black Republican Council in 1982, President Ronald Reagan summarized his critique of the American liberal tradition. He talked about the "broken will" of inner-city residents, whose desires for pride and independence were thwarted by misconceived government programs that had, "perhaps unintentionally," fostered dependency and "created a new kind of bondage for millions of American citizens." The Reagan perspective had some appeal for a nation just emerging from depression, and during the early 1980s about $45 billion was cut from food stamps, child nutrition, job training, Aid to Families with Dependent Children (welfare), housing, and other programs important to the central cities.

Has the welfare state produced "a new kind of bondage"? Not exactly, according to historian Stephanie Coontz, who finds some sort of dependency at the heart of the American experience—even, as she argues here, in that mythic stronghold of self-reliance, the 1950s suburb.

Coontz's provocative perspective raises as many questions as it answers: Are the kinds of subsidies shaping today's inner cities, including welfare, equivalent to those that helped build the postwar suburbs? If public assistance has not fostered poverty and dependence, why did Reagan make that argument in 1982, and why did so many Americans accept its validity? Finally, does Coontz's essay constitute an effective response to those who charge that the American family is in decline?

"They never asked for handouts," my grandfather used to say whenever he and my grandmother regaled me with stories about pioneer life in Puget Sound after George Washington Bush and Michael T. Simmons defied the British and founded the first American settlement in the area. But the homesteaders didn't turn down handouts either during that hard winter in 1852, when speculators had cornered almost all the already low supply of wheat. Fortunately, Bush refused to sell his grain for the high prices the market offered, reserving most of what he did not use himself to feed his neighbors and stake them to the next spring's planting.

The United States' successful claim to Puget Sound was based on the Bush-Simmons settlement. Ironically, once Bush had helped his community become part of the Oregon territory, he became subject to Oregon's exclusionary law prohibiting African Americans from residing in the Territory. His neighbors spearheaded passage of a special legislative bill in 1854, exempting Bush and his family from the law. Bush's descendants became prominent members of what was to become Washington state, and the story of Bush's generosity in 1852 has passed into local lore. Neither my grandparents' paternalistic attitudes toward blacks nor their fierce hatred of charity led them to downplay how dependent the early settlers had been on Bush's aid, but the knowledge of that dependence did not modify their insistence that decent families were "beholden to no one."

When I was older, I asked my grandfather about the apparent contradiction. "Well," he said, "that was an exception; and they paid him back by getting that bill passed, didn't they? It's not like all these people nowadays, sitting around waiting for the government to take care of them. The government never gave us anything, and we never counted on help from anybody else, either." Unless, of course, they were family. "Blood's thicker than water, after all," my grandparents used to say.

My grandparents are not the only Americans to allow the myth of self-reliance to obscure the reality of their own life histories. Politicians are especially likely to fall prey to the convenient amnesia that permits so much self-righteous posturing about how the "dependent poor" ought to develop the self-reliance and independence that "the rest of us" have shown. Sen. Phil Gramm, for example, co-author of the 1985 Gramm-Rudman-Hollings balanced budget amendment, is well known for his opposition to government handouts. However, his personal history is quite different from his political rhetoric.

Born in Georgia in 1942, to a father who was living on a federal veterans disability pension, Gramm attended a publicly funded university on a grant paid for by the federal War Orphans Act. His graduate work was financed by a National Defense Education Act fellowship, and his first job was at Texas A&M University, a federal land-grant institution. Yet when Gramm finally struck out on his own, the first thing he did was set up a consulting business where he could be, in his own words, "an advocate of fiscal responsibility and free enterprise." From there he moved on to Congress, where he has consistently attempted to slash federal assistance programs for low-income people.

Self-reliance is one of the most cherished American values, although there is some ambiguity about what the smallest self-reliant unit is. For some it is the rugged individualist; for most it is the self-sufficient family of the past, in which female nurturing sustained male independence vis-à-vis the outside world. While some people believe that the gender roles within this traditional family were unfair, and others that they were beneficial, most Americans agree that prior to federal "interference" in the 1930s, the self-reliant family was the standard social unit of our society. Dependencies used to be cared for within the "natural family economy," and even today the healthiest families "stand on their own two feet."

The fact is, however, that depending on support beyond the family has been the rule rather than the exception in American history, despite recurring myths about individual achievement and family enterprise. It is true that public aid has become less local and more impersonal over the past two centuries, but Americans have been dependent on collective institutions beyond the family, including government, from the very beginning.

A TRADITION OF DEPENDENCE ON OTHERS

. . . It was not a colonial value to avoid being beholden to others, even among the nonpoor. Borrowing and lending among neighbors were woven into the very fabric of life. The presence of outstanding accounts assured the continuing circulation of goods, services, and social interactions through the community: Being under obligation to others and having favors owed was the mark of a successful person. Throughout the colonies, life was more corporate than individualistic or familial. People operated within a tight web of obligation, debt, dependence, "treating," and the calling in of favors.

As America made the transition to a wage-earning society in the 1800s, patterns of personal dependence and local community assistance gave way to more formal procedures for organizing work and taking care of those who were unable to work, either temporarily or permanently. But the rise of a generalized market economy did not lessen dependency, nor did it make the family more able to take care of its own, in any sector of society.

Within the upper classes, family partnerships, arranged marriages, dowries, and family loans no longer met the need for capital, recruitment of trusted workers, and exploration of new markets. The business class developed numerous extrafamilial institutions: mercantile associations; credit-pooling consortia; new legal bodies for raising capital, such as corporations or limited liability partnerships; and chambers of commerce. Middle-class fraternal organizations, evangelical groups, and maternal associations also reached beyond kinship ties and local community boundaries to create a vast network of mutual aid organizations. The first half of the nineteenth century is usually called not the age of the family but the age of association.

For the working class throughout the nineteenth century, dependence was "a structural," almost inevitable, part of life. Among workers as well, accordingly, blood was not always thicker than neighborhood, class, ethnicity, or religion. Black, immigrant, and native-born white workers could not survive without sharing and assistance beyond family networks.

Working-class and ethnic subcommunities evolved around mutual aid in finding jobs, surviving tough times, and pooling money for recreation. Immigrants founded lodges to provide material aid and foster cooperation. Laborers formed funeral aid societies and death or sick benefit associations; they held balls and picnics to raise money for injured workers, widows, or orphans, and took collection at the mills or plant gates nearly every payday. Recipients showed the same lack of embarrassment about accepting such help as did colonial families. Reformer Margaret Byington, observing working-class life at the end of the nineteenth century, noted that a gift of money to a fellow worker who was ill or simply down on his luck was "accepted. . . very simply, almost as a matter of course." Among the iron- and steelworkers of Pittsburgh, "Innumerable acts of benevolence passed between the residents of the rows and tenements, . . . rarely remarked upon except for their absence." Some workers' cultures revolved around religious institutions, some around cooperative societies or militant unionism—but all extended beyond the family. Indeed, historian Michael Katz has found that in parts of early-twentieth-century Philadelphia, "Neighbors seemed more reliable and willing to help one another than did kin."

Among Catholic populations, godparenting was one way of institutionalizing such obligations beyond the family. In traditional Mexican and Mexican-American communities, for example, rites of baptism cut across divisions between rich and poor, Native American, mestizo, and Spanish. Godparents became *compadres* or *copadres* with the biological parents, providing discipline and love as needed. They were morally obliged to give financial assistance in times of need or to take on full parental responsibilities if the biological parents should die. Irish and Italian districts had similar customs. Some Native American groups had special "blood brother" rituals; the notion of "going for sisters" has long and still thriving roots in black communities.

Yet even ties of expanded kinship, class, neighborhood, and ethnicity were never enough to get many families by. Poor Americans, for example, have always needed support from the public purse, even if that support has often been inadequate. Indeed, notes one welfare historian, the history of dependence and assistance in America is marked by "the early and pervasive role of the state. There has never been a golden age of volunteerism."

By the end of the nineteenth century, neither poorhouses, outdoor relief, nor private charity could cope with the dislocations of industrial business cycles. As late as 1929, after nearly a decade of prosperity, the Brookings Institute found that the "natural family economy" was not working for most Americans: Three-fifths of American families earned $2,000 or less a year and were unable to save anything to help them weather spells of unemployment or illness. The Great Depression, of course, left many more families unable to make it on their own.

Even aside from times of depression, the inability of families to survive without public assistance has never been confined to the poor. Middle-class and affluent Americans have been every bit as dependent on public support. In fact, comparatively affluent families have received considerably *more* public subsidy than those in modest circumstances, while the costs of such subsidies have often been borne by those who derived the least benefit from them.

To illustrate the pervasiveness of dependence in American family history, I will examine in greater detail the two main family types that are usually held up as models of traditional American independence: the frontier family, archetype of American self-reliance, and the 1950s suburban family, whose strong moral values and work ethic are thought to have enabled so many to lift themselves up by their bootstraps. In fact, these two family types probably tie for the honor of being the most heavily subsidized in American history, as well as for the privilege of having had more of their advantages paid for by minorities and the lower classes. . . .

SELF-RELIANCE AND THE SUBURBAN FAMILY

Another oft-cited example of familial self-reliance is the improvement in living standards experienced by many Americans during the 1950s. The surge in home-ownership at that time, most people believe, occurred because families scraped together down payments, paid their mortgages promptly, raised their children to respect private property, and always "stood on their own two feet." An entire generation of working people thereby attained middle-class status, graduating from urban tenements to suburban homeownership, just as Lucille Ball and Desi Arnaz did in their television series.

The 1950s suburban family, however, was far more dependent on government handouts than any so-called "underclass" in recent U.S. history. Historian William Chafe estimates that "most" of the upward mobility at this time was subsidized in one form or another by government spending. Federal GI benefits, available to 40 percent of the male population between the ages of twenty and twenty-four, permitted a whole generation of men to expand their education and improve their job prospects without foregoing marriage and children. The National Defense Education Act retooled science education, subsidizing both American industry and the education of individual scientists. In addition, the surge in productivity during the 1950s was largely federally financed. More than $50 billion of government-funded wartime inventions and production processes were turned over to private companies after the war, creating whole new fields of employment.

Even more directly, suburban homeownership depended on an unprecedented enlargement of federal regulation and financing. The first steps were taken in the Great Depression, when the Home Owners Loan Corporation (HOLC) set up low-interest loans to allow people to refinance homes lost through foreclosure. The government began to underwrite the real estate industry by insuring private home-ownership lenders, loaning directly to long-term buyers, and subsidizing the extension of electricity to new residential areas. But the real transformation of attitudes and intervention came in the 1950s, with the expansion of the Federal Housing Authority and Veterans Administration loans.

Before the Second World War, banks often required a 50 percent down payment on homes and normally issued mortgages for only five to ten years. In the postwar period, however, the Federal Housing Authority (FHA), supplemented by the GI Bill, put the federal government in the business of insuring and regulating private loans for single-home construction. FHA policy required down payments of only 5 to 10 percent of the purchase price and guaranteed mortgages of up to thirty years at interest rates of just 2 to 3 percent on the balance. The Veterans Administration asked a mere dollar down from veterans. At the same time, government tax policies were changed to provide substantial incentives for savings and loan institutions to channel their funds almost exclusively into low-interest, long-term mortgages. Consequently, millions of Americans purchased homes with artificially low down payments and interest rates, courtesy of Uncle Sam.

It was not family savings or individual enterprise, but federal housing loans and education payments (along with an unprecedented expansion of debt), that enabled so many 1950s American families to achieve the independence of homeownership. Almost *half* the housing in suburbia depended on such federal financing. As philosopher Alan Wolfe points out: "Even the money that people borrowed to pay for their houses was not lent to them on market principles; fixed-rate mortgages, for example, absolved an entire generation from inflation for thirty years."

Yet this still understates the extent to which suburbia was a creation of government policy and federal spending. True, it was private real estate agents and construction companies who developed the suburban projects and private families who bought the homes. But it was government-funded research that developed the aluminum clapboards, prefabricated walls and ceilings, and plywood paneling that composed the technological basis of the postwar housing revolution. And few buyers would have been forthcoming for suburban homes without new highways to get them out to the sites, new sewer systems, utilities services, and traffic control programs—all of which were not paid for by the families who used them, but by the general public.

In 1947, the government began a project to build 37,000 miles of new highway. In 1956, the Interstate Highway Act provided for an additional 42,500 miles. Ninety percent of this construction was financed by the government. The prime beneficiaries of this postwar road-building venture, which one textbook calls "the greatest civil engineering project of world history," were suburbanites. Despite arguments that road building served "national interests," urban interstates were primarily "turned into commuter roads serving suburbia."

Such federal patronage might be unobjectionable, even laudable—though hardly a demonstration of self-reliance—if it had been available to all Americans equally. But the other aspect of federal subsidization of suburbia is that it worsened the plight of public transportation, the inner cities, poor families in general, and minority ones in particular.

Federal loan policies systematized and nationalized the pervasive but informal racism that had previously characterized the housing market. FHA redlining practices, for example, took entire urban areas and declared them ineligible for loans. Government policy also shifted resources from urban areas into suburban construction and expansion. At the same time, postwar "urban renewal" and highway construction reduced the housing stock for urban workers. Meanwhile, the federal government's two new mortgage institutions, the Federal National Mortgage Association (Fannie Mae) and the Government National Mortgage Association (Ginnie Mae), made it possible for urban banks to transfer savings out of the cities and into new construction in the South and West—frequently, again, into suburban developments. By the 1970s, for example, savings banks in the Bronx invested just 10 percent of their funds in the borough and only 30 percent elsewhere in the entire state.

In the 1950s and 1960s, while the general public financed roads for suburban commuters, the streetcars and trolleys that served urban and poor families received almost no tax revenues and thus steadily deteriorated, with results we are paying for today. In the nineteenth century, American public transport had been one of the better systems in the world, and one of the most used. In 1890, streetcar ridership in the United States was four times as great as that in Europe on a per capita basis. As late as 1953, a million and a half people traveled by rail each day. But expansion of the highway system undercut this form of public transport as well. Between

1946 and 1980, government aid to highways totaled $103 billion, while railroads received only $6 billion.

We should not overestimate the accessibility of earlier public transport to lower-income families—in the third quarter of the nineteenth century, most people walked to work—nor should we forget the pollution and overcrowding of streets filled with horse-drawn vehicles. Yet the fact remains that government transportation policy systematically fostered improvements in private rather than public conveyances, favoring suburban development over the revitalization of urban life. By the end of the 1950s, Los Angeles epitomized the kind of city such policies produced. Once served by an efficient and widely used mass-transit system, the city was carved up by multi-lane freeways, overpasses, and viaducts. By the end of the decade, two-thirds of central Los Angeles had been paved over to make room for cars.

THE MYTH OF SELF-RELIANT FAMILIES:
PUBLIC WELFARE POLICIES

The government subsidies discussed earlier, despite their ill effects on the cities and the poor, mobilized resources much more efficiently than older informal support networks had done, encouraging family formation, residential stability, upward occupational mobility, and high educational aspirations among those who received them. There is thus no intrinsic tendency of government subsidies per se to induce dependence, undermine self-esteem, or break down family ties, even though these charges are almost invariably leveled against one kind of subsidy: welfare for the poor.

During the 1960s, exposés such as Michael Harrington's *The Other America* (1962), as well as protests by poor people, stimulated attempts to ameliorate poverty and dampen social unrest. Along with reforms that lessened racial discrimination in welfare policies, the new government initiatives against poverty resulted in a substantial increase in the welfare rolls and a major extension of social insurance benefits during the 1960s and 1970s.

It is important to note that the most dramatic growth in government social expenditures since the 1960s has been in social insurance programs, such as worker's compensation, disability, and Medicare. Most benefits from these programs go to members of the white middle class. Although the programs are very important for the poor they do reach, even at the height of the Great Society antipoverty initiative, between 1965 and 1971, 75 percent of America's social welfare dollars were spent on the nonpoor. The proportion going to the poor has decreased substantially since then.

Yet in the late 1970s, as economic conditions tightened, a growing number of commentators began to argue that both the financial and the family afflictions of Americans existed because government had abandoned traditions of self-reliance and adopted overly generous subsidy programs for the poor. Ignoring the historical dependence of pioneer and suburban families on public support, as well as the continued reliance of industry on government handouts, some analysts asserted that the problems of poor families originated in the very fact that they received assistance at all.

Probably the most widely quoted of these commentators was Charles Murray, who wrote *Losing Ground: American Social Policy, 1950–1980*. Murray's arguments relied on the fact that "latent poverty" (the amount of poverty before any government welfare payments) declined rapidly during the 1950s and early 1960s, a period when government subsidies or transfer payments to the poor grew only slowly. During the late 1960s and 1970s, the rate of government social welfare expenditures increased, yet in this period latent poverty ceased to decline and eventually began to grow again. Asserting a causal connection between these trends, Murray argued that poverty decreased in the early period because government welfare payments remained modest, while poverty increased in the later period as a result of the increase in government payments. The Great Society initiative of Lyndon Johnson seduced the poor into dependence, eroded their commitment to self-reliance, family values, and the work ethic, and actually increased the poverty the programs were designed to alleviate. Welfare subsidies contained so many "disincentives" to marriage and work that they ensnared recipients in a tangled skein of dependence, demoralization, immorality, and self-destruction: "Cut the knot," Murray urged, "for there is no way to untie it." He advocated elimination of all social programs aimed at the poor, with the exception of unemployment insurance for the working-age population.

The phenomenal publicity and approval generated by Murray's book had more to do with the way it tapped into powerful cultural myths about self-reliance and dependency than with any connection to empirical evidence. It is true that the expansion of the economy between 1950 and 1965—itself partly a result of government subsidies—led to rising real wages, which, of course, meant a steady decrease in pretransfer poverty. But total poverty remained much higher in the 1950s than in the Great Society period. In 1964, after fourteen years of unprecedented economic growth, the poverty rate was still 19 percent; in 1969, after five years of relatively modest government welfare programs, it was down to 12 percent, a low that has not been seen since the social welfare cutbacks began in the late 1970s. In 1965, 20 percent of American children still lived in poverty; within five years, that had fallen to 15 percent. Between 1959 and 1969, the black poverty rate was reduced from 55.1 percent to 32.2 percent.

The economy weakened at the end of the 1960s, for reasons that had nothing to do with the minuscule amount of the gross national product being spent on welfare, but this makes the actual effectiveness of government assistance programs even more impressive. Despite the slowdown in economic growth, the most dramatic improvements for the poor came after the institution of new subsidy programs in the late 1960s. Even though infant mortality had been reduced very little prior to 1965, for example, it was cut in half between 1965 and 1980, during the period when Medicaid and other government-subsidized health programs were established. The gap in nutrition between low-income and other Americans had remained high throughout the 1950s and early 1960s. It narrowed significantly only between the mid-1960s and the late 1970s, as a direct result of the expansion of food stamp and school lunch programs. As late as 1963, 20 percent of Americans below the poverty line had *never* been examined by a physician; by 1970, this was true of only 8 percent of the poor.

Despite stagnant real wages in the 1970s, economists Sheldon Danziger and Peter Gottschalk point out, poverty reductions continued for groups who still received government assistance. It was in groups whose subsidies declined or stagnated that poverty grew. The fastest-growing government social welfare programs during the 1970s, and the largest in absolute terms, were those directed toward the elderly; they were so effective that they wiped out the historical tendency for elders to be the poorest sector of the population.

According to opponents of government aid to the poor, though, the material benefits of social welfare programs are simply not worth the social and psychological costs. Murray and others charge that relief grants and subsidies have created devastating changes in family structure and work patterns among the poor over the past two decades. Their claims conjure up ominous images of able-bodied men deserting their families so that they can sleep around without having to support their kids, and teenage girls popping out babies so that they can stay home, live off welfare, eat junk food, and watch television instead of work.

There *has* been an acceleration of urban deterioration, social decay, and family breakup in the past two decades But the claim that rising welfare subsidies caused this is not upheld by the facts. Although both single-mother families and the rolls of Aid to Families with Dependent Children (AFDC) have expanded since the mid-1950s, for example, these trends should be understood as separate responses to other socioeconomic and cultural changes, for there is no causal relationship between welfare benefits and single-parent families. Economists William Darity and Samuel Myers found that in any specific geographic area or time period from 1955 to 1972, the higher the welfare benefits, the *lower* were the rates of female headship and welfare participation. Since 1972, the correlations Murray made so much of have ceased to prevail even at the most general level. Between 1972 and 1980, the number of children living in female-headed households rose from 14 percent to almost 20 percent, but the number in AFDC homes held constant at about 12 percent. In the same period, the number of black children in female-headed families rose by nearly 20 percent, but the number in AFDC homes actually fell by 5 percent.

The image of teenage girls having babies to receive welfare checks is an emotion-laden but fraudulent cliché. If the availability of welfare benefits causes teen pregnancy, why is it that other industrial countries, with far more generous support policies for women and children, have far lower rates of teen pregnancy?

Welfare benefits do seem to increase the likelihood of unmarried teen mothers moving away from their parents' households, hence increasing the *visibility* of these mothers, but they bear little or no relation to actual birth rates for unmarried women. Harvard economists David Ellwood and Mary Jo Bane compared unmarried women who would be eligible for welfare if they had an illegitimate child with unmarried women who would not be eligible: Even by confining their analysis to states that gave the most generous welfare benefits to single mothers, they found no difference in the rates of illegitimacy between the groups. Mississippi, with the lowest welfare and food stamp benefits for AFDC mothers in the entire country (only 46 percent of the federal poverty guidelines), has the second-highest percentage of out-of-wedlock births in the country; states with higher AFDC benefits than the national average tend to have *lower* rates of illegitimacy than the national average.

Sociologist Mark Rank finds that "welfare recipients have a relatively low fertility rate" and that the longer a woman remains on welfare, whatever her age, the less likely she is to keep having babies. Mothers on AFDC have only one-fourth the number of births while they are on welfare as do mothers who are not on welfare.

Also, there is no clear evidence that welfare benefits encourage marital breakup, although here the findings are more mixed. Some studies have demonstrated a link between higher welfare payments and marital dissolution, but others have found only modest or insignificant correlations. In March 1987 the General Accounting Office released a report summarizing more than one hundred studies completed since 1975. The report concluded that "research does not support the view that welfare encourages two-parent family break-up" or that it significantly reduces the incentive to work. While researcher Robert Moffitt's 1990 review of welfare studies found some effects of welfare programs on marriage rates, it also showed that welfare explains neither the long-term decline in marriage rates nor the most recent increases in female headship.

Finally, the availability of welfare benefits and the size of grants cannot be shown to create a family cycle of dependency. A recent study of child poverty and welfare rates in both 1970 and 1980 found that "high-benefit states tend to have a relatively lower proportion of their children in poverty than low-benefit states." Census data from 1988 show that half the people on the welfare rolls in any month are off within a year. Two-fifths of those who leave eventually return for another spell, yet their total length of time on welfare still averages out to only two years or less. Only a small minority remain on the rolls for extended periods, and despite anecdotes about "welfare queens," this is not because payments are generous: The combined value of AFDC payments and food stamps is below the minimum poverty level in all but two states and one other county in America; nationally, the median worth of both benefits is only 73 percent of the poverty level. Most recipients live hand to mouth, sometimes going hungry near the end of the month or losing their housing if the welfare check is delayed for any reason. In light of this, if welfare benefits do encourage women to leave their husbands, this is a comment more on how bad their marriages must be than on how attractive the alternative of welfare is.

Obviously, there are serious problems with welfare policies and practices, but we cannot analyze these problems realistically if we cling to the myth that only the poor have ever been dependent on government aid, forgetting the near-universality of families' dependence on public assistance in American history. Few people would accuse government subsidies to middle- and working-class homeowners of destroying the recipients' work ethic, demoralizing their families, or wrecking the economy. When it comes to the poor, welfare researchers Richard Cloward and Frances Fox Piven suggest: "It is not receiving benefits that is damaging to recipients, but rather the fact that benefits are so low as to ensure physical misery and an outcast social status." Political scientist Robert Goodin reports: "Psychological studies show that aid which is given anonymously, which protects the autonomy of the recipient, and which allows him opportunities to reciprocate all have positive rather than negative effects upon the recipient—among them, encouraging subsequent attempts at self-help on his part."

Certainly there are debates to be held about welfare subsidies and practices. The extent to which expanded health coverage has been accompanied by ballooning hospital and specialists' charges deserves scrutiny. So do policies that penalize welfare recipients for working or saving by reducing the amount of their grants accordingly. The fact that AFDC payments to mothers do not have much impact on work-force participation may be positive from the point of view of the work ethic but negative in terms of the work mothers are forced to take and the inadequate child care they must use. Perhaps we should link payments in this case to *not* working. On the other hand, experiments with the negative income tax show that direct subsidies to youths below the age of twenty-one *do* have substantial effects on work-force participation. Perhaps here we should assist poor youth, given their high unemployment rates, but by providing educational scholarships or jobs rather than direct grants.

There are some situations, though, when it might make more sense to award direct cash grants. The Urban Affairs Center at Northwestern University, for example, recently calculated the total spending on poverty-related programs in Cook County, Illinois, during 1984, including salaries to welfare workers, doctors, social workers, psychologists, and security officers. Dividing the total ($4.8 billion) by the number of poor people in the county in that year (781,330), urban affairs professor John McKnight found that it averaged out to $6,209 per person, or $18,600 a year for a family of three. However, the poor received only one-third of this in actual financial assistance, since social service functionaries consumed two-thirds of the total.

To sustain the myth that only "abnormal" or "failed" families require public assistance, policymakers tend to smuggle into the budget the subsidies on which most families rely. Direct expenditures to the poor are debated to the last penny, accompanied by either agonized soul-searching or angry bombast about why the poor are unable to fend for themselves. But the same politicians unconcernedly vote for massive middle-class entitlement programs that are disguised as "earned" benefits (social security, for example) or slipped in as "off-budget" items whose costs are seldom tallied up until it is too late. Tax expenditures, for example, totaled $310 *billion* in fiscal year 1989, yet this massive government subsidy did not trigger the tax revolts and political upsets that have occurred over more readily comprehensible direct expenditures equaling only a tiny fraction of this sum.* As one economist points out:

> A dollar spent on housing, health care, or capital investment through the tax code has the same effects on the allocation of resources and the distribution of income as a dollar in direct spending for the same purposes. Yet, because tax expenditures are hidden and do not affect calculations of the "size of government" as measured by the ratio of outlays to GNP, they receive far less scrutiny than regular budget accounts.

---

*Recent agitation over funding for the National Endowment for the Humanities is a case in point: Federal spending on the arts in America amounts to less than 0.1 percent of the national budget, or less than is spent annually on the Pentagon's military band program; tax deductions for advertising that exploits sex to sell products cost the treasury billions of dollars each year.

One way that both direct expenditures and tax subsidies for nonpoor families are disguised is by attaching them, however tenuously, to an already existing work history, income level, or other personal characteristic. Or, instead of funding social services directly, the government may give tax breaks to families who purchase them privately. Such policies convey the false impression that the subsidies are somehow caused by, paid for, or *due* to the recipients because of their individual achievements. They also tend to tie the amount of public aid families and individuals receive to the amount of income or advantages they already have. Thus, even widely distributed tax deductions, such as the dependent child deduction so important to most working families, are set up in ways that aid the rich more than anyone else. The worth of a deduction depends on a person's tax bracket, so two children are "worth" twice as much to a family in the top bracket as they are to a family in more modest circumstances. For families too poor to pay taxes, of course, such deductions are totally meaningless.

The effect of distributing public subsidies through private income-boosting channels rather than through general social spending is that interest group lobbies become dominant in determining which families or sectors of the population receive subsidies. While businesses, unions, and retirement associations can form effective lobbies for the subsidies they desire, certain groups, such as children, have very little clout in these battles. They do not have the means to organize as interest groups or the private resources to take advantage of incentives, tax deductions, and so forth. This is one reason that, from 1978 to 1987, after adjusting for inflation, federal expenditures on the elderly grew by 52 percent, while those directed to children fell by 4 percent. Subsidies for children should not be taken from subsidies to the elderly, as some propose; however, "no other country has so large an age bias to its poverty rates nor so wide an age tilt to its allocation of resources." "What we've done in this country in the past few decades," comments economist Sylvia Hewitt, "is socialize the cost of growing old and privatize the cost of childhood. . . ."

DEBATING FAMILY POLICY: WHY IT'S SO HARD

Attempts to sustain the myth of family self-reliance in the face of all the historical evidence to the contrary have led policymakers into theoretical convolutions and practical miscalculations that are reminiscent of efforts by medieval philosophers to maintain that the earth, not the sun, was the center of the planetary system. In the sixteenth century, leading European thinkers insisted that the sun and all the planets revolved around the earth, much as Americans insist that our society revolves around family self-reliance. When evidence to the contrary mounted, defenders of the Ptolemaic universe postulated all sorts of elaborate planetary orbits, changes of direction, and even periodic loop-de-loops in order to reconcile observed reality with their cherished theory. Similarly, rather than admit that all families need public support, we have constructed ideological loop-de-loops that explain away each instance of dependence as an "exception," an "abnormality," or even an illusion. We have distributed public aid to families through convoluted bureaucratic orbits that have become impossible to track; and in some cases—most notably in the issue of subsidized homeownership—the system has become so cumbersome that it threatens to collapse around our ears.

Today, for example, economist Isabel Sawhill points out, purchases of new homes "absorb more than 100 percent of personal savings in the United States, compared to less than 25 percent as recently as 1970. Encouraging such purchases drains savings away from investments in the modernization of factories and equipment." Sawhill suggests that we either provide people with direct grants for purchases, a practice that would quickly expose how many of our housing subsidies go to the rich, or remove housing subsidies entirely and use them to reduce the deficit and/or increase low-income housing.

We urgently need a debate about the best ways of supporting families in modern America, without blinders that prevent us from seeing the full extent of dependence and interdependence in American life. As long as we pretend that only poor or abnormal families need outside assistance, we will shortchange poor families, overcompensate rich ones, and fail to come up with effective policies for helping families in the middle.

Family economic policy is not the only issue that could be debated more productively if we discarded the myth of the self-sufficient family. Many contemporary analysts explain almost every modern social, political, and cultural ill by the fact that individuals have supposedly abandoned the family as the basic unit of commitment, welfare, and morality. The decay of America's most cherished institutions, according to these commentators, has occurred because people have ceased to place the family at the center of their moral universe and to rely on family values for guidance in their political lives. As Rockford Institute President Allan Carlson puts it, America's founders

> understood the family to be the social unit that reconciled liberty with order, that kept the individual's interests in balance with the interests of community and posterity. We have already paid a huge price for forgetting that lesson, a price that ranges from high levels of crime to environmental degradation. The proper response, at both the policy and personal levels, is *a turn toward home.*

This solution has been tried before and found wanting. In the late nineteenth century, the ideals of economic and emotional family self-sufficiency that had begun to evolve in the eighteenth century were decisively severed from their original connection to larger principles of civic virtue, enlightened self-interest, and a gender division of labor whose social responsibilities extended beyond the family. Debates about political ethics and societal responsibilities became compressed into polemics about personal morality and family relations—a process that we have recently seen taken to painful extremes in election campaigns and partisan political disputes. The "turn toward home" did not solve, but actually exacerbated, the social problems in the Gilded Age of the 1870s and 1880s. A similar dynamic occurred with the rediscovery of traditional family values in what may be called the "second Gilded Age" of the 1970s and 1980s.

SOURCES

Families

The Nuclear Family

In this publicity photograph for MGM's *The Beginning or the End* (1946), the film's protagonists confront the threat of nuclear war with heterosexual coupling—the beginning of the "nuclear" families that would smother anxiety in havens of domesticity.

The Welfare Family: A Welfare Mother

Susan Sheehan

Carmen Rodríguez, the "welfare mother" in this account, arrived in the United States in 1959 from Puerto Rico, where she was a restaurant cook. She had three children by previous relationships, and two of them, Inocencia (b. 1958) and Felipe, lived with her in New York City. Within the year she had found a factory position and a "husband," Vicente Santana, who was also employed and whose mother cared for the children while Carmen and Vicente were at work. Within five years the couple had four more children: Vicente, Emilio, Gabriel, and María.

In 1961, Mrs. Santana's mother-in-law returned to Puerto Rico, leaving her without dependable baby-sitting; she quit her job; and her husband was temporarily laid off. Mrs. Santana applied for welfare. Over the next decade, the family received welfare department grants for food, shelter, utilities, and laundry and, until 1968, special grants for furniture and clothing. Vicente worked more or less regularly until 1968, when he stopped working altogether, claiming that he was unable to find a job and that his health was poor. Mrs. Santana had occasional factory jobs until 1963. In the late 1960s, she earned additional money selling numbers (and was arrested and jailed three times). By 1969 the couple's relationship had soured (Vicente had a drinking problem, and he was absent for long periods of time), and in 1971 Mrs. Santana took her children and moved to Brooklyn.

In the following selection, Susan Sheehan vividly describes Mrs. Santana's existence as a welfare mother in the mid-1970s. At this point she has found a new "husband," Francisco Delgado, but life remains difficult. How would you characterize Mrs. Santana's management of her finances and other aspects of her life? Could she do better than she does? Are her methods functional, or self-defeating? Based on this account, do you think the welfare system meets the needs of Mrs. Santana and the general society or that welfare has failed on both accounts?

On the fifth and the twentieth of every month, Mrs. Santana receives a check from the Department of Social Services for two hundred ninety-four dollars. Of that sum, eighty-five dollars is for half of her rent (she pays a hundred seventy dollars a month for her four-room apartment), and the remaining two hundred nine dollars is the semimonthly grant given to a welfare family of seven people in New York City. Twice a month, Mrs. Santana is also sent the authorization to buy one hundred fifteen dollars' worth of food stamps. She is able to buy the stamps for seventy-six dollars. Mrs. Santana is cheating the Department of Social Services in two ways.

She still receives support for her daughter Inocencia and Inocencia's first child, who was born in April of 1972, although they haven't lived with her since September of 1972. Instead of the grant for seven, Mrs. Santana should be getting only the New York City grant for a family of five, which is one hundred fifty-nine dollars every two weeks, plus authorization to buy food stamps. (Her food-stamp authorization would be for eighty-nine dollars; that amount of stamps would cost her fifty-seven dollars.) And she has not told the Department of Social Services that she is living with Francisco Delgado, who earns about a hundred fifty dollars a week working in a factory that makes automobile supplies. If the Department of Social Services were aware of Delgado's existence, it would not hold him responsible for supporting Mrs. Santana (because he isn't legally married to her) or her children (because he isn't their natural father), but it would attempt to make him liable for his share—a sixth—of the rent. Mrs. Santana would also be asked to declare whatever money he gave her as income, and that sum would be deducted from her welfare check. Mrs. Santana has no qualms about "cheating on the welfare." Almost everyone she knows cheats on the welfare. Most of her friends are cheating by continuing to live with men—who in most cases hold jobs and have fathered some of their children—after claiming that the men have deserted them. Other friends have undeclared incomes of their own; some have regular factory jobs, some sell cosmetics from door to door. A while back, one of Mrs. Santana's former caseworkers asked eighteen welfare mothers whether they were cheating on the welfare. All eighteen trusted him sufficiently to tell the truth. Twelve of the eighteen admitted that they had unreported incomes. Although the caseworker knows that welfare-cheating enrages middle-class workers and threatens to destroy the entire welfare system, he is not inclined to turn anyone in for cheating. "You can't stop the cheating until you give people decent grants," he says. "Welfare grants haven't kept up with inflation in recent years, so a lot of the cheating today is justified. For instance, between September of nineteen seventy and December of nineteen seventy-three, while food prices increased thirty-three and a half percent here, welfare grants decreased ten percent." Mrs. Santana considers the welfare grants inadequate. "Welfare gives you only enough money for food and rent," she says. "It's not enough to live on." Mrs. Santana knows of a few women who struggle to get by on just their welfare grants. She doesn't regard their honesty and thrift as virtues, because "they have to do without so much."

Despite the fact that Delgado buys his breakfast and lunch at work, and despite the fact that the four Santana children are entitled to free breakfasts and lunches at school, Mrs. Santana spends almost as much on food and household supplies as her entire legal grant for a family of five would be. Her semimonthly bill is never less than a hundred thirty dollars and sometimes runs as high as a hundred ninety dollars because her grown children and grandchildren eat at her apartment often. If Mrs. Santana knew as much about home economics as the people who draw up welfare budgets, and if she shopped judiciously once a week at the supermarket across the street from her apartment building, she could spend far less. Instead, she frequents a bodega a few doors away from the supermarket, and with good reason: when she runs out of money between welfare checks, as she inevitably does, the bodega will give her credit and the supermarket won't. There are no giant economy sizes, no specials, no money-saving house brands at the bodega, where prices of most items are about twenty percent higher than at the supermarket, but it has not been Mrs. Santana's experience that saving a few dollars on groceries has appreciably affected her situation.

Mrs. Santana shops the way Puerto Ricans have for generations—meal by meal and sometimes item by item. Early in the morning, she sends one of the children over to the bodega (after María's birth, Mrs. Santana began to suffer from chronic bronchitis, and she doesn't like to go up and down stairs any more than necessary) to buy whatever she thinks she will need for breakfast and lunch: half a pound of Bustelo coffee, a quart of milk, a loaf of Italian bread, a quarter of a pound of sliced ham, a quarter of a pound of sliced cheese, some margarine or mayonnaise, a bottle of Pepsi-Cola. If her children come home for lunch because they don't like the free meal the school is serving and she runs out of something, she sends them across the street to charge another loaf of bread, another quart of milk. After lunch, she buys whatever she thinks she will need for dinner. The children are constantly in and out of the bodega during the afternoon and evening—it is one of their main activities—charging snacks (potato chips, cupcakes, soda, ice cream) or replacements for whatever the household has just run out of: two rolls of toilet paper, a small bottle of cooking oil, a box of soap powder.

On the mornings of the fifth and the twentieth of the month, Mrs. Santana waits at her mailbox in the hall for the mailman to bring her welfare check. On a recent twentieth of the month, the mailman appeared at ten with two pieces of mail for Mrs. Santana. One was her welfare check, the other a letter from the public school attended by Vicente and Emilio saying that they were to be suspended the following week for "dangerous behavior." The letter asked her to come in at the end of the week, with the boys, to "discuss ways to improve their behavior so that they may be returned to school." Mrs. Santana puts the two envelopes in her pocketbook and set off immediately for a check-cashing place several blocks from her house, where she waited in line for fifteen minutes. Since the Department of Social Services has stopped sending out all welfare checks on the first and the sixteenth of the month and started staggering the checks in an attempt to cut down on check-stealing, the line was much shorter than it used to be. Mrs. Santana paid a dollar and fifty-seven cents to have her check cashed. At the same time, she bought two fifty-cent New York State Lottery tickets. There is a bank in her neighborhood that would cash her check free of charge, but it is a few blocks farther away. As soon as she had the money in hand, she put eighty-five dollars for the rent in a separate compartment of her pocketbook. Her landlord's representative has made it his business to master the new welfare-check schedule, and he never fails to appear on the mornings of the sixth and the twenty-first of the month to collect the rent. Since her move to Brooklyn, Mrs. Santana has always paid her rent on time, except when something in the apartment is broken and she withholds the rent money as a means of persuading the landlord to repair it. Mrs. Santana also put aside twenty-four dollars to reimburse three acquaintances—her numbers man, her superintendent, a neighbor—from whom she had borrowed five dollars, fourteen dollars, and five dollars to get through the previous week. She walked from the check-cashing place to the bodega. There the proprietor greeted her cordially, turned to the pages of his account book listing all the items the family had charged in the past fifteen days, and told her that her bill came to one hundred sixty dollars and fifty cents. Mrs. Santana sighed, because it was more than she had expected, and scanned the charges. One item—"Seven dollars cash"—displeased her. A few days earlier, she had dispatched Gabriel to the bodega to borrow five dollars; he had obviously asked for seven dollars, given her five dollars, and kept two dollars for himself. She shook her head and told the proprietor she would deal with Gabriel when he came home from school. She gave the proprietor her food stamps, and he deducted one hundred fifteen dollars from her account, leaving her with a new balance of forty-five dollars and fifty cents. Mrs. Santana never entirely wipes out her old balance on check days, but this was a higher balance than she wanted to have. Mrs. Santana's numbers man hangs out at the bodega. On her way out of the store, she gave him the five dollars she owed him and three dollars to play on three different numbers. Mrs. Santana likes to play the numbers. She plays them every day that she is solvent and some days that she isn't. She has never kept track of how much she spends playing the numbers in the course of a year, and so cannot compare that figure with her annual winnings, but she is happy each time she wins a small amount, and can cite every number on which she has won big—three hundred dollars or five hundred dollars—during the past three years. She also remembers the dreams she has had that prompted her to consult a dream book for proper numerical interpretations. Mrs. Santana has never saved a penny of her three-hundred-dollar and five-hundred-dollar winnings, but the windfalls have always been pleasant while they lasted. She has used the money for new linoleum, clothes for herself and the children, jewelry, beer and liquor for parties, trips to Puerto Rico, and deposits on new furniture.

From the bodega Mrs. Santana slowly walked four blocks (her bronchitis was bothering her, and she put the inhaler she always keeps in her pocketbook to her mouth) to a large furniture store. In June of 1974, she had dreamed about eggs, had learned from the dream book that 465 was the appropriate number to play when one had egg dreams, and had won five hundred dollars on 465. She had made a down payment of one hundred twenty-three dollars and ninety-five cents of her winnings on a washing machine, a coffee table, a lamp, a sofa, two easy chairs, and three plastic covers. The furniture cost a total of eight hundred seventy-three dollars and ninety-five cents, leaving a balance, including interest, of seven hundred fifty dollars, which she had been instructed to pay off at the rate of forty dollars a month. One payday in October of 1974, Delgado made a down payment of forty-two dollars and forty-five cents on a bed, a dresser, and a wardrobe costing a total of two hundred ninety-two dollars and forty-five cents, the balance of which was to be paid off at the rate of twenty dollars a month. Social reformers decry the exorbitant rates of interest charged in New York City's slums by furniture stores that sell on credit to poor blacks and Puerto Ricans, but Mrs. Santana doesn't even know how much of the two large purchase prices represent interest charges. The figures aren't broken down in her furniture-payment books, and she knows only the total purchase prices and the balances owed. Nor does Mrs. Santana resent having to make payments on furniture that is already worn out; she blames her children and grandchildren for the furniture's poor condition, rather than its shoddy construction. All her friends and relatives have the same sort of living room sets she has, protected by the same sort of plastic covers. Mrs. Santana likes furniture. As soon as she can afford the down payment on a new set, she looks forward to replacing her green and gold sofa and her aqua and gold and green and gold chairs with three almost identical orange and gold and red and gold pieces. It has never occurred to Mrs. Santana to save, go to a department store, pay cash, and obtain better value for her money; large department stores confuse her, and, besides, she has never succeeded in saving money for anything. The clerk to whom Mrs. Santana handed thirty dollars and her two furniture books recorded the payments in the books noncommittally. When Mrs. Santana recently skipped two payments in a row, no one at the store expressed concern over the missed payments or threatened to repossess the furniture—no doubt because it wasn't worth repossessing. Mrs. Santana has never worried when she has been short of cash and couldn't meet a payment. When she has had the money, she has paid; otherwise, not.

By the time Mrs. Santana left the furniture store, she had seventy-three dollars and forty-three cents in her pocketbook to cover the next fifteen days. Cash would be needed for food and other household supplies that the bodega didn't stock; for playing the numbers; for spending money for the children, who are always clamoring for a peseta (quarter) here, a peso (dollar) there; for transportation, most of her trips being either to her welfare center (where she has frequent business to attend to) or to the lower East Side (to visit friends and relatives); for emergency loans to friends and relatives (one has to be prepared to lend money to friends and relatives whenever one can, so that one can borrow money from them whenever one has to); and for a visit to the beauty parlor. Mrs. Santana dislikes her frizzy hair, and has it straightened and set as often as possible. Whenever she calls a person "handsome," like her second husband, Angel Castillo, the person's characteristics invariably include "good" hair—that is, hair that is straight.

Mrs. Santana's remaining cash wouldn't be sufficient to cover those expenses, much less the expenses Delgado usually took care of. Delgado's paychecks average a hundred and fifty dollars a week. He sends thirty dollars a week to his four children, who live back home in Yauco with his late wife's mother, and keeps a certain amount of money for his personal expenses—carfare, meals at work, clothes, cigarettes, beer, marijuana. He pays the gas-and-electricity bill and the phone bill. (The basic monthly charge for the phone is only seven dollars, but Mrs. Santana's older children often travel and call her long distance collect, so the phone bill sometimes runs as high as sixty dollars a month.) Each payday, he usually gives Mrs. Santana fifty dollars for the coming week for clothes for herself and the children, and for miscellaneous items. On a recent Friday evening, he gave her twenty dollars instead of the customary fifty. She didn't know why and didn't ask any questions.

From the furniture store, Mrs. Santana headed home along Havemeyer Street, one of Williamsburg's main shopping thoroughfares. It is a street lined with small Jewish, Puerto Rican, and Italian shops, which sell clothes, candy, pizza, cheese, fish, liquor, hardware, furniture, fruit and vegetables, and religious statues and other crockery bric-a-brac. In the streets of Mrs. Santana's neighborhood, in the late morning, children who should have been in school amused themselves by jumping on discarded mattresses; young men who could have been working souped up the motors of their Chevrolets or ogled the young women who sauntered along in threesomes and foursomes, inviting their attention; mothers wearily pushed their infants' strollers and held onto their toddlers' hands; scruffy mongrels foraged in the ubiquitous mounds of garbage, and stray cats suddenly ran out from under parked cars and from behind abandoned appliances; drug addicts shot up in vacant lots; heroin pushers went in and out of a local candy store, undisturbed by the cops on the beat, who were presumably being paid off not to disturb them; old men sipped from bottles wrapped in brown bags, or slept off last night's drunk on the sidewalk. Whenever Mrs. Santana spotted an acquaintance in the crowded street, she told her about her bodega bill, successfully soliciting her sympathy over the high cost of feeding a family. As she walked home, she looked longingly at the brightly-colored pants suits and see-through nightgowns in the windows of the clothing stores. Mrs. Santana has never subscribed to a magazine, owned a car, a rug, or an air conditioner, or bought insurance, but she and her children love clothes and spend about two thousand five hundred dollars a year to dress themselves in the latest styles. Mrs. Santana doesn't spend much on any single item for herself—her dresses cost about twelve dollars apiece—but the pegs in her bedroom hold an extensive collection of slacks, blouses, Bermuda shorts, sweaters, dresses, and satin undergarments. Mrs. Santana has been invited to attend the christening of Delgado's sister's baby. She doesn't look forward to going, because she may not have the money for a new long dress, and the other people who can be expected to attend have already seen all her other long dresses. Just as a light rain began to fall, Mrs. Santana stopped in at a small furniture store a block away from her apartment to look at a forty-dollar wardrobe she had priced many weeks earlier. She has never lived in a place that had closets, and her children had wrecked the last wardrobe she bought—the one on which she is still making payments—months ago. She hoped to have a spare forty dollars to replace the wardrobe before long, but she didn't have it then; perhaps she would hit a good number soon. Her last stop of the morning was at the bodega, where she charged a large white votive candle to her account.

The Statistical Family

In the 1950s, Americans searched for the "typical family," which not surprisingly turned out to be white, middle-class, northern, Anglo-Saxon, and suburban. There were many such families in the United States, but to label this family "typical" was to exclude millions of families that did not have some or all of these characteristics.

The notion of "family disintegration," so common in the 1970s and 1980s, presents similar problems. It paints with too broad a brush; it mystifies as much as it explains.

Statistics can help. They offer a sense of historical perspective, and they give some content to phrases such as "family disintegration." On this and the next page are four charts and tables, each having to do with some aspect of the recent history of the family. Look at each one separately, but also consider how they relate to one another.

U.S. Households, 1960, 1991, 2000

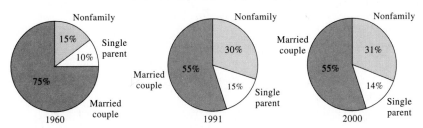

1960 — Nonfamily 15%, Single parent 10%, Married couple 75%
1991 — Nonfamily 30%, Married couple 55%, Single parent 15%
2000 — Nonfamily 31%, Married couple 55%, Single parent 14%

These pie charts reveal some dramatic changes in household structure over the last thirty years. What kinds of families would be included under "nonfamily" households? Would people in this category be more isolated, or less contented, than married couples? What might account for the growth of nonfamily households?

U.S. Median Age at First Marriage, 1890–1991

Year	Men	Women
1890	26.1	22.0
1900	25.9	21.9
1910	25.1	21.6
1920	24.6	21.2
1930	24.3	21.3
1940	24.3	21.5
1950	22.8	20.3
1955	22.6	20.2
1960	22.8	20.3
1965	22.8	20.6
1970	23.2	20.8
1975	23.5	21.1
1980	24.7	22.0
1985	25.5	23.3
1986	25.7	23.1
1987	25.8	23.6
1988	25.9	23.6
1989	26.2	23.8
1990	26.1	23.9
1991	26.3	24.1

What have been the major developments in the age at first marriage? How would you explain these developments? How would a higher age at first marriage affect household structure? Would it strengthen, or weaken, the family?

These materials are reprinted with permission from Dennis A. Ahlburg and Carol J. DeVita, *New Realities of the American Family* (Washington, D.C.: Population Reference Bureau, 1992).

Divorce and Marriage Rates, 1940–1990

The increase in divorce rate revealed in this graph is at the heart of claims that American family values have been eroding. How else might one account for a rising divorce rate? Could it have anything to do with the large number of marriages that took place years earlier? Does the timing of the divorce rate increase suggest that the responsibility lies with "no-fault" divorce laws (first passed in California in 1969) which made divorce simpler? Is the rising divorce rate a clear sign that Americans were unhappier in their marriages than ever before? Do you think the rising age at first marriage had something to do with the leveling off of the divorce rate after 1980?

U.S. Poverty Rates, 1959–1990

Poverty and the family are related in a variety of ways. For example, what relationship might there have been between poverty and divorce? and between divorce and poverty? between poverty and single-parent households? In general, is there any evidence that family "decline" was caused by increases in poverty?

TV Families

The photographs in this section are publicity images, generated by television programs about families in three widely separated periods of time. Although the images are of media families, they should be useful in giving us some sense of how Americans—or some group of them—thought about the family at different moments in the recent past. What desires, tensions, or other perspectives can you see in the photographs? From your knowledge of the content of these programs, what did each have to say about the family? How did each reflect social, economic, or even political conditions?

The Nelsons—Ozzie and Harriet and their children Ricky *(left)* and David—were one of television's most famous families in the 1950s and early 1960s. The Nelsons were also a real family, and on television they played themselves—more or less. On screen, Ozzie was charming and low-key; off screen, he could be a tyrannical boss. On screen, Ricky was a happy pop star; off screen, he was an increasingly resentful young man who wanted to play "authentic" rock 'n' roll. According to historian David Halberstam, the family was dysfunctional.
The Bettmann Archive.

All in the Family **first aired in January 1971, during Richard Nixon's first term. The Bunker family featured Archie (Carroll O'Connor), a lovable bigot; his wife Edith (Jean Stapleton); his daughter Gloria (Sally Struthers); and Archie's son-in-law Mike (Rob Reiner), a sociology student who was the spokesperson for youthful liberalism. What does the photograph reveal about the Bunker family? about the early 1970s?**
UPI/Bettmann.

Phylicia Rashad and Bill Cosby, stars of *The Cosby Show.* **From 1985 through 1989—in the midst of Reagan/Bush conservatism—***The Cosby Show* **was the most watched program on U.S. television. From your memories of the program, how do you explain its popularity? Why might the program have appealed to whites? to African-Americans? Were racism, or racial questions, a regular theme of** *The Cosby Show***? What did the show have to say about issues of gender?**
Mark MacLaren/Retna Ltd.

SUGGESTIONS FOR VIEWING AND LISTENING

Kramer vs. Kramer (1979)
An exploration of divorce and its consequences from the male perspective.

Working Girl (1988)
The catfight genre. A discussion of the "problem" of successful women.

Die Hard (1988)
Helpless woman rescued by macho man in postindustrial Los Angeles. Reagan-era values.

R.B. Greaves, "Ballad of Leroy" (1969)
The inner-city ghetto as pathology.

Anti-Nowhere League, "Woman" (1981)
Woman-bashing punk critique of middle-class values, including romance and marriage.

k.d. lang, "Nowhere to Stand" (1989)
A lesbian singer-songwriter reconsiders the nation's patriarchal "family tradition."

CHAPTER 10

The Reagan Revolution

"All of us recognize that these people who keep talking about the age of limits are really talking about their own limitations, not America's," said Ronald Wilson Reagan during his 1980 campaign for the presidency. Reagan's enthusiastic belief in America's future suited voters tired of the troubles and ambiguities of the last decade: the economic roller-coaster ride, the deceptions and ugliness of the Watergate years, the long, drawn-out defeat in Vietnam, the paralysis of the American government during the Iranian hostage situation. Reagan's election was also a rejection of at least some of the reforms generated by Lyndon Johnson's Great Society, a program that relied on the social sciences to deliver the Rooseveltian goal of a "changed concept of the duty and responsibility of government towards economic life." Instead, the Republican candidate offered a return to the conservative tradition of Robert Taft and Barry Goldwater, grounded in the vision of a "stateless society filled with self-regulating individuals."

Reagan, the Great Communicator, may have spoken to our own nostalgia for a simpler America: to our common vision of the past, a vision constructed by the art form of the twentieth century, the movies, and further validated by one of Hollywood's own as presidential candidate. He spoke of small towns with white picket fences, self-sufficient families, and old-fashioned American values reflected at home and in foreign policy. He was the new broom elected to sweep Washington, and he promised not only less government and more individualism, but a renewed faith in God and America. (As a conservative, Reagan might have been happy to think of himself as an "old broom" sweeping away new nonsense; he was the most aged man ever elected to the office.)

Reagan became the recognized voice of American conservatism following the defeat of Republican candidate Goldwater in 1964. His views, formulated during the Truman and Eisenhower presidencies, featured limited government, lower taxes, and increased vigilance against Communism and its associated evils— themes that remained the essence of the Reagan credo for the next thirty years. Although many voters were attracted to these ideas, Reagan's enormous popularity also had much to do with the depth of his commitment to the values he espoused.

262

No fact, no argument, no contradiction, no logical flaw, no opinion ever swayed his view of what was needed or what should be done. This unshakable faith was a devastating weapon, and the aura of personal purity and invulnerability that derived from his simple credo delivered in a sincere, telegenic format led Congresswoman Pat Schroeder to dub him the "Teflon President." His opponents frequently allowed themselves to be swayed by his confidence and their own inability to offer concrete solutions to highly complex problems. His supporters admired his style and argued that he was creating a model of presidential leadership, particularly in contrast to Jimmy Carter, who was almost universally perceived as politically inept. A new conservative voting bloc, sensing opportunity and sharing his sentimental visions, offered him unswerving loyalty.

Within two years of his election, Reaganomics was in full gear. Cuts in government programs, tax cuts for corporations, and increases in defense spending were all devised and implemented. The result was not as positive as many anticipated: the economy went into a recession, unemployment reached 10.5 percent in 1982, and federal expenditures began a steep climb. By 1984, the Reagan administration could claim it had rekindled the economy, but many of the new white-collar jobs that had been created were in financial and investment fields tied to the junk bond craze of the 1980s. Manufacturing continued to decline while service jobs increased, particularly low-paying ones. The one success story was the tremendous growth of the defense industry, predicated on Reagan's belief in the necessity of opposing the "Evil Empire" embodied in the Soviet Union. One result was the creation of a new federally funded technology, the Strategic Defense Initiative, credited by Reagan admirers with having played a significant role in ending the cold war. A corollary of Reaganomics was a tripling of the national debt and of the national deficit within the first four years of the Reagan presidency.

Most middle-class Americans did not see an immediate change in their economic or political situation resulting from the Reagan years, but Reagan did help transform the way they thought about government. Once understood as the solution to poverty, racial discrimination, and other social concerns, government was now perceived as *the problem*. Yet, a question remained: if government was not to be the arbiter of the rights, responsibilities, and duties of the citizen, then who was that arbiter to be? religion? the political parties? a social, cultural, and economic elite?

INTERPRETIVE ESSAY

David S. Meyer

Star Wars, Star Wars, and American Political Culture

The Reagan administration proposed the Strategic Defense Initiative (SDI) on March 23, 1983. The announced purpose of this anti-missile weapon was to create a giant umbrella that would protect Americans from incoming nuclear missiles. It was the largest single change in nuclear strategy since Eisenhower's decision to offer "more bang for the buck." The debate regarding the uses, advantages, and morality of nuclear weapons, visited in the late 1940s, was rekindled. But this time, morality did not take center stage. Instead, scientific feasibility and cost shaped political arguments and defined the options.

Critics argued that existing technology could not offer complete protection to the American public and that the cost of attempting to do so would be astronomical. They cited scientific studies, offered comparative examples, and derisively dubbed SDI "Star Wars." Nonetheless, the public was intrigued. The belief in the benefits of technology, the seemingly natural progression of finding a new technology to save the population from the "old" nuclear technology, and a natural propensity to believe in the genius of American scientists, all melded into popular support for the new weapons system.

In the following essay, David Meyer uses the Strategic Defense Initiative and the popular film trilogy Star Wars *(1977, 1981, 1983) to examine the American love affair with technology. Have Americans admired technology as the ultimate creation and expression of individual, human genius? or as a tool that reduces humans to efficient machines? Does the dichotomy—between technology as liberation and technology as control—have any counterpart in the political debate between conservatives and liberals? Do Americans have a forum to speak to the consequences of the Faustian bargain made by corporations in the name of workers? Can the arguments made about weapons systems also help us to understand our relationship to computers, or to the media?*

The small group of US Army officers who planned military strategy for the recent war in the Persian Gulf called themselves the "Jedi Knights," referring to the heroes of George Lucas' Star Wars films. Nearly a decade after the release of the last film, the name testifies to the cultural resonance of the trilogy. Indeed, *Star Wars* (1977), *The Empire Strikes Back* (1981), and *The Return of the Jedi* (1983) were

From David S. Meyer, "Star Wars, *Star Wars* and American Political Culture," *Journal Of Popular Culture,* 26 (Fall 1992): 99–115. Copyright © 1992 by Bowling Green University Popular Press. Reprinted by permission.

all among the most popular and profitable films in the history of cinema. It is not surprising then, that military and political figures have tried to use imagery from the films to build support for their policies. President Ronald Reagan's announcement of a new Strategic Defense Initiative, on March 23, 1983, is a case in point. Critics dubbed the Reagan program "Star Wars" in derision, contending that the president's vision of antimissile weapons in space was not simply fanciful, but also impossible, expensive, and dangerous.

Reagan readily accepted the critics' language, welcoming an association with the romanticism and the lure of technological advancement found in the films. The president's commitment to his Star Wars undermined at least one nuclear arms control agreement (the perhaps utopian Reykjavik proposals in 1986) and produced several less balanced budgets. At this writing, the Star Wars movie trilogy is available on videocassette for home use throughout the United States. Although not available for use in the home or elsewhere, the Department of Defense's Star Wars consumes some $2–4 billion annually, an increasing share of a declining budget, propped up by early, and probably overly optimistic, reports of the Patriot missile's effectiveness in the Gulf war.

"Star Wars" has stuck to an odd conglomeration of Pentagon programs with astonishing ease—indeed it is more frequently used than the official SDI acronym—but more than anything else this reflects a misreading and misinterpretation of the Lucas movies, which are seen to glorify and romanticize technology and, indeed, warfare. In this essay, I will argue that the Star Wars films suggest another reading that is far more skeptical of SDI's promises. In this essay I will examine the Star Wars trilogy in order to extract this critique. I begin with a brief review of each film and the political environment surrounding it, which helps to explain the incredible popularity of the series. I conclude with a discussion of several recurring themes in the trilogy and in contemporary American political culture.

STAR WARS

Released in 1977, *Star Wars* accompanied the first signs of a major military buildup as the United States government attempted to overcome the *malaise* of the Vietnam syndrome, that is, a general reluctance among the public to use military means to achieve political objectives abroad. Jimmy Carter presided over substantial increases in military spending and capabilities, even as he articulated a desire to rid the earth of nuclear weapons. He continued negotiations on a SALT II agreement with the Soviet Union, while providing for the development of new nuclear MX, cruise, Pershing II and Trident D-5 missiles. Carter defined the Persian Gulf as a "vital interest," and began organization of a "Rapid Development Force" which could defend it. Interestingly, however, filmmaker George Lucas began work on this film during the height of the Watergate scandal, imagining his work partly as a polemic against the corrupt Nixon administration. Indeed, Nixon was his initial inspiration for the insecure and repressive Emperor.

In *Star Wars,* we are drawn into a war between a loose rebel alliance, scattered across the galaxy, and the evil empire, whose imperial stormtroopers, faceless and dressed in either completely black or white armor, embody a totalitarian nightmare. Deliberately, the Empire's minions are without character or distinction, with the sole exception of Lord Darth Vader, commander of the Imperial forces and servant to the Emperor—who will not appear until the final film. Darth defines himself with austere excess, apparently muscular underneath his black armor and helmet, towering above all other characters, and blessed with the mechanically augmented baritone of James Earl Jones.

Darth and his troops chase and ultimately capture rebel leader Princess Leia, who has secret information about the Empire's Death Star, a superweapon which can destroy entire planets with a single blast. In pursuit, they destroy her home planet and numerous non-combatants along the way. Leia has sent a call for help with two robots, or "droids," R2-D2 and C3-PO, who are instructed to find the mysterious Jedi master, Obi-wan Kanobie. En route, pirates capture the droids and sell them to the trilogy's hero, young Luke Skywalker. As a hero, Luke is drawn no more subtly than villain Darth Vader. He is passionate, youthful, impatient and resolutely democratic. "Call me Luke," he tells C3, the protocol droid, who prefers to address his new owner as "Sir." Leia's message and the droids lead Luke to "Old Ben" Kanobie, a local hermit, who introduces Luke to the story and to the Force.

Ben enlists Luke's aid in finding and rescuing the princess. He also hires a pilot and a ship to evacuate them from the planet. Joining the rebels then, albeit only by hire, are Han Solo, a typical western hero, and his partner and intimate, Chewbacca, the large and hairy ape-like Wookiee. (Their relationship is deeply grounded in a long-tradition of American literature, in which the hero is paired with a non-white [nonhuman] male to allow the development of an intimate alliance without homoerotic overtones.) Solo is desperate for cash to pay off bad debts accumulated through smuggling, and to avoid bounty hunters pursuing the price on his head.

The Death Star captures Solo's ship, the *Millenium Falcon,* but the heroes view their predicament as an opportunity. Han, Luke, and "Chewey" set out to rescue Leia, a post-feminist princess who wields her own blaster and makes decisions, as Ben stealthily wanders the ship's corridors in his Jedi robes, looking for Darth. The rescue is successful, but only because Ben sacrifices his life (sort of) in a light sabre duel with Darth that allows the others the time to escape. They rejoin the rebel alliance and mount an attack on the Empire, aided by secret plans R2 copied from the Death Star's computer, which identify the Death Star's one vulnerability.

The rebel "snub fighters" are small enough to penetrate the Death Star's defenses, so the Empire sends out its own fighters. As the rebels make successive passes at their target, Ben's voice advises Luke to "trust [his] feelings." Luke rejects his computer targeting scope to feel the target instead. In the nick of time and against all odds, he destroys the Death Star. "Remember," says Ben, "the Force will be with you always." The movie ends with a formal ceremony in which Leia hugs and honors Han and Luke, and the final credits roll.

The movie was immensely popular, generating a line of spinoff toys, slogans and bumperstickers and infiltrating popular jargon. (I started thinking about this essay when I heard a man in the supermarket admonish his three year old son that "Jedi don't cry.") The technical wizardry of Lucas' team explains some of this popularity, but clearly the movie touched a deep nerve as well. It gave expression to popular myths in American culture. The heroic rebels succeeded by virtue not of technological advantages, but through greater commitment, diversity and justness of cause. Luke appeared to be both a common man and a master of science—much as Jimmy Carter (the peanut farmer and "nuculah" engineer) did in his presidential campaign. The heroes sought independence, not dominance, and personal affiliation was always a stronger motivation for action than obedience or ideology. Technology was less trustworthy than some mystical sense of self, and small was most assuredly beautiful.

THE EMPIRE STRIKES BACK

Released in 1980, during the electoral campaign between incumbent Jimmy Carter and challenger Ronald Reagan, the *Empire* promised a striking change in tone from the optimism of the new hope in *Star Wars.* The darkest and most confusing film of the trilogy, Empire and events separate and wound the heroes, and the film ends with a bare promise of retribution in a sequel as the heroes stare out into space. The Empire is still seeking to quash the rebellion, and to reconstruct the Death Star. Han's creditors pursue and capture him, while Luke seeks training as a Jedi Knight under the tutelage of Yoda, an elderly muppet living on a swamp planet.

Luke's training comprises the center of the film. Yoda instructs Luke in the use of the Force, aided periodically by Ben's apparition, while tormenting him with near zen challenges. In explanation and instruction Yoda is suitably cryptic, "You must unlearn what you have learned . . . my ally is the force. Life creates it . . . Its energy surrounds us and binds us . . . You must feel the force around you . . . everywhere . . . the rock, the tree . . ." Yoda then raises Luke's sunken ship through will. Luke is astounded. "I don't believe it," he says. Yoda responds sadly, "that is why you fail." The ship sinks below the swamp again. Faith is critical to make any of this work.

Against Yoda's counsel, Luke leaves training early to rescue Han and Leia, who he (correctly) senses are in trouble. Seeking help, they have travelled to Cloud City (the only place black people appear in the trilogy) to find Han's old friend, Lando Calrissian. Lando attacks, then embraces the heroes, before betraying them to the Empire; then, betrayed by Darth Vader, he helps Leia escape, incites a rebellion, and joins the rebel alliance. Darth freezes Han in carbonite, then gives the frozen Solo to bounty hunters. Luke arrives as the other heroes escape in the *Falcon,* and confronts Darth.

"You are not a Jedi yet," Darth reminds him, as they draw sabres and fight. Darth cuts off Luke's right hand, and invites him to join the Empire. He also tells him that he is Luke's father. Luke screams, cries and denies, but Darth has the Force with him, "Search your feelings," he says, "You know it to be true. We can rule the galaxy as father and son . . . come with me, it is the only way." But Luke finds another way, dropping off the side of the building. Hanging by a small piece of pipe, he calls to Leia telepathically, and the *Falcon* returns to rescue him. The film ends in disarray. Lando is off in the *Falcon* to rescue Han from his creditor, Jabba the Hut, while Leia visits Luke in the hospital, where he has been fitted with a new black mechanical hand, reminiscent of all of Darth.

Indeed, the disarray of *Empire* well reflected the political upheaval of 1980. The Carter presidency had reached a similar level of confusion, as the administration had jettisoned the more conciliatory aspects of its foreign policy, including restrained military spending, Secretary of State Cyrus Vance, participation in the Moscow Olympics, and arms control. Although Carter's new hawkishness may have helped him win the Democratic nomination for the presidency, it left him effectively defenseless against Ronald Reagan, the Republican nominee who promised a tougher foreign posture—and perhaps more importantly, a return to a mythic past of conventional values and Pax Americana. Carter offered only a softer version of his opponent's message, leaving voters with little apparent choice. Given this context, Carter's last minute attempt to raise the issues of nuclear proliferation and nuclear war, voiced through his daughter's concerns in a televised debate, seemed disingenuous.

Reagan took office in 1981, seeking to make good on his campaign promises in military and foreign policy, increasing Carter's already increased military budgets, continuing all of the weapons systems Carter had started and resurrecting a few Carter had cancelled, such as the B-1 bomber and two nuclear powered aircraft carriers. In 1982 and 1983 the situation appeared especially desperate, generating the strongest antinuclear movement the United States had yet seen. The last Star Wars film would emerge amidst a climate of conflict and confusion.

THE RETURN OF THE JEDI

The final installment of Star Wars, released early in 1983, shortly after Ronald Reagan announced his strategic defense initiative, *Return* is fittingly the most pantheist and primitivist in the series. In the face of insurmountable technological odds, the rebels, armed with the Force and primitive (even by 20th century standards) weapons, defeat the Empire, destroy the Emperor and redeem Darth Vader. Of course, it looks bleak at the outset. The Empire has virtually destroyed the rebel alliance and finished construction of the Death Star. Meanwhile, the rebels are dispirited and isolated. (It is *Star Wars* all over again.)

The rebels mount several attempts to rescue Han Solo who, still frozen in carbonite, is mounted on the wall of Jabba's den of hedonism, which is populated by all manners of slimy sycophantic types. As the rescues fail, Jabba gains custody of the droids, Chewbacca, Leia (who posing as a bounty hunter succeeds in thawing Han late one night) and eventually Luke. Jabba plans to use Leia (as a private dancer on a leash) and the droids (R2 has been reduced to selling drinks) and throw the others down a bottomless pit. Captive and apparently helpless, Luke, now a Jedi, demands that Jabba free them all or be destroyed. Jabba laughs, sealing his doom and that of his entire entourage. Effecting their escape by killing Jabba and his party, Luke and R2 return to Degna to complete the Jedi training with Yoda, while the others return to the *Millenium Falcon.*

Luke arrives to find Yoda on his deathbed. Yoda confirms that Darth is indeed Luke's father, formerly Anakin Skywalker, and notes that he must confront Darth in order to become a Jedi. "You will be the last of the Jedi," Yoda gasps, then dies and disappears. Ben's emanation comforts Luke, tells him that Leia is indeed his sister, with comparable Jedi potential, and encourages him to go on. Luke then returns to the rebel alliance, where the rebel command staff plans the final assault on the Death Star. Han, Luke (now both generals) and Princess Leia are to lead a ground attack to disable the power source for the Death Star's protective shield, and then General Lando Calrissian will lead the space attack.

On the ground, the rebels engage in a series of guerrilla battles with storm troopers, and are then captured by the Ewoks, tiny teddy bear-like creatures who plan to eat them, with the exceptions of Leia, who is a friend, and C3-PO, whom they worship as a god. The rebels escape the meal and forge an alliance with the Ewoks. Together, they defeat the imperial troops and disable the force shield. Luke then leaves to confront Darth directly; he plans to "turn" him to the good side of the force. Darth and the Emperor, aware of Luke's intent, plan to take advantage of his naivete and compassion.

Luke surrenders to Darth, who turns him over to the Emperor. The Emperor welcomes Luke, releases his handcuffs and sends the guards away, leaving the two alone with Darth. The Emperor orchestrates a duel between Darth Vader and Luke, who is reluctant to fight. He defends himself only, but far more effectively than in the previous film. Despite the Emperor's urging, however, Luke refuses to kill his father, throwing down his sabre and declaring "I am a Jedi like my father before me." His empire threatened, the Emperor himself now attacks Luke with electric rays and lightning bolts as Darth watches and Luke calls for help. At the last possible moment, Darth turns on the Emperor, and throws him down the reactor core of their ship, then breathes heavily and falls to the floor. Luke reaches Darth and holds him in his arms. The moral battle concluded, it remains only to sweep up the pieces.

The rebel fighters, under Lando's direction, blow up the Death Star. Recognizing his imminent death, Darth asks Luke to help him remove his helmet and mask, then tells him to leave him to die. Luke refuses, "I have to save you," he says. "You already have, Luke," Darth replies, then dies conveniently, as Luke exits. The Death Star explodes in a nova visible to the Ewoks on the planet below. The rebels rejoice, Han and Leia acknowledge their love, and absolutely everyone left alive is ecstatic. The Ewoks burn their dead heroes (and Anakin Skywalker) in a night ritual, dancing and beating drums, as the Jedi (Ben, Yoda and Anakin) look on approvingly.

STAR WARS IN POLITICS

Oddly, the political use of the Star Wars films is predicated on a reversal of terms. Ronald Reagan promised that his strategic defense initiative would one day end the threat of nuclear destruction by creating an impenetrable "peace shield" to protect the United States from any Soviet nuclear attack. Space-based defenses would destroy enemy nuclear missiles in space, providing a more stable security than the deterrence of mutually assured destruction (MAD). "Star Wars," at least in Reagan's vision, would end deterrence by retaliation and replace it with deterrence by defense. Rhetorically, it was an attractive notion, finding a technological *deus ex machina* to end the terror of the arms race. "Wouldn't it be better to save lives than to avenge them?" Reagan asked. Such an apocalyptic premise is clearly the province not of the often Luddite rebels, but of the evil Empire.

SDI was immediately confronted with opposition from a wide range of sources. Strategic theorists questioned the viability of a defense-based deterrence regime. Pentagon planners resented the commitment of large resources to a research effort with little immediate prospect of a military payoff. Peace activists wondered if the Star Wars technologies might be used offensively, worried that it would complicate or frustrate arms control, and rejected the notion of technological solutions to political problems.

The Star Wars plan had bypassed the institutional scientific establishment, including not only Lawrence Livermore and Los Alamos research laboratories, but even the President's science advisor. Many within the scientific establishment, including the laboratory directors, contended that the program had been oversold, and that the peace shield was a technological impossibility. Thus, much of the debate turned on the issue of whether or not Reagan's utopian vision was possible, rather than whether or not it was desirable, essentially conceding a kind of moral high ground to the administration. Framed in this way, SDI believers had a relatively safe rhetorical response: never doubt the imagination, initiative, and capabilities of American scientists; isn't it better to see what solutions they can devise?

THE ROMANCE OF TECHNOLOGY

At first glance, the Star Wars trilogy seems to support this approach. The movies are in themselves a technological tour de force, with spectacular special effects and innovative cinematic techniques. At the same time, however, the films explicitly and implicitly criticize faith in technology at every possible turn. Several themes emerge very clearly. First, small is beautiful, clearly reminiscent of the culture of the 1970s, when the trilogy was conceived. Second, initiative, creativity and risk-taking can always overcome superior technology. Third, technology is not to be trusted, for it corrupts human capacity and judgment.

Superweapons and impenetrable shields are the property not of the rebel alliance, but the evil Empire, which clearly possesses superior technological prowess. It is unable, however, to overcome the ingenuity (and moral superiority) of the rebels. The Empire's equipment never fails; its weapons never misfire, the scanners never report false information and the faceless stormtroopers (also part of the machinery of oppression) never disobey. Yet the Empire's forces are always frustrated by the smaller forces, less sophisticated weapons, and tactical innovation of the rebels. In contrast, the heroes are forced to make do with inferior equipment which frequently fails, patched together with ingenuity and tactics generally borne of desperation, that make the best of bad circumstances. It is a human or moral failure which makes the Empire vulnerable, the same element that allows the rebels to succeed.

This point is underscored by Lucas' decision to use the droids as the narrative center of the films. In the first few minutes of *Star Wars,* C3-PO calls R2-D2 a "malfunctioning little twerp." We then follow the droids across the galaxy and see them subject to the waves and whims of destiny, the Force and human agency. C3, sporting the only middle-Atlantic accent in the alliance, provides a running commentary of the audacity of the rebels by continually calculating (and reporting) the astronomical odds against success of every rebel operation. Yet Han Solo, Luke Skywalker and Princess Leia always go with their instincts rather than the odds (and they always win). The heroes also demonstrate an uncanny loyalty to their droids. In *Star Wars,* Luke is offered a fresh R2 unit to guide his fighter, but chooses to keep the battered R2-D2 because of their experiences together. In *Empire,* when C3 is blasted into hundreds of pieces, the Wookiee Chewbacca carries the pieces on his back while working to reassemble his friend.

It is not surprising that the Empire, with its focus on efficiency and efficacy, does not name its droids, but an even starker contrast is provided by the Empire's treatment of its people, who function as replaceable cogs in the Imperial machine. Darth Vader repeatedly demonstrates his willingness to execute commanders who allow the rebels any advantage, strangling them long-distance with the Force and giving battlefield promotions to terrified underlings. Darth greets the admission of error and acceptance of responsibility, tried by one admiral, with thanks—and death. In *Return,* we see that even Darth is deemed expendable by the Emperor, who invites Luke to kill and replace his father.

Throughout the battle scenes, the large Imperial weapons, walkers, battleships and Death Stars are frustrated by smaller and more versatile rebel equipment. Rebel fighters use harpoons and tow ropes to trip walkers in a desert battle and snub fighters to infiltrate the defenses of the Death Star. They are all small enough to avoid the major defenses and attacks of the Empire's weapons. Most impressive is Solo's smuggling ship, the *Millenium Falcon,* which is constantly beset by all kinds of technological failures. Chronically unable to achieve "hyper-drive" (light speed), Solo avoids destruction or capture by leading Imperial fighters through an asteroid field; he eludes the Death Star by landing on top of it, then drifting off with the garbage. The *Falcon's* odd construction allows the heroes a secret hiding place when searched by Imperial troops. Yet, despite its essential funkiness, the *Falcon* is the command ship of the final rebel attack on the Death Star.

As spectacular as the multi-ship space battles are, however, the most dramatic and critical scenes are duels between Jedi knights using light sabres. Clearly phallic, the will-powered laser, described by Obi-wan as "an elegant weapon of a nobler day," is disdained by all but the Jedi. Solo, who says that he would always prefer a good blaster, uses the sabre to slay and open a beast to keep Luke warm in the desert in *Empire.* It is the only non-Jedi use of the weapon in the films, possible because of Solo's strong feelings for Luke and the extreme circumstances. To become a Jedi, Luke must build his own sabre, developing his own distinctive green tinge. He uses it in hand-to-hand combat against both primitive beasts and imperial stormtroopers. It is with the light sabre that Darth Vader slays Obi-wan in the first film. Ben's blue light blade, shorter than Darth's red beam, flickers as Darth taunts him. "Your power is weak, old man," he says. Light sabre duels between Darth and Luke serve as the moral and dramatic cores of both *Empire and Return.*

The ultimate irony of technological advantage is demonstrated most dramatically in the final earth battle, in which the Ewoks defeat Imperial forces using sticks, rocks, spears, catapults, winged assault, ropes and hand-to-hand combat. With bravery and superior tactics, the tiny Ewoks are able to seize walkers, defeat stormtroopers and ultimately help disable the force shield to make the rebel victory possible. Importantly, after the battle the Ewoks are able to put down their weapons and hold an ecstatic dancing celebration around a fire. It's impossible to imagine the stormtroopers doffing their helmets and dancing similarly if they had won.

Ewok weaponry is versatile and subservient to Ewok designs. In contrast, Empire technology overwhelms both victims and perpetrators. Obi-wan tells Luke that the young man is mistaken about the good that might be in his father, for Darth is now "more machine than man." Luke's own mechanical right hand strains at the temptation of the dark side when the Emperor challenges him. Finally, as he dies, Darth asks Luke to help him remove his trademark helmet and faceplate, even though he knows it means his death, so that he can look at his son with his own eyes. The heavy breathing, pronounced footsteps and booming baritone now all disappear, as we see a middle-aged man relax and die, apparently redeemed—for he will appear in Jedi heaven in the last shot.

DARTH OR DAD?: IMAGES OF FATHERHOOD

Luke's development throughout the trilogy takes him through a series of surrogate fathers, as he struggles to grow up in a chaotic and hostile world. He is repeatedly orphaned and adopted, as he tries to discover his destiny, and with it his identity. In *Star Wars,* Luke feels trapped on his aunt and uncle's moisture farm. He is desperate to escape his pedestrian farm life and attend the space academy to become a pilot. His adoptive parents fear there may be too much of his father in him, that he is too reckless and wild, but the past is never discussed.

As resentful as he is about staying on the farm, he is unwilling to disobey his aunt and uncle, although he will complain. He is drawn into the adventure when he buys the droids from pirates for farmwork. Like all American farmboys, Luke is an inveterate tinkerer, working to keep the machinery intact. Trying to fix R2, he runs across Leia's message for help, and it is by following the droid that he ultimately meets "Old Ben" Kanobie, as clear a surrogate father figure as the American cinema has ever produced. Ben tells Luke about his real father, Anakin Skywalker, who had been Ben's friend and ally, and presents Luke with his father's light sabre, inviting him into Jedi training. Offering Anakin's legacy, the allure and mysticism of Jedi secrets, the promise of adventure and the appeals of the beautiful Princess Leia, Ben knows he has won Luke's commitment to the cause, even as he tells Luke that he must make his own choices.

The choice is preempted, however, when Luke learns that Imperial troops have killed his aunt and uncle. The option of choosing familial duty and staying on the farm has been foreclosed. Orphaned for the second time, Luke is now Ben's charge. The older man will initiate him into the ways of the Force, and protect him until Luke has reached maturity; he calls Luke, "Son." Jedi knighthood, and the strong relationship to the Force it entails, apparently includes a genetic component, for Ben repeatedly tells Luke that the Force is strong within him as it was for his father. We later learn Luke's sister Leia also has comparable Jedi potential (though in the "G" rated films, she never touches a light sabre). He urges the young man to find his strength within, to trust himself and to feel the Force in making decisions about tactics or ethics. Ben's tutelage is short-lived, however. Seeking to save rebel prospects for victory, represented in the persons of Luke, Leia and Han Solo, Ben allows himself to be slain by Darth Vader in a duel, knowing the ensuing confusion will give the others time to escape. "If you strike me down," Ben warns Darth, "I will become more powerful than you can imagine." Darth's light sabre passes through Ben's robe, but the old man disappears as his robe falls to the ground. (No Jedi corpses litter Star Wars' landscapes.) As Luke and his friends take off, Ben becomes a ghostly presence, his voice advising Luke to run.

This is, of course, hardly the stuff of engaged fatherhood. Luke seeks another surrogate in Han Solo, who calls him "Kid," but the model is flawed. Solo energetically expresses his disdain for the Force and for political causes generally, and vociferously maintains an explicit commitment to look out for himself rather than Luke or the rebel alliance. Further, both he and Luke are initially rivals for Princess Leia's affections. At best, he is an older brother, taunting, teasing and protecting. Luke has been orphaned, but oddly not abandoned, as Ben continues to serve as a conscience and an advisor—at least on general matters. In the succeeding space battle, when Luke is among numerous small snub fighter pilots attacking the giant Death Star, Ben's disembodied voice whispers instructions, telling Luke to feel the Force and trust his feelings. (Solo, who has promised to leave the battle to settle his debts, has a fit of conscience and returns to protect Luke.) And it is when Luke takes his mentor's advice, rejecting the targeting scope and computer on board to make a bombing pass on instinct, that he succeeds in destroying the Death Star and ending the dramatic conflict of the film.

The Empire Strikes Back is a film about Luke's continued search for his father. Instructed by the late Obi-wan to continue his Jedi training, Luke sets out for a distant swamp planet to find the Jedi master, Yoda. Wizened and small, Yoda is an unlikely trainer of warriors, and Luke doubts his identity from the start. The master's manner confuses him further, as Yoda whines and wheedles for food, hitting R2 with his cane. The bases of the master's instruction are much the same as Obi-wan's—feel the Force, trust your feelings, look within and believe. As Luke progresses in his training, he shows increasing deference to his master, who informs him that he must enter a swamp cave to complete his training, bringing in no weapons, for the cave contains only what one brings inside. There are no reflections of eternal truth in this parable; rather, Luke confronts his own fears in a vision of Darth Vader. The two duel with light sabres, and Luke decapitates the evil vision, only to find his own visage in Darth's helmet. Terrified, he runs out to find Yoda.

He finds the courage to confront the actual Darth Vader only when he feels his friends in jeopardy. The aspiring Jedi, armed with his father's sabre, seeks out and finds Darth Vader, whom he knows is at the center of the Empire's evil. Obi-wan had told him that Darth, another Jedi, had killed Luke's father, Anakin Skywalker. As they duel, Darth explains that the story is slightly different, that he is Anakin, Luke's father. Luke refuses to believe, but Darth—in true Jedi fashion—tells him to look inside himself for the truth. Luke is enraged, and attacks Darth with an abandon which proves to be his undoing, for Darth is stronger and more controlled. Luke lunges at Darth with his sabre in both hands, while Darth easily parries Luke's thrust with one hand. He strikes at Luke, severing the young Jedi's right hand, and with it his sabre and connection to the Force. It is an horrific masturbation fantasy. Darth has robbed Luke of his Jedihood, reminding him of his youth and effective impotence. Outside Cloud City, Luke clings with his remaining hand to the edge of a bridge, as Darth approaches slowly, inviting his son to join him in ruling the Empire. The dark side beckons, and Luke, disarmed, demoralized and maimed, seems to have little choice: surrender (morally as well as tactically) or die. He releases his hold on the building, choosing not to choose.

Although he is rescued by Leia and Lando in the *Falcon,* Luke is not the same. He has fallen from innocence, and now distrusts not only his father, but also his surrogates, who kept him from knowing of Darth's paternity. Symbolically, his right hand has been replaced by a black mechanical one similar to Darth Vader's. He is, he knows now, his father's son, supremely conscious of his own vulnerability, both in battle against Darth and from within. The movie ends darkly.

In *Return,* Luke identifies himself as a Jedi; he has made his own sabre and wears the monk's robes of a Jedi master. Armed with knowledge of the Force, he is able to duplicate some of Ben's tricks, winning entrance to Jabba's lair by controlling the minds of his guards, and demonstrating the skill with a light sabre that only a Jedi knows. After effecting the rescue of Han and his friends, however, Luke returns to Yoda's planet in hopes of completing his training. The master is on his deathbed, however, and tells Luke that the younger man now knows everything. Lamenting Luke's rush through his training, Yoda's last words are naturally about the Force. "Remember," he says, "a Jedi's strength flows from the Force . . . once you start down the dark path, forever will it dominate your destiny . . . Don't underestimate the Emperor's power or your father's fate you will follow." The prediction of following in father's footsteps is surely first the fantasy then the nightmare of most young boys.

Orphaned yet again, Luke is confused and desperate until Ben's emanation reappears, comforting him and telling him that Yoda will always be with him. He apologizes for concealing Darth's true identity, and tells him of his twin sister, whom Luke instantly realizes is Princess Leia. The master's advice suddenly reverses, "Bury your feelings deep down, Luke. They do you credit, but they could be made to serve the Emperor." Luke's confusion is understandable. His masters have consistently told him that his feelings were the source of his power and his relation to the Force. Ben has now acknowledged that they are also a weakness, a route to the dark side and must be controlled. He has also said that he must confront and destroy his own father in order not only to reach maturity, but to save the Empire.

Affecting a reversal, Luke decides to confront Darth by not fighting, turning himself in to Imperial troops, "knowing" that Darth will not betray him to the Emperor. He challenges Darth's paternity, empathy and ethics rather than his martial skills. Luke surrenders his light sabre to Darth, addressing him as "Father," but Darth renounces the name, and without apparent hesitation hands the sabre (and Luke) over to the Emperor. Almost sighing in recognition of the complexities of life in the real world, Darth explains, "It's too late for me, son. The Emperor will show you the true nature of the Force. He is your master now." Luke is shocked and disappointed that Darth expresses powerlessness in the face of the larger world, that his commitments to the Empire supersede any feelings he might have for his son. "My father is truly dead," he says.

The Emperor claims his role as Luke's new master, determined to teach him all about the dark side, alternately offering Luke a position alongside his father and the opportunity to replace him. He appeals to Luke's rage, showing him the battle between the rebels and the Empire, and taunting Luke to intervene and do something about it. Luke gazes longingly at his sabre, as the Emperor narrates, "You want this, don't you. The hate is swelling within you now. Take your Jedi weapon. Use it. I am unarmed . . . Give in to your anger . . . It is your destiny. You, like your father, are mine."

With obvious sexual overtones, this is a story about adulthood. The phallic sabre and the feelings and power associated with it make Luke different, but they do not free him from a social role, at least as the Emperor tells it. He must accept his father's failings and recognize his limits. Destiny means accommodation, and acceptance of an appropriate role within a rigidly structured hierarchy. "Your over-confidence is your weakness," Luke tells the Emperor. "Your faith in your friends is yours," The Emperor responds. Destiny is a solitary affair.

As they watch the battle going badly for the rebels, the Emperor continues taunting Luke, calling for him to go for his weapon, to acknowledge his feelings and temptations, to recognize, in effect, his mortality. Led by his own mechanical hand, Luke reaches for his sabre, but Darth is quickly there to parry his son's strike against the Emperor. The two are quickly enmeshed in a sabre battle. Almost in parody of Yoda and Ben, the Emperor provides commentary and instruction to Luke: "Use your aggressive feelings. Let the hate flow through you." Luke puts his weapon down, refusing to fight his father, confining himself to parrying his father's blows. Now Darth is tired; he swings his sabre with both hands, while Luke provides the commentary. "Your feelings betray you father. I feel the good in you, the conflict." The Emperor laughs, and Darth pursues Luke, calling upon him to give in to the dark side. Suddenly, from Luke's mind, Darth realizes he also has a daughter. Suddenly Luke is much less important, there is another Skywalker who may be turned.

Luke loses all control thinking about his sister confronted by Darth, and moves to attack Darth. He cuts off Darth's right hand, evening the score from the previous picture. The Emperor laughs. "Your hate has made you powerful," he announces. "Now fulfill your destiny and take your father's place at my side." Luke nervously feels his own mechanical hand twitching (runaway technology), then throws down his weapon. "Never!" Luke responds, "You've failed . . . I'm a Jedi like my father before me."

The Emperor now attacks Luke with lightning bolts, and Luke is dependent upon Darth Vader for rescue. Darth kills the Emperor and saves his son, but at the cost of his own life. Darth's sacrifice makes the rebel victory possible, and also vindicates Luke's faith in his father. A moment of conversion has redeemed an entire life. This kind of moral equation, however, is difficult to balance. We can't imagine Luke visiting his father in retirement, discussing space-based crabgrass.

Nor can Luke make him answer for his life in service to the Emperor. Luke's father must die, but he does so after abandoning the mask and the identity of Darth Vader. He looks upon his son through Anakin's eyes, then dies conveniently, allowing Luke the dilemma and the freedom of discovering his adult identity alone.

GROWING UP: PERSONAL AND POLITICAL MATURITY

Although the droids are the narrative center of the story, and the romance of Han and Leia a major plot device, the moral center of the films is Luke's search originally for roots, and ultimately for identity. We see Luke struggle from adolescent longing to arrive at Jedi knighthood. Importantly, however, arriving means recognizing the limits of his achievements. There is a profound uneasiness in Luke's maturity. His role models, Ben and Yoda particularly, have been killed; his father resurrected only to die almost immediately afterward.

The real story is that Luke recognizes that his achievements have come through recognizing other ways of doing battle. In stark contrast with the technological escalations that drive the arms race, Luke's battles are fought with progressively less sophisticated weapons. His triumph in *Star Wars,* destroying the Death Star with a bomb dropped from his snub fighter, occurs only when he rejects computer targeting and following Ben's disembodied advice, trusts his feelings and feels his target. In *Empire,* he confronts Darth with a light sabre in hand-to-hand combat—and he is defeated. Although he is able to demonstrate considerably more sabre skill in *Return,* the climactic battle in the final film is fought and won with moral suasion. The Emperor is defeated by rallying the conscience of his servants, not by beating him or those servants down. (It is a prescient predictor of the fall of state communist governments throughout the Eastern bloc.) Luke essentially rejects even the sabre in the final reel, triumphing by not fighting.

We might read in Luke's process of maturation an allegory of the United States growing up as a nation. Like Luke, the United States's early development was defined by playing enemies and allies off each other, even as George Washington sounded the warning about entangling alliances. The post-World War II period was defined by the creation of progressively stricter alliances, and the development of increasingly sophisticated weaponry. Its purported cold war victory, like Luke's triumph over the Emperor, took place not because the East bloc was overwhelmed by force, but because the citizens of East bloc nations were moved to undermine their own governments, and importantly, it was the international softening which made their efforts possible.

Political leaders in the United States have been reluctant to recognize this; such a realization would call for dramatic policy changes. Instead, the government has sought to legitimate building an Empire (or "new world order") with the trappings of innocence and rebellion. Politically we demand both dominance and the sympathy reserved for underdogs, ostensibly to be earned with moral superiority. Reagan promised to "give" the completed star wars system once complete—albeit twenty to thirty years later—to the Soviet Union, cloaking the strategic defense system in the language of apocalyptic promise. American troops in the Persian Gulf are said to have triumphed by virtue of superior cause and skill, ignoring the massive firepower advantage. They were led not by a lord, but the very human "Storming Norman." In contrast, the Iraqi dead, both civilian and military, remain nameless and faceless, as do future enemies. We need to confront the ambiguity and conflict here, and the films suggest a way to do so.

We recognize Luke's maturity when he realizes that the faster scooter or even the more deft swordsmanship are not marks of maturity, but rather maturity is marked by the ability to lay the weapons down. This is, of course, no easy feat. Luke learns from his Jedi masters and from the Empire that technological advancement, no matter how sophisticated, comes always with a cost; that it distorts judgment while making its own demands. He sees no military or technical advantage, no matter how lopsided it appears, can ensure victory, and that there are in fact more powerful weapons. Contrary to the Emperor's expectations, Luke's compassion proves not to be his vulnerability, but the strength which makes it possible to topple the Empire. We learn that even the Emperor's cruelest servant, Darth, was redeemable via love and faith, not power. Considering the prospects for strategic defense, we might also do well to consider Luke's lessons.

SOURCES

Cartoon Commentary: Star Wars

Reagan's commitment to national defense was fundamental; he believed it was the most legitimate function of government. Thus, when the new administration came to office, one of its imperatives was to strengthen the military. In 1983, without conferring with the departments of Defense, State, or Treasury, Reagan launched a totally new concept, the Strategic Defense Initiative (SDI). Its premise was simple. American scientists would create a technological solution to the bomb they had created forty years before. They would move the nuclear confrontation to outer space, using laser-beam technology to destroy incoming missiles, and thus create a protective umbrella for the American population.

President Reagan's commitment to this new technique grew out of two different motivations. He wanted to "save lives rather than to avenge them," as he said in one speech. He also wanted to defend the American way of life against the evils of Communism, without "offensive" military establishments.

The cartoons on these pages present "Star Wars" through the eyes of both critics and advocates. How did advocates defend the concept? How did critics attack it? What was the basic premise underlying all of the cartoons? Why was "Star Wars" such a tempting idea?

Reprinted courtesy of the Seattle *Post-Intelligencer.*

Reprinted with the permission of Chuck Asay and the *Colorado Springs Sun*.

Reaganomics

The big economic issue that hovered over the 1970s was stagflation, a condi-
tion involving both rising prices and falling production. Reagan's solution
was supply-side economics. Supply-siders argued that federal tax cuts for
corporations would jump-start the economy, as corporations invested in new
plants and technology and hired more workers. While seeking the nomination
in 1980, George Bush had labeled the plan "voodoo economics." Besides tax
cuts, the Reagan administration employed deregulation and the relaxation of
environmental laws to create this new economy. Everyone expected there
would be some revenue shortfalls, but in the long run, greater efficiencies in
the private sector would end stagflation and reduce government intervention
in the economy.

David Stockman, Director of the Office of Management and Budget and
the man responsible for creating the miracle, soon discovered that the num-
bers did not work. Over time, they indicated a growing, indeed tripling, of the
budget deficit. In 1981, Stockman admitted publicly that he was no longer
confident of the outcome, and with good reason. By 1984, the United States
had become the world's largest debtor nation, a condition not seen since the
presidency of Woodrow Wilson.

The following charts illustrate the growth of the deficit, median income in the U.S., and a breakdown of income by region. In what years did the United States experience a surplus? Where did the curve have its greatest changes? With what events did this coincide? Might there be situations in which it would be helpful, or even necessary, to have a deficit? What do you first notice about median income? What change do you see from 1973 to the present? What observations can one make about regional income?

Annual Surpluses and Deficits of the U.S. Government
for Selected Years, 1955–1996

1955	−2,993,000,000
1960	301,000,000
1965	−1,411,000,000
1970	−2,842,000,000
1975	−53,242,000,000
1980	−73,835,000,000
1985	−212,334,000,000
1990	−221,384,000,000
1992	−290,403,000,000
1993	−254,670,000,000
1994 (est.)	−234,758,000,000
1996 (est.)	−169,564,000,000

Median Income in the United States, 1970–1992
(constant 1992 dollars)

	All Households	White	Black	Hispanic
1970	29,670	30,903	18,810	na
1975	29,458	30,806	18,494	22,131
1980	30,191	31,851	18,350	23,271
1985	30,796	32,478	19,323	22,773
1990	32,142	33,525	20,048	23,970
1992	30,786	32,368	18,660	22,848

Income Summary by Region, 1989–1992
(in 1992 dollars)

	1989	1991	1992	Percent Change
Northeast	36,934	34,471	33,194	−10.1
Midwest	32,529	30,828	30,911	−5.0
South	29,271	27,996	27,741	−5.2
West	35,172	33,226	33,621	−4.4

The Reagan Mystique

Peggy Noonan

What I Saw at the Revolution

Although Reagan won in 1980 with only 50.7 percent of the popular vote, it was soon clear that he would be among the most popular of American presidents. Following an attempt on his life in March 1981, his popularity shot up by 11 percent, and thereafter he was nearly untouchable. In the following account, Peggy Noonan, one of Reagan's speechwriters, offers something of the flavor of Ronald Reagan and some suggestions about why Americans were so fond of him. What qualities attracted people to Reagan? How do you explain the empathy so many people experienced when meeting him? What do you make of the charges of coldness to family and to long-term aides?

You may notice that many of Reagan's most admired qualities—his easy charm, his actor's craft—are precisely those condemned by his critics. Was Reagan the strong leader of a political revolution, or was he an empty suit, a hollow man playing the role of a lifetime? Or is it possible to tell?

Here he is, at his desk in the Oval Office, a bright, rounded room of gravity and weight.

He is answering his mail. He looks up as you enter and blinks his moist eyes. His suit is brown, of a dense, substantial weave, his white shirt as bright and uncreased as a shirt in a department store; a tie striped in earth colors is knotted at his neck. You imagine him patting down the collar and trying out a smile.

"Well," he says, as he stands and rounds the desk. He walks toward you softly (I never remember hearing his footsteps).

"Hello!" you say smiling, as he puts out his hand. As your hands touch and then clasp you think: I am standing here shaking hands with the president of the United States, right now, this second. The thought so takes you that you forget to let go. He lets you keep shaking. He is used to this. He rarely lets go first.

He stands there in his tall brown suit looking down with soft, kind eyes, and you are surprised by the pinkness, the babylike softness of his skin. The soft neck, and something you hadn't expected: the air of frailty.

He gleams; he is a mystery. He is for everyone there, for everyone who worked with him. None of them understand him. In private they admit it. You say to them, Who was that masked man?, and they shrug, and hypothesize.

James Baker said, He is the kindest and most impersonal man I ever knew.

An aide said, Beneath the lava flow of warmth there is something impervious as a glacier.

Mother Teresa said, In him, greatness and simplicity are one.

A friend said, Behind those warm eyes is a lack of curiosity that is, somehow, disorienting.

A power source cool at the core. A woman who knew him said, He lived life on the surface where the small waves are, not deep down where the heavy currents tug. And yet he has great powers of empathy. There is a picture of the president and his aides watching TV moments after the shuttle *Challenger* blew up. It is shot from the angle of the television set. On the faces of the men around the president we see varying degrees of interest, curiosity, consternation. Only on the face of Reagan do we see horror, and pain.

Through the force of his beliefs and with a deep natural dignity he restored a great and fallen office.

He was so humble and unassuming that his aides were embarrassed a few days after he was shot to find him in a little bathroom off his hospital room, down on his hands and knees on the cold tile mopping up some water he'd spilled from the sink. He hated to make a mess for the nurse, he said. He wanted to clean it up before she came back, and could they get him some more towels?

Imagine a president with no personal enemies. This has never happened before.

Imagine a man nobody hates, or no one who knows him. He was never dark, never mean, never waited for the sound of the door closing to say, "What a fool," didn't seethe, had no malice. People could tell he trusted their motives. It brought out the best in the best of them, who acted better for the compliment, and the worst in the worst of them: They nodded with mild surprise when they saw his trust, looked into his eyes, and saw . . . nothing. They thought he was an empty house, and they were second-story men.

I'll tell you something surprising: This sunny man touched so many Americans in part because they perceived his pain. They saw beyond the television image, they saw the flesh and blood, they felt those wounds, they caught that poignance.

The reporters and correspondents and smart guys, they missed it. But the people saw. They thought, Look at the courage it took at his age to be shot in the chest by a kid with a gun and go through healing and therapy and go out there again and continue being president, continue waving at the crowds as he walks to the car. Think of the courage that old man had!

Stop shaking his hand for a moment. Stop loving him. This is what you should say: "So where did you come from, Mr. President, and who are you, really? What are the forces that shaped you, and why are you so odd?"

"I'm not odd," he would say. "I'm only odd for a president." . . .

"What you have to remember is that this boy was a loner. He was often alone, reading and dreaming. He looks back on his boyhood with nostalgia, but it's very clear in his writings, his autobiography and interviews, that he always had a place to be alone.

"Look at that childhood, the mom a do-gooder who took part in the local plays, who was strongly Christian and devout. Always taking in strays, and scolding people who weren't helping the poor or taking people in. And minorities. She was always down in the local hospital or the jail, volunteering." . . .

"He's so nonjudgmental. He doesn't judge people's motives or morals, he doesn't cast aspersions on how they live and what they do. He got this from his mother."

—Nancy Reynolds, a longtime Reagan friend

His career both in Hollywood and Washington was devoted in part to celebrating the traditional family, but he didn't come from one. The Reagan children called their parents Nell and Jack, who in turn called their sons Moon and Dutch. They were always moving. Jack had jobs but no profession. The mother was dominant; she ran the home. It was, all in all, more like a Reagan era family than a family typical of its time.

"I think he must have suffered a terrible hurt in his youth, because he closed himself off. He didn't become involved with people. The people he worked with, they were all interchangeable. He didn't become immersed in their lives, and they didn't touch his. He was closed off."

—an aide to Ronald Reagan

The father was an alcoholic but the son rarely speaks of it. He offers, when pressed, a memory: He was coming home from somewhere one day when he was a teenager, and saw his father passed out on the porch. In front of everybody, the whole neighborhood. He dragged him inside and closed the door. It is part of the lore.

"Kids of alcoholics," said Nancy Reynolds, "are hurt. Their mothers are always so embarrassed, and they're hurt for them. There's shame and embarrassment and pity. The shame that you're so ashamed. And it's a little frightening, because alcoholics are scary." . . .

He was a compulsive entertainer: He couldn't not do it. Before he entered a room, he would pause at the entrance and prepare. He sucked in his breath, straightened his shoulders, sucked in his stomach—he would sort of blow himself up. His upper body would get higher, and when he turned he was sort of swiveling. Then he would walk that smooth walk. (A screenwriter told me, "Actors always try to get the walk first. John Travolta told me he knew he had Tony Manero when he got the walk.")

He would bound into a room, acknowledge the applause with a nod, and begin his remarks. He needed a joke at the top to relax him; he still had some stage fright. He would make a small speech, put the cards back into his pocket, wave and nod again, and as he left he would walk backward, edging out of the room like a vaudeville hoofer shuffling off stage right. All he needed was a cane, a straw hat, and a glove—*Is everybody happy?*

Right up until the end, right up until they were closing the door, he maintained eye contact with the people in the room—the audience—and if he saw an unsmiling eye he stopped and tarried. (It was a generous impulse, wasn't it, to want to give people a lift? Or was it only or partly that he needed that laugh, needed the approval?)

It was the lonely empty middle of America and he wanted out, so he joined the migration of ambitious kids out of the small towns and into the media of the big cities. (They were already including this cultural phenomenon in the movies, with Jack Carson sprawled across the counter telling the soda jerk he was going to get out of this one-horse town, this two-bit hamlet.)

It was lonely where he came from and he turned to the world, to a place where the world was synthesized, distilled, where a Swiss mountain village was just down the block from a western town, where life was denser. He turned to Hollywood, the Hollywood of the Depression—the place that cheered up a nation.

He came of age in the middle of the most eager-to-please city in the most eager-to-please era in the most eager-to-please country in the history of the world. Scott Fitzgerald summed up the ethos when he said of one of his heroes, Dick Diver, "He had the American disease—he wanted to be loved."

In Hollywood in those days movie stars knew the names of the heads of the state chapters of their fan clubs, and they were happy to cooperate with the fanzines and the popular press—no one punched photographers in those days— and they were happy to give autographs, and movie posters were colorful with the stars smiling out, and there would be a zany blonde with her eyes crossed in comic confusion and a dancer hurtling himself against a wall to make 'em laugh, and it was zany, hilarious, tons of fun. . . .

And there was little sense of "I can't offend my own dignity," no sense that you were stooping to entertain. There seemed nothing embarrassing about making yourself a little silly for a laugh, to cheer people up. His adult sensibility was shaped in this place.

Maybe there was a sense of imported dignity, of class, in the British colony, but the mood of Hollywood in the thirties was also set by the refugees from vaudeville and burlesque, the Bert Lahrs and Jack Bennys. In the show business of Lahr's youth an out-of-work actor would smudge the collar of his shirt with greasepaint before he walked down Forty-second Street, so every one would think he had a job. (The young Reagan, eclipsed by the mischievous Errol Flynn in a publicity photo, quietly built up a mound of dirt around his feet as the photographer changed the film and the setups, so that by the time the last picture was taken he was taller than most—and even with Flynn.) . . .

For years I had an intuition that his idea of the presidency and how to be president was influenced by a scene in *Yankee Doodle Dandy,* the big hit of 1942. An actor playing FDR gives a presidential medal to George M. Cohan in a private little ceremony in a room in the president's house.

Jimmy Cagney, as Cohan, is properly awed. The FDR character is down-to-earth and expansive—he has all the time in the world as he makes the visitor feel at home. They reminisce. Cagney/Cohan speaks of his birth—born red-faced and squalling on the Fourth of July as the cannon went off in the public square in celebration.

The FDR character listens, adding in his rich radio announcer's voice that there's something special about the Irish, they wear their love of country right out there where everyone can see it. He gives Cagney/Cohan the medal, saying it is for his contribution to American patriotism through the writing of such classics as "Over There" and "Grand Old Flag."

Cohan is so moved he can barely speak. He stands, takes the president's hand. "My mother thanks you," he says, in the family's old vaudeville sign-off, "my father thanks you, my sister thanks you and, I assure you, I thank you."

He takes his leave, is handed his hat and coat by an old Negro butler, and begins his descent down the broad white stairs. But he cannot contain his emotion, the jaunty habit of a lifetime asserts itself: He begins to dance down the stairs. Soon he is doing a wonderful, joyous step-by-step tap, as the music builds. He walks on to Pennsylvania Avenue, where a parade of soldiers is passing by. He joins the parade and joins in the song they are singing, "Over There."

The scene in the president's office is one of the most beautifully played in all the history of the movies, the dancing down the stairs one of the most moving.

And I always thought—I knew—that that was the movie and those were the scenes that Reagan kept in his mind as he greeted his visitors and sang their praises. It gave him a beautiful sense of how to be president, how to make people comfortable, how to make them aware of their own bigness, as if America noticed their work and appreciated it.

A lot of people, after meeting him, wanted to dance down the stairs.

He didn't work from the inside out, he worked from the outside in. He saw the role and put it on, like a costume. He had respect for the set and respect for the character he played, or rather the title and circumstances of the character. He really always played himself; the vivid have no choice. That's why he seemed both phony and authentic. Because he was. He was really acting but the part he played was Ronald Reagan.

The White House always seemed like a set. "I used to feel sometimes it was a stage," said a man who worked there. I wasn't surprised when I heard what Reagan said twenty years earlier, when he was asked, "What kind of governor will you be?" He answered, "I don't know, I've never played a governor."

When Al Haig left—he'd repeatedly threatened to resign, and finally they accepted—the president had to go into the pressroom and take questions. He'd just been given the letter of resignation, had read it, and now he was telling jokes and making everyone laugh as he ambled toward the pressroom. "Whoa there" said James Baker as they approached the door, "we better get serious here."

"Oh don't worry, I'll play it somber," said the president—who stepped, in the next second, in front of the reporters with a face so serious you could call it . . . well, somber. An aide who stood behind him noticed how he held his feet—one curled nonchalantly around the other, as if he didn't have a care in the world. But from out front you couldn't see. . . .

He wasn't only a man who had to be loved. He had courage.

All through the fifties and early sixties, when he had his last chance to become a star, all through that time the convictions he held were unfashionable. The important people, the sophisticated people who'd been successful, who produced and directed the serious movies and who owned the great newspapers and produced the hit sitcoms, all looked down on his politics.

But he held to the unfashionable. This man who wanted to be loved stood fast to his views and voiced them even though he knew the cultural leaders (by whom he wanted to be accepted, in whose movies he wanted to star) had contempt for what he thought.

He could have adopted the corporate liberalism of Hollywood, the happy conviction as they raked in the money that they really cared about the working man.

But he wouldn't play. At the dinner table at the dinner party it was, "Isn't the asparagus wonderful, isn't this lovely wine?," but then when someone made a reference to Communists and someone else said, "At least they're trying to help the little man," he'd answer, "Well, I got to know them in my union days and you can be sentimental about them but they sure won't be sentimental about you, or the proletariat, or the workers, or whatever they're calling them. They aren't sentimental people; they're hard as nails. And kickers, also. Look at Poland, look at Stalin and the kulaks, and they count on us not to notice. But . . ."

And the crystal would hit the linen ever so softly, and his cultural betters would think, He's obviously sincere, but he's so . . . simplistic. Or: unsophisticated. Or: such a radical, and dangerous.

Look at him on abortion. It took courage to oppose an option that at least 20 million Americans had exercised since *Roe v. Wade,* when the issue isn't a coalition-builder but an opposition creator, when the polls are against you and the boomers want it and when you've already been accused of being unsympathetic to women and your own pollster is telling you your stand contributes to a gender gap. . . .

But he puzzled it out on his own, not like a visionary or an intellectual but like a regular person. He read and thought and listened to people who cared, and he made up his mind. And suddenly when they said, "The argument is over when life begins," he said, "Well look, if that's the argument: If there's a bag in the gutter and you don't know if what's in it is alive, you don't kick it, do you?"

Well no, you don't.

He held to his stand against his own political interests (where were the anti-abortion people going to go?) and against the wishes of his family and friends. Nancy wasn't anti-abortion, the kids weren't anti-abortion, and people like the Bloomingdales and his friends in Beverly Hills—they did not get where they are through an overfastidious concern for the helpless. He was the only one of his group who cared.

You forget what it takes to think the unpopular thing, for a politician. But they all want love, that's their game, they want to agree and build bridges and reach out. They all suffer from the American disease.

There's a funny thing in life, but one way to keep people close to you is by not giving them enough. I used to wonder if he ever noticed that with people who give a lot of themselves, you sometimes lean back—but with people who give little you often lean forward, as if they're a spigot in the desert and you're the empty cup. It is the tropism of deprivation: We lean toward those who do not give. Did he ever think in these terms? (What did they teach him on the soundstage at Warner Bros.? Always leave 'em wanting more.)

Ronald Reagan: A Photo Essay

*Strong presidents inspire either great affection or strong dislike, in part be-
cause they act as lightning rods for our emotions about the nation and its politics. Ronald Reagan somehow managed to escape the trap; his personal popularity remained high even while he led an administration responsible for a
great many unpopular actions and policies. Pundits, editorialists, and historians have sought explanations for this contradiction. Historian Gary Wills has
suggested that Reagan's career as a movie actor had tied him firmly to Americans' common past. As a result, the public experienced an unusual degree of
comfort and familiarity with him, as though a trusted family friend had become
president. Other commentators have reflected that Reagan's mature and masculine appearance inspired confidence and admiration in the public. Glance at
these pictures and list your one-word impressions. What do you think?*

**Ronald Reagan reading his morning papers while eating breakfast in the Oval Office.
1982.**
Ronald Reagan Library.

Ronald Reagan after a day's work on the ranch. 1983.
Ronald Reagan Library.

Ronald Reagan riding at the ranch. 1983.
Ronald Reagan Library.

Ronald and Nancy Reagan taking a boat ride at the ranch. 1983.
Ronald Reagan Library.

SUGGESTIONS FOR VIEWING AND LISTENING

Raiders of the Lost Ark (1981)
The mythic quest, so popular in the 1980s.

E.T.—The Extra-Terrestrial (1982)
Christ as E.T. All you need is faith.

Rambo: First Blood, Part 2 (1985)
The hard, overbuilt male body was a Reagan-era staple, and a sign of a crisis in masculinity. Americans reimagined the Vietnam war through the POW issue.

Kenny Rogers, "Coward of the County" (1980)
Americans are tired of being pushed around. Echoes of the Iranian hostage crisis.

Dead Kennedys, "We've Got a Bigger Problem Now" (1984)
Punk rock view of the Reagan presidency as fascism.

Manowar, "Defender" (1987)
Heavy metal perspective. What it takes to be a man in the modern world.

DePeche Mode, "People Are People" (1984)
One of many "one world" songs of the mid-1980s.

CHAPTER 11

Culture Wars

When he took office as president in 1981, Ronald Reagan had many constituencies. As the oldest man ever to assume the presidency, he was the candidate of the elderly. His promises to restore American "strength" and "pride" brought him the support of millions of working-class and middle-class Americans who could not understand or accept the defeat in Vietnam, humiliation at the hands of the Arab nations, or the nation's weakness in the international marketplace. Reagan appealed to the business community and to growing numbers of other Americans who believed that welfare, the welfare state, liberalism, big government, unions, or high taxes were responsible for the nation's ills. And he had the support of fundamentalist Christians, who interpreted the nation's troubles as a fall from grace and sought a remedy in the restoration of traditional values and practices: an end to abortion, prayer in the public schools, sexual abstinence before marriage, old-fashioned gender roles, censorship of the pornographic or salacious.

For twelve years Reagan and his successor, George Bush, held this curious coalition together. They did it with style, bravado, and posturing, amd by playing on cold war anxieties that had been part of the American psyche for decades. They did it with taxing, spending, and social policies that seemed, for a time at least, to have stemmed American economic decline and that promised to restore the nation to its former greatness. And they did it by convincing large numbers of people that the country's problems were somehow related to the sphere of culture—to the photographs they took, the pictures they painted, the languages they learned, the words they used, the books they read, the music they listened to, the television programs they watched, the way they presented and thought about the past.

It was probably wrong to blame "culture" for the nation's ills, and perhaps misguided to look to the cultural arena for solutions to social problems that had more to do with poverty, racism, and misogyny. Even so, there was ample evidence that the tone of American life was increasingly antagonistic and evidence, too, of deterioration in the quality and civility of cultural expression. Facing the economic uncertainties that were part of the ordinary round of life, Americans turned mean, aggressive, and deadly. Violent crimes—assaults, murders, and rapes—became commonplace events in major cities, and the ghettos of some cities, where drug traffic was heavy, became zones of terror, where people were afraid to leave their homes. Despite Bush's call for a "kinder, gentler" nation, all manner of real and fictitious Americans—talk-show hosts, comedians, rock stars, cartoon characters—seemed to revel in insults, abuse, and hate-mongering. The victims were predictable: blacks, women, Asians, Arabs, welfare recipients, Jews, homosexuals, and (for rap artists like N.W.A.) the police. It was—and is—an ugly age.

As the twenty-first century approached, the search for ways of understanding the nation's difficult recent history increasingly took the form of forays into the realm of culture. One set of conservative critics attacked the emerging "multicultural" focus of the high schools and universities, calling for a return to a traditional curriculum that emphasized the nation's European roots. Book-banning made a comeback when fundamentalist, "pro-family" groups went to court to prove that some school districts were using public-school textbooks to teach the "religion" of secular humanism. Under Reagan and Bush—but not Clinton—the National Endowment for the Arts withdrew its support from projects—usually ones with some erotic content—that did not have "the widest audience."

One of the more interesting cultural battles of the 1980s was waged by Tipper Gore, the wife of Albert Gore, Jr., the Tennessee senator who would become Clinton's vice president. Working through a variety of family groups, including her own Parents' Music Resource Center, Gore focused her criticism on heavy metal rock music, a genre she claimed was characterized by harmful images of sadism, brutality, and eroticism. After congressional hearings in 1985, the record industry agreed to a voluntary system of warning labels. Later in the decade and into the 1990s, cultural censors turned their guns on the misogynist lyrics of "gangsta rap." In the 1990s, conflict over culture often took the form of debates over the interpretation, presentation, and teaching of American history. Historians and other liberals attacked plans by the Walt Disney Company to build a historical theme park, "Disney's America," in northern Virginia and questioned the content of Hollywood films that claimed the mantle of history, including *Pocahontas* (1995) and Oliver Stone's *JFK* (1991). When Republican Senator Robert Dole lashed out at the newly issued National History Standards for too often mentioning the Ku Klux Klan and other examples of historical conflict, it seemed likely that culture—and history—would play a role in the 1996 presidential election.

Americans have always had a prudish streak, and perhaps the culture wars of the 1980s and 1990s were just another outbreak of the nation's obsession with morality. More likely they are the other face of the American postindustrial economy. One face—whether under Reagan, Bush, or Clinton seems to make no difference—looks outward toward a new, post-American world in which the United States is just another player in the international marketplace. The other face looks inward, contemplating the damage already wrought by these changes and anticipating problems to come. It is this face—the face of a pervasive anxiety about the future—that seeks some modicum of control in the "culture wars."

INTERPRETIVE ESSAY

Culture Wars

James Davison Hunter

In this thoughtful analysis of recent controversies over art, music, television, and other aspects of culture, James Davison Hunter offers us a picture of two cultural camps, one conservative and "orthodox," the other liberal and "progressivist." Because each camp has its own idea of what is vital and important, they appear in this story almost as shadowboxers, struggling furiously against their opponents yet somehow never landing a blow.

While reading Hunter's essay, look for evidence that would indicate the author's sympathies. Is Hunter consistently evenhanded, or does his account lean toward the orthodox or progressivist camp? Consider, too, the meaning of Hunter's overall analysis for American history in the late twentieth century. That is, what kind of society does Hunter describe? Is it healthy or sick? Furthermore, if the culture wars are, indeed, "the struggle to define America" (the words of the subtitle of Hunter's book), which definitions of America have been offered in this debate? Perhaps more significant, which definitions have been left out? In the end, can anything significant be accomplished through wars over culture?

One does not need to endure a thousand bleary-eyed evenings with Dan Rather or Tom Brokaw to understand how important a role the media of mass communications play in our lives. Television, radio, magazines, newspapers, news magazines, the popular press, as well as music, film, theater, visual arts, popular literature, do much more than passively reflect the social and political reality of our times. Like the institutions of public education . . . , these institutions actively define reality, shape the times, give meaning to the history we witness and experience as ordinary citizens. This outcome is unavoidable in many ways. In the very act of *selecting* the stories to cover, the books to publish and review, the film and music to air, and the art to exhibit, these institutions effectively define which topics are important and which issues are relevant—worthy of public consideration. Moreover, in the *substance* of the stories covered, books published and reviewed, art exhibited, and so on, the mass media act as a filter through which our perceptions of the world around us take shape. Thus, by virtue of the decisions made by those who control the mass media—seemingly innocuous decisions made day to day and year to year—those who work within these institutions cumulatively wield enormous power. In a good many situations, this power is exercised unwittingly, rooted in the best intentions to perform a task well, objectively, fairly. Increasingly, however, the effects of this power have become understood and deliberately manipulated. Is it not inevitable that the media and the arts would become a field of conflict in the contemporary culture war?

There are at least two matters to consider here. First, the contest to define reality, so central to the larger culture war, inevitably becomes a struggle to control the "instrumentality" of reality definition. This means that the battle over this symbolic territory has practically taken shape as a struggle to influence or even dominate the businesses and industries of public information, art, and entertainment—from the major television and radio networks to the National Endowment for the Arts; from the Hollywood film industry to the music recording industry, and so on. But there is more. At a more subtle and symbolic level, the tensions in this field of conflict point to a struggle over the meaning of "speech" or the meaning of "expression" that the First Amendment is supposed to protect. Underlying the conflict over this symbolic territory, in other words, are the questions "What constitutes art in our communities?" "Whose definition of entertainment and aesthetic appreciation do we accept?" "What version of the news is fair?" And so on.

TAKING ON THE ESTABLISHMENT

We begin by considering a brief vignette of an event that occurred at a pro-life march in Washington, D.C. The day was filled with speeches from politicians, religious leaders, pro-life leaders, and other luminaries. Several hundred thousand people listened attentively, cheered, chanted, prayed, and sang songs. Such are the rituals of modern political rallies. At one point during the rally, however, a number of pro-life advocates spontaneously turned toward a television news crew filming the event from atop a nearby platform and began to chant in unison, "Tell the truth!" "Tell the truth!" "Tell the truth!" What began as a rumble within a few moments had caught on within the crowd. Soon, tens of thousands of people were chanting "Tell the truth!" "Tell the truth!" "Tell the truth!" Of all the aspects of the rally covered in the newscast that evening or in the newspapers the following day, this brief and curious event was not among them.

The story highlights the conviction held by virtually everyone on the orthodox and conservative side of the new cultural divide that the media and arts establishment is unfairly prejudiced against the values they hold dear. They do not tell the truth, the voices of orthodoxy maintain, and what is worse, they do not even present opposing sides of the issues evenhandedly. . . .

Exaggerated [though] they may be, the general perceptions are not totally born out of illusion. Studies of the attitudes of media and entertainment elites, as well as of television news programming and newspaper coverage of various social issues and political events, have shown a fairly strong and consistent bias toward a liberal and progressivist point of view. The field over which these particular battles are waged, then, is uneven—and the contenders recognize it as such. One contender takes a position of defending territory already won; the other strives to reclaim it.

There are three major ways in which traditionalists have sought to reclaim this symbolic (and institutional) territory.

One way has been in a direct assault against the media and arts establishment. Acquiring a large-circulation newspaper or a network was something that had been "a dream of conservatives for years," according to Howard Phillips of the Conservative Caucus. Early in 1985, such an assault was made. After years of frustration with what it called "the liberal bias" of CBS, a group called Fairness in Media (FIM) spearheaded a move to buy out the television network. . . . Ultimately, of course, the bid to take over the network failed, but those who supported the idea were not put off. "It may take a while to accomplish [this goal]," one editorialized, "but it's a goal well worth waiting—and striving—for."

The persistent effort of the orthodox alliance to hold the media establishment accountable for the content it presents is another strategy. Numerous national and local organizations are committed to this task, covering a wide range of media. Morality in Media, for example, is an interfaith organization founded in 1962 by three clergymen in order to stop traffic in pornography and to challenge "indecency in media" and to work "for a media based on love, truth and good taste." Accuracy in Media has, since 1969, sought to combat liberal bias by exposing cases where the media have not covered stories "fairly and accurately." The Parents' Music Resource Center, established in 1985, is concerned to raise the awareness of parents about the content of modern rock music, especially heavy metal music. Its specific focus is, according to one of its founders, "not the occasional sexy rock lyric . . . [but] the celebration of the most gruesome violence, coupled with explicit messages that sadomasochism is the essence of sex." One of the most visible of all media watchdog groups is the American Family Association and the affiliated CLeaR-TV, or Christian Leaders for Responsible Television. Founded by the Reverend Donald Wildmon, the American Family Association membership claims ordinary believers and religious leaders from all Christian faiths, Protestant, Catholic, and Orthodox, and together they propose to combat the "excessive, gratuitous sex, violence, profanity, [and] the negative stereotyping of Christians."

These organizations are joined by many others both national and local, including town and city councils around the country that share a similar concern about the content of public information and entertainment. They are effective because they are grass roots in orientation (or at least they pose as being locally connected to the grass roots), and they make use of proven techniques of popular political mobilization: letter writing, boycott, countermedia exposure, and the like.

As much a support structure for the various orthodox and conservative subcultures as a weapon in the culture war, communities within the orthodox alliance have created an entire network of alternative electronic media. These alternative media challenge the media and arts establishment a third way, then, through competition, offering programming that defines a fundamentally different and competing reality and vision of America. . . .

. . . Vigorous challenges have been made by the Evangelical-dominated television and radio industry. Within the Evangelical subculture alone there were over 1300 religious radio stations, over 200 religious television stations, and 3 religious television networks broadcasting in the United States by the early 1990s. The

Catholic place in this industry is relatively small by comparison, but it does make an important contribution. The programming goes far beyond televised religious services or radio broadcasts of sacred music to include religious talk shows, soap operas, drama, Bible studies, and news commentary. In addition to these enterprises is a billion-dollar book industry (made up, within the Evangelical orbit alone, of over eighty publishing houses and over 6000 independent religious bookstores) that publish and market books on, for example, how to be a better Christian, how to raise children, how to cope with a mid-life crisis, not to mention a sizable literature on what is wrong about America and what you can do about it. And a multimillion-dollar music industry extends far beyond the latest rendition of "Blessed Assurance" by George Beverly Shea to Hasidic and Christian rock and roll, folk, heavy metal (groups called Vengeance, Petra, or Shout singing such releases as "In Your Face"), and even rap music.

THE POLITICS OF FREE SPEECH

What makes these battles over the media and arts especially interesting is that they reveal a conflict that is several layers deeper. The first layer of conflict concerns the nature and meaning of art and music, as well as the nature and meaning of information. Inevitably this conflict leads to the more philosophical and legal disputes over the nature of "speech" and "expression" protected by the First Amendment. There is no end to the number of "headline cases" in which these sorts of issues are worked out. The fact is that each dispute contains within it all the underlying philosophical and legal tensions as well. Collectively, they make the matter a crisis over which actors on both sides of the cultural divide urgently press for resolution.

To demonstrate how this conflict is played out at these different levels, it is necessary to get down to specific cases. . . .

The Avant-Garde and Its Discontents

It begins with the quest for novelty. This impulse is undeniably a driving force in the arts, entertainment, and news media. The quest is based on the premise that the new will somehow be better than the old, a premise that fits well with America's utilitarian demand for improvement. The expectation that the media and arts will continue to innovate keeps an audience coming back for more. Cultural tensions, of course, inhere within the quest and on occasion they erupt into full-blown controversy.

Art

Out of a budget of more than $150 million a year, the National Endowment for the Arts funds literally hundreds upon hundreds of projects in theater, ballet, music, photography, film, painting, and sculpture. In the late 1980s, however, it became widely publicized that the National Endowment for the Arts had indirectly funded two controversial photographic exhibits. One project, by Andres Serrano, included, among others, a photograph of a crucifix in a jar of Serrano's urine, entitled *Piss Christ* [see p. 307]; the other project, by Robert Mapplethorpe, included, among many others, a photograph that turned an image of the Virgin Mary into a tie rack as well as a number of homoerotic photos (such as one showing Mapplethorpe with a bullwhip implanted in his anus and another showing a man urinating in another man's mouth). All of this was well publicized. Avant-garde? To say the least! But Serrano and Mapplethorpe are, their defenders maintained, "important American artists." One critic called the photograph *Piss Christ* "a darkly beautiful photographic image." Likewise, the director of the Institute of Contemporary Art in Boston concluded of Mapplethorpe's exhibit, "Mapplethorpe's work is art, and art belongs in an art museum."

For those in the various orthodox communities, the controversial aspects of the Serrano and Mapplethorpe exhibits were not art at all but obscenity. "This so-called piece of art is a deplorable, despicable display of vulgarity," said one critic. "Morally reprehensible trash," said another. Of Serrano himself, a third stated, "He is not an artist, he is a jerk. Let him be a jerk on his own time and with his own resources." The American Family Association responded with full-page advertisements in newspapers asking, "Is this how you want your tax dollars spent?"

These voices had a sympathetic hearing in the halls of government as well. In response to the National Endowment for the Arts funding of these projects and the likelihood that it would fund still other such projects in the future, Senator Jesse Helms introduced legislation that would forbid the endowment from supporting art that is "obscene or indecent." The National Endowment for the Arts agreed to make grants available only to those who pledge not to do anything of this nature. The endowment, a Helms ally argued in support of this proposal, should not showcase "artists whose forte is ridiculing the values . . . of Americans who are paying for it." Conservative columnist Doug Bandow argued similarly. "There's no justification for taxing lower-income Americans to support glitzy art shows and theater productions frequented primarily by the wealthy." Still others cited Thomas Jefferson's dictum that it is "sinful and tyrannical" to compel a person to contribute money for the propagation of opinions with which he or she disagrees.

Music

Rap is just one more innovation in youth-oriented music that began decades before with rock and roll. Serious questions were raised about the form and content of this innovation, however, with the 1989 release of *As Nasty As They Wanna Be* by the Miami-based rap group 2 Live Crew. On just one album, there were over 200 uses of the word *fuck,* over 100 uses of explicit terms for male and female genitalia, over 80 descriptions of oral sex, and the word *bitch* was used over 150 times. And what about the work of groups like Mötley Crüe, which invokes images of satanism, and the rap group the Beastie Boys, who mime masturbation on stage, or N.W.A., who sing about war against the police (in "Fuck tha Police"), or Ozzy Osbourne, who sings of the "suicide solution"? Was this really music?

The arts establishment responded with a resounding "yes." Its endorsements were positive and sympathetic. Notwithstanding the violence and irreverence, one essay in the *Washington Post* described rap in particular as "a vibrant manifestation of the black oral tradition. . . . You cannot fully understand this profane style of rapping if you disregard the larger folklore of the streets." A review of 2 Live Crew and rap in general in the *New York Times* claimed that this form of musical expression "reveals the tensions of the communities it speaks to. But with its humor, intelligence and fast-talking grace, it may also represent a way to transcend those tensions." Even at its grossest, one critic wrote in *Time,* this entire genre of music represents "a vital expression of the resentments felt by a lot of people."

Needless to say, the opinions within the orthodox communities were less enthusiastic. One American Family Association member called the work of the rap poets of 2 Live Crew as well as other exemplars of popular music, such as the heavy metal of Mötley Crüe, Twisted Sister, and the like, "mind pollution and body pollution." An attorney involved in the controversy commented, "This stuff is so toxic and so dangerous to anybody, that it shouldn't be allowed to be sold to anybody or by anybody." Because this album was being sold to children, he continued, the group's leader, Luther Campbell, was nothing less than "a psychological child molester." Judges in Florida agreed with the sentiment, finding the lyrics to *As Nasty As They Wanna Be* to violate local obscenity laws. Police arrested Campbell for performing the music in a nightclub after the decree, as well as record store owners who continued to sell the album. In response, Campbell promised two things: a legal appeal and a new album—"this one dirtier than the last."

Television

Every year during the ratings sweep, the major networks display their raciest and most innovative programming. In years past, television shows like "Miami Vice," "Dream Street," "Knots Landing," "thirty-something," "A Man Called Hawk," "The Cosby Show," among many others have made strong showings within the national television audience. These, in turn, become strong draws for corporations wanting to advertise their products. Critics admit that the amount of sexual intimacy outside marriage, violence, and profanity portrayed on some of these shows is very high, yet they also have been quick to point out that many of these shows are technically innovative and treat many issues such as homosexuality, child abuse and incest, and the ambiguities of ethical behavior in law enforcement, marriage, student culture, and the like, with great sensitivity.

Sensitivity is the last thing these television shows display, in the view of many with orthodox commitments. To the contrary, "television," claimed a letter from the American Family Association, "is undermining the Judeo-Christian values you hold dear and work hard to teach your children." For this reason, leaders from CLeaR-TV visited with executives from the three major networks in order to express their concerns. According to Reverend Wildmon, "They used the same words that I used, but we certainly didn't mean the same thing by them." From this point on, the leaders decided to approach the advertisers rather than the networks. "Advertisers don't give you a cold shoulder. They want to be your friend." In line with this strategy, the American Family Association and CLeaR-TV began to approach advertisers. Sponsors who did not respond positively to their concerns very often faced the threat of a boycott. PepsiCo, for example, pulled a commercial featuring pop star, nude model, and actress Madonna and their promotion of her world tour; General Mills, Ralston Purina, and Domino's Pizza pulled advertising from "Saturday Night Live"; Mazda and Noxell were also influenced in this way; and of the 400 sponsors of prime-time television in the 1989 ratings sweeps, CLeaR-TV focused on the Mennon Company and the Clorox Corporation, pledging to boycott their products for a year for their sponsorship of programs containing sex, violence, and profanity. . . .

Decoding Art and the Avant-Garde

The preceding examples are but a few well-publicized illustrations of cultural warfare in various media and forms of public expression. The point of reviewing them was to demonstrate, across media, certain patterns of cultural conflict. Despite the variations of situation and media, one can trace a common and consistent thread of sentiment on each side of the new cultural divide.

On the progressivist side, there is a tendency to value novelty and the avant-garde for their own sake. This in itself is not controversial. What is controversial is *how* avant-garde is defined. Progressives implicitly define the "avant-garde" not so much as the presentation of classic social themes in new artistic forms, but rather as the symbolic presentation of behavior and ideas that test the limits of social acceptability. More often than not this means the embrace of what the prevailing social consensus would have called "perverse" or "irreverent," what Carol Iannone calls "the insistent and progressive artistic exploration of the forbidden frontiers of human experience." Lucy Lippard acknowledges as much in her review of the Serrano corpus in *Art in America:* "His work shows," she contends, "that the conventional notion of good taste with which we are raised and educated is based on an illusion of social order that is no longer possible (nor desirable) to believe in. We now look at art in the context of incoherence and disorder—a far more difficult task than following the prevailing rules." A similar theme can be found in each of the other cases reviewed. In rap music and in television programming, the boundaries of social consensus around human relationships are tested through excessive sex and violence. . . . In each case, an earlier consensus of what is "perverse" and what is "irreverent" is challenged, and as it is challenged, it inevitably disintegrates.

The issue is sharpened when considering the special case of art. Here too the underlying controversy is over how art is to be defined. In general, progressivists tend to start with the assumption that there is no objective method of determining what is art and what is obscene. Historical experience demonstrates time and again that even if a consensus declares that a work has no enduring artistic value, the consensus may change; the work could, over time, come to be viewed as art. For this reason one must recognize and at all times respect and defend the autonomy of the artist and of artistic effort. Artists should not be bound by legal constraints or inhibited by social conventions, for artistic genius may yet emerge, if it is not already evident. Indeed, modern criticism does regard art "as a 'sacred wood,' a separate universe, a self-contained sovereignty" and the artist, in writer Vladimir Nabokov's words, as responsible to no one but himself. One artist expressed this theme when he said, "It is extremely important that art be unjustifiable."

Out of this general perspective comes the implicit understanding that a work is art if "experts" are willing to call it art and if it symbolically expresses an individual's personal quest to understand and interpret one's experience in the world. Both themes were evident in the expert testimony given at the 1990 obscenity trial of the Contemporary Arts Center in Cincinnati where the question "What is art?" was posed directly in view of the Mapplethorpe retrospective. Jacquelynn Baas, director of the University Art Museum at the University of California at Berkeley, responded to the question of why one should consider Robert Mapplethorpe's work as art by declaring: "In the first place, they're great photographs. Secondly, in this work he dealt with issues that our society, modern society is grappling with . . . what it means to be a sexual being, and also race, that was an important part of the show." . . .

For the orthodox and their conservative allies, expert opinion is not a reliable measure of artistic achievement and the artist's intentions are completely irrelevant to determining whether a work is art. Rather, artistic achievement is measured by the extent to which it reflects the sublime. Critic Hilton Kramer endorses this view in speaking of federal funding for art that reflects "the highest achievements of our civilization." George F. Will similarly favors the view that art, at least art worthy of support, is recognized in its capacity to "elevate the public mind by bringing it into contact with beauty and even ameliorate social pathologies." Art worthy of government funding, therefore, should be justifiable on the grounds that it serves this high public purpose. Congressman Henry Hyde, in reflecting about his role in the public policy process, argues that "art detached from the quest for truth and goodness is simply self-expression and ultimately self-absorption." . . .

In sum, for the orthodox and their conservative allies artistic creativity is concerned to reflect a higher reality. For their opponents, art is concerned with the creation of reality itself. Art for the progressivist is, then, a statement of being. To express oneself is to declare one's existence. Hilton Kramer may be correct that the professional art world maintains a sentimental attachment to the idea that art is at its best when it is most extreme and disruptive, but he is probably wrong if he believes this to be its chief or only aim. More fundamentally, if only implicitly, the contemporary arts project is a statement about the meaning of life, namely that life is a process of self-creation. As this enterprise takes public form, however, contemporary art and the avant-garde come to represent nothing less than the besmearing of the highest ideals of the orthodox moral vision.

When all is said and done, however, the events taking place in each of the contexts mentioned earlier—the action and reaction of progressivists and cultural conservatives—represent only the first state in the development of a deeper debate about the limits of public expression in American society.

CENSORSHIP

Progressivist Accusations

The immediate reaction of the progressivists is that those who complain about art do so because they "do not know enough about art," or simply "do not care about art." All the protest demonstrates, as the *Washington Post* put it, "the danger of a cultural outsider passing judgment on something he doesn't understand." Such comments may sound elitist (and undoubtedly are), but their significance goes beyond implying that those who do not share progressive aesthetic taste are simple philistines. The real significance of such sentiments is that they reaffirm the basic characteristic of the contemporary culture war, namely the nigh complete disjunction of moral understanding between the orthodox and progressivist communities—in this case, on what constitutes art. The progressivist communities and the arts establishment display a certain arrogance in believing that their definitions of "serious artistic merit" should be accepted by all, and this leads them to categorize various cultural conservatives as "Know-Nothings," "yahoos," "neanderthals," "literary death squads," "fascists," and "cultural terrorists."

The response of progressivists to this situation, however, quickly evolves beyond this. In a way, what we hear after this initial response is less an argument than a symbolic call to arms, a "Banzai!" that reveals a spontaneous, unified, and passionate indignation every bit as deep as that expressed by the orthodox in reaction to tarnishing of their ideals. Irrespective of the circumstances or media, the orthodox protest evokes among progressives the cry of "censorship."

Nowhere has this alarm sounded more loudly than in the case of the protest against network television. People for the American Way, Americans for Constitutional Freedom, *Playboy,* and many others have viewed the boycotting of corporate advertisers of television programming as acts of "economic terrorism" that are tantamount to censorship. "What is more intrusive than the attempt by fundamentalist censors to dictate what we can watch in the privacy of our own homes?" asked the founder of Fundamentalists Anonymous. Donald Wildmon, whom *Playboy* called the "Tupelo Ayatollah," is nothing short of "dangerous." Said the executive director of Americans for Constitutional Freedom, "We intend to do everything to prevent him from setting himself up as a censor who can remake America in his own image."

Similar accusations are leveled in every other situation where the orthodox protest the content of public media. The music industry viewed the efforts of the Parents' Music Resource Center to have albums labeled "contains explicit lyrics" as an act of censorship. Frank Zappa called it a conspiracy to extort. . . . And, finally, efforts to prohibit flag burning have been called political censorship.

Implicit within this accusation, of course, is the legal judgment that the constitutionally guaranteed right to freedom of speech is either threatened or actually violated by conservative protest. For this reason, the Bill of Rights is almost always invoked by progressives or by artists themselves. When, for example, Nikki Sixx of Mötley Crüe was told in an interview that there were those who objected to the band stating on stage that their "only regret is that [they] couldn't eat all the pussy [they] saw here tonight, he responded, 'I say fuck 'em. It's freedom of speech; First Amendment!'" Thomas Jefferson himself might not have put it quite that way or even necessarily agreed with the application, but without fail, the legacy of Jefferson directly informs the content of the progressivist reply. Luther Campbell of 2 Live Crew echoed this sentiment when he said, "We give America what they want. Isn't there such a thing as free enterprise here? Isn't there such a thing as freedom of speech?" The record store owner in Florida arrested for selling *As Nasty As They Wanna Be* put the matter in a slightly larger context. "We tell the Lithuanians, you know, fight for freedom. . . . And yet, we're trying to censor our own country. . . . We don't need nobody to censor us and they're violating our civil rights and our freedom of speech. And next—what else will it be next?" . . .

The pounding repetition of this accusation is in accord with the general position taken by the People for the American Way, who believe that this brand of censorship is not only on the increase, it "has become more organized and more effective" with haunting implications. The very language employed by cultural conservatives when they insist it is time to "clean up our culture" or to "stop subsidizing decadence" is, as several writers contend, "chillingly reminiscent of Nazi cultural metaphors." Robert Brustein, writing in the *New Republic,* goes so far as to dismiss the distinction between censorship and the effort to influence the distribution of taxpapers' money (as in the effort to defund "offensive art" at the National Endowment for the Arts), insisting that defunding art is a form of censorship. He concludes that "only government—in a time when other funding has grown increasingly restrictive and programmatic—can guarantee free and innovative art. And that means acknowledging that, yes, every artist has a First Amendment right to subsidy."

The progressivist response to this backlash has gone beyond rhetoric into direct political action as well. Full-page newspaper ads criticizing the censorious impulse have appeared. Individual artists, the ACLU [American Civil Liberties Union], Playboy Enterprises, *Penthouse,* the American Booksellers Association, and many other individuals and organizations have initiated litigation against a number of organizations, such as Concerned Women for America and the American Family Association. . . .

Orthodox Counteraccusations

To the accusation of censorship, the reply of cultural conservatives is "nonsense!" *Christianity Today* editorialized that the media and arts establishment

> use freedom of speech as a means to flout standards of common public decency. We must not throw in the towel. Christians must unite in mounting a counteroffensive through our families, churches, schools, and other institutions. The legal issues surrounding public standards may be complex, but the moral imperatives are not. We must not abandon the ring of public debate to those who would use freedom of speech as an excuse to be as morally offensive as they "wanna" be.

Implicit here and in much of the orthodox and conservative rhetoric is the view that communities have the right to decide for themselves what standards will be used to discriminate between art and obscenity. If, through the democratic process, standards are agreed upon, why should communities not be entitled to uphold them through official means?

Donald Wildmon also rejects the idea that he and his compatriots are somehow violating the First Amendment protections of free speech, but he takes a slightly different tack. He insists that artists do have the right to express themselves as they please but that he too has a right to speak out against them. This posture is expressed paradigmatically in his rationale for acting against Pepsi for its plans to fund the Madonna tour.

> Here is a pop singer who makes a video that's sacrilegious to the core. Here's a pop star that made a low-budget porn film. Here's a pop star who goes around in her concerts with sex oozing out, wearing a cross. Now Pepsi is saying to all the young people of the new generation, "Here is the person we want you to emulate and imitate." They can do that. They've got every right to give Madonna $10 million dollars, put it on television every night if they want to. All I'm saying is "Don't ask me to buy Pepsi if you do it." . . .

Tipper Gore of the Parents' Music Resource Center called the cry of censorship "a smoke screen," a dodge for taking corporate responsibility for their product. In asking for labels on record albums, her group claimed, they were asking for more information, not less. The group's approach, then, "was the direct opposite of censorship." Morality in Media takes the argument one step further in maintaining that "freedom of expression is not the exclusive right of producers, publishers, authors or a handful of media executives. Freedom of expression belongs . . . to the entire community. . . . [it is only a] vocal, unremitting, organized community expression [that] will bring about a media based on love, truth and good taste." . . .

Some complain that progressivists and a liberal educational establishment censor, through exclusion, material on traditional religion in the public school textbooks. . . . The same kind of de facto censoring occurs, it is maintained, when major magazines and newspapers, through editorial edict, refuse to review books written and published by conservative Catholics or Evangelical Protestants, or deny them the recognition they deserve by not including these works on their best-seller lists. The Evangelical writer Francis Schaeffer, for example, sold over 3 million copies of his books in the United States, and yet his books were never reviewed in the *New York Times Book Review* or *Time* and never counted on any best-seller list. The same was true of Hal Lindsey's *Late Great Planet Earth,* a book that was the top nonfiction seller in America in the 1970s—for the entire decade. The book was not reviewed by the literary establishment nor did it appear on weekly best-seller lists until it was later published by a secular publishing house. For publishing elites to ignore this literature, for whatever reasons—even if they do not believe such works constitute "serious literature or scholarship"—is, they say, to "censor." . . .

Decoding Free Speech

Back and forth the arguments go. After a time, the details of this conflict become tediously predictable. One side claims that a work is "art"; the other claims it is not. One claims that a work has enduring aesthetic or literary appeal; the other claims it appeals only to the eccentric interests of a deviant subculture. At least on the face of it, one is tempted to agree with Justice John Marshall Harlan, who concluded that "one man's vulgarity is another's lyric." Such relativism may not be desirable but it seems to be the necessary outcome of the present cultural conflict. In this light, it is entirely predictable that each side would claim that the other side is not committed to free speech but to a systematic imposition of its values and perspectives on everyone else. Alas, one person's act of "censorship" has become another's "commitment to community standards."

Thus, in the contemporary culture war, regard for rights to the freedom of speech has become a matter of "whose ox is being gored" at the moment. The fact is, both sides make a big mistake when they confuse *censuring* (the legitimate mobilization of moral opprobrium) with *censoring* (the use of the state and other legal or official means to restrict speech). Censuring, say through economic boycott or letter-writing campaigns, is itself a form of political speech protected by the First Amendment and employed legally all the time whether in boycotts against South Africa, Nestle's, or California lettuce growers, or against the purveyors of sexually explicit or theologically controversial art. But the finer points of distinction are lost on many of the activists in this debate. Even when the protest is merely the expression of disapproval, what each side invariably hears are the footsteps of an approaching cadre of censors. In most cases, however, neither side presents a genuine threat to the rights of the other to free expression. The cry of censorship from both sides of the cultural divide, then, becomes an ideological weapon to silence legitimate dissent.

This being said, it must also be stated that real censorship *is* taking place and the voices of both cultural conservatism and progressivism perpetuate it in their own ways. Censorship, again, is the use of the state or other official means to restrict speech. In every case it is justified by the claim that "community standards" have been violated. The use of the police to arrest the members of 2 Live Crew in Florida and the use of law to shut down the Contemporary Arts Center in Cincinnati because they violated community standards of obscenity are, then, textbook cases of such censorship. Censorship is also perpetuated on the other side of the cultural divide. It is seen in the efforts of student groups and universities to prohibit, in the name of community standards, defamatory remarks and expressions against minorities, gays, and women. (Would progressives throw their support or legal weight behind a similar code that prohibited say, unpatriotic, irreligious, or sexually explicit "expressions" on the community campus?) Censorship is also seen, to give another example, in the suspension of Andy Rooney from his job at CBS in 1990 for making remarks against gays. On both sides of the cultural divide, the concept of "community standards" is invoked as an ideological weapon to silence unpopular voices. Understanding how the standards of one moral community can be so diametrically opposed to the standards of the other takes us back to the root of the culture war itself.

ART, EXPRESSION, AND THE SACRED

A critic quoted earlier warned of the danger of a cultural outsider passing judgment on something he does not understand. The reality of the culture war is that the cultural conservative and the progressivist are each outsiders to the other's cultural milieu. Accordingly, each regularly and often viciously passes judgment on the other. That judgment is not at all bad in itself. Such is the back and forth of democratic discourse. The danger is not in passing judgment but in the failure to understand why the other is so insulted by that judgment. *That* is the measure of their mutual outsiderness.

The orthodox, for example, demonstrate such a position when they view certain artistic work in isolation from the larger aesthetic project of an artist and label it obscene, pornographic, and prurient. Who are these people, progressivists ask, to label the life work of Serrano and Mapplethorpe as vulgarity? That they cannot see the "enduring artistic achievement" of an artist's oeuvre is a gauge of their alienation from "high art" discourse. The same kind of obtuseness is found among progressivists. Consider the controversy surrounding *The Last Temptation of Christ. A Washington Post* editorial stated with no equivocation that audiences would not find the film blasphemous. Another reviewer, from *Newsweek,* said, "One can think of hundreds of trashy, thrill-happy movies devout Christians could get upset about. Instead, they have taken to the airwaves to denounce *the one movie that could conceivably open a viewer's heart to the teachings of Jesus.*" Still another reviewer, from Newhouse Newspapers, called the film, "The most realistic biblical film ever made." Who are these people, orthodox Christians ask, to proclaim universally that *The Last Temptation of Christ* was not blasphemous? For millions of Americans it certainly was, and it was a measure of progressives' outsiderness that they could not acknowledge it to be.

This kind of mutual misunderstanding reveals once more that the conflict over the media and the arts is not just a dispute among institutions and not just a disagreement over "speech" protected by the First Amendment. Ultimately the battle over this symbolic territory reveals a conflict over world views—over what standards our communities and our nation will live by; over what we consider to be "of enduring value" in our communities; over what we consider a fair representation of our times, and so on. As a bystander at the Contemporary Arts Center in Cincinnati observed during the controversy over the Mapplethorpe exhibit, "This isn't just an obscenity prosecution. This is a trial of a good part of American culture."

But even more, these battles again lay bare the tensions that exist between two fundamentally different conceptions of the sacred. For those of orthodox religious commitments, the sacred is obvious enough. It is an unchanging and everlasting God who ordained through Scripture, the church, or Torah, a manner of life and of social relationship that cannot be broached without incurring the displeasure of God. On the other side of the cultural divide, the sacred is a little more difficult to discern. Perhaps Tom Wolfe had it right when he observed that art itself was the religion of the educated classes. Maybe this is why Broadway producer Joseph Papp said as he observed the police coming into the Cincinnati Contemporary Arts Center to close the Mapplethorpe exhibit, "It's like an invasion. It's like they're coming into a church or coming into a synagogue, or coming into any place of worship. It's a violation." Such an insight makes sense if we see art as a symbol of conscience. To place any restrictions on the arts, therefore, is to place restrictions on the conscience itself; it is to place fetters on the symbol of being. Such an insight also makes sense if we see art as a symbol of immortality—of that which will outlive us all. To place restrictions on art is to place restrictions on the (secular) hope of eternity. Perhaps this is why the procedural guarantee of freedom of expression has also acquired a sacred quality in progressivist circles.

The idea that the battle over the arts is related to the tensions between two different conceptions of the sacred is not far-fetched. How else can one explain the passion and intensity on both sides of the cultural divide were it not that each side, by its very being and expression, profanes what the other holds most sublime? If this is true, we are again reminded of the reasons that the larger culture war will not subside any time soon.

Andres Serrano, "Piss Christ," 1987.
Paula Cooper Gallery.

SOURCES

The Battleground of History

Since the mid-1960s, a new generation of historians has been rewriting American history. What has emerged is less an account of politics, economics, the nation, big business, and presidents of the United States and more the story of ordinary people, minorities, local contexts, everyday lives, and popular culture. Although the people responsible see this new perspective as much more accurate and truthful than the old one, there are others who believe that the new emphases distort the American experience and encourage people to see themselves as African-Americans or Asian-Americans or women, rather than as simply "Americans."

The selections that follow feature two of the great speechmakers of the 1980s, Ronald Reagan and African-American leader Jesse Jackson, functioning here partly as historians, probing the American past in very different ways. Focus on the sections of each speech that deal with American history. What "history" does each speaker present? What kinds of people populate Reagan's version of the American past? Or Jackson's? Does one man's version of American history seem more accurate to you than the other?

Second Inaugural Address, January 21, 1985

Ronald Reagan

Senator Mathis, Chief Justice Burger, Vice President Bush, Speaker O'Neill, Senator Dole, Reverend Clergy and members of my family and friends, and my fellow citizens: This day has been made brighter with the presence here of one who for a time has been absent. Senator John Stennis, God bless you and welcome back.

There is, however, one who is not with us today. Representative Gillis Long of Louisiana left us last night. And I wonder if we could all join in a moment of silent prayer.

Amen.

There are no words to—adequate to express my thanks for the great honor that you've bestowed on me. I will do my utmost to be deserving of your trust.

This is, as Senator Mathias told us, the fiftieth time that we, the people, have celebrated this historic occasion. When the first president, George Washington, placed his hand upon the Bible, he stood less than a single day's journey by horse-

Vital Speeches of the Day, February 1, 1985.

back from raw, untamed wilderness. There were four million Americans in a Union of thirteen states.

Today we are sixty times as many in a Union of fifty states. We've lighted the world with our inventions, gone to the aid of mankind wherever in the world there was a cry for help, journeyed to the moon and safely returned.

So much has changed. And yet we stand together as we did two centuries ago.

When I took this oath four years ago, I did so in a time of economic stress. Voices were raised saying that we had to look to our past greatness and glory. But we, the present-day Americans, are not given to looking backward. In this blessed land, there is always a better tomorrow.

Four years ago I spoke to you of a new beginning, and we have accomplished that. But in another sense, our new beginning is a continuation of that beginning created two centuries ago when, for the first time in history, government, the people said, was not our master. It is our servant; its only power that which we, the people, allow it to have.

That system has never failed us. But for a time we failed the system. We asked things of government that government was not equipped to give. We yielded authority to the national government that properly belonged to states or to local governments or to the people themselves. We allowed taxes and inflation to rob us of our earnings and savings and watched the great industrial machine that had made us the most productive people on earth slow down and the number of unemployed increase.

By 1980 we knew it was time to renew our faith, to strive with all our strength toward the ultimate in individual freedom consistent with an orderly society.

We believed then and now there are no limits to growth and human progress when men and women are free to follow their dreams. And we were right. And we were right to believe that. Tax rates have been reduced, inflation cut dramatically and more people are employed than ever before in our history.

We are creating a nation once again vibrant, robust and alive. But there are many mountains yet to climb. We will not rest until every American enjoys the fullness of freedom, dignity, and opportunity as our birthright. It is our birthright as citizens of this great republic.

And if we meet this challenge, these will be years when Americans have restored their confidence and tradition of progress; when our values of faith, family, work, and neighborhood were restated for a modern age; when our economy was finally freed from government's grip; when we made sincere efforts at meaningful arms reductions by rebuilding our defenses, our economy, and developing new technologies helped preserve peace in a troubled world; when America courageously supported the struggle for individual liberty, self-government, and free enterprise throughout the world and turned the tide of history away from totalitarian darkness and into the warm sunlight of human freedom.

My fellow citizens, our nation is poised for greatness. We must do what we know is right and do it with all our might. Let history say of us, these were golden years—when the American Revolution was reborn, when freedom gained new life and America reached for her best.

Our two-party system has solved us—served us, I should say, well over the years, but never better than in those times of great challenge, when we came together not as Democrats or Republicans but as Americans united in the common cause.

Two of our Founding Fathers, a Boston lawyer named Adams and a Virginia planter named Jefferson, members of that remarkable group who met in Independence Hall and dared to think they could start the world over again, left us an important lesson. They had become, in the years spent in government, bitter political rivals. In the presidential election of 1800, then years later, when both were retired and age had softened their anger, they began to speak to each other again through letters.

A bond was reestablished between those two who had helped create this government of ours.

In 1826, the fiftieth anniversary of the Declaration of Independence, they both died. They died on the same day, within a few hours of each other. And that day was the Fourth of July.

In one of those letters exchanged in the sunset of their lives, Jefferson wrote, "It carries me back to the times when, beset with difficulties and dangers, we were fellow laborers in the same cause, struggling for what is most valuable to man, his right of self-government. Laboring always at the same oar, with some wave ever ahead threatening to overwhelm us, and yet passing harmless we rode through the storm with heart and hand." . . .

The time has come for a new American emancipation, a great national drive to tear down economic barriers and liberate the spirit of enterprise in the most distressed areas of our country. My friends, together we can do this, and do it we must, so help me God.

From new freedom will spring new opportunities for growth, a more productive, fulfilled and united people and a stronger America, an America that will lead the technological revolution and also open its mind and heart and soul to the treasuries of literature, music and poetry, and the values of faith, courage, and love. . . .

Now there is another area where the federal government can play a part. As an older American, I remember a time when people of different race, creed, or ethnic origin in our land found hatred and prejudice installed in social custom and, yes, in law. There's no story more heartening in our history than the progress that we've made toward the brotherhood of man that God intended for us. Let us resolve: There will be no turning back or hesitation on the road to an America rich in dignity and abundant with opportunity for all our citizens.

Let us resolve that we, the people, will build an American opportunity society in which all of us—white and black, rich and poor, young and old—will go forward together, arm in arm. Again, let us remember that, though our heritage is one of blood lines from every corner of the earth, we are all Americans pledged to carry on this last best hope of man on earth.

And I have spoken of our domestic goals, and the limitations we should put on our national government. Now let me turn to a task that is the primary responsibility of national government—the safety and security of our people.

Today we utter no prayer more fervently than the ancient prayer for peace on earth. Yet history has shown that peace does not come, nor will our freedom be preserved, by good will alone. There are those in the world who scorn our vision of human dignity and freedom. One nation, the Soviet Union, has conducted the greatest military buildup in the history of man, building arsenals of awesome offensive weapons. . . .

I have approved a research program to find, if we can, a security shield that will destroy nuclear missiles before they reach their target. It wouldn't kill people, it would destroy weapons. It wouldn't militarize space, it would help demilitarize the arsenals of earth. It would render nuclear weapons obsolete. We will meet with the Soviet [leaders] hoping that we can agree on a way to rid the world of the threat of nuclear destruction.

We strive for peace and security, heartened by the changes all around us. Since the turn of the century, the number of democracies in the world has grown fourfold. Human freedom is on the march, and nowhere more so than in our own hemisphere. Freedom is one of the deepest and noblest aspirations of the human spirit. People worldwide hunger for the right of self-determination, for those inalienable rights that make for human dignity and progress.

America must remain freedom's staunchest friend, for freedom is our best ally, and it is the world's only hope to conquer poverty and preserve peace. Every blow we inflict against poverty will be a blow against its dark allies of oppression and war. Every victory for human freedom will be a victory for world peace. . . .

My friends, we, we live in a world that's lit by lightning. So much is changing and will change, but so much endures and transcends time.

History is a ribbon, always unfurling; history is a journey. And as we continue on our journey we think of those who traveled before us. We stand again at the steps of this symbol of our democracy, or we would've been standing at the steps if it hadn't gotten so cold. Now, we're standing inside this symbol of our democracy, and we see and hear again the echoes of our past.

A general falls to his knees in the hard snow of Valley Forge; a lonely president paces the darkened halls and powers, ponders his struggle to preserve the Union; the men of the Alamo call out encouragement to each other; a settler pushes west and sings a song, and the song echoes out forever and fills the unknowing air.

It is the American sound: It is hopeful, big-hearted, idealistic—daring, decent and fair. That's our heritage, that's our song. We sing it still. For all our problems, our differences, we are together as of old. We raise our voices to the God who is the author of this most tender music. And may he continue to hold us close as we fill the world with our sand, sound—in unity, affection and love. One people under God, dedicated to the dream of freedom that he has placed in the human heart, called upon now to pass that dream on to a waiting and a hopeful world.

God bless you and may God bless America.

Address to the Democratic Convention, July 19, 1988

Jesse Jackson

Thank you. Thank you. Thank you. Tonight, we pause and give praise and honor to God for being good enough to allow us to be at this place at this time. When I look out at this convention, I see the face of America, red, yellow, brown, black and white. We are all precious in God's sight—the real rainbow coalition. All of us—all of us who are here think that we are seated. But we're really standing on someone's shoulders. Ladies and gentlemen. Mrs. Rosa Parks. The mother of the civil rights movement. . . .

My right and my privilege to stand here before you has been won—won in my lifetime—by the blood and the sweat of the innocent. . . .

Dr. Martin Luther King Jr. lives only a few miles from us tonight. Tonight he must feel good as he looks down upon us. We sit here together, a rainbow coalition—the sons and daughters of slavemasters and the sons and daughters of slaves sitting together around a common table, to decide the direction of our party and our country. His heart would be full tonight.

As a testament to the struggles of those who have gone before; as a legacy for those who will come after; as a tribute to the endurance, the patience, the courage of our forefathers and mothers; as an assurance that their prayers are being answered, their work have not been in vain, and hope is eternal, tomorrow night my name will go into nomination for the Presidency of the United States of America.

HIGHER GROUND

We meet tonight at the crossroads, a point of decision.

Shall we expand, be inclusive, find unity and power; or suffer division and impotence.

We've come to Atlanta, the cradle of the old south, the crucible of the new south.

Tonight there is a sense of celebration because we are moved, fundamentally moved from racial battlegrounds by law, to economic common ground, with the moral challenge to move to higher ground.

Common ground! . . .

When people come together, flowers always flourish—the air is rich with the aroma of a new spring.

Take New York, the dynamic metropolis. What makes New York so special?

It's the invitation of the Statue of Liberty—give me your tired, your poor, your huddled masses who yearn to breathe free.

Not restricted to English only. . . .
Common ground!
That's the challenge of our party tonight.
Left wing. Right wing. Progress will not come through boundless liberalism nor static conservatism, but at the critical mass of mutual survival. . . .

SALUTE FOR DUKAKIS

When we divide, we cannot win. We must find common ground as a basis for survival and development and change and growth. The day when we debated, differed, deliberated, agreed to agree, agreed to disagree, when we had the good judgment to argue a case and then not self-destruct, George Bush was just a little further away from the White House and a little closer to private life.

Tonight I salute Governor Michael Dukakis. He has run—He has run a well-managed and a dignified campaign.

No matter how tired or how tried, he always resisted the temptation to stoop to demagoguery. I have watched a good mind fast at work, with steel nerves, guiding his campaign out of the crowded field without appeal to the worst in us.

I have watched his perspective grow as his environment has expanded. I've seen his toughness and tenacity close up, knew his commitment to public service. . . .

His foreparents came to America on immigrant ships. My foreparents came to America on slave ships. But whatever the original ships, we are in the same boat tonight. . . .

Our choice? Full participation in a democratic government or more abandonment and neglect. And so this night, we choose not a false sense of independence, not our capacity to survive and endure. Tonight we choose interdependency, and our capacity to act and unite for the greater good.

SETTING AN AGENDA

Common good is finding commitment to new priorities to expansion and inclusion. A commitment to expanded participation in the Democratic Party at every level. A commitment to a shared national campaign strategy and involvement at every level.

A commitment to new priorities that insure that hope will be kept alive.

A common ground commitment to a legislative agenda for empowerment—for the John Conyers bill, universal, on-site, same-day registration everywhere. A commitment to D.C. statehood and empowerment, these we deserve, statehood. A commitment to economic set-asides. A commitment to the Dellums bill for comprehensive sanctions against South Africa. A sad commitment to a common direction. . . .

We find common ground at the plant gate that closes on workers without notice. We find common ground at the farm auction where a good farmer loses his or her land to bad loans or diminishing markets. Common ground at the school yard where teachers cannot get adequate pay, and students cannot get a scholarship, and can't make a loan. Common ground at the hospital admitting room, where somebody tonight is dying because they cannot afford to go upstairs to a bed that's empty waiting for someone with insurance to get sick.

We are a better nation than that. We must do better than that. . . .

A QUILT OF UNITY

Common ground. America is not a blanket, woven from one thread, one color, one cloth. When I was a child growing up in Greenville, South Carolina, and grandmomma could not afford a blanket, she didn't complain and we did not freeze. Instead she took pieces of old cloth—patches—wool, silk, gaberdine, crockersack—only patches, barely good enough to wipe off your shoes with. But they didn't stay that way very long. With sturdy hands and a strong cord, she sewed them together into a quilt, a thing of beauty and power and culture. Now, Democrats, we must build such a quilt. . . .

Reaganomics. Based on the belief that the rich had too little money and the poor had too much. That's classic Reaganomics. They believe that the poor had too much money and the rich had too little money so they engaged in reverse Robin Hood—took from the poor and gave to the rich, paid for by the middle class. We cannot stand four more years of Reaganomics in any version, in any disguise.

How'd I document that case.—Seven years later—the richest 1 percent of our society pays 20 percent less in taxes. The poorest 10 percent pay 20 percent more. Reaganomics.

Reagan gave the rich and the powerful a multibillion-dollar party. Now the party's over, he expects the people to pay for the damage.

I take this principal position . . . let us not raise taxes on the poor and the middle-class, but those who had the party, the rich and the powerful must pay for the party. . . .

CHALLENGE OF OUR DAY

Leadership must meet the moral challenge of its day. What's the moral challenge of our day? We have public accommodations. We have the right to vote. We have open housing. What's the fundamental challenge of our day? It is to end economic violence. Plant closings without notice. Economic violence. . . .

Most poor people are not lazy. They're not black. They're not brown. They're mostly white and female and young. But whether white, black or brown, a hungry baby's belly turned inside out is the same color. . . .

Most poor people are not on welfare. Some of them are illiterate and can't read the Want Ad section and when they can, they can't find a job that matches the address. They work hard everyday. I know, I live amongst them . . . They catch the early bus. They work every day. They raise other people's children. They work every day. They clean the streets. They work every day. . . .

No, no, they're not lazy. Someone must defend them because it's right and they cannot speak for themselves. . . .

DRUG POLICY

We need a real war on drugs. You can't just say no. It's deeper than that. You can't just get a palm reader or an astrologer. It's more profound than that.

We are spending $150 billion on drugs a year. We've gone from ignoring it to focusing on the children. Children cannot buy $150 billion worth of drugs a year. A few high-profile athletes, athletes are not laundering $150 billion a year. Bankers are.

I met the children in Watts who unfortunately in their despair, their grapes of hope have become raisins of despair and they're turning on each other and they're self-destructing. . . .

They say we don't have Saturday night specials anymore. They say, We buy AK47's and Uzis the latest make of weapons. We buy them across the counter on Long Beach Boulevard. You cannot fight a war on drugs unless until you're going to challenge the bankers and the gun sellers and those who grow them. Don't just focus on the children. Let's stop drugs at the level of supply and demand. . . .

REVERSE THE ARMS RACE

. . . Leadership must face the moral challenge of our day. In the nuclear age, buildup is irrational. Strong leadership cannot desire to look tough and let that stand in the way of the pursuit of peace.

Leadership must reverse the arms race. At least we should pledge no first use. Why? Because first use begets first retaliation. And that's mutual annihilation. That's not a rational way out. . . .

NEVER STOP DREAMING

I am often asked, Jesse, why do you take on these toughies? They're not very political. You can't win that way. If an issue is morally right, it will eventually be political. It may be political and never be right. . . .

We can win. We must not lose to the drugs, and violence, premature pregnancy, suicide, cynicism, pessimism and despair. We can win. Wherever you are tonight, now I challenge you to hope and to dream. Don't submerge your dreams. Exercise above all else—even on drugs, dream of the days you are drug free. Even in the gutter, dream of the day that you will be up on your feet again. You must never stop dreaming. . . .

Dream of peace. Peace is rational and reasonable. War is irrational . . . and unwinnable.

And I was not supposed to make it. You see, I was born of a teen-age mother, who was born of a teen-age mother. I understand. I know abandonment, and people being mean to you, and saying you're nothing and nobody and can never be anything. I understand. . . .

Wherever you are tonight, you can make it. Hold your head high. Stick your chest out. You can make it. It gets dark sometimes, but the morning comes. Don't you surrender. Suffering breeds character, character breeds faith, in the end faith will not disappoint.

You must not surrender. You may or may not get there but just know that you're qualified and you hold on and hold out. We must never surrender.

America will get better and better. Keep hope alive. Keep hope alive. Keep hope alive for tomorrow night and beyond. Keep hope alive. I love you very much. I love you very much.

Debacle at the Smithsonian

The different versions of American history held by Ronald Reagan and Jesse Jackson seem almost academic compared with the passions aroused by the plans of the Smithsonian, America's national museum, to mark the fiftieth anniversary of the dropping of the atomic bomb on Japan. The museum intended to display the fuselage of the Enola Gay, *the plane that dropped the first*

Enola Gay Exhibit.

Hiroshima/ground zero.

bomb, as well as photographs and artifacts of Ground Zero, all tied together by a lengthy script that offered the most recent historical interpretations of Truman's decision to use the weapon. Under enormous pressure from the Air Force Association and the American Legion, which found the museum's approach offensive to veterans, and threatened with cuts in funding, the Smithsonian capitulated. The script was abandoned, and the Enola Gay *fuselage was displayed without context or commentary.*

Rap Wars

Rap music emerged in the South Bronx ghetto in the late 1960s and was first recorded in 1979. During the mid-1980s, rap entered the mainstream, and by 1988, white ten-year-olds in the suburbs were plugged into "wholesome" black rappers like Young MC or white rappers like Vanilla Ice. At the same time, however, a new generation of confrontational, hard-core rappers—among them Public Enemy, N.W.A., and 2 Live Crew—had begun to record forms of rap music that many thought were simply unacceptable. In 1990, 2 Live Crew's album As Nasty As They Wanna Be *was ruled obscene by a U.S. District*

Court in Florida, and the band was arrested and tried on obscenity charges for its performance at an adults-only concert in Hollywood, Florida.

Concerned about the content and tone of rap music, Tipper Gore (see the introduction to this chapter) offered her thoughts in a January 1990 editorial in the Washington Post; *the piece was written before the controversy over 2 Live Crew erupted. Henry Louis Gates, Jr., professor of English at Duke University and an authority on African-American culture, joined the fray six months later, when 2 Live Crew was at the center of things, with a brief column for the* New York Times.

Is Gates's defense of 2 Live Crew convincing? Do his arguments address Tipper Gore's concerns?

Hate, Rape and Rap

Tipper Gore

Words like bitch and nigger are dangerous. Racial and sexual epithets, whether screamed across a street or camouflaged by the rhythms of a song, turn people into objects less than human—easier to degrade, easier to violate, easier to destroy. These words and epithets are becoming an accepted part of our lexicon. What's disturbing is that they are being endorsed by some of the very people they diminish, and our children are being sold a social dictionary that says racism, sexism, and antisemitism are okay.

As someone who strongly supports the First Amendment, I respect the freedom of every individual to label another as he likes. But speaking out against racism isn't endorsing censorship. No one should silently tolerate racism or sexism or antisemitism, or condone those who turn discrimination into a multimillion-dollar business justified because it's "real."

A few weeks ago television viewers saw a confrontation of depressing proportions on the Oprah Winfrey show. It was one I witnessed firsthand; I was there in the middle of it. Viewers heard some black American women say they didn't mind being called "bitches" and they weren't offended by the popular rap music artist Ice-T when he sang about "Evil E" who "f—ed the bitch with a flashlight/pulled it out, left the batteries in/so he could get a charge when he begins." There is more, and worse.

Ice-T, who was also on the show, said the song came from the heart and reflected his experiences. He said he doesn't mind other groups using the word nigger in their lyrics. That's how he described himself, he said.

Some in the audience questioned why we couldn't see the humor in such a song.

Will our kids get the joke? Do we want them describing themselves or each other as "niggers?" Do we want our daughters to think of themselves as "bitches" to be abused? Do we want our sons to measure success in gold guns hanging from thick neck chains? The women in the audience may understand the slang; Ice-T can try to justify it. But can our children?

Washington Post, January 8, 1990. © *The Washington Post*

One woman in the audience challenged Ice-T. She told him his song about the flashlight was about as funny as a song about lynching black men.

The difference is that sexism and violence against women are accepted as almost an institutionalized part of our entertainment. Racism is not—or at least, it hasn't been until recently. The fact is, neither racism, sexism nor antisemitism should be accepted.

Yet they are, and in some instances that acceptance has reached startling proportions. The racism expressed in the song "One In A Million" by Guns N' Roses, sparked nationwide discussion and disgust. But, an earlier album that featured a rape victim in the artwork and lyrics violently degrading to women created barely a whisper of protest. More than 9 million copies were sold, and it was played across the radio band. This is only one example where hundreds exist.

Rabbi Abraham Cooper of the Simon Wiesenthal Center, who also appeared on the Oprah Show, voiced his concerns about the antisemitic statements made by Professor Griff, a nonsinging member of the rap group Public Enemy; statements that gain added weight from the group's celebrity. "Jews are wicked," Professor Griff said in an interview with the *Washington Times*. . . . [Responsible for] "a majority of wickedness that goes on across the globe."

The Simon Wiesenthal Center placed a full-page ad in *Daily Variety* calling for self-restraint from the music industry, a move that prompted hundreds of calls to the center. Yet Rabbi Cooper's concerns barely elicited a response from Oprah Winfrey's audience.

Alvin Poussaint, a Harvard psychiatrist who is black, believes that the widespread acceptance of such degrading and denigrating images may reflect low self-esteem among black men in today's society. There are few positive black male role models for young children, and such messages from existing role models are damaging. Ice-T defends his reality: "I grew up in the streets—I'm no Bryant Gumbel." He accuses his critics of fearing that reality and says the fear comes from an ignorance of the triumph of the street ethic.

A valid point, perhaps. But it is not the messenger that is so frightening, it is the perpetuation—almost glorification—of the cruel and violent reality of his "streets."

A young black mother in the front row rose to defend Ice-T. Her son, she said, was an A student who listened to Ice-T. In her opinion, as long as Ice-T made a profit, it didn't matter what he sang.

Cultural economics were a poor excuse for the south's continuation of slavery. Ice-T's financial success cannot excuse the vileness of his message. What does it mean when performers such as Ice-T, Axl Rose of Guns N' Roses and others can enrich themselves with racist and misogynist diatribes and defend it because it sells? Hitler's antisemitism sold in Nazi Germany. That didn't make it right.

In America, a woman is raped once every six minutes. A majority of children surveyed by a Rhode Island Rape Crisis Center thought rape was acceptable. In New York City, rape arrests of thirteen-year-old boys have increased 200 percent in the past two years. Children eighteen and younger now are responsible for 70 percent of the hate crime committed in the United States. No one is saying this happens solely because of rap or rock music, but certainly kids are influenced by the glorification of violence.

Children must be taught to hate. They are not born with ideas of bigotry—they learn from what they see in the world around them. If their reality consists of a street ethic that promotes and glorifies violence against women or discrimination against minorities—not only in everyday life, but in their entertainment—then ideas of bigotry and violence will flourish.

We must raise our voices in protest and put pressure on those who not only reflect this hatred but also package, polish, promote, and market it; those who would make words like nigger acceptable. Let's place a higher value on our children than on our profits and embark on a remedial civil rights course for children who are being taught to hate and a remedial nonviolence course for children who are being taught to destroy. Let's send the message loud and clear through our homes, our streets and our schools, as well as our art and our culture.

2 Live Crew, Decoded

Henry Louis Gates, Jr.

Durham, N.C.

The rap group 2 Live Crew and their controversial hit recording *As Nasty As They Wanna Be* may well earn a signal place in the history of First Amendment rights. But just as important is how these lyrics will be interpreted and by whom.

For centuries, African-Americans have been forced to develop coded ways of communicating to protect them from danger. Allegories and double meanings, words redefined to mean their opposites (*bad* meaning *good,* for instance), even neologisms (*bodacious*) have enabled blacks to share messages only the initiated understood.

Many blacks were amused by the transcripts of Marion Barry's sting operation, which reveals that he used the traditional black expression about one's *nose being opened.* This referred to a love affair and not, as Mr. Barry's prosecutors have suggested, to the inhalation of drugs. Understanding this phrase could very well spell the difference (for the Mayor) between prison and freedom.

2 Live Crew is engaged in heavy-handed parody, turning the stereotypes of black and white American culture on their heads. These young artists are acting out, to lively dance music, a parodic exaggeration of the age-old stereotypes of the oversexed black female and male. Their exuberant use of hyperbole (phantasmagoric sexual organs, for example) undermines—for anyone fluent in black cultural codes—a too literal-minded hearing of the lyrics.

This is the street tradition called *signifying* or *playing the dozens,* which has generally been risqué, and where the best signifier or "rapper" is the one who invents the most extravagant images, the biggest "lies," as the culture says. (H. "Rap" Brown earned his nickname in just this way.) In the face of racist stereotypes about black sexuality, you can do one of two things: you can disavow them or explode them with exaggeration.

2 Live Crew, like many "hip-hop" groups, is engaged in sexual carnivalesque. Parody reigns supreme, from a take-off of standard blues to a spoof of the black power movement; their off-color nursery rhymes are part of a venerable western tradition. The group even satirizes the culture of commerce when it appropriates popular advertising slogans ("Tastes great!" "Less filling!") and puts them in a bawdy context.

2 Live Crew must be interpreted within the context of black culture generally and of signifying specifically. Their novelty, and that of other adventuresome rap groups, is that their defiant rejection of euphemism now voices for the mainstream what before existed largely in the "race record" market—where the records of Redd Foxx and Rudy Ray Moore once were forced to reside.

Rock songs have always been about sex but have used elaborate subterfuges to convey that fact. 2 Live Crew uses Anglo-Saxon words and is self-conscious about it: a parody of a white voice in one song refers to "private personal parts," as a coy counterpart to the group's bluntness.

Much more troubling than its so-called obscenity is the group's overt sexism. Their sexism is so flagrant, however, that it almost cancels itself out in a hyperbolic war between the sexes. In this it recalls the intersexual jousting in Zora Neale Hurston's novels. Still, many of us look toward the emergence of more female rappers to redress sexual stereotypes. And we must not allow ourselves to sentimentalize street culture: the appreciation of verbal virtuosity does not lessen one's obligation to critique bigotry in all its pernicious forms.

Is 2 Live Crew more "obscene" than, say, the comic Andrew Dice Clay? Clearly, this rap group is seen as more threatening than others that are just as sexually explicit. Can this be completely unrelated to the specter of the young black male as a figure of sexual and social disruption, the very stereotypes 2 Live Crew seems determined to undermine?

This question—and the very large question of obscenity and the First Amendment—cannot even be addressed until those who would answer them become literate in the vernacular traditions of African-Americans. To do less is to censor through the equivalent of intellectual prior restraint—and censorship is to art what lynching is to justice.

Censored! The Most Banned
Books of the 1990s

Herbert N. Foerstel

The list below appears in Herbert N. Foerstel, Banned in the U.S.A. *(1994). Foerstel compiled it from listings of banned books by People of the American Way and the American Library Association's Office of Intellectual Freedom. From what you know of the content of individual books, why do you think they appear on the list? What themes were of most concern to those seeking to ban books?*

Herbert N. Foerstel, *Banned in the U.S.A.* Reprinted with permission of Greenwood Publishing Group, Inc., Westport, CT. Copyright © 1994 by Herbert N. Foerstel.

THE MOST BANNED BOOKS OF THE 1990s

1. *Impressions,* ed. Jack Booth (a language arts textbook for young children)
2. *Of Mice and Men,* by John Steinbeck (1937)
3. *The Catcher in the Rye,* by J.D. Salinger (1951)
4. *The Adventures of Huckleberry Finn,* by Mark Twain (1885)
5. *The Chocolate War,* by Robert Cormier (1974)
6. *Bridge to Terabithia,* by Katherine Paterson (1977)
7. *Scary Stories to Tell in the Dark,* by Alvin Schwartz (1981)
8. *More Scary Stories to Tell in the Dark,* by Alvin Schwartz (1984)
9. *The Witches,* by Roald Dahl (1983)
10. *Daddy's Romance,* by Michael Willhoite (1990)
11. *Curses, Hexes, and Spells,* by Daniel Cohen (1974)
12. *A Wrinkle in Time,* by Madeleine L'Engle (1962)
13. *How to Eat Fried Worms,* by Thomas Rockwell (1973)
14. *Blubber,* by Judy Blume (1974)
15. *Revolting Rhymes,* by Roald Dahl (1982)
16. *Halloween ABC,* by Eve Merriam (1987)
17. *A Day No Pigs Would Die,* by Robert Peck (1972)
18. *Heather Has Two Mommies,* by Leslea Newman (1989)
19. *Christine,* by Stephen King (1983)
20. *I Know Why the Caged Bird Sings,* by Maya Angelou (1969)

SUGGESTIONS FOR VIEWING AND LISTENING

Heaven's Gate (1980)
An effort to present the nation's history, but at a moment in time when there was no shared understanding of America's past.

Full Metal Jacket (1987)
Part of the struggle for "control" of the meaning of the Vietnam war.

The Last Temptation of Christ (1988)
A very human Jesus, confused and suffering. Fundamentalists were appalled.

Public Enemy, "Welcome to the Terrordome" (1990)
Anti-semitic verses often noted by critics.

N.W.A., "——— the Police" (1988)
Police harrassment of ghetto blacks, with a suggestion of deadly retaliation.

Schoolly D., "No More Rock 'n' Roll" (1988)
Blacks reject the dominant tradition in American popular music. The meaning of that rejection is the issue.

CHAPTER 12

Trouble in Multicultural America

In the mid-1970s, a reasonable person could look back on the social upheaval of the previous decade as a disturbing memory, but a memory nonetheless. The war that had divided Americans had ended, and the riots that had devastated inner-city ghettos and alarmed the nation were no more. To be sure, Watergate was an unseemly mess, but here, too, the excesses of the Nixon White House could be traced to the president's anxieties about demonstrations, leaks of classified information, and other concerns that were arguably unique to the 1960s. With pressures to have both guns and butter subsiding, even the troubled economy would right itself. And the nation would come together once again.

It didn't happen that way. Indeed, by the mid-1990s the nation was more divided—by race, class, gender, sexuality, religion, ethnicity, age, region, and ideology—than it had been two or three decades earlier. Some of these divisions were products of the social ferments of the 1960s. Unlike the war in Vietnam, the conflict between men and women could not be ended by treaty. Instead, it produced a series of protracted struggles over abortion, the Equal Rights Amendment (defeated in 1982), access to the workplace, and sexual harassment. The latter emerged as a major public issue in 1991, when Anita Hill testified that she had been the victim of improper advances by Clarence Thomas, recently nominated to the Supreme Court. Black nationalism was at the core of black cultural expression in the 1970s and 1980s, whether in hip-hop, break-dancing, graffiti, rap music, literature, or film, and by the 1990s had produced a controversial "Afrocentric" approach to the study of African-American history and culture that downplayed the European heritage.

By the mid-1980s, the term *multiculturalism* was in common use, especially by those who preferred to see division as diversity, and for whom racial, gender, ethnic, and other differences were grounds for celebration. But others were less positive. In an important 1978 essay, Kevin Phillips used the term "balkanization" to describe everything from the demands of Native Americans for "Red Power" and the organization of older Americans for "Gray Power" to the growing conflicts over energy policy and resources between the Sun Belt and the Frost Belt. A kind of geographic balkanization was also at work in and around the nation's cities, where the continued migration of the white middle and upper classes to suburban communities left the cities—and their deteriorating school systems—to minorities and the poor. Eventually, even suburban isolation proved insufficient, and by the 1990s the trend was toward "gated" housing developments, with fences and guards to keep out those who did not belong.

Fragmentation also had something to do with how Americans felt about government and the state. In 1961, when John Kennedy announced that "we shall pay any price, bear any burden, meet any hardship, support any friend, oppose any foe to assure the survival and the success of liberty," his words reflected a twofold consensus: that international Communism required a unified, national response and that government could accomplish whatever it chose to. As this consensus dissolved, government became suspect and dangerous. The revolt against government was apparent on the state level in 1978, when California voters used the initiative process to pass Proposition 13, which slashed real estate taxes statewide. Ronald Reagan cultivated an anti-government, individualist ideology, and under his leadership Americans who had money or aspired to having it revelled in selfishness, instant gratification, and consumption, ignoring the public sphere. His successor, George Bush, cared less about wealth and its display, yet the slogan most identified with his administration—"a thousand points of light"—was a reminder that Bush's vision of a good society was no less fragmented and individualistic than Reagan's. When the cold war ended in the early 1990s, Americans lost the "evil empire" that had enforced consensus and focused the nation's aggressive impulses since 1945. And in 1995 right-wing fanatics, convinced that the American government was the true enemy of liberty, bombed the federal building in Oklahoma City, killing more than 200 people.

The city of Los Angeles, the focus of this chapter, is in many respects the quintessence of a multicultural, balkanized America. As the nation's foremost user of highways and automobiles, Los Angeles had by the 1950s become a dispersed and centerless city, an aggregation of farflung suburbs. Since the 1930s the city had been home to strangers—first migrants from other states, then, during and after World War II, immigrants from Guatemala, the Philippines, Iran, Korea, and, of course, Mexico. By 1970, Los Angeles could call itself the third largest Mexican city in the world, and the enormous influx of Hispanics had just begun.

As the city's industrial base declined and the Reagan and Bush administrations cut funds for urban programs, the city of angels seethed with racial, ethnic, and nativist hostilities. Blacks boycotted Korean grocers in their neighborhoods, poor whites resented Hispanic newcomers on public assistance, and urban planners tried to wall off the downtown core from the poor, ethnic neighborhoods that surrounded it. Out in the San Fernando Valley, where the white middle class had fled from the heterogeneity of the city, developers created dozens of gated communities. When in April 1992 a jury in one of those outlying communities found four white policemen innocent of using excessive force on a black man, Rodney King, Los Angeles erupted in days of rioting and looting. The mirror-image verdict of acquittal in the O.J. Simpson double-murder trial, delivered by a mostly black jury in October 1995 and triggered by the racism of investigating detective Mark Fuhrman, produced no similar episode of violence. But reactions to the Simpson verdict—white outrage, black celebrations—confirmed how bitterly divided the nation was, and how little remained of the public sphere.

INTERPRETIVE ESSAY

Melvin L. Oliver, James H. Johnson, Jr., and Walter C. Farrell, Jr.

Anatomy of a Rebellion
A Political-Economic Analysis

The 1992 Los Angeles rebellion had its immediate origins in a violent confrontation between white police officers and Rodney King, a twenty-five-year-old black man. On the night of March 3, 1991, King was pulled over by Los Angeles police officers following a long high-speed chase. He was drunk and had been smoking marijuana and, according to witnesses, he was laughing and dancing as he got out of his car. The police were not amused. In eighty-one seconds—every one of them on videotape—King was kicked or beaten by four police officers over fifty times and received several blasts from a stun-gun. While ten other police officers stood watching, King's skull was fractured in nine places, his eye socket shattered, and his leg and cheekbone broken.

During the trial that ensued, police officers explained their conduct in several ways. At 6'3" and 200 pounds, King was big (a "bear" and "bear-like") and, therefore, dangerous. He might have been on a drug called PCP. And one juror said the videotape, played in slow motion by the defense, revealed that King's body was in "complete control" and that King had chosen the moment when he "wanted" to be handcuffed. To most of those who had seen the videotape (it was made widely available on television), these claims seemed ludicrous. Nonetheless, in April 1992 the four officers were acquitted, the verdict igniting thirty-six hours of violence, looting, and burning in the black and Hispanic district of South Central Los Angeles.

In the selection that follows, a team of urban studies scholars examines the "Rodney King" rebellion from a variety of demographic, geographic, and political perspectives. While reading the essay, think about whether the verdict in the King beating was central, or peripheral, to the rebellion. Could the rebellion have occurred in any American city, or was it determined by forces unique to Los Angeles? As American society becomes increasingly multiethnic and multiracial, are rebellions likely to happen more frequently? What kinds of policies or programs, if any, might have prevented the rebellion from occurring?

Excerpted from Melvin L. Oliver, James H. Johnson, Jr., and Walter C. Farrell, Jr., "Anatomy of a Rebellion: a Political-Economic Analysis," *Reading Rodney King/Reading Urban Uprising,* ed. Robert Gooding-Williams (New York: Routledge, 1993). Used with permission of Walter C. Farrell, Jr., Professor of Educational Policy and Community Studies and Member of the Graduate Faculty in Urban Studies, University of Wisconsin–Milwaukee.

It is quite impossible to understand the events surrounding the acquittal of the four police officers accused of brutally beating Rodney King without placing them within the local and national circumstances and forces that have deepened class and racial inequalities over the past two decades. Both at the local and national level, the trajectory of economic, political, and social trends has exacerbated the ever-so-fragile social fabric of our nation's cities, making ripe the conditions that kindled the social explosion that occurred in Los Angeles on 29 April 1992.

In this essay, we reflect on the Los Angeles civil disorder of 1992 from an urban political economy perspective. It is our contention that the course and magnitude of changes in the urban political economy of American cities in general, and Los Angeles in particular, were crucial in bringing to the forefront the contradictions underlying the Los Angeles urban rebellion. Thus, this essay is an anatomy of the civil unrest that seeks to unravel its relationship to rebellions of the past, highlighting both the ever-changing and unchanging nature of the relationship of black Americans to the economic and political order, and the consequences of the introduction of new actors into the sociopolitical mix of large American cities. In order to accomplish this, we situate the civil unrest within the broader context of the recent demographic, social, and economic changes occurring in the Los Angeles milieu. The object of this analysis is to ground the rebellion in the context of a political system that is frayed at the edges in its attempt to integrate new voices into the body politic, and, at the same time, is incapable of bringing into the economic mainstream significant portions of the African-American community (traditionally one of the most economically marginal segments of American society). Can the efforts that have been spawned as a consequence of the urban rebellion achieve a modicum of success in confronting these difficult challenges? We address this issue in a brief but critical review of existing policies and proposals that have been advanced to "rebuild" Los Angeles. Finally, we outline our own strategy for redeveloping South Central Los Angeles, one which is designed to address the real "seeds" of the civil unrest.

ANATOMY OF THE REBELLION

The recent civil unrest in Los Angeles was the worst such event in recent U.S. history. None of the major civil disorders of the 1960s, including the Watts rebellion of 1965, required a level of emergency response or exacted a toll—in terms of loss of life, injuries, and property damage and loss—comparable to the Los Angeles rebellion of 1992. The burning, looting, and violence that ensued following the rendering of a not-guilty verdict in the police-brutality trial required the deployment of not only the full forces of the Los Angeles Police Department (LAPD) and the Los Angeles County Sheriff's Department, but also 10,000 National Guardsmen and 3,500 military personnel. The Fire Department received 5,537 structure fire calls and responded to an estimated 500 fires. An estimated 4,000 businesses were destroyed. Fifty-two people died and 2,383 people were injured, including 20 law-enforcement and fire personnel. Property damage and loss have been estimated at between $785 million and $1 billion.

In contrast to the civil disorders of the 1960s, this was a multiethnic rebellion. This diversity is reflected in those arrested during the rebellion. Between April 30 and May 4, 36.9% of those arrested by the Los Angeles Police Department and the Sheriff's Department were Latino; 29.9% were Black; 6.8% were white; and 26.4% were of undetermined or unknown race or ethnicity. It has been estimated that 1,200 of the 16,000 plus arrested were illegal aliens, roughly 40% of whom were handed over to INS [Immigration and Naturalization Service] officials for immediate deportation. More than 75% of those deported were from Mexico. Also in contrast to the civil disorders of the 1960s, the burning and looting were neither random nor limited to a single neighborhood; rather, the response was targeted, systematic, and widespread, encompassing much of the legal city. This fact has lead us to purposefully and consistently refer to the civil unrest as a rebellion as opposed to a riot.

THE VERDICT AND THE REBELLION IN RETROSPECT

We think it is safe to say that both the verdict rendered in the police-brutality trial, and the widespread burning, looting, and violence which ensued after the jury issued its decision, shocked most Americans. In retrospect, however, we would like to suggest that both the verdict and the subsequent rebellion were quite predictable. The treatment of black suspects by the police and black defendants by the courts represents a continuity in the experience of blacks in relationship to the criminal-justice system.

The outcome of the trial, in our view, was predictable for two reasons. The first pertains to the defense attorneys' successful bid for a change of venue for the trial. Simi Valley, the site of the trial, and Ventura County more generally, is a predominantly white community known for its strong stance on law and order, as evidenced by the fact that a significant number of LAPD officers live there. Thus, the four white police officers were truly judged by a jury of their peers. Viewed in this context, the verdict should not have been unanticipated.

The second development that made the outcome of the trial predictable, in retrospect, was the defense attorneys' ability to put Mr. King, instead of the four white police officers, on trial. (We should note here, parenthetically, that the media is also guilty in this regard, as evidenced by its consistent characterization of the case as "the Rodney King trial.") The defense attorneys, in effect, played the so-called "race card"; they painted Mr. King as unpredictable, dangerous, and uncontrollable, much as Mr. Bush, in the 1988 presidential campaign, used Willie Horton, the convicted rapist released on a temporary work furlough only to commit another heinous crime, to paint Mr. Dukakis as being soft on crime.

In today's society, the Willie Horton stereotype, recent surveys tell us, is often applied categorically to black males, irrespective of their social and economic status, but especially if they reside in the inner city. It is our contention that the jury agreed with the defense attorneys' portrayal of Mr. King as dangerous and uncontrollable, and thus rendered a verdict in favor of the four white police officers, notwithstanding the seemingly irrefutable videotaped evidence.

Why do we think, in hindsight, that the civil unrest following the verdict in the police-brutality trial was predictable? We believe that the response was not about the verdict in the police-brutality trial per se; rather, the civil unrest reflected the high degree of frustration and alienation that had built up among the citizens of South Central Los Angeles over the last 20 years. The rebellion, as we view it in retrospect, was a response not to a single but rather to repeated acts of what is widely perceived in the community to be blatant abuse of power by the police and the criminal-justice system more generally.

The civil unrest was also a response to a number of broader, external forces which have increasingly isolated the South Central Los Angeles community, geographically and economically, from the mainstream of Los Angeles society. These forces include: recent structural changes in the local (and national) economy; wholesale disinvestment in the South Central Los Angeles community by banks and other institutions, including the local city government; and nearly two decades of conservative federal policies which have simultaneously affected adversely the quality of life of the residents of South Central Los Angeles and accelerated the decline and deterioration of their neighborhoods.

Moreover, these developments were occurring at a time when the community was experiencing a radical demographic transformation, an unprecedented change in population accompanied by considerable tensions and conflict between long-term residents and the more recent arrivals. Viewed from this perspective, the verdict in the police-brutality trial was merely the proverbial straw that broke the camel's back.

SEEDS OF THE REBELLION

The videotaped beating of Mr. Rodney King was only the most recent case in which there were serious questions about whether LAPD officers used excessive force to subdue or arrest a black citizen. For several years, the City of Los Angeles has had to pay out millions of taxpayers' dollars to settle the complaints and lawsuits of citizens who were victims of LAPD abuse. Moreover, the black citizens of the city of Los Angeles have been disproportionately victimized by the LAPD's use of the choke hold, a tactic employed to subdue individuals who are perceived to be uncooperative. During the 1980s, 18 citizens of Los Angeles died as a result of LAPD officers' use of the choke hold; 16 of them reportedly were black.

Accordingly, the not-guilty verdict rendered in the police-brutality trial was also only the most recent in a series of cases in which the decisions emanating from the criminal-justice system were widely perceived in the black community to be grossly unjust. This decision came closely on the heels of another controversial verdict in the Latasha Harlins case. A videotape revealed that Ms. Harlins—an honor student at a local high school—was fatally shot in the back of the head by a Korean shopkeeper following an altercation over a carton of orange juice. The shopkeeper received a six month suspended sentence and was ordered to do six months of community service.

These and related events have occurred in the midst of drastic demographic change in South Central Los Angeles. Over the last two decades, the community has been transformed from a predominantly black to a mixed black and Latino area. Today, nearly one-half of the South Central Los Angeles population is Latino. In addition, there also has been an ethnic succession in the local business environment, characterized by the exodus of many of the Jewish shopkeepers and a substantial influx of small, family-run Korean businesses. This ethnic succession in both the residential environment and the business community has not been particularly smooth. The three ethnic groups—blacks, Latinos, and Koreans—have found themselves in conflict and competition with one another over jobs, housing, and scarce public resources.

Part of this conflict stems from the fact that the Los Angeles economy has undergone a fairly drastic restructuring over the last two decades. This restructuring includes, on the one hand, the decline of traditional, highly unionized, high-wage manufacturing employment; and on the other, the growth of employment in the high-technology-manufacturing, the craft-specialty, and the advanced-service sectors of the economy. South Central Los Angeles—the traditional industrial core of the city—bore the brunt of the decline in manufacturing employment, losing 70,000 high-wage, stable jobs between 1978 and 1982.

At the same time these well-paying and stable jobs were disappearing from South Central Los Angeles, local employers were seeking alternative sites for their manufacturing activities. As a consequence of these seemingly routine decisions, new employment growth nodes or "technopoles" emerged in the San Fernando Valley, in the San Gabriel Valley, and in El Segundo near the airport in Los Angeles County, as well as in nearby Orange County. In addition, a number of Los Angeles–based employers established production facilities in the Mexican border towns of Tijuana, Ensanada, and Tecate. Between 1978 and 1982, over 200 Los Angeles–based firms, including Hughes Aircraft, Northrop, and Rockwell, as well as a host of smaller firms, participated in this deconcentration process. Such capital flight, in conjunction with the plant closings, has essentially closed off to the residents of South Central Los Angeles access to what were formerly well-paying, unionized jobs.

It is important to note that, while new industrial spaces were being established elsewhere in Los Angeles County (and in nearby Orange County as well as along the U.S.-Mexico border), new employment opportunities were emerging within or near the traditional industrial core in South Central Los Angeles. But, unlike the manufacturing jobs that disappeared from this area, the new jobs are in competitive sector industries, which rely primarily on undocumented labor and pay, at best, minimum wage.

In part as a consequence of these developments, and partly as a function of employers' openly negative attitudes toward black workers, the black-male jobless rate in some residential areas of South Central Los Angeles hovers around 50%. Whereas joblessness is the central problem for black males in South Central Los Angeles, concentration in low-paying, bad jobs in competitive sector industries is the main problem for the Latino residents of the area. Both groups share a common fate: incomes below the poverty level. Whereas one group is the working poor (Latinos), the other is the jobless poor (blacks).

In addition to the adverse impact of structural changes in the local economy, South Central Los Angeles also has suffered from the failure of local institutions to devise and implement a plan to redevelop and revitalize the community. In fact, over the last two decades, the local city government has consciously pursued a policy of downtown and westside redevelopment at the expense of South Central Los Angeles. One needs only to look at the skyline of downtown and the so-called Wilshire corridor—that twenty-mile stretch extending along Wilshire Boulevard from downtown to the Pacific Ocean—to see the impact of this policy.

Finally, the seeds of the rebellion are rooted in nearly two decades of conservative policy making and implementation at the federal level. Many policy analysts talk about the adverse impact on minorities and their communities of Democratic president Lyndon Johnson's "War on Poverty" programs of the 1960s, but we must not lose sight of the fact that the Republicans have been in control of the White House for all but four (the Carter years) of the past 20 years. A number of public policies implemented during the period, and especially during the years when Mr. Reagan was president, we contend, served as sparks for the recent civil unrest. Three of these policy domains are worthy of note here.

The first pertains to the federal government's establishment of a laissez-faire business climate in order to facilitate the competitiveness of U.S. firms. Such a policy, in retrospect, appears to have facilitated the large number of plant closings in South Central Los Angeles and capital flight to the U.S./Mexico border and various Third World countries. Between 1982 and 1989 there were 131 plant closings in Los Angeles, idling 124,000 workers. Fifteen of these plants moved to Mexico or overseas.

The second involved the federal government's dismantling of the social safety net in minority communities. Perhaps most devastating for the South Central Los Angeles area has been the defunding of community-based organizations (CBOs). Historically, CBOs were part of that collectivity of social resources in the urban environment which encouraged the inner-city disadvantaged, especially disadvantaged youth, to pursue mainstream avenues of social and economic mobility and discouraged dysfunctional or antisocial behavior. In academic lingo, CBOs were effective "mediating" institutions in the inner city.

During the last decade or so, however, CBOs have become less effective as mediating institutions. The reason for this is that the federal support they received was substantially reduced. In 1980, when Mr. Reagan took office, CBOs received an estimated 48% of their funding from the federal government. As part of the Reagan Administration's dismantling of the social safety net, many CBOs were forced to reduce substantially programs that benefited the most disadvantaged in the community. Inner-city youth have been most adversely affected by this defunding of community-based initiatives and other safety-net programs.

It should be noted, moreover, that the dismantled social safety net has been replaced with a criminal dragnet. That is, rather than allocate support for social programs that discourage or prevent disadvantaged youth from engaging in dysfunctional behavior, over the past decade or so, the federal government has pursued a policy of resolving the problems of the inner city through the criminal-justice system.

Given this shift in policy orientation, it should not be surprising that, nationally, 25% of prime-working-age young black males (ages 18–35) are either in prison, in jail, on probation, or otherwise connected to the criminal-justice system. Although reliable statistics are hard to come by, the anecdotal evidence suggests that at least 25% of the young black males in South Central Los Angeles have had a brush with the law. What are the prospects of landing a job if you have a criminal record? Incarceration breeds despair and in the employment arena, it is the scarlet letter of unemployability.

Educational initiatives enacted during the late 1970s and early 1980s, which were designed to address the so-called "crisis" in American education, constitute the third policy domain. There is actually a very large body of social-science evidence which shows that such policies as tracking by ability group, grade retention, and the increasing reliance on standardized tests as the ultimate arbiter of educational success have, in fact, disenfranchised large numbers of black and brown youth. In urban school systems, they are disproportionately placed in special-education classes and are more likely than their white counterparts to be subjected to extreme disciplinary sanctions.

The effects of these policies in the Los Angeles Unified School District (LAUSD) are evident in the data on school-leaving behavior. For the Los Angeles Unified School district as a whole, 39.2% of all the students in the class of 1988 dropped out at some point during their high-school years. However, for high schools in South Central Los Angeles, the drop-out rates were substantially higher, between 63% and 79%. It is important to note that the dropout problem is not limited to the high-school population. According to data compiled by LAUSD, approximately 25% of the students in the junior high schools in South Central Los Angeles dropped out during the 1987–88 academic year.

Twenty years ago it was possible to drop out of school before graduation and find a well-paying job in heavy manufacturing in South Central Los Angeles. Today, however, those types of jobs are no longer available in the community, as we noted previously. Juxtaposing the adverse effects of a restructured economy and the discriminatory aspects of education reforms, what emerges is a rather substantial pool of inner-city males of color who are neither at work nor in school. These individuals are, in effect, idle; and previous research shows us that it is this population which is most likely to be in gangs, to engage in drug trafficking, and to participate in a range of other criminal behavior. Moreover, we know that it is this population of idle, minority males that experiences the most difficulty forming and maintaining stable families, which accounts, at least in part, for the high percentage of female-headed families with incomes below the poverty level in South Central Los Angeles.

EXPLAINING THE SOURCES OF A MULTIETHNIC REBELLION

The most distinctive aspect of the Los Angeles rebellion was its multiethnic character. While blacks were the source of the disturbances as they broke out on the first night of the rebellion, by the second evening it was clear that the discontent that emerged initially was shared by many of the city's largest racial group, the

Latino community. As we have just pointed out, the economically depressed Latinos in Los Angeles are comprised of a working-poor population, characterized by a large and significant core of Mexican and Central American immigrants. But what is interesting is that the rebellion did not encompass the traditional Mexican-American community of East Los Angeles. Indeed, the fires and protest were silent in these communities as political leaders and local residents ardently cautioned residents against "burning your own community." Nevertheless, Latinos in South Central Los Angeles did not hesitate to participate in looting, particularly against Korean merchants. How do we explain this pattern?

One important element necessary to explain the uneven participation of Latinos in the rebellion is to place the Latino experience into the context of struggles to incorporate that community politically into the electoral system in Los Angeles city and county. With the largest Latino population outside of Mexico City, Latinos have been severely underrepresented in city and county governments. In a struggle emanating from the 1960s, Latinos, particularly Mexican Americans, have been involved in protesting this situation, in ways ranging from street-level, grass-roots activity to highly coordinated court challenges to racially biased redistricting schemes that have unfairly diluted Latino voting strength. That struggle has just recently begun to bear fruit. In the important court case *Garza et al. v. County of Los Angeles,* Los Angeles County was found guilty of racial bias in the redistricting process and ordered to accept an alternative redistricting plan that led to the election of Gloria Molina as the first Latino(a) to serve on the powerful five-person Los Angeles County Board of Supervisors. Recent maneuvering at the city level will ensure significant representation of Latinos on the Los Angeles City Council, but not without considerable conflict between entrenched black and Latino City Council leaders over communities that are racially mixed. Los Angeles is a city in flux politically.

While it is clear that an emerging Latino majority will assume greater political power over time, the political-empowerment process has left several portions of the Latino population behind. In particular, Mexican Americans in Los Angeles, who have a longer history there and are more likely to constitute greater portions of the voting-age-citizen population, are the key recipients of the political spoils that have come in the Latino struggle for electoral power. All the elected officials to come into power as a consequence of these struggles are Mexican, and while they articulate a "Latino" perspective on the issues, they also tend to represent a narrow "Mexican" nationalism. The growing Central American population, which is residentially based in South Central Los Angeles and not in the traditional core of East Los Angeles, has not benefited for the most part from the political empowerment of Mexicans in Los Angeles. They are recent immigrants, not able to vote, and thus have become the pawns in negotiations with the county and city over the composition of political districts. Black and white politicians now represent districts with up to 50% of the population being Latino. But because they are unable to vote, a declining black or white population of 25% to 35% can maintain control over these districts without addressing the unique need of a majority of the community. The upshot has been the political neglect of a growing community whose problems of poverty have been just as overlooked as those of the black poor.

This contrast was easily observed during the rebellion as traditional Mexican-American community leaders were either silent or negative toward the mass participation of Latinos in the rebellion. Those Latinos in South Central had little stake in the existing political and economic order while East Los Angeles was riding the crest of a successful struggle to incorporate their political demands into the electoral system. Just as the black community is divided into a middle and a working class that are connected to the system by way of their political and economic ties, the Latino community in Los Angeles is increasingly divided by income, ethnicity, and citizenship.

The second element necessary to understand the involvement of Latinos, particularly Central American and Mexican immigrants, in the rebellions is the existence of interethnic hostilities between these groups and Korean Americans. While much is made of African-American and Korean-American conflict, little is said about an equally and potentially more volatile conflict between Latinos and Koreans. While the crux of African-American and Korean-American conflict is based on the uneasy relationship between merchant and customer, the Latino-Korean conflict has the added dimensions of residential and workplace conflict. Latino involvement in the rebellion was most intense in Koreatown. Koreatown is an ethnic enclave demarcated by both the Korean control of businesses and a dwindling Korean residential presence. The community, in fact, is residentially mixed, with large portions of Latinos and Koreans. Latinos in this community come into contact with Koreans on multiple levels and, from all we know from current research, experience considerable hostility in each level. First, in terms of residence, Latinos complain of discrimination on the part of Korean landlords as buildings and apartments are rented according to racial background. Second, as customers in Korean establishments, Latinos complain of forms of disrespectful treatment similar to that about which black customers complain. Third, as employees in Korean small businesses, Latinos point to high levels of exploitation by their employers. Thus, in this context, it was not surprising to see the vehemence and anger that the Latino community in South Central Los Angeles expressed, especially toward the Korean community.

THE FEDERAL BLUEPRINT

How do we simultaneously deal with the seeds of the rebellion, as we have characterized them above, and rebuild the physical infrastructure of South Central Los Angeles? In attempting to answer this question, we shall limit the discussion here to the federal government's blueprint, as the local "Rebuild L.A." initiative remains somewhat vague in both scope and content.

In the aftermath of the rebellion, the Bush administration presented a plan to revitalize the South Central Los Angeles community. In actuality, the main elements of the plan constitute what Secretary of Housing and Urban Development Jack Kemp termed, prior to the Los Angeles rebellion, his blueprint for a "Conservative War on Poverty."

Mr. Kemp promotes enterprise zones as being the key to job creation and retention in the inner cities. He proposes to eliminate capital-gains taxes and reduce levies for business that will locate in specified inner-city areas. However, there is no history of success of such strategies in poor communities like South Central Los Angeles.

Moreover, recent research has indicated, as we noted earlier, that those white businesses in the inner city are especially reluctant to hire black males. Employer responses to a field survey in Chicago showed that they generally embrace the prevailing racial stereotypes about this group—that they are lazy, lack a good work ethic, are ineducable, and perhaps most important, dangerous.

Couple this social reality with the fact that the major priorities for businesses when making locational decisions are access to markets, access to a quality labor force (code words for no blacks), infrastructure, and crime rates. These business factors are considered to be much more important in site selection than tax rates. And where enterprise zones have been successful, employers have brought their work force with them rather than employing community residents, or they have used these enterprise locations as warehouse points where there is a need for few workers.

Secretary Kemp has had a long-term commitment to empowering the poor by making them homeowners—the theory being that individuals will have a stronger commitment to maintaining that which they own and to joining in other efforts to enhance their general neighborhood environment. Project HOPE, as it is called, would make home ownership affordable. This idea had languished in the Bush administration for the last four years, until the Los Angeles rebellion pushed it to center stage.

However, this program would lock poor people into communities that are isolated, socially and economically, from mainstream employment and educational opportunities. And it would do nothing to expand the housing stock. Project HOPE is analogous to the reservation status provided to Native Americans in the government's effort to empower them. As a result, in part, of their isolation over time, Native Americans currently have some of the highest rates of unemployment, alcoholism, and domestic abuse of any American ethnic or racial group.

The federal blueprint also includes monies to give the poor, inner-city residents of South Central Los Angeles greater choice in deciding what school their children will attend. The encouragement of educational choice among public and private schools—using public dollars—needs to be carefully monitored. Although promoted as the solution to the crisis in public education, poor parents are at risk of being losers in a system where choice is "unchecked." The much-heralded Wisconsin Parental Choice Plan has achieved a modicum of success because this public/private initiative was carefully designed to meet the educational needs of poor children.

The Wisconsin legislature structured this plan to mandate that private educational providers develop their recruitment strategies and curricular offerings specifically to accommodate poor students. Since nonpoor youngsters already had a wide range of educational choice, it was appropriate that poor children—who are the least well served in our educational system—have their interests served. Educational choice should be driven by the needs of the poor if we are to revitalize education in inner cities.

Finally, the Bush administration proposes to spend $500 million on a "Weed and Seed Program," which is designed to rid the community of the violent criminal element and to provide support for programs like Headstart and the Job Corps which are known to benefit the urban disadvantaged and their communities. As it is currently envisioned, however, the program places too much emphasis on the "weed" component and not enough on the "seed" component. Of the $500 million proposed for the program, only $109 million is targeted for "seed" programs like Headstart. With nearly 80% of the proposed funding targeted for the "weed" component, the primary goal of the program is, clearly, to continue the warehousing of large numbers of poor inner-city youth in the penal system.

This, in our view, is a misplaced programmatic focus, as it is ever so clear that harsher jail and prison terms are not deterrents to crime in inner-city areas like South Central Los Angeles. What is needed in South Central Los Angeles, instead, is more "seed" money; to the extent that increased police power is deployed in South Central Los Angeles, it should be via a community policing construct where officers are on the street, interfacing with community residents prior to the commission of a crime.

We are, quite frankly, dubious of the so-called conservative war on poverty and, in particular, of its likely impact in South Central Los Angeles. The federal blueprint, and apparently the local "Rebuild L.A." initiative headed by Mr. Peter Ueberroth as well, is built on the central premise that, if the proper incentives are offered, the private sector will, in fact, play the leading role in the revitalization and redevelopment of South Central Los Angeles. We do not think this is going to happen for the reasons state earlier; the types of governmental incentives currently under consideration in Washington are not high on private businesses' locational priority lists.

In view of these facts, and the social-science evidence is clear on the ineffectiveness of enterprise-zone legislation both in Britain and in 36 states in this country, we firmly believe that what is needed to rebuild South Central Los Angeles is a comprehensive public-works service-employment program, modeled on President Roosevelt's Works Progress Administration program of the 1930s. Jobs to rebuild the infrastructure of South Central Los Angeles can provide meaningful employment for the jobless in the community, including the hard-core disadvantaged, and can be linked to the skilled trades' apprenticeship-training programs.

To incorporate the hard-core disadvantaged into such a program would require a restructuring of the Private Industry Council's Job Training Partnership Act Program (JTPA). The program must dispense with its performance-based approach in training where funding is tied to job placement. This approach does not work for the hard-core disadvantaged because training agencies, under the current structure, have consistently engaged in creaming—recruiting the most "job-ready" segment of the inner-city population—to ensure their continued success and funding. Meanwhile, the hard-core unemployed have received scant attention and educational upgrading.

We are now convinced that a WPA-type initiative, combined with a restructured JTPA program, will go a long way toward resolving the chronic jobless problem, especially among young males of color in the community, and toward rebuilding the infrastructure of South Central Los Angeles.

Such a program would have several goals that would enhance the social and economic viability of South Central Los Angeles. First, it would create meaningful jobs that could provide the jobless with skills transferable to the private sector. Second, it would rebuild a neglected infrastructure, making South Central Los Angeles an attractive place to locate for business and commerce. Finally, and most important, by reconnecting this isolated part of the city to the major arteries of transportation, by building a physical infrastructure that could support the social and cultural life of this richly multicultural area (e.g., museums, public buildings, housing), and by enhancing the ability of community and educational institutions to educate and socialize the young, this plan would go far in providing a sustainable "public space" in the community. For it is our contention, that only when South Central Los Angeles is perceived as a public space that is economically vibrant and socially attractive will the promise of this multicultural community be fulfilled. Thus far, private-sector actions and federal-government programs and proposals have done nothing to bring us nearer to reaching this goal.

CONCLUSIONS

The fires have been extinguished in South Central Los Angeles and other cities, but the anger and rage continue to escalate, and they are likely to reemerge over time to the extent that the underlying political and economic causes are left to fester. While political, business, and civic leaders have rushed to advance old and new strategies and solutions to this latest urban explosion, much of what is being proposed is simply disjointed and/or déjà vu.

Clearly there is a need for additional money to resolve the underlying causes of this urban despair and devastation, but money alone is not enough. Government is constitutionally mandated to ensure "domestic tranquility," but government alone cannot empower poor communities. And although blacks and other people of color have a special role and obligation to rebuild their neighborhoods because they are the majority of the victims and the vandals, they cannot solely assume this burden of responsibility.

What is needed, in our view, is a reconceptualization of problem solving where we meld together, and invest with full potential, those strategies offered from liberals and conservatives, from Democrats and Republicans, and from whites and people of color. Three cities (Milwaukee, Los Angeles, and Detroit, respectively) have served, individually and collectively, as urban laboratories where we have engaged in action research and proffered solutions to the urban problems which have generated violent outbursts.

The contentious state of police/minority-community relations has served as the linchpin of urban unrest in each instance. While relations have improved in several large cities in recent years, the Los Angeles Police Department has been frozen in time. Black and Hispanic males have been particularly brutalized in their encounters with police, the majority of whom are white males. But more disconcerting is the fact that poor, central-city minority communities have become more crime-ridden of late. Thus, minorities find themselves in the ambiguous situation of needing greater police service on the one hand and protection from the excesses of those same services on the other. This contradictory situation had kept relations between these groups at a race/class boiling point.

More police officers are desperately needed in high-crime communities that are disproportionately populated by the poor. Local, state, and federal dollars (federal funds for this initiative are in the crime bill before Congress) need to be allocated quickly toward this end. At present, violent felons are beginning to outnumber police officers in many of our urban centers. As we noted previously, this increase in police power should be deployed via a community policing program. Such an effort can serve to control minor offenses and to build trust between police and community residents. Community policing has evidenced positive results in Detroit and Philadelphia and is showing encouraging signs in Milwaukee and numerous other large and small cities. In addition, the intensive recruitment of minority officers and specific, ongoing (and evaluated) diversity training will further reduce police/minority community tensions. But most important in this effort is enlightened, decisive leadership from the office of the chief, a position of abysmal failure in Los Angeles.

The national administration's initial response to the rebellion was to blame it on deficiencies among the urban poor, particularly on the supposed lack of "family values" and the predominance of female-headed households. This jaundiced view ignores the real sources of the conflict and concentrates instead on the symptomatology of growing up in concentrated-poverty communities where the social resources and assistance necessary to negotiate mainstream society successfully are either totally lacking or insufficient. Thus, the policy implication that needs to be drawn from the rebellion is that, in order to bring the poor and disenfranchised into mainstream society, in order to enhance their acceptance of personal responsibility, and in order to promote personal values consistent with those of the wider society, we must find a way to provide a comprehensive program of meaningful assistance to this population. But clearly, a change in personal values alone, as suggested by some right-wing analysts, will not substitute for job training, job creation, and the removal of racial stereotypes and discrimination. The spatial concentration of contemporary poverty presents significant challenges to policy makers and human-service providers alike. Although numerous programs and initiatives have been instituted to combat these problems, they suffer from three important weaknesses.

First, there is a lack of coordination among programs aimed at improving the life chances of citizens in poor communities. Second, no systematic steps have been taken to evaluate existing efforts, to ensure that the programs are effectively targeting the "hardest to serve," adults with low skills and limited work history, and youth who are teen parents or school dropouts. Third, there is no comprehensive strategy for planning future resource allocations as needs change and as these communities expand in size.

A recent national study of training and employment programs, under the Job Training Partnership Act, revealed that little has been done to address the remedial educational needs of high-school drop-outs and that those with the greatest need for training and employment services are not targeted. However, overcoming these and other program weaknesses is not sufficient to solve these complex problems. A strategic plan is needed to alleviate the social ills associated with concentrated poverty.

There is a need to conduct a comprehensive inventory of agencies and institutions that provide services to populations in poverty areas. We also need to assess and evaluate the service providers' performance in an attempt to identify strengths, weaknesses, and missing links in their service-delivery systems. On the basis of these findings, a strategy should be devised for a more effective and coordinated use of existing resources and for generating new resources to address unmet needs. Finally, we need to propose a plan of action that would encourage development in the 1990s that links together the various program initiatives.

And, most important, representatives of the affected ethnic and racial groups must be in key decision-making roles if these efforts are to achieve success. Citizens of color, individually and through their community, civic and religious institutions, bear a responsibility to promote positive values and lifestyles in their communities and to socialize their youth into the mainstream. But they cannot do this alone.

They cannot be held accountable for the massive plant closings, disinvestments, and exportation of jobs from our urban centers to Third World countries. There must be an equality in status, responsibility, and authority across race and class lines if we are to resolve our urban crises. Government, in a bipartisan fashion, must direct its resources to those programs determined to be successful with the poor, the poor must be permitted to participate in the design of programs for their benefit, and society at all levels must embrace personal responsibility and a commitment to race and gender equity.

How likely are these reforms to be implemented? If one were to analyze the prospects of these changes from the perspective offered in this essay, the answer would not be an optimistic one. However, an important consequence of the rebellion was to shake the very foundation of the taken-for-granted quality of our discourse and practice about race and class in American society. It opens up the opportunity for reassessing positions, organizing constituencies, and collectively engaging issues that have been buried from sight until now. Given these new openings, the Los Angeles urban rebellion of 1992 gives us all the opportunity to work on building a society in which "we can all get along."

SOURCES

The Los Angeles Rebellion: A Photo Essay

What does each photograph reveal about the Los Angeles rebellion? In each case, what did the photographer want to convey? The photographs are presented with original captions.

A California national guardsman stands watch in front of a graffiti-covered wall in Los Angeles April 30 [1992] as two days of rioting tore through the area in the wake of the acquittal of four L.A. police officers in the beating of motorist Rodney King. The graffiti reads "for Rodney King."
Reuters/Bettmann.

Los Angeles police officers train their guns on a suspect in South Central Los Angeles April 30 [1992] as two days of rioting followed the acquittals of four LAPD in the beating of Rodney King.
Reuters/Bettmann.

Looters carry away goods from a store in a riot-torn area of South Central Los Angeles April 30 [1992] as two days of rioting tore through the city in the wake of the acquittal of four L.A. police officers in the beating of motorist Rodney King.
Reuters/Bettmann.

Private Korean security guards ready for patrol duty in Los Angeles' Koreatown district as the jury continues its sixth day of deliberations in the Rodney King beating case, April 15 [1993]. Korean businesses were targeted during the riots following the 1992 trial.
Reuters/Bettmann.

Hunger of Memory
The Education of Richard Rodriguez

Richard Rodriguez

By 1982, when Richard Rodriguez published this autobiographical account, the idea of multiculturalism had emerged to represent a rapidly growing admiration for "cultures." Cultures were arguably infinite in variety: ethnic, racial, based on gender, class, sexual orientation, religion, geography, age, language—you name it. As a way of thinking about the past, multiculturalism helped historians to open up and explore one new field after another, including women's history, working-class history, ethnic history, gay history, and the history of Native

*Americans. In the schools, there were many advocates of bilingualism, an effort
to recognize and nurture the languages and cultures of minority groups.*

*Based on his experiences growing up Hispanic in Sacramento, Califor-
nia, in the 1950s, Rodriguez took a different, and widely debated, position.
What was it that convinced him that bilingualism was a mistaken policy?
Having made his life decision, what did Rodriguez sacrifice? What assumptions governed that decision? Do you think Rodriguez was correct?*

I remember to start with that day in Sacramento—a California now nearly thirty
years past—when I first entered a classroom, able to understand some fifty stray
English words.

The third of four children, I had been preceded to a neighborhood Roman
Catholic school by an older brother and sister. But neither of them had revealed
very much about their classroom experiences. Each afternoon they returned, as
they left in the morning, always together, speaking in Spanish as they climbed the
five steps of the porch. And their mysterious books, wrapped in shopping-bag
paper, remained on the table next to the door, closed firmly behind them.

An accident of geography sent me to a school where all my classmates were
white, many the children of doctors and lawyers and business executives. All my
classmates certainly must have been uneasy on that first day of school—as most
children are uneasy—to find themselves apart from their families in the first institution of their lives. But I was astonished.

The nun said, in a friendly but oddly impersonal voice, 'Boys and girls, this is
Richard Rodriguez,' (I heard her sound out: *Rich-heard Road-ree-guess.*) It was the
first time I had heard anyone name me in English. 'Richard,' the nun repeated more
slowly, writing my name down in her black leather book. Quickly I turned to see
my mother's face dissolve in a watery blur behind the pebbled glass door.

Many years later there is something called bilingual education—a scheme proposed in the late 1960s by Hispanic-American social activists, later endorsed by a
congressional vote. It is a program that seeks to permit non-English-speaking children, many from lower-class homes, to use their family language as the language
of school. (Such is the goal its supporters announce.) I hear them and am forced to
say no: It is not possible for a child—any child—ever to use his family's language
in school. Not to understand this is to misunderstand the public uses of schooling
and to trivialize the nature of intimate life—a family's 'language.'

Memory teaches me what I know of these matters; the boy reminds the adult. I
was a bilingual child, a certain kind—socially disadvantaged—the son of working-
class parents, both Mexican immigrants.

In the early years of my boyhood, my parents coped very well in America.
My father had steady work. My mother managed at home. They were nobody's
victims. Optimism and ambition led them to a house (our home) many blocks
from the Mexican south side of town. We lived among *gringos* and only a block
from the biggest, whitest houses. It never occurred to my parents that they
couldn't live wherever they chose. Nor was the Sacramento of the fifties bent on
teaching them a contrary lesson. My mother and father were more annoyed than

intimidated by those two or three neighbors who tried initially to make us unwelcome. ('Keep your brats away from my sidewalk!') But despite all they achieved, perhaps because they had so much to achieve, any deep feeling of ease, the confidence of 'belonging' in public was withheld from them both. They regarded the people at work, the faces in crowds, as very distant from us. They were the others, *los gringos.* That term was interchangeable in their speech with another, even more telling, *los americanos.*

Supporters of bilingual education today imply that students like me miss a great deal by not being taught in their family's language. What they seem not to recognize is that, as a socially disadvantaged child, I considered Spanish to be a private language. What I needed to learn in school was that I had the right—and the obligation—to speak the public language of *los gringos.* The odd truth is that my first-grade classmates could have become bilingual, in the conventional sense of that word, more easily than I. Had they been taught (as upper-middle-class children are often taught early) a second language like Spanish or French, they could have regarded it simply as that: another public language. In my case such bilingualism could not have been so quickly achieved. What I did not believe was that I could speak a single public language.

Without question, it would have pleased me to hear my teachers address me in Spanish when I entered the classroom. I would have felt much less afraid. I would have trusted them and responded with ease. But I would have delayed—for how long postponed?—having to learn the language of public society. I would have evaded—and for how long could I have afforded to delay?—learning the great lesson of school, that I had a public identity.

Fortunately, my teachers were unsentimental about their responsibility. What they understood was that I needed to speak a public language. So their voices would search me out, asking me questions. Each time I'd hear them, I'd look up in surprise to see a nun's face frowning at me. I'd mumble, not really meaning to answer. The nun would persist, 'Richard, stand up. Don't look at the floor. Speak up. Speak to the entire class, not just to me!' But I couldn't believe that the English language was mine to use. (In part, I did not want to believe it.) I continued to mumble. I resisted the teacher's demands. (Did I somehow suspect that once I learned public language my pleasing family life would be changed?) Silent, waiting for the bell to sound, I remained dazed, diffident, afraid. . . .

Three months. Five. Half a year passed. Unsmiling, ever watchful, my teachers noted my silence. They began to connect my behavior with the difficult progress my older sister and brother were making. Until one Saturday morning three nuns arrived at the house to talk to our parents. Stiffly, they sat on the blue living room sofa. From the doorway of another room, spying the visitors, I noted the incongruity—the clash of two worlds, the faces and voices of school intruding upon the familiar setting of home. I overheard one voice gently wondering, 'Do your children speak only Spanish at home, Mrs. Rodriguez?' While another voice added, 'That Richard especially seems so timid and shy.'

That Rich-heard!

With great tact the visitors continued, 'Is it possible for you and your husband to encourage your children to practice their English when they are home?' Of course, my parents complied. What would they not do for their children's well-being? And how could they have questioned the Church's authority which those women represented? In an instant, they agreed to give up the language (the sounds) that had revealed and accentuated our family's closeness. The moment after the visitors left, the change was observed. *'Ahora,* speak to us *en inglés,'* my father and mother united to tell us. . . .

Again and again in the days following, increasingly angry, I was obliged to hear my mother and father: 'Speak to us *en inglés.' (Speak.)* Only then did I determine to learn classroom English. Weeks after, it happened: One day in school I raised my hand to volunteer an answer. I spoke out in a loud voice. And I did not think it remarkable when the entire class understood. That day, I moved very far from the disadvantaged child I had been only days earlier. The belief, the calming assurance that I belonged in public, had at last taken hold.

Shortly after, I stopped hearing the high and loud sounds of *los gringos.* A more and more confident speaker of English, I didn't trouble to listen to *how* strangers sounded, speaking to me. And there simply were too many English-speaking people in my day for me to hear American accents anymore. Conversations quickened. Listening to persons who sounded eccentrically pitched voices, I usually noted their sounds for an initial few seconds before I concentrated on *what* they were saying. Conversations became content-full. Transparent. Hearing someone's *tone* of voice—angry or questioning or sarcastic or happy or sad—I didn't distinguish it from the words it expressed. Sound and word were thus tightly wedded. At the end of a day, I was often bemused, always relieved, to realize how 'silent,' though crowded with words, my day in public had been. (This public silence measured and quickened the change in my life.)

At last, seven years old, I came to believe what had been technically true since my birth: I was an American citizen.

But the special feeling of closeness at home was diminished by then. Gone was the desperate, urgent, intense feeling of being at home; rare was the experience of feeling myself individualized by family intimates. We remained a loving family, but one greatly changed. No longer so close; no longer bound tight by the pleasing and troubling knowledge of our public separateness. Neither my older brother nor sister rushed home after school anymore. Nor did I. When I arrived home there would often be neighborhood kids in the house. Or the house would be empty of sounds. . . .

The silence at home, however, was finally more than a literal silence. Fewer words passed between parent and child, but more profound was the silence that resulted from my inattention to sounds. At about the time I no longer bothered to listen with care to the sounds of English in public, I grew careless about listening to the sounds family members made when they spoke. Most of the time I heard someone speaking at home and didn't distinguish his sounds from the words people uttered in public. I didn't even pay much attention to my parents' accented and ungrammatical speech. At least not at home. Only when I was with them in public would I grow alert to their accents. Though, even then, their sounds caused me less and less concern. For I was increasingly confident of my own public identity. . . .

Today I hear bilingual educators say that children lose a degree of 'individuality' by becoming assimilated into public society. (Bilingual schooling was popularized in the seventies, that decade when middle-class ethnics began to resist the process of assimilation—the American melting pot.) But the bilingualists simplistically scorn the value and necessity of assimilation. They do not seem to realize that there are *two* ways a person is individualized. So they do not realize that while one suffers a diminished sense of *private* individuality by becoming assimilated into public society, such assimilation makes possible the achievement of *public* individuality.

The bilingualists insist that a student should be reminded of his difference from others in mass society, his heritage. But they equate mere separateness with individuality. The fact is that only in private—with intimates—is separateness from the crowd a prerequisite for individuality. (An intimate draws me apart, tells me that I am unique, unlike all others.) In public, by contrast, full individuality is achieved, paradoxically, by those who are able to consider themselves members of the crowd. Thus it happened for me: Only when I was able to think of myself as an American, no longer an alien in *gringo* society, could I seek the rights and opportunities necessary for full public individuality. The social and political advantages I enjoy as a man result from the day that I came to believe that my name, indeed, is *Rich-heard Road-ree-guess.* It is true that my public society today is often impersonal. (My public society is usually mass society.) Yet despite the anonymity of the crowd and despite the fact that the individuality I achieve in public is often tenuous—because it depends on my being one in a crowd—I celebrate the day I acquired my new name. Those middle-class ethnics who scorn assimilation seem to me filled with decadent self-pity, obsessed by the burden of public life. Dangerously, they romanticize public separateness and they trivialize the dilemma of the socially disadvantaged.

My awkward childhood does not prove the necessity of bilingual education. My story discloses instead an essential myth of childhood—inevitable pain. If I rehearse here the changes in my private life after my Americanization, it is finally to emphasize the public gain. The loss implies the gain: The house I returned to each afternoon was quiet. Intimate sounds no longer rushed to the door to greet me. There were other noises inside. The telephone rang. Neighborhood kids ran past the door of the bedroom where I was reading my schoolbooks—covered with shopping-bag paper. Once I learned public language, it would never again be easy for me to hear intimate family voices. More and more of my day was spent hearing words. But that may only be a way of saying that the day I raised my hand in class and spoke loudly to an entire roomful of faces, my childhood started to end.

The New, New Immigration

The "new" immigration refers to the great wave of immigrants from southern and eastern Europe—Italians, Slavs, Russians, Poles—who came to the United States between 1880 and 1915. What we have called the "new, new" immigration was partly a result of the Hart-Cellar Act of 1965. This law abolished most of the quotas based on national origins that had been at the heart of U.S. immigration law since the 1920s. The new law gave preference to the immediate relatives of U.S. citizens and permanent resident aliens, encouraged political refugees, and imposed quotas on western hemisphere countries. As a result, the share of foreign-born persons in the United States rose each year after 1970, reaching almost 8 percent in 1990.

Use the graphs in this section to explore further the "new, new" immigration. What conclusions can you draw about U.S. immigration in the twentieth century? about the role of the Hart-Cellar Act? about the content of the post-1965 immigration? Do you think recent immigration patterns had anything to do with the Rodney King/Los Angeles rebellion? Does anything here lead you to believe that immigration should be restricted?

Rate of Immigration by Decade, 1821–1990

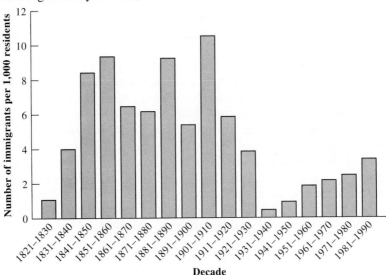

The materials on immigration in this chapter are from Reed Ueda, *Postwar Immigrant America*, Copyright © 1994. Reprinted with permission of St. Martin's Press, Incorporated.

Immigrants Admitted as Immediate Relatives of U.S. Citizens, 1970–1990

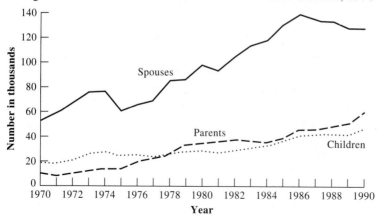

Immigrants Admitted to the United States by Occupational Group, 1976–1990

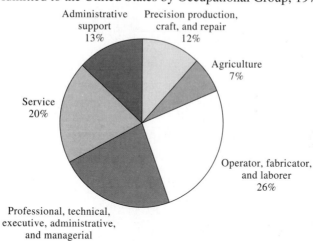

Immigrants Admitted by Region of Birth, Selected Years, 1955–1990

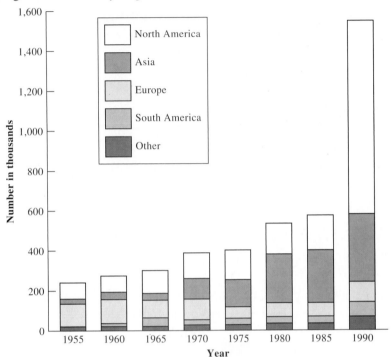

Population Growth of Asian and Hispanic Ethnic Groups, 1980–1990

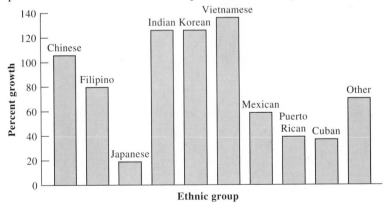

SUGGESTIONS FOR VIEWING AND LISTENING

Blade Runner (1982)
Sci-fi *noir* set in the bleak Los Angeles of 2019.

Do the Right Thing (1989)
Koreans, Italians, and African-Americans trying—and failing—to work things out in Brooklyn's Bedford-Stuyvesant.

Grand Canyon (1993)
New Age ways of thinking transcend the social realities of contemporary Los Angeles.

Boyz 'N the Hood (1991)
Gangs and drugs in L.A.'s black ghetto.

Los Lobos, "Will the Wolf Survive?" (1984)
Chicano band from Los Angeles sings metaphorically about endangered species.

War, "Low Rider" (1975)
African-American group from Long Beach, with a song about Chicano car customizers.

John Cougar Mellencamp, "Small Town" (1985)
Postindustrial nostalgia.

CHAPTER 13

The New World Order

It was an extraordinary moment. In 1989, nearly a half-century after Winston Churchill announced that an "iron curtain" had descended over the European continent, the cold war ended. Appropriately, it ended first where it had begun, in central and eastern Europe. In Poland, voters crossed out names of Communist candidates and gave Lech Walesa's political action union, Solidarity, a thunderous majority. In Hungary, a new generation of students forced deliberations on a new constitution and helped bring into being a new republic. In Berlin, balls and chains smashed into the wall that since 1961 had divided one of the great cities of the world and come to symbolize the cold war itself. And by the end of 1991, the Soviet Union had disintegrated into more than a dozen independent states. First with curiosity, and then with disbelief, Americans had watched these events unfold, night after night, as images on television screens. They were finally able to understand that a cold war undertaken, in the words of Dean Acheson, "to create and to maintain an environment in which the American experiment in liberty could flourish and exist," was over. Except for China, where a geriatric oligarchy continued to hold the reins of power, and for Cuba, where Fidel Castro remained in control, Communism was dead. The West had won.

With victory came opportunity. Generations of Americans who had grown up practicing air raid drills, building bomb shelters in their basements, or wondering if the presence of Soviet missiles in Cuba would mean nuclear war, looked forward to the possibility of life without fear of nuclear holocaust. Those who had lived through the postwar Red Scare or witnessed the government's use of state agencies against political dissidents in the 1960s anticipated the dismantling of the enormous security apparatus that had grown up to keep the United States, and much of the rest of the world, free from Communism. There was talk of the "peace dividend," as Americans imagined alternatives uses for the billions upon billions of dollars that had each year been spent to create and operate the largest military establishment in the history of the world. Freed from the necessity of opposing Communism at every turn, of living defensively, the nation would now be free to pursue a foreign policy based on its own ideals.

A world accustomed to American political and moral leadership was startled to discover that there was no plan. There was to be no reassessment of America's military strength, no discussion of the necessity for nuclear weapons control, no dismantling of the Central Intelligence Agency or other security bureaucracies, and no thoughtful reassessment of foreign policy alternatives. The peace dividend proved a chimera; by the mid-1990s, a Republican-led Congress was cutting social programs rather than committing the nation to new ones. The only focus of America's future was economic growth, pursued globally through free trade or regionally through free trade zones such as that created by the North American Free Trade Agreement (1994). George Bush's grandiose call for a "new world order" was little more than a shopkeeper's agenda for a stable business environment.

Free trade required a stable world order in which players accepted assigned roles and statuses. It was too much to expect. One of the first challenges to post–cold war stability came from the Middle East, where Iraq, led by Saddam Hussein, threatened Western access to the rich petroleum deposits of the region. Another, more serious challenge arose in the former Yugoslavia, where the end of Soviet hegemony produced a complex and bloody struggle between Serbs, Croats, Bosnians, Muslims, and Christians. In a conflict in which "ethnic cleansing" returned to the vocabulary of government leaders and religion was the basis for persecution, the single-minded American concern with free trade seemed worse than no policy at all. A third challenge to the "new world order" emerged on the domestic front, where efforts to dismantle the cold war military infrastructure—to reallocate resources from military to civilian purposes—revealed how much postwar economic growth had come to depend on military expenditures. Both George Bush and Bill Clinton began the process of reducing the size of the military, but the political and economic costs have been, and continue to be, considerable.

To the American hope that the end of the cold war would bring the triumph of the "new world order," there was a final challenge, perhaps the most important of all: the economic condition of the United States. The United States had won the cold war, but at a staggering cost to its domestic economy: it had failed to modernize its infrastructure, ignored declining productivity, and used entitlement programs to put societal problems on hold instead of amending the conditions that made for permanently disadvantaged classes. In addition, a series of huge budget deficits rolled up in the 1980s made the United States the world's largest debtor nation. As a debtor, the country was beholden to its creditors—investors from Japan and Germany, Saudi Arabia and Switzerland—and dependent on a booming world economy to fund past, present, and future expenditures. There was in all of this a kind of balance, or reciprocity: America provided the world order, the structure and philosophy under which the world economy functioned; successful economies supported the American debt.

Although the "new world order" had the ring of a major shift in policy, it came with a set of constraints that sharply limited the nation's options. To be sure, Democrats and Republicans took different approaches. Clinton and his socially progressive wife, Hillary, spent much of the first two years of his presidency in an unsuccessful effort to convince the nation to invest in the health of its citizenry through a program of national insurance; the Republicans took the opportunity to blame the nation's economic woes on welfare and the welfare state and to call for huge cuts in social expenditures. Yet both parties agreed on the key ingredients of the "new world order": free trade, economic growth, and deficit reduction. Whether Republican or Democratic, the nation's political leadership had failed at the crucial task of producing a foreign policy commensurate with that glorious moment in 1989—when the cold war ended, and the "new world order" was to begin.

INTERPRETIVE ESSAY

Ronald Steel

Temptations of a Superpower

The "American Century" heralded by Time *publisher Henry Luce in 1941 turned out to be a half-century effort to impede the growth of Communism. In defense of a free world, most Americans accepted a policy of expansion and global military intervention that was costly and, in the case of the Vietnam war, socially divisive.*

The end of the cold war brought mixed reactions, even a kind of national disorientation. In Washington, there was a good deal of jubilation and self-congratulation, and many gave credit for the victory to the Reagan adminis-tration. They argued that Star Wars, by raising the spending ante, was the proverbial straw that broke the Soviet Union's back. Foreign observers, both European and Soviet, gave more credit to the diplomacy of West German Chancellor Willie Kohl and to Soviet leader Mikhail Gorbachev for the blood-less collapse of the Communist system, while proposing that both the Soviet Union and the United States were brought to their knees (in the words of his-torian Paul Kennedy) by a severe case of imperial overstretch.

The euphoria over the collapse of Communism was limited by the revela-tion that the end of the cold war had removed the most important rationale for America's policy of global intervention. Without an "evil empire" to fight, Americans could no longer conceive of any compelling reason to support an interventionist posture abroad. Expenditures that had once seemed entirely appropriate in a cold war context—for military bases abroad, for foreign aid, for exchange programs, for costly weapons—now seemed burdensome obliga-tions for a nation deeply in debt.

Cutting back would be difficult. Unlike Great Britain in 1947, or France in 1954, the United States did not have a formal empire that it could disman-tle in order to place itself on the path to fiscal probity. To cut back on the costs of its own version of empire would mean rethinking its role in the world order—the "new world order" on which it was very much dependent.

At this critical juncture in the nation's history, Americans reflected on a variety of issues. What had been the price of victory in the cold war? How should the United States respond to the new circumstances? Could, and should, the nation continue its interventionist role? Or should it turn to some-thing resembling isolationism? If the United States was not to be the world's policeman, then who should be?

More than forty years ago Dean Acheson, in retirement as secretary of state, lectured the British that they had "lost an empire but not yet found a role." The United States, he made it clear, had taken over their old role of being the world's chief banker, umpire, and police enforcer. Now it was up to them to scale back their ambitions to accord with their financial means.

His words were tough, but not inaccurate. British officials thought that he was rude, and spent the next decades trying to ignore the truth of his observation. What Acheson was telling them was simply that the world had moved on, other powers had come to the fore, and though they were a great nation, they could no longer run the show. They would have to adjust. Resisting the reality of their altered situation, often filled with nostalgic bluster, they have been searching for a role ever since.

Today we find ourselves in a similar situation. Yet unlike Britain in 1945, we have not been superseded by a more powerful challenger. It is not as though someone new has come along to beat us at the old game. If that were the case it might be enough simply to try harder. The problem is that the game itself has changed.

With the passing of the Cold War, the United States no longer enjoys either its old authority or its freedom of action. It needs the Europeans and Japanese, who were once so dependent on American protection, to buy the Treasury bonds that finance its persistent deficits. American presidents are loath to mount expensive military operations, as the Gulf war revealed, unless others help pay for them. And they do not want to get bogged down in open-ended "peacekeeping"—or, even less, "peace*making*"—forays into unruly regions unless others share responsibility, and also blame when things go awry.

If the end of the Cold War has rendered old rivalries obsolete, it has done the same for old power equations as well. Military might is now only one component of national power, and not nearly as great a one as it used to be. While the president can call out the army or unleash the CIA, these are not likely to be of much help in reducing Japanese trade barriers or taming the deficit.

The forum of competition among the major powers has, at least for the time being, moved from the military to the economic realm. It is no longer fought over pretensions of ideology, no longer governed by delicate military balances, and no longer conducted through military interventions. Increasingly it is one of technology, finance, trade, and innovation. In this realm we have seen old foes, like Russia, become alarmingly weak dependents, while our Cold War allies are becoming increasingly formidable trade rivals.

This dramatic shifting of the world power balance will not be easy for an American economy distorted by a half century of reliance on military spending, nor for an American public now deprived of an enemy to serve as reason for its sacrifices. Above all it will not be easy for American political elites which had come to take for granted that they had both the right and the duty to lead the rest of the world.

With the demise of our Soviet adversary and the breakdown of the old alliances, we are, in one sense, reverting to earlier patterns of international life: regional wars, power balances, coalitions, and spheres of influence. At the same time, traditional cultural and economic barriers among nations are being steadily eroded as an embryonic international society takes form.

The fragmentation of what only a few years ago seemed to be a politically stable, if divided, world is proceeding with frightening speed. The Cold War has given way, on the one hand, to an ever more integrated global economy of industrialized nations, and on the other hand to an ancient political primitivism marked by blood feuds, systemic breakdowns, and even wars of all against all.

Everywhere the nation-state is under assault—either from those who consider it anachronistic and would merge it into larger entities, such as the Europeans are attempting, or from those who decry it as a prison of tribes and nationalities and would smash it into ethnically "purer" parts. Sometimes in a single place both movements are going on simultaneously.

Yet even as the old order crumbles, the United States, from a military point of view, has never been more secure. For the first time in half a century we face no serious security threat from abroad. We are as near to being invulnerable as a nation can get. "There are no significant hostile alliances," Republican hopeful and former defense secretary Dick Cheney has stated. "The strongest and most capable countries in the world remain our friends."

Yet policymakers continue to be preoccupied by notions of threat and credibility. Even Bill Clinton, who cut his political teeth on opposition to the Vietnam war, periodically succumbs to the Cold War vocabulary. In announcing the American withdrawal from the ill-fated expedition to Somalia, he declared that it must be gradual and, in effect, disguised as a victory. Otherwise, he explained, "our own credibility with friends and allies would be damaged" and "our leadership in world affairs would be undermined."

The term "credibility" once meant that we wanted the Russians to take our resolve seriously, lest they miscalculate and set a dire train of actions in motion: like the Cuban missile crisis. What does it mean today—and directed toward friends and allies? "Credibility" was ostensibly what we were trying to demonstrate in Vietnam.

The notion of credibility, like that of leadership, is linked to the way that the foreign policy establishment defines security. By "national security" it means not merely the physical protection of the nation, or the welfare and liberties of its citizens. Beyond that it means the defense of what it calls a "security environment." The special quality of such an environment is that it can be defined as big as one wishes. In the vagueness of the term lies its utility.

The environment can be one's own country, or the countries that surround it, or the countries and even oceans and air spaces that lie beyond that, or, for that matter, the entire world. A security environment, if defined large enough, embraces everything. This is what happened during the Cold War when the United States, facing a challenger of global ambitions, constructed a global definition of its own security.

Yet we were not the first to define security by the length of our reach or the depths of our pockets. The Victorians, as two British historians have recounted in a masterly study of the British Empire, started out with the intention of protecting their core interests overseas. Yet the defense of their colonies inevitably drew them into ever-wider circles of engagement.

To protect their investments in India they had to guard the Himalayas and the frontiers of Central Asia. To ensure safe transit for their ships they had also to control the Suez Canal. This meant policing Egypt, on whose soil the Canal was located, and the nearby countries of the Middle East, which could pose potential problems for the Canal. Ultimately, as the concentric rings grew ever-larger, this drew them as far afield as the east coast and even the interior of Africa.

Unfortunately the peoples of these areas were not always content with British rule. This obliged the British to police them, and also to provide benefits that would keep the natives happy. They became policemen imposing order on these areas, and eventually in lands adjacent to them, from which disorder spilled.

Soon they were engaged in tribal conflicts in the heart of Africa—ostensibly to protect their position in India. Since each link was considered vital, the chain got longer and longer until they were running an African empire.

In the end they never felt secure, no matter how much they controlled. The "frontiers of insecurity," in the historians' telling phrase, expanded indefinitely. It was governed not by any explicit definition of vital interest—nothing they could explain coherently to a concerned citizen. Rather it was governed by the ability of imperial England, then at the height of its pride and wealth, to project power.

Small nations, by contrast, take a more parsimonious approach to threats than do great ones. They first define their interests narrowly. Then they respond to situations which are threatening to those interests. The Swedes, for example, are greatly concerned with hostile submarines in the Baltic and have impressive measures to deal with them. They are not at all troubled by the political complexions of warring factions in Southeast Asia.

Powerful nations such as ours, particularly when they define themselves as "superpowers," are different. They turn the equation around. They perceive all unwelcome changes as threats. Then they declare that their "interests" require them to counter such "threats."

The result is to make interests universal. This was a hallmark of the American approach to the Cold War. Places became "crisis areas" when their governments were under attack from the left, or when their rulers threatened to "go communist" unless "saved" by large infusions of American dollars and military equipment. Under this definition, dozens, and even scores, of nations were deemed to be "vital" to our interests, and to some of them, such as South Korea and South Vietnam, we even sent our soldiers to fight in their wars.

During the Cold War the ultimate threat, however broadly defined, was the Soviet Union. This was what dictated most of our military strategy, the mission of our forces, the size of our defense budgets. When it disappeared, the logic of the strategy went with it. A new blueprint for American strategy had to be devised. Naturally it was assumed that, in the absence of an enemy, defense budgets would shrink and that there would be a "peace dividend."

In the fall of 1993 the Pentagon produced what it called a "bottom up" review of U.S. defense plans. Frankly admitting that, with the demise of communism, "the threat . . . is gone," it recognized that "in the post Cold War period perhaps [the] most important set of dangers that U.S. strategy must confront is economic."

Nonetheless, the planners were willing to cut less than seven percent from the five-year force plan devised during the Cold War. They would make some cuts in the army, but increase the size of the Marines, and retain twelve aircraft carrier battle groups originally designed to keep open sea lanes, even though, in the document's words, "without the Soviet navy, no one challenges us for control of the seas."

To provide what it calls "reassurance" for Cold War allies, the Clinton administration, like the Bush administration before it, plans to keep at least 100,000 American troops in Europe and maintain forces permanently in Korea, Japan, and the Persian Gulf. Some $90 billion a year is earmarked for the protection of Gulf potentates—a sum that raises serious questions about the real price of "cheap" oil.

While the current defense budget of $253 billion is down fractionally from the previous year, it is still 85 percent of the average Cold War level. This makes it as large as that of all the other nations of the world *combined.* Of the total, about half is geared for the defense of Cold War allies in Europe and Asia against the now-defunct Soviet Union.

Given the collapse of the nation that inspired the military budgets of the Cold War, what justifies them now? According to the Pentagon planners, it is the threat of "aggression by major regional powers with interests antithetical to our own," or smaller conflicts driven by "ethnic or religious animosities." To cope with such potential problems, the planners propose that the United States "be able to win two major regional conflicts that occur nearly simultaneously."

Which particular regional conflicts does the Pentagon have in mind? One possibility is a threat to the oil kingdoms. But neither Iran nor Iraq, the leading candidates, is a major power, and the greatest danger to the ruling families of these countries comes from dissidents bearing the Koran. Another area of contention is the two Koreas. Yet even should North Korea develop nuclear weapons, South Korea remains covered by the American nuclear guarantee. Should conventional war break out again, South Korea has more than ample manpower to deal with its northern cousins: it has twice the population of the North and ten times the wealth. In any case, rather than war between the two Koreas we will more likely see reunification, with the South taking over the North (and its nuclear capacity) just as West Germany took over the East.

Since the nations of Europe are more secure from aggression than they have been in sixty years, and since neither Russia nor any Asian power challenges vital American interests, it is hard to refute the conclusion of one analyst that the Pentagon's "planning 'requirements' have been invented to justify the forces and structures we have rather than to cope with the world we face." Indeed, this view seems to be supported, however inadvertently, even by defense secretary William Perry. In presenting the new strategy to the House armed services committee in the spring of 1994, he suggested that the Congressmen not fret about a gap between the two-war strategy and our ability to execute it, since "it's an entirely implausible scenario that we'd fight two wars at once."

Why do we need Cold War defense budgets when there is no more Cold War? One answer lies, of course, in the desire of bureaucracies to defend and perpetuate themselves. The military is no different in this regard than private industry or any other branch of government. It is well known that the first law of bureaucracy is survival.

Yet the rationale can also be found in politics and strategy. The Cold War was not merely a struggle against communism, but an international system. The United

States dominated that system through a network of regional alliances. Other industrialized nations that might have been tempted to act independently instead chose to defer to Washington. In an age of contending superpowers it was prudent to ally with the strongest and most friendly.

Absent a menacing enemy, that alliance system is difficult to maintain. Countries like Japan, China, and Germany have the potential to be major military powers. This would not only threaten American leadership, but (at least theoretically) increase the possibility of regional conflict in Europe and Asia.

What does this have to do with the U.S. defense budget? Everything. This is because political strategists have all along been concerned not only with containing communism, but with creating an integrated global system, resting on a political and an economic base, orchestrated from Washington. The end of the Cold War has loosened the cement holding that system together, but not its underlying rationale.

That rationale was made explicit in a Pentagon planning document that was leaked to the press in 1992. In blunt language, not intended for a general audience, its authors argued that the United States must "discourage the advanced industrial nations from challenging our leadership or even aspiring to a larger regional or global role."

The explanation for this immodest ambition is that any effort by other industrialized nations, even friendly ones, to exert more influence in their regions might lead to competition and strife with their neighbors. This could cause political instability, inhibit the flow of global trade, and upset a host of cooperative international agreements.

Thus the argument is that American hegemony is ultimately good for everyone, even though it may involve a heavy burden for the United States. This is ostensibly America's duty. Or as the Pentagon strategists argue, the United States must "retain the preeminent responsibility for addressing . . . those wrongs which threaten not only our interests, but those of allies or friends, or which could seriously unsettle international relations."

This is at least part of the explanation of a paradox: why the end of the Cold War does not mean the end of Cold War military budgets, or why the disappearance of the Soviet Union and the conversion of China to capitalism presumably do not reduce the specter of global threats.

Whereas the American arsenal was once directed primarily against the Soviet Union, it would now be directed against everybody. Whereas it was once intended to contain communism, its goal now is nothing less than the containment of global disorder. If communism could at least be localized, disorder is epidemic everywhere. Thus it is not surprising that it should require forces comparable to those used to hold off the Soviet Union. The suppression of disorder requires an enormous array of weapons capable of engagement against wrongdoers everywhere.

The suffocation of disorder—or, to use the new terminology, the creation of a "stable international environment"—has now replaced the out-of-date containment doctrine as the national security establishment's formula for the 1990s.

It was not easy for the Pentagon to explain to the Europeans and the Japanese why they must be discouraged from "challenging our leadership or even aspiring to a larger global or regional role." For this reason embarrassed officials later put out a sanitized version of the report. Yet the central argument remained in place. It was in everyone's interest that the United States smother conflict everywhere, and thereby ostensibly remove the need for other major powers to build up their armed forces.

There are a number of problems with this strategy, even in terms of its own dubious premises.

First, does the prosperity of the industrialized nations really depend on a tranquil international environment? History would seem to demonstrate the opposite. Nations are rarely so prosperous as when engaged in war or the preparation for war. Factories are humming full blast, unemployment lines disappear, contentious ethnic and social groups are joined in common purpose.

It was the Korean war and the subsequent rearmament drive that lifted the cloud of another depression from the American economy. That same war persuaded American occupation officials to remove the restrictions on Japanese cartels and war criminals so that they could provide the equipment the United States needed to fight in Korea. That in turn set in motion the reindustrialization that has become the Japanese juggernaut. Similarly, West Europe's economy moved into high gear with the launching of the Cold War.

Second, if we are the international cop on the beat, how do we decide which nation to protect? Let us assume that China and Japan get into a fight, or China and Russia. How do we decide which one should win? We trade with all of them. They trade with each other. When we take one side, we alienate the other. The alienated side will not see us as a friendly arbitrator, but as an enemy. It will not feel "reassured," but threatened. Instead of being a "regional balancer and honest broker," to use a Pentagon official's phrase, we will have become a meddlesome belligerent.

Third, why would any major nation turn over its military security—that is, the defense of its vital interests—to another nation in the absence of a compelling reason to do so? We certainly would not. No nation normally relinquishes that power, no matter how friendly its protector might be, except in grave emergencies. Even during the Cold War, Britain and France kept their separate nuclear arsenals, despite our guarantees to protect them.

Fourth, in an effort to "reassure" its trading partners by punishing "malefactors," Washington can make them more anxious. For example, in 1994 the United States put itself on a collision course with North Korea over that nation's nuclear program. Fearful that the North Koreans might be producing a bomb, Washington pushed for economic sanctions and skirted military confrontation. The nations most affected, however—South Korea and Japan—were far more cautious. They feared that North Korea might collapse, flooding them with refugees, or that, feeling cornered, it might lash out irrationally. We sought to be tough to "reassure" our allies. They warned that we were making the situation worse. When the reassurer rocks the boat, who offers reassurance?

Fifth, playing international gendarme is an expensive proposition that the world's biggest debtor nation can ill afford. It is also a dangerous one. It means that the United States will be perpetually involved in quarrels around the globe in which it has no direct interest, and over causes it will often misunderstand. It was precisely the fear of being dragged into such a conflict, and not being able to emerge without frustration, casualties, and dissension at home, that stayed the hand of the Clinton administration in Bosnia.

The "reassurance" policy so appealing to strategists ignores the fact that our major trading partners have political as well as economic ambitions. They have no objection to being defended by the United States. But they also want the freedom to make decisions and to undertake actions to which the U.S. government might be opposed. They need to be able to act independently of the "friendly superpower," and even in defiance of it.

For this they need strong armed forces of their own not subject to American control. Thus we see that Japan and China are significantly increasing their military capabilities. This is not because they do not trust the United States, but because they want freedom of action to pursue their political goals. Pentagon planners may argue that they are doing others a favor by exercising a friendly hegemony. But in a world of rising regional powers—Japan, China, a German-led Europe, and ultimately a revived Russia—it will not be delegated that authority.

An attempt to police the world, even if intended to be in "everybody's best interests," would have the effect of undermining American interests. Cold War defense budgets have starved our civilian industries of investment funds and increased the power of trade rivals enjoying the benefits of our military umbrella. As they grow relatively stronger, we grow relatively weaker. As illustration, simply consider our relationship with Japan. The end result, as analyst Benjamin C. Schwartz has explained, is that the system we are trying to protect ultimately creates powerful rivals that will weaken our control and replace us—just as we replaced Britain.

The cost of "reassuring" allies does not come cheap. Currently it costs $100 billion a year for Europe, and another $46 billion for Japan and South Korea. Today more than 50 percent of all discretionary federal spending is still devoted to defense, even in the absence of an enemy. While other nations invest for production, the United States borrows for consumption—and in the process becomes ever further indebted to the trade rivals whose interests it determinedly seeks to protect.

For most Americans the defense budget is a mystery, and foreign policy elites would just as soon keep it that way. Patriotic appeals to national defense keep appropriations high. So does the fact that millions of jobs are linked to Pentagon contracts. Despite whatever theories strategists may spin, the defense budget is now, to a large degree, a jobs program. It is also a cash cow that provides billions of dollars for corporations, lobbyists, and special interest groups. Even Bill Clinton, championing "new priorities" during his campaign, pledged to build two weapons systems the Bush administration wanted to cut: the $2.5 billion Seawolf submarine and the tilt-rotor V-22 plane.

All during the Cold War it was considered unpatriotic to question the size of the defense budget. The habit lingers. The public, fearful about jobs and mystified by geopolitical theories, defers to the strategists. The Congress defers to the special interest groups. And the White House, seeking to avoid enemies, defers to everyone.

The defense budget flows from both habit and strategy. To pare it down to size for a world without serious enemies for the United States means to break the habit and confront the strategy. To ask whether we still need to devote so much of our resources to defense is to ask whether the strategy we pursue makes sense in the post-communist, economically competitive world.

The decision has to rest not only on what we can afford. In fact, we can afford a great deal. At times in the past we spent a far bigger chunk of our GNP on defense than today. And we happily throw away tens of billions of dollars for cat food, cologne, and colas. When the nation is in real danger we spend what we must.

But it is not now in danger. Thus the real question is how much defense we need, and against what. This cannot be answered until we figure out what our interests are. Only then can we determine what kind of foreign policy we ought to have. To do that we have to get rid of a considerable amount of intellectual baggage.

SOURCES

Contract with America

Newt Gingrich, Dick Armey, and House Republicans

The election of 1994 transformed the political landscape. For the first time since 1932, congressional leadership passed from Democrats to Republicans. The change signaled the growing belief that government (especially the federal government) was the cause of many of the nation's most pressing problems, including the increasing cost of social services, the declining wages of working-class white men, and rising rates of crime and teenage pregnancy. In 1932, very different problems had led to the election of Democrat Franklin Delano Roosevelt and to the New Deal. In 1994, they brought the Republicans—and their Contract with America—to power.

The Contract with America was the result of a massive Republican effort, involving dozens of members of the House of Representatives, to give Republicans a banner under which they could rally in the 1994 campaign, and to show America that a new spirit animated the Grand Old Party. To emphasize its self-proclaimed status as a contract, on September 27, 1994, hundreds of members of Congress gathered on the steps of the Capitol in a public ceremony and signed the document. House Majority Leader Newt Gingrich (R.-Georgia) was the organizing force behind the ceremony and the contract, although others, including Rep. John Boehner (R.-Ohio) and Peter Hoekstra (R.-Michigan), also helped plan strategy. When both houses of Congress were won by Republicans, Gingrich became Speaker of the House and the most influential politician in the country, and the contract (with 367 Republican signatures) became a powerful lever of political action.

The contract's intent was to restate the GOP's principles and vision and to create a sense of trust between voters and their elected representatives. The following section of the Contract with America lists and describes the measures that Republicans believed were necessary. What is the philosophical focus of the contract? How does it differ from earlier reform efforts such as the Great Society? How did Republicans intend to change government? What was their objection to bureaucracy? According to the contract, what are the most important problems in American society?

On the first day of the 104th Congress, the new Republican majority will immediately pass the following major reforms, aimed at restoring the faith and trust of the American people in their government:

First, require all laws that apply to the rest of the country also apply equally to the Congress;

Second, select a major independent auditing firm to conduct a comprehensive audit of Congress for waste, fraud, or abuse;

Third, cut the number of House committees, and cut committee staff by one-third;

Fourth, limit the terms of all committee chairs;

Fifth, ban the casting of proxy votes in committee;

Sixth, require committee meetings to be open to the public;

Seventh, require a three-fifths majority vote to pass a tax increase;

Eighth, guarantee an honest accounting of our federal budget by implementing zero baseline budgeting.

Thereafter, within the first hundred days of the 104th Congress, we shall bring to the House Floor the following bills, each to be given full and open debate, each to be given a clear and fair vote, and each to be immediately available this day for public inspection and scrutiny.

The Fiscal Responsibility Act

- A balanced budget/tax limitation amendment and a legislative line-item veto to restore fiscal responsibility to an out-of-control Congress, requiring them to live under the same budget constraints as families and businesses.

The Taking Back Our Streets Act

- An anti-crime package including stronger truth in sentencing, "good faith" exclusionary rule exemptions, effective death penalty provisions, and cuts in social spending from this summer's crime bill to fund prison construction and additional law enforcement to keep people secure in their neighborhoods and kids safe in their schools.

The Personal Responsibility Act

- Discourage illegitimacy and teen pregnancy by prohibiting welfare to minor mothers and denying increased AFDC for additional children while on welfare, cut spending for welfare programs, and enact a tough two-years-and-out provision with work requirements to promote individual responsibility.

The Family Reinforcement Act

- Child support enforcement, tax incentives for adoption, strengthening rights of parents in their children's education, stronger child pornography laws, and an elderly dependent care tax credit to reinforce the central role of families in American society.

The American Dream Restoration Act

- A $500-per-child tax credit, begin repeal of the marriage tax penalty, and creation of American Dream Savings Accounts to provide middle-class tax relief.

The National Security Restoration Act

- No U.S. troops under UN command and restoration of the essential parts of our national security funding to strengthen our national defense and maintain our credibility around the world.

The Senior Citizens Fairness Act

- Raise the Social Security earnings limit, which currently forces seniors out of the workforce, repeal the 1993 tax hikes on Social Security benefits, and provide tax incentives for private long-term care insurance to let older Americans keep more of what they have earned over the years.

The Job Creation and Wage Enhancement Act

- Small business incentives, capital gains cut and indexation, neutral cost recovery, risk assessment/cost-benefit analysis, strengthening of the Regulatory Flexibility Act and unfunded mandate reform to create jobs and raise worker wages.

The Common Sense Legal Reforms Act

- "Loser pays" laws, reasonable limits on punitive damages, and reform of product liability laws to stem the endless tide of litigation.

The Citizen Legislature Act

- A first-ever vote on term limits to replace career politicians with citizen legislators.

Global Symbolism

Every era has its symbols or icons. The 1920s are associated with art deco, slim (near pencil-like representations of) women, representations of conspicuous wealth; the 1930s convey images of the depression: people selling apples on corners, men in lines waiting for jobs, boys riding freight trains; the 1940s are closely tied to World War II: combat, loss, A-bombs, family reunions; the 1950s with rock 'n' roll, suburbia, and poodle skirts. Images are kept alive for later generations through media such as film, art, and graphics.

Political graphics is a medium experiencing a period of renewed interest. This art form has been in existence for centuries, renewing itself during periods when people are questioning the "rules of the game." Graphics use simple line drawings of cultural symbols to create a mass idiom. If they are to become global idiom in the post–cold war world, the symbols must be simple and easy to recognize.

Two examples illustrate the point. One graphic is a protest against the Gulf war in 1990. What cemeteries does this graphic remind you of? What audience does it target? How many people would "see" this message? The second graphic protests the public silence over AIDS and its impact. What symbols does it use? How many people would understand its significance?

George Bush, "The Education President," by *Guerilla Girls—Conscience of the Art World.*

Silence = Death: Vote
ACT UP/NEW YORK.

The New World Order Comes to America: A Statistical Essay

Americans are inundated daily with polls, news, and data. Despite the sheer volume of information, recent studies have shown that Americans, though drowning in numbers and information, have very little real appreciation for the actual conditions under which their fellow citizens live.

The following statistics allow you to draw your own conclusions about life in the United States. Who is represented in these charts? How do the categories compare with one another? After examining these materials, how would you describe American society?

Gross National Product, by Country, 1985–1991
(in constant 1991 dollars)

	1985	1989	1990	1991	Per Capita
	(in billions of dollars)				(constant 1991 dollars)
Canada	501	576	571	563	20,840
China (mainland)	965	1,347	1,424	1,528	1,327
France	1,019	1,158	1,182	1,191	20,900
Germany*	1,313	1,461	1,531	1,586	19,830
Japan	2,584	3,082	3,242	3,386	27,300
Saudi Arabia	118	101	114	118	7,151
South Africa	94	104	104	105	2,573
Soviet Union*	2,642	2,870	2,767	2,531	8,639
Switzerland	214	239	242	242	35,590
United Kingdom	887	1,023	1,025	1,002	17,400
United States	5,057	5,714	5,765	5,695	22,550

*Germany in 1991 includes East Germany; Soviet Union in 1991 is estimated.

Child Poverty Rates, 1979–1986
(Selected countries)

Countries/Year	Percentage of All Children (under 17) Regardless of Living Arrangements
U.S. '79	14.7
'85	20.4
Canada '81	10.2
'87	9.3
Australia '81	8.6
'85	9.0
Sweden '81	2.1
'87	1.5
West Germany '79	1.3
'84	2.8
Netherlands '83	4.0
'87	3.8
France '79	4.7
'84	4.6
United Kingdom '86	3.3
'86	7.4

Average Earnings of Year-round, Full-time Workers, 1992
(in 1992 dollars)

Education	Male	Female
Less than 9th	19,853	13,647
9th-12th	23,529	15,300
HS diploma	28,944	19,965
Some college	34,456	23,437
Associate degree	35,315	26,083
Bachelor's or more	52,920	34,552

Children under 6 Years Old below Poverty Rates
by Family Type and Race, 1992

Race and Family Type	All Children		Children below Poverty Level	
	Number, in Millions	Percent	Number, in Millions	Percent
All Races				
All family types	23.2	100%	5.6	24%
married-couple	17.0	73.4%	2.2	12.7%
single-parent	6.2	26.6%	3.4	55.2%
mother-only	5.4	23.3%	3.2	58.9%
White, non-Hispanic				
All family types	15.7	100%	2.3	14.4%
married-couple	12.9	82.3%	1.1	8.4%
single-parent	2.8	17.6%	1.2	42.2%
mother-only	2.3	14.6%	1.1	47.0%
Black, non-Hispanic				
All family types	3.6	100%	1.8	50.7%
married-couple	1.3	34.7%	0.2	19.3%
single-parent	2.3	65.3%	1.6	67.5%
mother-only	2.2	61.3%	1.5	83.6%
Hispanic				
All family types	2.9	100%	1.3	44.0%
married-couple	2.0	69.1%	0.7	34.3%
single-parent	0.9	30.9%	0.6	65.5%
mother-only	0.8	26.9%	0.5	68.6%

Average Hourly Earnings of Production Workers in
Manufacturing Industries, 1980–1993
(in dollars)

1980	7.27
1985	9.54
1987	9.91
1988	10.19
1989	10.48`
1990	10.83
1991	11.18
1992	11.46
1993	11.76

War and the New World Order: A Photo Essay

The end of the cold war destabilized American defense. Strategists, faced with the sudden end of the bipolar contest, had to develop new defense plans for a period marked by insecurity and instability. How were they to define and fore-see potential threats to the national security of the United States? Indeed, given the multitude of issues in a multipolar world, which ones should rank first? As strategists groped to define America's long-term interests and secu-rity needs, the world issued a series of challenges.

The first was thrown by Saddam Hussein, leader of Iraq, in his attempt to annex Kuwaiti oil fields to restore his country's finances. The Gulf war brought together, under the umbrella of the United Nations, many of the allies that had constituted the free world during the cold war. The basis of the al-liance was a desire to defend the status quo. The war was quick and efficient and it visually demonstrated the destructive power of technology. It also showed the rest of the world the symbiotic relationship between money, tech-nological weaponry, and the definition of first world status. It signified that the world order created by the "free world" during the cold war would con-tinue to direct the development of the world.

More complicated questions about the structure of the world order were raised in later conflicts. Somalia, where civil order had degenerated into con-flict between competing warlords, raised the issue of humanitarian responsi-bility. But whose job was it to guide these countries toward "free world" de-velopment? the United Nations'? the ex-colonials'? the United States' as lone superpower? the nations themselves? The answers did not quickly come to mind, but policy makers could console themselves with the view that Africa was both far away and not very relevant to maintaining world order. Eastern Europe seemed more central. The breakdown of Yugoslavia into ethnic groups of Bosnians, Serbs, and Croats was not totally unexpected, but when ethnic conflicts were joined by religious hostilities between ethnic Christians and ethnic Muslims, the possibility of restoring some sense of nation and order be-came remote. Again, the question of responsibility was raised. To whom did one turn when trying to maintain order in Europe? At first, American and Eu-ropean public sentiment favored a European solution, but as the killing esca-lated and Europe hesitated, both of the world institutions—the United Nations and the United States—appeared weak through indecision, and doubts were voiced as to their ability to resolve the problem. Was this failure to accept re-sponsibility the defining characteristic of the "new world order"?

The following pictures illustrate the media-sanitized view of warfare under the "new world order." What is missing? What theme is most repre-sented in these pictures? How does this compare with written descriptions of war? Although technology has been touted as a transformer of warfare, what kinds of weapons appear most frequently in these pictures? Who is most likely to encounter and suffer from these weapons?

U.S. soldiers in Saudi Arabia. Test of mine clearing line charge (MCLC), used to clear mine fields; 2,000 lbs. of C-4 plastic explosive on a line attached to a rocket explodes as 16th engineers view it in the desert.
Reuters/Bettmann.

A soldier from the United States Army 1st Armor Division fires an automatic weapon with a gas mask during a live fire exercise near the front lines February 9. The military continues to drill with gas masks as Iraq still threatens the use of gas during any possible ground offensive in Kuwait.
Reuters/Bettmann.

A Yugoslav Federal Army soldier guards the main gate at the blockaded Marshall Tito barracks November 20. Several hundred Serbian-led members of the army are unable to move from this barracks in the Croatian capital.
Reuters/ Bettmann.

U.S. Marine guards weapons and grenades that were found and confiscated in a department store near the market square in Mogadishu on January 11. Around 858 Marines searched the market for weapons.
Reuters/Bettmann.

SUGGESTIONS FOR VIEWING AND LISTENING

Reality Bites (1994)
The frustrations of Generation X.

Thelma & Louise (1991)
The end of the open road.

Regarding Henry (1993)
A new era brings forth new, more sensitive men.

Counting Crows, "Mr. Jones" (1994)
Thinking about fame—negatively.

Enigma, "Return to Innocence" (1994)
Plugging into the primitive, the cosmos.

Guns 'n' Roses, "One in a Million" (1989)
As external enemies fade, internal conflicts emerge. The new xenophobia.

CHAPTER 14

(Post) Modern America

This chapter is organized around the concept, or idea, of postmodernism. The word itself is a curious one, because it seems to be descriptive only in a negative way; the word appears to define postmodern America less by what it *is* than by what it is *not* (that is, it is not "modern," it is after the modern). There are other difficulties. Although the term *postmodern* has been in circulation since the late 1940s, and in common usage in scholarly circles since about 1980, it is more frequently used to depict developments in art, architecture, and literature than to characterize politics or describe history. Indeed, historians seldom use the term. Moreover, scholars disagree not only about what is meant by postmodernism, but also about whether it ought properly to be praised or condemned. Nonetheless, postmodernism is a rich and useful idea, and one that can help give meaning and focus to many of the events and developments examined in previous chapters.

Beginning in the late 1960s, literary critics began using the term *postmodern* to describe the fictional works of John Barth, Thomas Pynchon, Donald Barthelme, Rudolph Wurlitzer, and other writers whose work was then called "experimental." Most earlier novelists had employed traditional narrative forms; that is, they told "stories" with a beginning, a middle, and an end, stories in which events had some causal relationship to other events. For the new breed of experimental novelists, this traditional narrative no longer seemed a reasonable way of writing about a world that seemed to lack order and continuity. "If I could remember a story," wrote Wurlitzer, "I would tell it. That always helps to hold ground, to pass the time. . . . Stories in the dead of night are always fabricated, pointing to relief, to a way out, to a cozy direction. . . . [But] I am unable to bring it all together, to say something clear, that I can remember."

Instead of coherent and comforting stories that moved through time (that were "linear"), postmodern writers offered works that mixed fact and fantasy and eschewed any consistent chronology or development in favor of shapelessness or repetition. In place of strong protagonists that could change the course of history (or, at the very least, affect their own lives), postmodernism presented a universe governed by contingency and fate. "In the end," writes postmodern theorist

Lawrence Grossberg, "the only possible story is the one that does not let you take any story too seriously."

The postmodern sensibility also involved a new relationship to popular or "mass" culture. During the first half of the twentieth century, most "modern" artists—Picasso, for example, or Jackson Pollock and the abstract expressionists of the 1940s—kept their art as separate as possible from the "corrupting" influences of popular culture and the media, perhaps because they feared being swallowed up by the expressions and values of capitalism. In contrast, artists in the postmodern vein increasingly embraced the popular and used it in their art. Andy Warhol led the way in the early 1960s, when he painted rows of Campbell soup cans or made multiple images of the face of the recently deceased Marilyn Monroe. Other artists used techniques of collage and juxtaposition to demonstrate that the materials and detritus of ordinary life could be assembled in new and meaningful ways. Whether Warhol and those who followed him had found a worthy avenue of social criticism, or whether they had simply capitulated to the power of consumer capitalism, is still hotly debated.

The most important scholarly disagreement is over how one should interpret the developments that we label *postmodern*. Optimists argue that postmodernism should be understood as one face of a society that is increasingly decentralized, heterogeneous, and multiple—in effect, the cultural expression of feminism, black nationalism, and the post-1965 immigration (see Chapter 12). According to this view, the traditional unidimensional narrative has been replaced by a multiplicity of narratives that reflect and speak to a diverse population. This process began in the nineteenth century when rising rates of literacy made the printed word available to many ordinary people, and it accelerated in the twentieth century, with the emergence of an image- and media-based culture of film and television that was accessible even to the illiterate. By the late twentieth century, new technological developments—the computer internet, cable television, the VCR—had further democratized cultural expression and reception, until Americans could select from an almost unlimited array of meaningful cultural offerings, from evangelical television to the Great Books, from Harlequin romances to rap music. From this perspective, American cultural life in the 1990s is more open and variegated than it was in the 1940s, when the pressures of war meant censorship, and more diverse than in the 1950s and early 1960s, when the cold war and the cult of domesticity produced a stifling social consensus.

Pessimists present an altogether different picture. In their framework, postmodernism is the understandable expression of a society wracked by anxiety, instability, and uncertainty. This view foregrounds the events of the 1940s: the Holocaust, the use of the atomic bomb against Japan, the enormous toll of war dead (see Chapter 1). It also underscores the ways in which the Vietnam war, urban violence, international terrorism, industrial decline, rising rates of divorce, and a host of other problems and developments have led to a climate of hopelessness in which people wear T-shirts that proclaim "Life is hard and then you die" or display bumper stickers that announce, "Shit Happens."

According to this perspective, the postmodern interest in collage and juxtaposition is neither liberating nor genuinely innovative. Rather, it reflects the artist's (or architect's) lack of confidence in his or her ability to create new forms—that is, to imagine the future. Lacking this confidence, artists follow the strategy of re-assembling the products of eras more creative and self-possessed than the present one. Filmmakers do the same, repackaging films (the *Rocky* and *Batman* series, for example) for audiences that cannot tolerate or imagine the new—who feel more confident going "back to the future." By the mid-1980s, consumers inhabited what journalist Tom Shales called the "Re Decade," as fashion turned "retro" and Block-buster offered racks of videos from every decade since the Great War. When peo-ple lack the courage to deal with the present and face the future, narrative not only multiplies, but also disintegrates, until human events, as writer Jack Solomon has put it, become represented and understood as "a narrativeless and nonsensical se-ries of skits . . . one long episode of 'Monty Python.'" It follows, too, that ambiva-lence, cynicism, and irony become the only acceptable positions. As Madonna said of her own stage presentation, "It's not insincere—you just can't take it seriously."

It is only fair to say that not everyone believes that postmodernism is a useful concept for describing and interpreting the postwar world. Perhaps the most cogent and sensible criticism is that every feature of postmodernism seems to have existed in an earlier era. For example, the breakdown in the novel's narrative coherence is clearly apparent in James Joyce's *Ulysses,* written in the 1910s. If images, adver-tising, and consumerism are central to the postmodern sensibility, then surely its appearance would coincide with the invention of the camera in the nineteenth cen-tury or the emergence of advertising as a major industry after World War I. And if postmodernism is about the emergence and proliferation of heretofore unheard voices, then arguably one should make room within the concept for the Harlem re-naissance of the 1920s or for the working-class voices of the Great Depression.

It may be, then, that the postmodern isn't so very new after all. Even so, it seems clear that postmodernism is more than smoke and mirrors, more than a clever idea proposed by literary theorists. Perhaps one should think of it as an in-terpretation of American society and culture, rooted in postwar history and shaped by postwar currents and developments. But what history? and what developments?

INTERPRETIVE ESSAY

Postmodernism
Roots and Politics

Todd Gitlin

In this brief and synthetic account, sociologist and historian Todd Gitlin pro-
vides a useful catalog of the components of postmodernism and offers two dif-
ferent kinds of historical explanations: one that places postmodernism against
a backdrop of premodernism and modernism, and another that sets postmod-
ernism in the context of historical developments in the United States after
1945. Although his list of things postmodern is mostly cultural, Gitlin argues
that the postmodern aesthetic has some relationship to politics. One might
begin by exploring that relationship: Is postmodernism a political statement?
Is it identified with the politics of any particular group? It might be helpful to
know that Gitlin was part of the New Left in the 1960s, organizing demonstra-
tions against the Vietnam war and heading the Students for a Democratic Soci-
ety (SDS) for a time. How might Gitlin's politics have shaped his understand-
ing of the historical origins of postmodernism? In particular, what role do
events of the 1960s play in his account? Finally, thinking back to the introduc-
tion to this chapter, does Gitlin belong with the optimists or the pessimists?
Does his account make the postmodern "orientation" seem useful, or useless?

Something must be at stake in the edgy debates circulating around and about
something called postmodernism. What, then? Commentators pro, con, serious,
fey, academic, and accessible seem agreed that something postmodern has happened, even if we are all (or virtually all) Mr. Jones who doesn't know what it is.
(At times the critical world seems to divide between those who speak with assurance about what it is and those who are struggling to keep up.) The volume and
pitch of the commentary and controversy seem to imply that something about this
postmodern something *matters*. In the pages of art journals, popular and obscure,
abundant passion flows on about passionlessness. It would be cute but glib and
shortsighted to dismiss the talk as so much time-serving space-filling, the shoring
up of positions for the sake of amassing theoretical property, or propriety, or priority. There is *anxiety* at work and at play here. I think it is reasonable, or at least interesting, to assume that the anxiety that surfaces in the course of the discussion—
and I confess I share in it—is called for. A certain anxiety is entirely
commensurate with what is at stake.

"Postmodernism" usually refers to a certain constellation of styles and tones in
cultural works: pastiche; blankness; a sense of exhaustion; a mixture of levels,

Reprinted from *Dissent* with permission of the author and publisher.

forms, styles; a relish for copies and repetition; a knowingness that dissolves commitment into irony; acute self-consciousness about the formal, constructed nature of the work; pleasure in the play of surfaces; a rejection of history. It is Michael Graves's Portland Building and Philip Johnson's AT&T, and hundreds of more or less skillful derivatives; it is photorealism, David Hockney, Rauschenberg's silkscreens, Warhol's multiple-image paintings and Brillo boxes, Larry Rivers's erasures and pseudopageantry, Sherrie Levine's photographs of "classic" photographs; it is Disneyland, Las Vegas, suburban strips, shopping malls, mirror glass facades, William Burroughs, Italo Calvino, Jorge Luis Borges, Donald Barthelme, Monty Python, Don DeLillo, Isuzu "He's lying" commercials, *Star Wars,* Spalding Gray, David Byrne, Twyla Tharp, the Flying Karamozov Brothers, George Coates, the Kronos Quartet, Frederick Barthelme, Laurie Anderson, David Letterman, John Ashbery, Paul Auster, the Centre Pompidou, the Hyatt Regency, *The White Hotel, Less Than Zero,* Kathy Acker, Philip Roth's *The Counterlife* (but not *Portnoy's Complaint*), the epilogue to Fassbinder's *Berlin Alexanderplatz;* it is Michel Foucault, Jacques Derrida, Jacques Lacan, Jean Baudrillard; it is bricolage fashion; it is news commentary cluing us in to the image-making and "positioning" strategies of the candidates; it is remote-control-equipped viewers "zapping" around the television dial.

To join the conversation I am going to use the term to refer to art located somewhere in this constellation. But I am also going to argue that what is at stake in the debate—and thus the root of the general anxiety—goes beyond art: it extends to the question of what sort of disposition toward the contemporary world is going to prevail throughout Western culture. Postmodernism in the arts corresponds to postmodernism in life, as sketched by the French theorist Jean-François Lyotard: "[o]ne listens to reggae, watches a western, eats McDonald's food for lunch and local cuisine for dinner, wears Paris perfume in Tokyo, and 'retro' clothes in Hong Kong." The entire elusive phenomenon that has been categorized as postmodernism is best understood not just as a style but as a general orientation, as a way of apprehending and experiencing the world and our place, or placelessness, in it. (Just whose place or placelessness is at issue is an entirely legitimate question I shall return to.) Likewise, controversies about postmodernism—the whole of what inevitably has to be called "the postmodernism discourse"—are in no small part discussions about how to live, feel, think in a specific world, our own: a world in nuclear jeopardy; a world economically both alluring and nerveracking for the fitful middle classes; a world two decades from the hopes and desperate innocence of the sixties; a world unimpressed by the affirmative futurology of Marxism. Not for the first time, debates over cultural politics intersect with larger intellectual and political currents, prefiguring or tracing conflicts that have emerged, or ought to emerge, in the sphere of politics strictly understood. When the *Partisan Review* embraced modernism in the 1930s, for example, it took a position on more than style: it took a position on reason, the State, the (ir)rationality of history; finally, it drove a revisionary wedge into left-wing politics in the large. Postwar American versions of modernism, as artistic practice and critical exegesis, can also be understood as a way to inhabit a drastically changed political space.

I am going to take the position that the discussion of postmodernism is, *among other things,* a deflected and displaced discussion of the contours of political thought—in the largest sense—during the seventies and eighties. The aesthetics of postmodernism are situated, historical. The question is, What is postmodernism's relation to this historical moment, to its political possibilities and torments?

I want to broach some intersecting questions: What do we mean by postmodernism? Why has it come to pass? What is troubling about it? Finally, postmodern is pre-what? What is the relation between postmodern aesthetics and a possible politics?

WHAT IS POSTMODERNISM?

Things must be made to look crystalline for a moment before complications set in. Here, then, is one person's grid—hopelessly crude, in the manner of first approximations—for distinguishing among premodernism (realism), modernism, and postmodernism. These are ideal types, mind you, not adequate descriptions. And they are not necessarily ideal types of the work "itself"; rather, of the work as it is understood and judged by some consensus (albeit shifting) of artists, critics, and audiences.

The premodernist work aspires to a unity of vision. It cherishes continuity, speaking with a single narrative voice or addressing a single visual center. It honors sequence and causality in time or space. Through the consecutive, the linear, it claims to represent reality. It may contain a critique of the established order, in the name of the obstructed ambitions of individuals; or it may uphold individuals as the embodiments of society at its best. In either event, individuals matter. The work observes, highlights, renders judgments, and exudes passions in their names. Standing apart from reality, the work aspires to an order of beauty, which, in a sense, judges reality. Lyrical forms, heightened speech, rhythm and rhyme, Renaissance perspective, and compositional "laws" go to work in the interest of beauty. Finally, the work may borrow stories or tunes from popular materials but it holds itself (and is held by its audience) above its origins; high culture holds the line against the popular.

The modernist work still aspires to unity, but this unity, if that is what it is, has been (is still being?) constructed, assembled from fragments, or shocks, or juxtapositions of difference. It shifts abruptly among a multiplicity of voices, perspectives, materials. Continuity is disrupted, and with enthusiasm: it is as if the work is punctuated with exclamation marks. The orders of conventional reality—inside versus outside, subject versus object, self versus other—are called into question. So are the hitherto self-enclosed orders of art: poetry vs. prose, painting vs. sculpture, representation vs. reality. The work is apocalyptic, often fused with a longing for some long-gone organic whole sometimes identified with a fascist present or future. The protagonist is not so much wholeheartedly opposed as estranged. Instead of passion, or alongside it, there is ambivalence toward the prevailing authorities. The work composes beauty out of discord. Aiming to bring into sharp relief the line between art and life, modernism appropriates selected shards of popular culture, quotes from them.

In the postmodernist sensibility, the search for unity has apparently been abandoned altogether. Instead we have textuality, a cultivation of surfaces endlessly referring to, ricocheting from, reverberating onto other surfaces. ("Surface is illusion but so is depth."—David Hockney.) The work calls attention to its arbitrariness, constructedness; it interrupts itself. Instead of a single center, there is pastiche, cultural recombination. Anything can be juxtaposed to anything else. Everything takes place in the present, "here," that is, nowhere in particular. Not only has the master voice dissolved, but any sense of loss is rendered deadpan. The work labors under no illusions: we are all deliberately playing, pretending here, get the point? There is a premium on copies; everything has been done. Shock, now routine, is greeted with the glazed stare of the absolute ironist. The implied subject is fragmented, unstable, even decomposed; it is finally nothing more than a crosshatch of discourses. Where there was passion or ambivalence, there is now a collapse of feeling, a blankness. Beauty, deprived of its power of criticism in an age of packaging, has been reduced to the decoration of reality, and so is crossed off the postmodernist agenda. Genres are spliced; so are cultural gradations. Dance can be built on Beach Boys songs (Twyla Tharp, "Deuce Coupe"); a circus can include cabaret jokes (Circus Oz); avant-garde music can include radio gospel (David Byrne and Brian Eno, *My Life in the Bush of Ghosts*). "High culture" doesn't so much quote from popular culture as blur into it. . . .

Postmodernism is known by the company it succeeds. It shadows modernism. Modernism lurks in its sequel, haunts it. The very fact that a phenomenon is called "postmodernism"—that it differs from modernism by nothing more than a prefix—pays tribute to the power of modernism's cultural force field and suggests that postmodernism might be no more (or less) than an aftermath or a hiatus.

So what's new? It has been argued, with considerable force, that the lineaments of postmodernism are already present in one or another version of modernism, that postmodernism is simply the current incarnation, or phase, in a still unfolding modernism. Roger Shattuck, for example, has recently made the point that Cubism, Futurism, and artistic spiritualists like Kandinsky "shared one compositional principle: the juxtaposition of states of mind, of different times and places, of different points of view." Collage, montage: These are of the essence of modernism high and low. Then what is so special about (1) Philip Johnson's AT&T building, with its Chippendale pediment on high and quasi-classical columns below; (2) the Australian Circus Oz, which combines jugglers who comment on their juggling and crack political jokes along with (their list) "Aboriginal influences, vaudeville, Chinese acrobatics, Japanese martial arts, fireman's balances, Indonesian instruments and rhythms, video, Middle Eastern tunes, B-grade detective movies, modern dance, Irish jigs, and the ubiquitous present of corporate marketing"; (3) the student who walks into my office dressed in green jersey, orange skirt, and black tights?

Put it this way: Modernism tore up unity and postmodernism has been enjoying the shreds. Surely nothing is without precedent; surely modernism had to set asunder what postmodernism is mixing in and about. Modernism's multiplication of perspective led to postmodernism's utter dispersion of voices; modernist collage made possible postmodernist genre-splicing. The point is not only juxtaposition but its attitude. The quality of postmodern juxtaposition is distinct: There is a deliberate self-consciousness, a skating of the edge dividing irony from dismay or endorsement, which makes up a distinct cultural mood. Picasso, Boccioni, Tatlin, Pound, Joyce, Woolf in their various ways thundered and hungered. Their work was radiant with passion for a new world/work. Today's postmodernists are blasé; they've seen it all. They are bemused (though not necessarily by bemusement). The quality of deliberateness and the sense of exhaustion in the postmodern are what set it apart.

It might be objected that we are talking about nothing more than a fad. We read in a "Design Notebook" column in the *New York Times* of March 12, 1987, that "Post-Modernism Appears to Retreat." Apparently *Progressive Architecture* is no longer giving its awards to pastiches of columns, capitals, and cornices; the writer suggests that the popularization of the premium architectural style of the last ten years signals its uniformity, mediocrity, and impending end. Actually, postmodernism as a stylistic avant-garde movement in architecture had probably already reached a plateau (but does this mean it ended?) at the moment when photographs of Michael Graves's buildings were featured in the *New York Times Magazine.* But what is interesting about postmodernism goes beyond the fashion in architecture—for the recombinatory thrust, the blankness, the self-regarding irony, the play of surfaces, the self-referentiality and self-bemusement that characterize postmodernism are still very much with us. What is interesting is not a single set of architectural tropes but postmodernism as what Raymond Williams called a "structure of feeling"—an interlocking cultural complex, or what he called "a pattern of impulses, restraints, tones"—that forecasts the common future as it colors the common experience of a society just at or beneath the threshold of awareness. In this flickering half-light, postmodernism is significant because its amalgam of spirits has penetrated architecture, fiction, painting, poetry, planning, performance, music, television, and many other domains. It is one wing, at least, of the zeitgeist.

WHY THIS POSTMODERNISM?

If this is so, the interesting question is, Why? We can distinguish more or less five approaches to an answer. These are not at all necessarily incompatible. To the contrary: Several forces are converging to produce the postmodernist moment.

The first is the bleak Marxist account sketched with flair in a series of essays by Fredric Jameson. The postmodernist spirit, with its superseding of the problem of authenticity, belongs to, is coupled to, corresponds to, expresses—the relation is not altogether clear—the culture of multinational capitalism, in which capital, that infinitely transferable abstraction, has abolished particularity as such along with the coherent self in whom history, depth, and subjectivity unite. Authentic use value has been overcome by the universality of exchange value. The characteristic machine of this period is the computer, which enthrones (or fetishizes) the fragment, the "bit," and in the process places a premium on process and reproduction that is aped in postmodernist art. Surfaces meet surfaces in these postmodern forms because a new human nature—a human second nature—has formed to feel at home in a homeless world political economy.

Postmodernists ransack history for shards because there is no here here; be-

cause historical continuity is shattered by the permanent revolution that is capitalism (which, by the way, I find it clumsy and inconsistent to call "late capitalism," a
formulation haunted by a peculiar nostalgia for sequential time—as if we could
know whether it is late early, middle, or early late). Uprooted juxtaposition is how
people live: not only displaced peasants cast into the megalopolis, where decontex-
tualized images proliferate, but also TV viewers confronted with the interruptus of
American television as well as financial honchos shifting bits of information and
blips of capital around the world at will and high speed. Art expresses this abstract
unity and vast, weightless indifference through its blank repetitions (think of
Warhol or Philip Glass), its exhausted anti-romance, its I've-seen-it-all, striving, at
best, for a kind of all-embracing surface that radiates from the world temple of the
postmodern, the glorious Centre Pompidou in Paris.

A second stab at explanation calls attention to our political rather than strictly economic moment. In this light, the crucial location of the postmodern is *after the
1960s*. The postmodern is an aftermath, or a waiting game, because that is what we
are living in: a prolonged cultural moment that is oddly weightless, shadowed by
incomplete revolts, haunted by absences—a Counterreformation beating against an
unfinished, indeed barely begun, Reformation. From this point of view, postmodernism rejects historical continuity and takes up residence somewhere beyond it
because history *was* ruptured: by the Bomb-fueled vision of a possible material
end of history; by Vietnam, by drugs, by youth revolts, by women's and gay movements; in general, by the erosion of that false and devastating universality embodied in the rule of the trinity of Father, Science, and State.

   It was faith in a rule of progress under the sway of that trinity that had underlain
our assumptions that the world displays linear order, historical sequence, and moral
clarities. But cultural contradiction burst open the premises of the old cultural complex. The cultural upwellings and wildness of the sixties kicked out the props of a
teetering moral structure, but the new house has not been built. The culture has not
found a language for articulating the new understandings we are trying, haltingly, to
live with. Postmodernism dispenses with moorings, then, because old certitudes have
actually crumbled. It is straining to make the most of seriality, endless recirculation
and repetition in the collective image warehouse, because so much of reality *is* serial.
As Donald Barthelme's fiction knows, we live in a forest of images mass-produced
and endlessly, alluringly empty. Individuality has become a parody of itself: another
word for a fashion choice, a life-style compound, a talk-show self-advertisement
logo. It might even be argued that postmodernism plays in and with surfaces because
that is what it must do to carry on with its evasions: because there are large cultural
terrors that broke into common consciousness in the sixties and there is no clear way
to live out their implications in a conservative, contracting period.

   From this point of view, postmodernism is blank because it wants to have its
commodification and eat it. That is, it knows that the cultural industry will tailor
virtually any cultural goods for the sake of sales; it also wants to display its knowingness, thereby demonstrating how superior it is to the trash market. Choose one:
the resulting ironic spiral either mocks the game by playing it or plays it by mocking it. A knowing blankness results; how to decode it is a difficult matter. Take, for

instance, the "Joe Isuzu" commercials in which the spokesman, a transparently slick version of the archetypal TV huckster, grossly lies about what the car will do, how much it costs, and so on, while the subtitles tell us he's lying, and by how much. The company takes for granted a culture of lies, then aims to ingratiate itself by mocking the conventions of the hard sell.

Or consider the early episodes of *Max Headroom* during the spring of 1987, which in nine weeks melted down from a blunt critique of television itself to a mishmash of adorability. "20 Minutes into the Future"—so the pilot film shows us—the computer-generated Max fights the tyranny of the ratings-crazed Network 23, whose decidedly sinister (shot from below with wide-angle lens) board-room tycoons will stop at no crime in their pursuit of profits. (Cherchez la japanoise: the venal Zik-Zak corporation that brings on the ratings panic is conveniently Japanese.) Is Max a revolutionary guerrilla or a sales gimmick? In the British prototype, he throws in with a revolution against Network 23; in the American version, the self-proclaimed revolutionaries are thuggish terrorists, as despicable as the Network bosses. In any event, Max in his early American weeks reaches out of the fictional frame to yawn in the face of ABC's impending commercials. As the weeks pass, however, Max loses his computerized bite and becomes regressively cuter. The same Max is marched forward to promote Coca-Cola over Pepsi, as if Coke were both subversive and mandatory (the "wave" to be "caught")—to an audience encouraged to laugh at the distinction and still, as consumers, act on it. Commerce incorporates popular cynicism and political unease while flattering the audience that is has now, at last, seen through all the sham: Cynicism, Inc., Mark Miller has named it. Andy Warhol would have grasped the point in a second, or fifteen.

A third approach to explaining postmodernism is a refinement of the second: an argument not about history in general but about a specific generation and class. Postmodernism appears as an outlook for (though not necessarily *by*) Yuppies— urban, professional products of the late baby boom, born in the late fifties and early sixties. Theirs is an experience of aftermath, privatization, weightlessness: They can remember political commitment but were not animated by it—more, they suspect it; it leads to trouble. They cannot remember a time before television, suburbs, shopping malls.* They are accustomed, therefore, to rapid cuts, discontinuities, breaches of attention, culture to be indulged and disdained at the same time. They grew up taking drugs, taking them for granted, but do not associate them with spirituality or the hunger for transcendence. Knowing indifference is their "structure of feeling"—thus a taste for cultural bricolage. They are, though, disabused of authority. The association of passion and politics rubs them the wrong way. Their idea of government is shadowed by Vietnam and Watergate. *Their* television runs through *Saturday Night Live* and MTV. Their mores lean toward the libertarian and, at least until the AIDS terror, the libertine. They like the idea of the free market as long as it promises them an endless accumulation of crafted goods, as in the (half-joking?) bumper sticker: "The One With the Most Toys Wins." The

---

*Cecilia Tichi argues that the blank-toned fiction of Ann Beattie, Bret Easton Ellis, Bobbie Ann Mason, and Tama Janowitz, among others, is the anesthetized expression of a TV-saturated generation.

idea of public life—whether party participation or military intervention—fills them with weariness; the adventures that matter to them are adventures of private life. But they are not in any conventional sense "right-wing": They float beyond belief. The important thing is that their assemblage of "values" corresponds to their class biographies.

A fourth approach starts from the fact that postmodernism is specifically, though not exclusively, *American*. Andreas Huyssen makes an interesting argument that carries us partway but needs to be extended. Postmodernism couldn't have developed in Germany, because postwar Germans were too busy trying to reappropriate a suppressed modernism. Where it developed in France at all, it did so without antagonism to or rupture from modernism. But in America, the artistic avant-garde, in order to break from cold war orthodoxy and corporate-sponsored smugness, had to revolt against the officially enshrined modernism of the postwar period, had to smash the Modern Art idol. I would add the obvious: that postmodernism is born in the U.S.A. because juxtaposition is one of the things we do best. It is one of the defining currents of American culture, especially with Emancipation and the rise of immigration in the latter part of the nineteenth century. (The other principal current is the opposite: assimilation into standard American styles and myths.) Juxtaposition is the Strip, the shopping mall, the Galleria, Las Vegas; it is the marketplace jamboree, the divinely grotesque disorder, amazing diversity striving for reconciliation, the ethereal and ungrounded radiance of signs, the shimmer of the evanescent, the good-times beat of the tall tale meant to be simultaneously disbelieved and appreciated; it is vulgarized pluralism; it is the cultural logic of laissez-faire but perhaps, the suspicion arises, even more—of an elbows-out, noisy, jostling, bottom-up version of something that can pass as democracy. We are, central myths and homogenizations and oligopolies notwithstanding, an immigrant culture, less melting pot than grab bag, perennially replenished by aliens and their singular points of view. As long ago as 1916, Randolph Bourne wrote that "there is no distinctively American culture. It is apparently our lot rather to be a federation of cultures." Hollywood and the radio and TV networks flattened the culture, but there is still life in Bourne's vision. The postmodernist, from this point of view, is hitching high art to the raucous, disrespectful quality that accompanies American popular culture from its beginnings. And indeed, the essential contribution of postmodernist art is that it obliterates the line—or the brow—separating the high from the low. What could be more American? . . .

SOURCES

The Architecture of Postmodernism:
A Photo Essay

Architect Philip Johnson, admiring a model of his AT&T building, constructed in New York City in 1982. Although most of the building looks like any "modern" sky-scraper, the arched entryway and, especially, the unusual Chippendale top, a refer-ence to the eighteenth-century English cabinetmaker, warrant the designation *post-modern.* **Why did Johnson add these details?**
Library of Congress.

The Portland Public Services Building (1983), designed by Michael Graves, is considered a standard postmodern structure. How does it differ from typical modern structures, such as the Empire State Building or the United Nations Building? What makes the building's appearance unusual? Do you think the Portland Building is the work of a society at the peak of its strength? or at a moment of weakness?
Courtesy, City of Portland, Oregon, Bureau of General Services.

The photographs on this and the following page are of an addition to Reed Library on the campus of the State University of New York at Fredonia. The addition opened in 1994. The interior photograph features the exposed heating ducts, steel beams, and open stairways typical of many postmodern buildings, including the United Airlines terminal at Chicago's O'Hare airport.

Except for the benches and the shape jutting out from the left (parts of a modern structure built in the 1960s), the exterior photograph features the juxtaposition of forms and styles characteristic of postmodernism. What historical periods does this architecture invoke? Why the round tower? the triangular top? What purpose does the tiny balcony (center right) *have? Does this building share any features with the Portland Building? Does it present a similar message?*

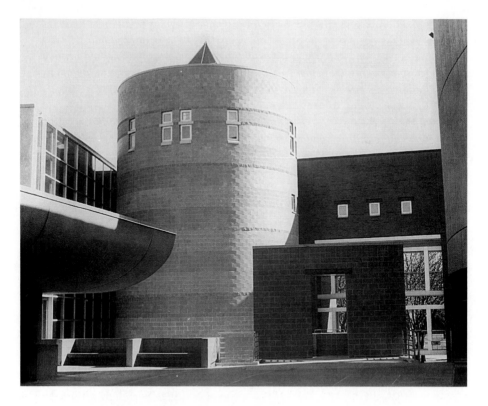

Slacker

Richard Linklater

Richard Linklater is best known as the writer, producer, and director of the 1991 film Slacker. *Although most critics either ignored the film or railed against its lack of plot and development,* Slacker *rose to the status of minor cult classic, at least among younger viewers. In this selection, Linklater attempts to explain and justify the attitudes of the cohort which writer Douglas Coupland has labeled "Generation X," defined here as a post–baby boom group born after about 1960. Consider Linklater's ideas in relationship to Todd Gitlin's account of postmodernism. Does Linklater's "slacker" generation share the postmodern sensibility? or is it in revolt against it? What events or developments have shaped Linklater's perspective, or that of the "slackers" in his film? Do you think Linklater is more or less alienated from dominant social values than David Letterman (see the following section)? Is his alienation of a different kind?*

PROFESSIONAL MOUTH SECTION

One minute you're a filmmaker hoping your film will speak for itself and you can get on to something else, the next you're on national television with Generation X *author Doug Coupland helping to explain to moms why their twenty-four year olds are still at home. In between, you're informed that you have to do lots of interviews and talk endlessly about the film and "whatever else" someone might want to discuss. Somewhere along the way I begin to see it all as filler between ads on a page. Anyway, what follows are bits from that "whatever else" file—much of it speaking about the generation that doesn't want to be spoken for.*

"There has always been this part of the population that was on the margins, that was intentionally outside society, or at odds with what was expected of it. They have been pretty much ignored for the past twenty years—millions of intelligent, creative people who just don't buy into their preordained traditional roles in society. They maybe haven't found out what they want to do yet, but they know what they don't want. You see what your options are in the world, and if none of them look appealing, then you just retreat into your own thing for a while. I like that because it's you rejecting society before society rejects you."

"I guess there was something in the air . . . making the movie it really came out. . . . This incredible kind of, what? Dissatisfaction, or total nonbelief in everything, but with an interesting sense of humor and irony about it all."

"I think many people are getting away from the old thoughts about how to change things, the ol' 'If you don't like the way things are, then why don't you change things' post-sixties protest isn't nonexistent, it just looks different. I like the kind of protest that took place in the early eighties when Reagan was thinking about going into Central America and renewed conscription and no one signed up. Not a lot of hoopla, just a direct message that they couldn't count on us to do their dirty work down there. The mass noncompliance and the public's attitude in general basically forced the government agenda underground. The army itself, however, could always be bought—just start a multijillion-dollar Be All That You Can Be ad campaign. There will always be plenty of kids with no opportunities that can be coerced."

"It's kind of fun to be relegated to the margins: there's a lot less pressure, and there's more room for other things. It can be more optimistic, ultimately. Some people might think it's kind of naive, but it's all about a certain openness to new possibilities."

"There are less of us—statistically there's a difference between generations. We grew up in a different time and have been through a different epic at a different age. I'm not saying our human needs are any different or people have changed in one generation. But we play off a whole different scenario."

"There's a little element of truth in each encounter. It was an idealized world of sorts. That no matter what somebody would say, no matter how crazy it seemed, someone else would listen."

"I've always felt regular life was worthy of a movie. I think people feel alienated from most movies because it's far from what we experience. You come away thinking, My life's no good, let other people entertain me and tell me what's important. *Slacker* is a celebration of day-to-day life. Especially the last scene, with the all-night partiers driving around and filming each other. It's a microcosm of the whole film, ordinary people saying, 'Hey, my life's worthy of cinema.'"

"*Slacker* was really kind of made similar to the energy that is put forth into making something happen musically. You hook up with the right people and see what happens. I think a lot of the musicians in the movie could relate to it in that way. Kind of the spirit of creating something that doesn't really fit into the marketplace, just something that is worthwhile to do: a *Slacker*-type project. It's not a goal, it's just something fun. A lot of people value that kind of immediate activity."

"People judge them as lazy, but actually they are aggressive nonparticipants in a society they don't see much point in. A realm of activity that more closely corresponds to one's desire is never a bad thing."

"The boomers grew up with a kind of fifties postwar abundance as a foundation. It seemed to have a solid framework and a certain code of belief in the president, the media, and every official word from above. I guess the assassinations and political upheaval that happened in the sixties and early seventies, the things we grew up with, left us without any of that false innocence to return to. It's hard to think nostalgically about our country when we were kids because there was nothing calm or reassuring about it. The previous generation still hasn't gotten over their initial realization that they'd been lied to and that everything was irrevocably fucked. We grew up knowing all that."

"I slept on a double-size mattress on the floor for about five years. Why, am I supposed to say *futon*?"

". . . It's the old consumer terror—the fear of not having enough money to get in line to buy the recent stuff. That's what they've implanted in us from day one: that freedom means the ability to choose between all the different models and gadgets. It takes a real conscious shift of priorities to forget that whole way of thinking, that treadmill you get on and can't get off. Because it is self-perpetuating. Once you commit to a certain thing, you're committing to the inevitable upgrade."

"I think this generation has drifted farther away from any kind of ideologies: seeing all official systems of thought as alienations. And when you look at the American political system, there's nothing to feel aligned with, you're not represented. I think that's become more and more clear to more and more people. It's someone else's game for their own agenda . . . I mean, how can a thinking person really buy in wholeheartedly to something like a political party or think something as unimaginative as the political discourse that goes on in this country can change their lives for the better?"

"The way *Slacker* was made really grew out of my own personality and the people I was making the film with. There was a strong methodical element to *Slacker*, very rational and planned out. The entire structure had to be intricately planned, which is probably one part of my personality. Within each scene, however, there was a freedom and openness. In the rehearsal process and all the way up to the time the camera rolled, we were always spontaneous and open to new ideas or inspiration. That is probably another side of me. I think we all have those two sides, one rational, and one more poetic and open to anything."

"Work isn't mandatory in our society. There's no law that says you must work.

You can get by if you can do without. If you're willing not to have a family, a new car, nice living conditions, nice clothes, and eat out every night; if you're willing to go, "I just want to work part-time or not at all and spend most of my time making music, writing, reading, or watching movies," you can consciously drop out. There's still enough freedom left where you can maneuver. The freebies and hand-me-downs in this society are probably the best in the world. For example, I was never really a student at the University of Texas, but that's a great facility. I'd get my library card for thirty bucks a year and have access to one of the bigger libraries in the South. Just being a citizen, you can take advantage of a lot of things in this culture. You can be a parasite for a while, but hopefully, what you gain out of it you'll return eventually in some form or another. It's like an extended loan."

"Daydreaming doesn't sound very productive, but it's where many of your breakthrough thoughts come from. It's in this daydreaming state that you can imagine an ideal life for yourself or the ideal society you want to live in. Where will that ever come from if you don't give yourself room to think about it?"

"I wasn't consciously saying that this group was less goal oriented, but I think that if you look at the film, you can tell that they are not ambitious in that way. They have a different kind of ambition or productivity. You can work hard and do all these things and the payoff you were after can still elude you. There's a lot of dissatisfaction in that group before us—whatever you call them: the Yuppies, the Me group, or the Boomer crowd. The psychic toll of all that activity seemed so high."

"I had always thought of a story that would go from one completely different situation to the next—and how that would be permission to include so many disparate things. It was a total experiment that could very well have not worked. It's the kind of risk you could only take on an underground, no-budget level."

"That's not to say that everybody in the film is unemployed; the film doesn't necessarily say that about these people. I mean, they're all kind of getting by. A key difference is that if they have a job, the job usually doesn't have them. They might not be doing much occupationally, but they are still educating themselves. There's a lot of cerebral activity; they're still in that idea environment. And it's not like they aren't trying to do anything with their ideas. They might not have too much to show for it right now, but there is some potential there."

"I used to have a sticker on my phone that said, Assume This Phone Is Tapped. But no. Why would they tap my phone? Maybe now, actually. I heard Spike Lee talks by pay phone. He always has a lot of quarters."

"I don't judge them as right or wrong. It's to be looked at in a completely different way. Like the rap at the beginning by the guy in the cab. You're led to believe that if he'd gotten off at a different street it would have been an entirely different movie. It's not to be agreed or disagreed with but thought of from a more aesthetic viewpoint. So on one level, the film's a blunt realism unfolding in front of us in an almost real-time fashion. But what's being talked about is suggesting infinite levels. We're stuck with one reality right in front of us, but who knows what's really going on? You change your mind, and you create a whole new world where everything is the same but you're different. That kind of open-ended thinking creates something else. There are thoughts that can change your life. They recalibrate your mind."

"It's a deprogramming period that's good to go through. I know that it gave me a new angle on my life. It was during that period that I really discovered cinema and had the time to totally immerse myself in it."

"They're people who have experienced a lot of thinking in their adult lives through secondary sources—books, movies, and TV. They're overloaded with information that they don't always know how to use in a socially acceptable manner."

"Lazy? No, no, no! Not at all! That's a total misconception. Slackers, in one way, are on a track to something much better . . ."

"I guess I can see how some people think the movie is a bit depressing. It certainly has its dark areas. But what gives me eternal hope and, in a way, what the film really depicts is that our society still has a strong individual vitality at heart, intellectual and otherwise. Habitual energy can equal optimism. We as individuals and as a society have the ability to revitalize ourselves."

"I had a job about three years ago working at a hotel. I was the graveyard-shift bellman. But, you know, who checks into a business hotel after eleven at night? So basically, I'd just sit in this large coat closet and read and write. I had this little electronic typewriter, and I worked on scripts. I got away with it for about ten months before they finally figured out I wasn't doing anything and canned me."

"I was interested in the subject matter of the movie just from living in this neighborhood and always thinking about film. So I always knew there was a movie there somewhere. There's a kind of energy that's never really captured on film, just the whole idea of a lot of thought and energy and activity that isn't really close to action or traditional drama. It's just talk, but in itself, to me, that was worthy of cinema, that could be a film."

"Even with environmentalism, it's like, Let's buy some more environmentally safe products. Let's buy a new environmentally safe bag that will be really good to carry things in. If you want to save the environment, don't buy anything. But that's one thing that's never questioned in the system. The question's always WHAT to buy. It's never WHETHER to buy or not. The cardinal sin is to question consumerism in the first place. Yet now I'm in a position where I have a movie I want people to come see. On that level, it's out there in the evil world as a commodity to be consumed."

"I wanted to make films but had nothing to show for it. Watching three movies a day, reading, and shooting a lot of Super 8 doesn't sound productive to most people, but it got me here. It's different now that I'm making bigger films, but even talking to a lawyer is still like play to me because it's still part of doing what I want."

"I can't commit to a specific message other than that this kind of world exists. There are people in the margins that most either don't pay attention to or pretend don't exist. But if you live there, if you are into it, then it's very legitimate. It's a way to live. It's about people who are not buying in but are not completely dropping out either. It's not that they don't want to be part of society at all; they're just kind of looking for a sort of coexistence. I like the idea of millions of personal revolutions and people doing what they feel most free doing and then shaping their worlds to conform to society in only the most obligatory, painless way."

"I wanted to capture how your mind works as you go through a certain day, how you interact with certain people and how you just sort of drift. After it's all finished, you sort of put it all together. Unlike theater, cinema captures something so real you don't have to force it on people. I've always been fascinated with showing real people in real time. No big drama, just the things we all do, such as walking down the street or getting in a car. But the style also came out of my economic restrictions.

"I'm surprised. The film seems to be finding an audience. You don't think about it when you're making the movie. I just wanted to make it. Pretty soon you're watching the finished film and going, 'Hmmm . . . well, it's a pretty difficult film.' It is. It demands a lot. I feel lucky the film ever got out there."

"The movie is a study in communication, verbal and otherwise, because I do think everybody does want to connect. The old anarchist character knows immediately that he's found a kindred spirit, that kid was him however many years ago. And the young burglar realizes that this older guy is worthwhile, he can learn something from him. So he just walks with him and listens."

"There is a large amount of alternative social and cultural experimentation going on. It's in the process of slowly being recognized and in many cases working its way into the mainstream. It's at the fun stage because nobody's quite got a grip on it. I mean, for a film like *Slacker* to gross well over a million at the box office, for *Generation X* to sell more than a hundred thousand copies, for Lollapalooza [Jane's Addiction, Butthole Surfers, etc.] to be the biggest tour of last summer, for Nirvana to be at the top of the charts. I just kind of think, yeah, something IS going on and a lot of people are participating. And if it isn't anything new, then it's at least a new emphasis, a new combination."

Entertainment Tonight
Modern/Postmodern

According to Todd Gitlin, David Letterman, host of Tonight with David Letterman *since 1982, exemplifies the postmodern sensibility, while Johnny Carson, who hosted* The Tonight Show *from 1962 through 1992, does not. Your focus should be on Letterman, whose program was promoted not long ago as "an hour of celebrities talking about themselves constantly interrupted by commercials. Hey America, the pride is back." Among other things, consider the content of Letterman's humor, his interview style, the way his show utilizes the world outside the studio and—taking the cue from the photograph—the window behind Letterman and the "city" it overlooks. Examine the Carson photograph for what it might convey about the star and his values. In addition, compare Carson's real, functioning office with the barren Letterman office that often appears on his programs. What is postmodern about the way Letterman presents his office?*

Johnny Carson, c. 1970.
Library of Congress.

David Letterman as he hosts the premiere of the NBC-TV show *Late Night with David Letterman,* **February 1, 1982.**
UPI/Bettmann.

SUGGESTIONS FOR VIEWING AND LISTENING

Blue Velvet (1986)
Reality appears innocent—on the surface.

Stranger than Paradise (1984)
Minimal editing produces "real time" feeling, as well as the knowledge that one is watching something that was filmed.

True Stories (1986)
David Byrne stars and directs. The ironic sensibility of the postmodern.

Slacker (1991)
No central narrative, no plot.

Brian Eno and David Byrne, *My Life in the Bush of Ghosts* (album) (1979)
Erasing boundaries, linking what was heretofore separate.

R.E.M., "Radio Free Europe" (1983)
Unintelligible lyrics, producing a new consciousness on the part of the listener.

Police, "Message in a Bottle" (1979)
A song that never ends, casting into doubt the concepts of endings, narratives, and history.